ROADSIDE AMERICA

The Automobile
in Design
and Culture

ROADSIDE AMERICA

The Automobile in Design and Culture

Edited by JAN JENNINGS

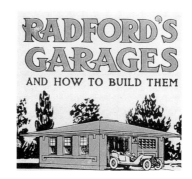

Published by IOWA STATE UNIVERSITY PRESS,
Ames, Iowa, for the
SOCIETY FOR COMMERCIAL ARCHEOLOGY

This publication was funded in part by a grant from the
Graham Foundation for Advanced Studies in the Fine Arts.

Manufactured in the United States of America

∞ This book is printed on acid-free paper.

First edition, 1990

Library of Congress Cataloging-in-Publication Data

Roadside America : the automobile in design and culture /
   edited by Jan Jennings.—1st ed.
        p.   cm.
     Selected papers from the 1988 SCA conference held in
   Dearborn, Mich., and co-sponsored by the Henry Ford Museum.
      ISBN 0-8138-0131-1 (alk. paper)
      1. Automobiles—Social aspects—United States—His-
   tory—Congresses. 2. Automobiles—Design and construction—Social aspects—United States—History—Congresses.   I. Jennings, Jan, 1946– . II. Society for
   Commercial Archeology (U.S.) III. Henry Ford Museum and
   Greenfield Village.
   HE5623.R62   1990
   303.48'32—dc20   90-32517
                                                              CIP

Book design by Joanne Elkin Kinney

Contents

Preface

Since its founding in 1978, the Society for Commercial Archeology (SCA) has operated nationally as a promoter of public awareness, as an information clearinghouse, and as a preservation advocate for the commercial landscape. *Roadside America: The Automobile in Design and Culture* represents a new departure for the organization. It is the outcome of the most successful conference in its history and commemorates the tenth year anniversary. Although the SCA has encouraged scholarship, primarily through its journal, the publication of these essays represents the membership's first effort to promote the formal study of the roadside.

These essays were selected from the 1988 SCA conference, "Americans and the Automobile," held in Dearborn, Michigan, and co-sponsored by the Henry Ford Museum. The museum proved to be an exciting setting to celebrate the society's tenth year anniversary and the automobile's impact on America. On the way to the paper sessions, conference participants were stimulated by the museum's newest exhibit, The Automobile in American Life, with its shiny sedans, a roadside diner, a drive-in theater, and bright neon signs.

Thematically, the Dearborn conference took a broad point of view and sought to establish an alliance between the automobile and its impact on culture and the environment. There is a body of literature that deals with the effect of the automobile on popular culture, but this anthology, while extending those studies, also includes much description about how the automobile was accommodated in everyday life. Therefore, the thrust of these papers is more physical than symbolic.

For the society, coming to terms with the automobile has always implied the need to conserve and preserve the commercial landscape—the brash and forceful arena of commodities and services that has been discounted often by amateur and professional preservationists alike. Some assume that these structures are not old enough to be considered eligible for the National Register of Historic Places, but, in fact, by the 1930s, the roadside culture was well established throughout the country. Much of the roadside landscape is modern in style, its form and materials susceptible to change. Indeed, these artifacts are disappearing rapidly. It is our hope that these essays will help provide the historical context that preservationists need to evaluate these resources.

The eighteen articles are divided into four multi-disciplinary themes: building types, arts and literature, technology and geography, and road and street. The essays speak of our love-hate relationship with the automobile, and they chronicle the profound, and irrevocable, changes it brought to rural regions, small towns, and cities. Americans wanted to drive everywhere. They needed new roads, better bridges, and sophisticated maps to get there. Because the car gave us the most mobility we had ever known, Americans connected with each other through cross-country road trips or through a library system on wheels. New building types, such as the residential garage, the parking garage, motels, and drive-in theaters, sprang up to accommodate our prized possession. Aerodynamic imagery influenced both architectural form and ornamentation. Celebrated designers, anonymous builders, and manufacturers gave us new commercial structures. Automobile production modernized manufacturing. Overall, we saw automobiles as extensions of ourselves, a second skin we could live in.

We watched movies in it, we had our pictures taken in it, and we read adventure stories about being in it.

Viewing the essays in total, it becomes clear that most of the authors relied on ephemeral sources as primary material for their research. Trade catalogs and papers, advertising materials, builder's journals, photographs, postcards, popular magazines, books, and sheet music become the basis for automobile culture. Originally produced for commercial use only, these documents recreate the context of the roadside for the contemporary scholar.

Many people contributed to the preparation of this book. The SCA expresses its sincere appreciation to the Graham Foundation for Advanced Studies in the Fine Arts, which provided partial funding for the publication. I am grateful to the Iowa State University Press, for not only making the book a reality but also for making my editorial responsibilities less difficult. I would especially like to thank Richard R. Kinney, the Press's director, for his enthusiastic support and to William Silag, who kept the project on track.

During various stages of development, the following readers offered thoughtful and knowledgeable counsel: William Allen, Arkansas State University; Daniel M. Bluestone, Columbia University; Gina Crandell, Iowa State University; Herbert Gottfried, Iowa State University; David Heymann, Iowa State University; Michael Jackson, Illinois Historic Preservation Agency; Albert Larson, University of Illinois at Chicago; Richard Longstreth, The George Washington University; Michael Marsden, Bowling Green State University; Michael Mendelson, Iowa State University; Darrell A. Norris, State University of New York at Geneseo; David Roberts, Iowa State University; Sidney K. Robinson, University of Illinois at Chicago; Dan Scully, Dan V. Scully, Architect; William Silag, Iowa State University Press; and Tania Werbizky, the Preservation League of New York State. Finally, I am endebted to the Department of Art and Design at Iowa State University for their generous support.

Jan Jennings

1

TECHNOLOGY
AND
GEOGRAPHY

The Automobile

CHAPTER 1

FOLKE T. KIHLSTED

*A Bridge between Engineering
and Architecture*

The automobile has become a fixture of our daily lives and a ubiquitous presence in our society. It has affected our activities and our thinking in both obvious and obscure ways. One of these ways, as one considers architecture, is that the car has contributed to linking architecture and engineering and has helped to close the rift between these two professions that developed in the nineteenth century. Many still believe that the pragmatic and functionally determined designs of a structural engineer lack aesthetic merit when placed against the intuitive and formally conceived designs of the architect. Nevertheless, recent developments in architecture indicate that a new alliance between engineering and architecture has taken place.[1]

The automobile has played an important role in fostering this alliance: first, through the European architects who held up automotive design as exemplary, a way to lead them out of the stylistic historicism of architectural design; and second, in America where the ubiquitous presence of a car demanded many changes in our architecture and encouraged communication between architects and engineers.

In a most basic sense, the automobile shares the qualities of machine and building—the rightful territories of the engineer and the architect. The automobile is powered by a machine. Moreover, as with the machine, it is replicable for wide distribution and its major function is one of moving from one place to another. On the other hand, the automobile envelops functional space—space for sitting, and even sleeping and living; and its roof, a stamped steel shell, is a form-resistant structure. As a hybrid, sharing qualities of both machine and structure, the car has been the focus of designs by both engineers and architects.[2]

In bridging the traditional gap between engineering and architecture, the car has prompted us to question such basic assumptions of architecture as permanence and immobility. It has challenged the way we think of and perceive large commercial buildings as well as the private house.[3] One of these challenges has led to a fundamental change in the relationship between the machine and the building.

Today, we think nothing of driving an automobile into the most elegant of buildings, and it has become a necessity to incorporate innumerable machines into our architecture. In the nineteenth century, however, the machine's relationship to architecture usually was perceived as antithetical. Even in the most utilitarian of buildings, such as factories, engines first were located outside of the main buildings. Only later did the factory eliminate its separate engine-house and house both its machinery and the power source under one roof. In essence, the factory became a machine, and one could talk about going in in the morning and "turning the building on," as if it were, indeed, the machine. If, in the nineteenth century, the industrial revolution introduced the concept of the building as a machine, it was only for the factory; and this building type was not considered to be architecture.

A broader definition of architecture, which embraced engineering technology and the machine, emerged in the twentieth century; the engineer, the factory, and the machine aesthetic provided a base for the modernist movement after the second decade. Le Corbusier called the house "a machine for living in," and the frontispiece to his chapter on the automobile as a model for architecture set the tone for architectural theory in the following decades.

Above the chapter title, "Eyes Which Do Not See: III, Automobiles," Le Corbusier pictured a cutaway drawing of the axle, brake, and wheel hub of a De-lage automobile.[4] The car was important to Le Corbusier not only for its style and mechanical perfection, but also for the way in which engineers posed the problem of its design and overcame it. "The point then was," he later wrote, "that our eyes did not see . . . the building of a new [mechanized] world full of strength and confidence."[5]

A decade earlier than Le Corbusier's book, Walter Gropius designed the model factory for the Werkbund exposition in Cologne (figure 1.1). The Werkbund yearbook for that year, 1914, was dedicated to transportation, and Gropius had been searching for examples of pure form in automobiles and airplanes for that issue.[6] His factory grew out of this search, and although it may seem an idealized and generic factory, this temporary building acknowledged the automobile in some revealing ways.

Connecting the administration building and the worksheld were a series of open garages or carports. These formed a type of atrium. In fact, the total layout of Gropius's model factory parallels that of the prototypical early Christian basilica (figure 1.2). In this sense, the administrative offices serve as the triumphal-arch entrance to the complex; the garages form the atrium; the place of actual line production becomes the nave; and, to the left, off-axis, the octagonally shaped Deutz motor pavilion is positioned where the early Christian baptistery would have been. This relationship is more than coincidental; and it is fitting that the Deutz pavilion, the place for the manufacturing of the gasoline engine, becomes associated with the baptistery, the place for the rebirth of the faithful. Where a contemporary such as Marcel Duchamp would have embraced

the irony of such a juxtaposition and metamorphosis, Gropius developed it with studied subtlety and with the seriousness of a true initiate of the machine age.

1.1. Walter Gropius (and Adolf Meyer), Cologne, Werkbund model factory, 1913–14, plan. The place of mass production had a spatial layout that hints at sacred processionals.

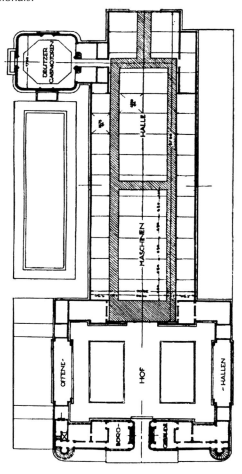

1.2. Rome, Old St. Peter's, ca. 320–330 (with later additions to ca. 500), plan. Every modern architect would know this plan as an example of early sacred architecture.

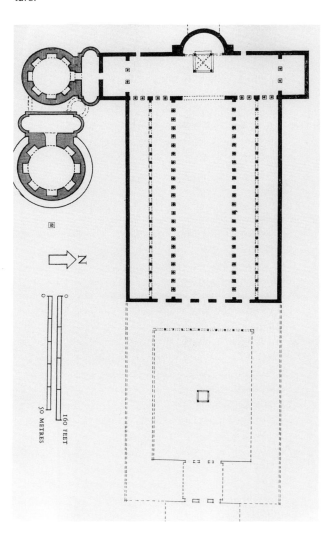

These examples are European, and the theoretical impulse for associating the car with modern architecture first made itself felt in Europe. By the 1920s, however, the car had become a powerful technological, social, and cultural force in America, much more so than in Europe. The mass-produced car was a consumer item, an object of everyday use. Here it was less an object of reverence than it was in Europe. For example, in the 1920s, before European modernist attitudes took hold in the United States, our architects were not as ready to correlate the style of automobile showroom buildings with the form of the ever-sleeker automobiles they displayed. Laprade and Bazin's Garage Marbeuf (figure 1.3), a Citroën showroom in Paris of 1929, has no match at its date across the Atlantic. Our most advanced showrooms still were highly eclectic or conservatively classical designs.

Modernist theories may not yet have affected the design of the architecture for our automobiles in the 1920s, but we sure knew what to do with the car itself! Le Corbusier theorized about the machine for living in; but in precisely the same year, the Dietz Lumber Company built the house for driving in (figure 1.4). Of course, this modification of a Ford Model T was simply an advertisement to promote house ownership as equivalent to automobile ownership. Ironically, it encouraged the continued dependency on wasteful handicraft building and thus "drove" in opposition to Le Corbusier's call to arms for mass-production housing.

Mobility was the key word in the 1920s in America. The automobile had become a metaphor for individual progress through speed, personal freedom, and sleek beauty. Automobility was the predominant progressive force of the time.[7] Thus Warren G. Harding could call the motorcar "an indispensable instrument in our political, social, and industrial life;"[8] and, maybe more apt as a reference to its offer of freedom, a Chevrolet ad of 1924 asked, "How can Bolshevism flourish in a motorized country?"[9]

1.3. Albert Laprade and L.-E. Bazin, Paris, Garage Marbeuf, 1929, interior view. Fifty cars could be kept on display in this ultra-modern building served by elevators.

1.4. C. N. Dietz Lumber Company, Omaha, Nebraska, "Own Your Home," modified Model-T chassis, 1923. The model of mass production was used to advertise traditional craft-built houses.

The values fostered by automobilism and its mobility—privatism, freedom of choice, the extending of one's control over the physical and social environment—are evidenced in innumerable examples of car chassis that have been modified into traveling homes and bungalows ever since the second decade of the century. Each one of these is a personal statement, a recrafting of the mass-produced machine into an individualized structure.

In contrast to these private, idiosyncratic modifications of the car, the automobile also played an architectural role in the field of prefabricated housing, where it was held up as an inspirational paradigm, and in the design of trailers and mobile homes, where it was the *raison d'etre* for their existence. The efficiency of mass production demonstrated by Ford's Highland Park factory generated calls from every profession for a major systems revolution in the way we make houses. Bolstered by his visit to America, Le Corbusier found himself "in a kind of daze . . . on leaving the Ford factory at Detroit. . . . When I, an architect," he mused, "pay ten thousand francs to a contractor it doesn't even cover the cost of one room. Yet here for ten-thousand francs Ford delivers the marvellous car [the Model A] that we all know."[10]

Even General Motors (GM) president Alfred P. Sloan gave his blessing to "the manufacture and assembly of machine-made houses" in 1934, houses that would be factory-equipped with the most sophisticated technology for living, learning, and recreation.[11] Although here, right from the top, was interest in assembling houses like cars, GM never ventured into prefabricated housing. Many architects did, however. Howard T. Fisher, for example, patterned his General Houses on the automotive industry and offered many types so owners might think of trading up. A contemporary analyst described the more elaborate of these as the Cadillac of his system, whose "details or mechanism and construction will compare with the most expensive motor cars"; and Fisher himself, in the previous decade, predicted that the house of the future would soon become "as fine an expression of our age as the modern automobile."[12] Another prefabricated brochure boasted, "It won't be long now before houses will be punched, pounded and pressed out at factories precisely as Henry Ford ground out the model T—millions of 'em."[13] Emulating the automobile, some of these prefabs had roll-down windows; some had window frame and wall components stamped out of steel (figure 1.5); some called their structural frames chassis; some boasted trading-in or trading-up; some imitated the entire GM system of distribution, sales, delivery, and finance; and one touted the idea of machine efficiency by boasting, "There is also to be an electric cigarette lighter so that a busy woman can rush in the front door, glance at the clock and with one switch light her cigarette and turn on the radio."[14]

In the opinion of a *Fortune* commentator, we were on the threshold of a triumphant modern architecture in which "the common citizen will expect motorcar perfection in house engineering, and motorcar honesty in house appearance."[15] The automobile was the thirties' challenge to the house. It demonstrated that prefabricated housing could be the palliative for the social instability and economic hardship of the Depression. Yet none of the prefabricated housing systems survived across the war years and into the 1950s.

The type of "prefabricated" dwelling that did manage to survive the war and grow thereafter was the mobile home. Skyline Corporation, which incorporated in 1951, began as a mobile home builder and today is the largest house builder of any sort in the United States.[16] It, and its ilk, began as did the automobile—as the common "invention" of numerous individuals. Small-scale manufacture began by the early thirties. The product was what we today would call a trailer. Nevertheless, examples such as that of car designer and general inventor William B. Stout expanded into sizable units. It could be packed and folded for the road in about twenty minutes.

Here was the American version of a "machine for living in," issuing first out of technological inge-

1.5. O. Kline Fulmer, Middletown, Ohio, residence of George T. Creech, ca. 1933–34, exterior view. A prize-winner in the Better Homes in America Small House Competition, this house has 20-gauge rolled steel, factory-fabricated floor and wall units; its exterior is porcelain enamel sheet steel with stainless-steel clip joints.

nuity rather than abstract theorizing. Stout's prototype mobile home was truly mobile, much more flexible, and certainly more modern in its material, rounded forms and clean lines than Le Corbusier's venture into prefabrication, the Maison "Voisin" of 1920.[17] Moreover, Stout's design should be perceived as part of a transportation package—the other half being his radical, streamlined, rear-engined Scarab automobile (figure 1.6).

1.6. William B. Stout, Scarab automobile and prototype mobile home, 1936, exterior view, unfolded. The trailer, 16 by 6½ feet road-ready, could be unfolded by one person in twenty minutes to a 20-by-13-foot home with reception hall, bedroom, living room and kitchen. It weighed under three thousand pounds and had alloy metal walls screwed to a steel tubular frame.

Stout's design may be anomalous, but even the more prosaic mobile home of the 1930s was built, sold, financed, taxed, depreciated, and traded in just like the automobile, which of course provided its motive power. It began as a consumer item and not merely a different kind of architecture; this insured its longevity. So also, as a consumer item, it could be sleekly modern, like Stout's or the Curtiss Aerocar, without offending those traditional sensibilities that customers bring to the design of permanent houses. Today, the mobile home has evolved, as has the original Skyline trailer, into all aspects of prefabricated housing: modular, sectional, and systems building. Many architects have tried their hand at designing or using mobile homes, and Paul

Rudolph has called it our vernacular form, the "twentieth-century brick" (figure 1.7).[18]

More importantly, the mobile home has given us a new concept for architecture—the plug-in. Contrary to what one may expect, this idea didn't originate in the 1960s with Rudolph or the many other architects who stacked mobile homes horizontally and vertically, nor with Archigram, the British group that popularized the plug-in. Rather, it began with the etiquette of trailer travel and lot leasing in mobile home parks. The ubiquitous Airstream, for example, "plugged in" to other structures whenever possible, and the numerous publicity photographs for Wally Byam's world tours show Airstreams camping in the Roman forum at Jerash, Jordan, for instance, with each unit neatly inserted into the intercolumniations of the colonnaded stoa. But even when occupying an empty trailer park lot, the mobile home must "plug in" to the permanent utilities hidden below the ground. In fact, thirty years before the 1960s mania for plug-in architecture, cartoonist Alan Dunn anticipated that architecture with a tongue-in-cheek proposal that clearly recognizes the mobile home's potential. He drew a nine-story, open, steel skyscraper frame on top of which a crane was busy hauling up trailer homes and slotting them into the frame. A sign on the structure advertised, "Now Renting. 1½–2 Room Trailer Apartments," while on the sidewalk some pedestrians converse: "Maybe the people aren't ripe for it yet—," and another trailer, still hitched to its car, awaits its turn. Today this scene is hardly fantasy. We regularly plug in prefabricated housing units, some of which remain the unmodified mobile home prototype, others of which adapt its form and dimensions to massive reinforced-concrete units.[19]

The architectural forms and ideas looked at so

far have derived from the machine side of engineering technology. Can one look at structures, the other side of engineering technology, and find connections between the automobile and architecture? Now, the paradigmatic engineering structure of the nineteenth century is the suspension bridge. Proposals for suspension roofs existed in that century, but they really had to wait for a developed steel technology to become practical. One of the best-known early examples of the suspension principle applied to architecture is Buckminster Fuller's Dymaxion House of 1927. Hung from a central mast containing all its mechanical support systems, this was to be an autonomous dwelling weighing a mere three tons and requiring no connections for fuel, electricity, water, or sewage. Although its technology was more strongly connected to the airplane than the car, it was intended to be mass-produced like the car, and Bucky boasted that its $1,500 price tag was "roughly the price of a typical American motorcar."[20] Moreover, this "4-D" house was to come with its own 4-D transportation unit, the Dymaxion car of which Bucky made three prototypes in 1933–34. Fuller's pioneering work on the integration of automobile and dwelling was an influence on Stout in the next decade. Also, his suspension principle was soon picked up by younger architects. In 1929, for example, Simon Breines proposed an automobile filling station based on the suspension principles of the Dymaxion house (figure 1.8).

In the next decade, the best examples of the suspension structure adapted to architecture come from Chicago and are responses to the theme of transportation and the automobile. The Travel and Transportation Building at the Century of Progress International Exposition exposed its structure as a positive aesthetic feature. Leon Moisseiff, as con-

sulting engineer, allowed the dome to adjust to uneven wind or snow loading while its twelve braced columns, each 150 feet high, could also move on rocker bearings.[21] Outside of unexecuted Russian Constructivist projects, this building to house machines of transportation was the most dramatic example of architecture-as-structure of the period.

1.7. Paul Rudolph, New Haven, Oriental Masonic Gardens, 1970, exterior view from above. To provide low-income housing, 12-foot-wide mobile home modules were clustered to form two- to five-bedroom apartments; the 148 units, which were trucked in from Maryland, demonstrate the architect's concept of the "twentieth-century brick."

Five years later, architect Bertrand Goldberg built prototype suspended structures that combined Fuller's ideas of lightweight forms with the mobility of the automobile. His North Pole Ice Cream Store was a trailer that could be towed and unfolded at its destination, its expanded roofs and walls suspended from a mast that was hinged on the trailer roof (figure 1.9). A mother truck, in which ice cream was made, would have served this and other stores, and all units would have folded up and evacuated their parking lot stations to head south for the winter. In the same spirit of serving the automobile through advanced (and suspended) structures, Goldberg also built a gasoline station at Clark and Maple in Chicago in which its two service bays were hung from double masts.[22]

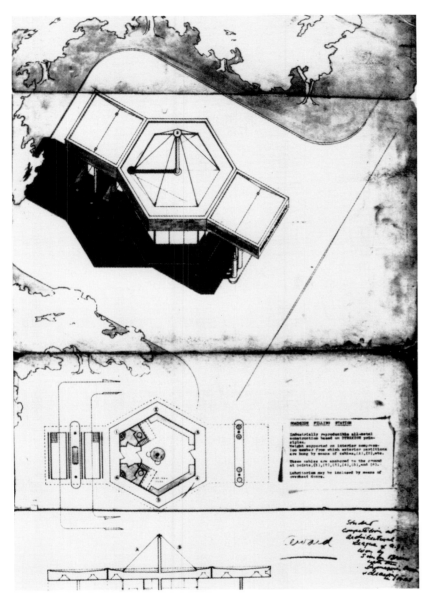

A very different type of structure, one that has been exclusively the domain of the civil engineer, is the road or highway. Once again, we can first look to Europe for the integration of architecture and road. When Giovanni Agnelli restructured Fiat after World War I, architect Mattè-Trucco designed the Lingotto factory with a dramatic continuous ramp leading to a roof test track. This immediately became the inspiration for everyone who sought tangible examples of machine-age architecture, and it was illustrated in nearly all the major texts of the modern movement.

1.8. Simon Breines, Project for a Roadside Filling Station based on Fuller's Dymaxion principles, 1929, bird's eye perspective, plan and elevation. The hexagonal central pavilion is supported by cables from a central mast; it won the New York Architectural League award for 1929. (Courtesy Buckminster Fuller Estate, Los Angeles)

1.9. Bertrand Goldberg, River Forest, Illinois, North Pole Ice Cream Store, 1938, exterior view. The architect describes this as "a trailer (not a building) to be towed by a truck tractor and 'unfolded' at its destination."

It is one thing, however, to design an automobile factory with an access ramp to a roof track. After all, Mattè-Trucco's design is an efficient solution to the functional demands of the factory and its crowded semi-urban setting. It is quite another to project buildings that incorporate the road as part of the larger fabric of an increasingly highway-oriented society. But this is how we must look at such projects as Frank Lloyd Wright's Automobile Objective of 1923 for Sugarloaf Mountain, Maryland, or the numerous contemporary projects that combine the structures of elevated highway and skyscraper.[23] The technological optimism of these projects would soon be tempered by the economic realities of the Depression; but these vast multiuse structures incorporating road and skyscraper and serving traffic, commerce, and residence reveal the extent to which the car was altering our perceptions of architecture.

Possibly the most dramatic example of the road-building, because it became a reality for two years, is the Ford Building and its "Road of Tomorrow," designed by Walter Dorwin Teague and Albert Kahn for the 1939 New York World's Fair (figure 1.10). The main building was semicircular with pylon buttresses radiating from its periphery, which made it look like a toothed gear. The road issued from its upper level on a straightaway, spiraled to the ground, and curved back to the other side to define the building plan as a double-apsed oblong. Thousands of people were able to drive this half-mile road on and through the building in new Ford automobiles. Here they could experience, first-hand, the World of Tomorrow—the theme of the fair. That world was symbolized by the automobile, and its new architecture was defined by the road.

The clearest example of the integration of machine and building in the service of the automobile is a structure for parking. The automatic car park in Chicago has long since departed from its Monroe Street site, where it was erected in March of 1932 (figure 1.11). Here was a structure that was really a machine, a modern version of the endless chain. It had been developed by Westinghouse in 1929 for small lots and for installation in office and apartment buildings. It even could be coin-operated and so didn't need an attendant.

Its inventor, Westinghouse engineer H. D. James, envisioned these parking stations spread throughout cities and inserted in all new buildings as a way to enhance driver convenience and alleviate traffic congestion. "The time is coming soon," he wrote, "when each building must care for the automobiles of its tenants as well as for the tenants themselves."[24] In reference to his Monroe Street car park, James claimed the Ferris wheel as its ancestor.

Appropriately, then, this machine-as-building first went public in Chicago, where the Ferris wheel first appeared on the midway of the World's Columbian Exposition in 1893.

That same Westinghouse machine was transformed by the Whiting Corporation for the Nash Motors exhibit at the Century of Progress International Exposition of 1933 (figure 1.12). Now encased in glass, it could assume the modernist stamp of approval. In fact, it may well be the first totally glass-sheathed tall building actually built—housing cars before people.

1.10. Albert Kahn and Walter Dorwin Teague, New York, New York World's Fair, 1939–40, Ford Building, exterior, view at night. Road and building are united in a dramatic design done cooperatively by architect and industrial designer.

Today, our architecture and our perceptions of what is appropriate for architecture have changed, both subtly and overtly. We are comfortable exposing novel structures rather than masking them in traditional materials. We are also more prepared to view architecture as a machine than were most clients of the earlier decades. By the mid-1960s, a François Dallegret, in his "Anatomy of a House," can draw a house as consisting merely of its infrastructure of pipes, ducts, and other service equipment; or a Yona Friedman can propose a "Spatial City," which is no more than a continuous three-dimensional space-frame raised above the ground and capable of being moved or reassembled.[25] With these examples, house as well as city have taken on the engineering aspect of pure structure.

Similarly, Mike Webb's "Cushicle" and Peter Cook's "Blow-out Village" transform house and city into the engineering aspect of pure machines, at once ubiquitous, mobile, and dynamic. Webb, for example, describes his "Cushicle" as "basic clothing skin that can be inflated to make a chaise-longue or further inflated to make a room [for] in principle an overcoat is a house, is a car when a motor's clipped on."[26] This is radical stuff—a perception of architecture so changed that it would have been alien even to the modernists of the 1920s.

Architecture has become dynamic, moving, and capable of changing form and size. Roads move in to it and serve it exclusively, becoming part of the architectural fabric, as in the Contemporary Resort Hotel at Walt Disney World, or the Union Carbide Headquarters in Danbury, which even has its own traffic cop.

Today, an architectural firm such as Future Systems can conceive designing a private house like a crane, a kinetic living unit that can follow the sun

or change the view out its living-room window, which is actually a windshield (figure 1.13). Meanwhile, plug-in architecture has become fairly common and has created new formal configurations, as in Moshe Safdie's Habitat in Montreal, which presents an agglomerative stacking of prefabricated concrete boxes—irregular, yet pleasing and most

reminiscent of some Mediterranean or Aegean hillside village.

One architect who has carried the plug-in and its relationship to the automobile to a literal extreme is Dan Scully, whose projects have transformed the house into road and car. The project called "End of the Road, or Reeling in the Dotted Line" has a garage door that swings up to admit his pickup truck, which possesses the best seats in the house and the only radio (figure 1.14). Thus the road, which paves the main space of the house, the vehicle, which plugs into the main space and contains some of the essentials of comfortable living, and the house, which envelops and shelters the vehicle, merge as inseparable parts of a whole. Scully designed another project named "'55 Stayin' Alive" for his 1955 Chevrolet panel wagon, which backs into a neoprene, weathertight opening to become the master bedroom of this house. In this case, the automobile becomes an extrusion of the house, and it drives off whenever the owner travels.

Possibly the ultimate examples in this shift in architectural thinking come when architects design private houses or entire cities that move on their own, as in Ted Bakewell and Mike Jantzen's "Autonomous Dwelling Vehicle" of 1980 and Ron Herron's 1966 project for "Cities Moving."[27] In these cases, the structure is also the machine. The car, which had acted as the catalyst for changing our perceptions about architecture, has been dispensed with. It is no longer needed.

1.11. H. D. James, Chicago, Westinghouse car parking machine, installed in March 1932 on Monroe Street between State and Dearborn. This is the ultimate pragmatic design by an engineer of the machine as building in the service of the automobile. (See also figure 15.12.)

1.12. Whiting Corporation, Chicago, Century of Progress International Exposition, 1933–34, Nash Motors exhibit, exterior view. The same car park machine was given an architectural face-lift and an advertising mission.

Many of these projects are not yet realizable. Many also may remain merely as ideas, for our social structure is not quite ready for what Louis Armand called an "era of a world in movement."[28] But to the extent that this new approach to architecture as movable and removable has helped to break down the professional barriers between architect and engineer (a process that should extend much farther into our society), our built environment will benefit and our changing social needs will be better met. As Stephen Bayley of the Conran Foundation recently wrote in an article on the automobile as a built environment, "You get static-controlled environment and you call it architecture. You get mobile-controlled environment and you call it a car."[29] It would seem to me that if we can combine the two, as more of our young architects are proposing, you get the engineered architecture of the next century—an architecture reunited with engineering and one in which, indeed, house and car have become synonymous.

1.13. Future Systems (Jan Kaplicky and David Nixon), Project 124: "The Peanut," ca. 1984, perspective. This high-tech, movable living unit can follow the sun and change its position and view.

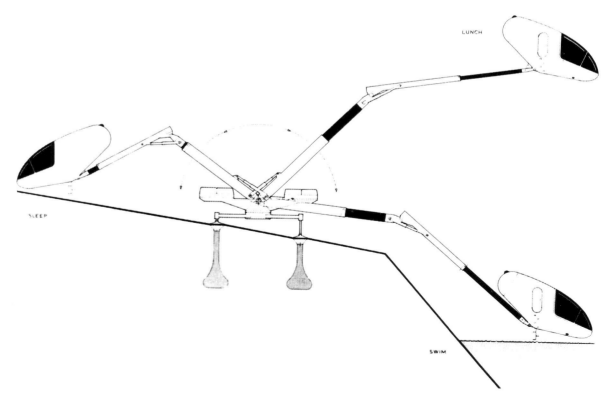

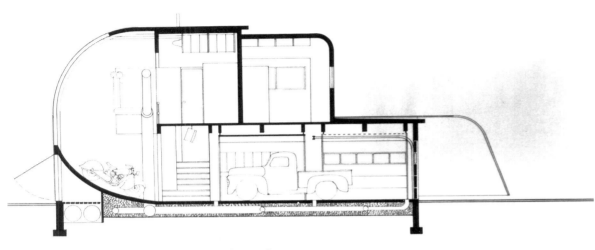

1.14. Daniel Scully, "End of the Road, or Reeling in the Dotted Line," 1976, cross section. The driveway, with a painted dotted line, continues into the house, where the parked pickup truck becomes furniture. To either side of the central room are overhead garage doors that roll up to reveal kitchenette and storage closets.

Notes

Research for this paper has been supported by a grant from the Graham Foundation for Advanced Studies in the Visual Arts.

1. See, for example, such recent buildings as Foster Associates' Renault Centre and their Hong Kong and Shanghai Bank, Richard Rogers and Partners' Patscenter in Princeton, or Jean Nouvel et al., Arab World Institute in Paris.

2. On the distinctions between machine and structure as two sides of engineering technology, see David P. Billington, *The Tower and the Bridge: The New Art of Structural Engineering* (New York: Basic Books, 1983), 11. On the split between architecture and engineering, see Peter Collins, *Changing Ideals in Modern Architecture* (Montreal: McGill-Queens Univ. Press, 1965), 128–46, 185–97.

3. See F. T. Kihlstedt, "The Automobile and the Transformation of the American House, 1910–1935," in David L. Lewis and Laurence Goldstein, eds., *The Automobile and American Culture* (Ann Arbor: University of Michigan Press, 1983), 160–75.

4. Le Corbusier, *Towards a New Architecture,* trans. Frederick Etchells (London: Architectural Press, 1927), 121.

5. Le Corbusier, *Aircraft* (London: The Studio, May 1935), 5. Corbusier grasped the distinction between structure and machine in his Citrohan house projects of the early 1920s and clearly saw them as machines when he said the house could be located anywhere and in any environment, from the Argentine pampas to the Parisian suburb. See Stanislaus von Moos, *Le Corbusier: Elements of a Synthesis* (Cambridge: M.I.T. Press, 1975), 90.

6. Sigfried Giedion, *Walter Gropius: Work and Teamwork* (New York: Reinhold, 1954), 22.

7. James J. Flink, *The Car Culture* (Cambridge: M.I.T. Press, 1975), 41.

8. Flink, 140.

9. Jane Stern and Michael Stern, *Auto Ads* (New York: Random House, 1975), 21.

10. Le Corbusier, *Oeuvre complète, 1934–1938* (Zurich: Girsberger, 1938), 24.

11. Alfred P. Sloan, Jr., "The Forward View," *Atlantic*

Monthly 154 (Sept. 1934): 260.

12. F. R. S. Yorke, *The Modern House,* 2d ed. (London: Architectural Press, 1935), 260; H. T. Fisher, "New Elements in House Design," *Architectural Record* 66 (Nov. 1929): 403.

13. "Housing and Prefabrication," *Pencil Points* 17 (June 1936): 308.

14. American Houses, Inc., *The New American Motohome* (New York: John Wanamaker, 1935), 8.

15. Sheldon Cheney and Martha Chandler Cheney, *Art and the Machine: An Account of Industrial Design in 20th Century America* (New York: McGraw-Hill, 1936), 157.

16. Some of the mobile home firms that did incorporate in the 1930s and continued after the war were the Palace Corporation, from 1935 into the mid-1960s; Vagabond Coach Company, from 1931 to 1964, when it was sold to Guerdon Industries; Traveleze Industries, Inc., from 1931 and still in business; Trotwood Trailers, 1932, and still in business; and Redman Industries, 1937, and now one of the largest producers of mobile and modular houses. See Carlton M. Edwards, *Homes for Travel and Living* (East Lansing, Mich.: C. E. Edwards, 1977), 125–33.

17. See Le Corbusier-Saugnier, "Les Maisons 'Voisin'," *L'Esprit Nouveau,* no. 2 (1920; reprint, New York: Da Capo Press, 1968), 211–15; for Stout, who licensed construction of his mobile home to the Palace Coach and Trailer Co. of Flint, Mich., to be redesigned for factory-housing production during World War II, see William B. Stout, *So Away I Went!* (Indianapolis: Bobbs-Merrill, 1951), 288.

18. Paul Rudolph, "The Mobile Home Is the 20th-Century Brick," *Architectural Record* 143 (Apr. 1968): 145; and "Twentieth Century Bricks," *Architectural Forum* 136 (June 1972): 49.

19. For the former, see such vernacular housing solutions as Skye Rise Terrace, St. Paul, Minnesota, erected in 1970 by Elmer Frye, the so-called father of the 10-wide; and for the latter, see Moshe Safdie's Habitat of 1967 in Montreal or Cerna Garza and Raba's Palacio del Rio Hilton of 1968 in San Antonio, Texas.

20. James Ward, ed., *The Artifacts of R. Buckminster Fuller,* vol. 1 (New York: Garland, 1985), 53.

21. The architects for the Travel and Transportation Building were Bennett, Burnham, and Holabird, and this domed suspension building was for the display of locomotives. See Folke T. Kihlstedt, "Formal and Structural Innovations in American Exposition Architecture: 1901–1939" (Ph.D diss., Northwestern University, 1973), 209–13.

22. In a letter to me dated January 4, 1983, Goldberg noted that the owner of the North Pole was a wealthy young client who lost interest in the operation, even though it "'worked' just as it was supposed to," and it disappeared. See also, Michel Ragon, *Goldberg. Dans la ville. On the City* (Paris: Paris Art Center, 1985), 148–49.

23. Among these latter skyscraper-bridge projects are those by Louis Mullgardt of 1924, a skyscraper bridge across the San Francisco Bay; by Charles Morgan of 1928 (for D. H. Burnham and Co.), a skyscraper bridge over the Chicago River; by Raymond Hood of 1929, a proposal for Manhattan bridge with apartments; and by Hugh Ferriss, also of 1929, apartments on bridges for New York City of the Future. All of them integrate bridge, apartment building, and automobile highway.

24. See *The American City* 41 (Nov. 1929): 100; and H. D. James, "Westinghouse Vertical Parking Machine," memorandum of 5/26/32, Westinghouse Historical Collection, Pittsburgh, Pa. James, although an engineer, was also interested in architecture and wrote on modern architecture, albeit from a technological perspective in which he stresses "efficient performance" in houses; see his "If I Were Building a House," *Popular Mechanics* 60 (Dec. 1933): 826–30ff.; and *Architectural Record* 73 (Jan. 1933): 67.

25. For Dallegret, see Reyner Banham, "A Home Is Not a House," *Art in America* (Apr. 1965): 71; for Friedman, see Michel Ragon, "Prerequisites for a New Urbanism: Mobile Architecture," *Landscape* 13 (Spring 1964): 20.

26. Michael Webb and David Greene, "Drive-In Housing," *Architectural Design* 36 (Nov. 1966): 573.

27. For the Bakewell project, see *Domus* 610 (1980): 42–43; for the well-known Herron project, see Lampugnani (ed.), *L'Aventura delle Idee nell'architettura: 1750–1980* (Milan: XVII Triennale, 1985), 209.

28. See Ragon, 21.

29. Stephen Bayley, "Grace . . . Pace . . . Space: The Architecture of the Car," *Architectural Review* 176 (Nov. 1984): 76. Bayley claims that "inside a car, you get a perfect little exercise in interior design, a controlled environment more perfect than most homes."

Transportation Imagery and Streamlined Moderne Architecture

ROBERT M. CRAIG

A Case for a Design Typology

When one surveys the modern architectural forms in America between World War I and World War II, one discovers among the various expressions of "Modern" (International Style), "Art Deco," or "Depression Modern" designs, a distinctive architectural style of the 1930s that is determined by the progressive forms of automobiles and other transportation machines of the day. The imagery of this class of buildings is both modern and progressive, and although the characteristic architectural makeup can suggest ornamental parallels with *l'art decoratif* of the late 1920s, the functional and aesthetic links to transportation and streamlining help to identify a unique building style, a style that mirrors an increasingly mobile American society. Borrowing their formal language from industrial design, the typical buildings of this distinctive "Streamlined Moderne" style distinguish themselves from contemporary modernistic or Art Deco architecture. As buildings served by and serving the automobile, the architecture of the Streamlined Moderne constitutes a unique design typology of the 1930s and beyond. This essay, therefore, proposes that the embracing of streamlining by architecture resulted in the creation of more than just another modernistic building style. The following sets forth a definition of an architectural design typology that links streamlined form and transportation-oriented functions expressive of the patterns of an increasingly automobile-centered American way of life.

Recent Historiography of American Twenties and Thirties Styles

Bracketed by two world wars, the decades of the 1920s and 1930s seem quite naturally a single period despite the obvious social, economic, and aesthetic differences between years of boom and crash, of jazz-age prosperity and depression. As a whole, the interwar years were above all a period in which the machine, in its various manifestations, was playing an increasingly central part in the lives of Americans.[1] In architecture, as "The Machine Age" co-curator Richard Guy Wilson has described, 1920s–1940s design offered an aesthetic of progress and modernity, evidenced in several building styles, each reflecting differing influences of the machine on form, space, materials, and ornament. More than this, machine imagery of the day gave expression to the building's progressive and more modern functionalism. Machine Age architecture thrust skyscrapers higher than ever before (or rarely since), revolutionized architectural "open plans," and incorporated technical advances in modern houses that were intended to solve social and ecological problems. To be sure, many Machine Age buildings share with contemporary painting and sculpture (or, for that matter, with photography, fashion, industrial design, and the cinema, etc.) a modern abstraction,[2] but neither the common themes of machine imagery nor tendencies toward abstraction can alone define this pluralistic modern Machine Age.

Professor Wilson organized his discussion of architecture in the Machine Age by distinguishing styles, or at least aesthetic approaches to design, which he identified as the moderne (or the "machine-as-parts" approach), the International Style, the Streamlined, and "stripped classical modernism." These are four categories with which I have little argument, as they coincide substantially with distinctions I drew in 1980 when I defined four

American modern architectural styles of the period, which I then labeled Art Deco, International Style, Streamlined Moderne, and WPA (or PWA) Classic.[3] I sought to clarify distinct styles that informed modernistic American architecture between the world wars but that had often been homogenized by historians who embraced all of the modern styles under collective terms such as *Art Deco* or *Moderne.*

Publications from the mid-1970s have clarified the various machine aesthetics that marked the interwar period, and for purposes of the present essay, perhaps Donald Bush's discussion of "the streamlined decade" is the most significant.[4] Bush focused on streamlining as an aesthetic impulse that affected industrial design, and in particular the forms of transportation machines. Although Bush discussed a few buildings, he presented them merely as architectural reflections of "the spirit of the age." What emerges clearly from Bush's study, however, is the formal shift away from the angularity and syncopation of the twenties to the aerodynamic teardrop forms and lines of speed that by the thirties symbolized progress, efficiency, and a new kinetic functionalism.

In describing the populist commercial architecture of the American Main Street, therefore, it was no longer possible to depict a homogenous Art Deco or modernistic period between the wars, and even Machine Age architecture does not offer *a specific typology* that links certain building types to the respective styles, in particular to the streamlined aesthetic. Cervin Robinson and Rosemarie Haag Bletter had suggested a typology for Art Deco in describing the "skyscraper style" in New York, although their study did not extend to the wealth of Art Deco five-and-ten-cents stores, boutiques, department stores, and movie theaters built at a pedestrian scale throughout the country.[5] Among the four Machine Age styles, I submit, the Streamlined Moderne presents a body of work for which a typology can be defined. Streamlined Moderne architecture is unlike the first—the highly pluralistic, fundamentally formalist, and ornamental Art Deco building tradition; is unlike the second—the volumetric abstractions of the Bauhaus-inspired International Style; and is unlike the third—the stripped-down, classically imbued Depression Modern of thirties civic buildings. This fourth style, Streamlined Moderne architecture, evidences a direct and specific (sometimes literal) aesthetic transfer from transportation machines—ships, trains, airplanes, and especially automobiles—to roadside buildings that serve these machines.

Art Deco Versus Streamlined Moderne

By means of a transference of streamlining in industrial design—including, most significantly, automobile design—to building form and ornament, the Streamlined Moderne especially isolates itself from Art Deco architecture, with which it has generally been associated. Art Deco's fundamentally cosmetic character reflects its reliance on color and ornament for decorative effect. Art Deco designers crown the skyline of skyscrapers with floral abstractions and machine-cut chevrons, and Deco artists surface jazz-age theaters, office building lobbies, department stores, and boutiques with zigzag patterns, stylized animal or plant shapes, and even exotic, Mayan-inspired surface incisions and sculptural relief work. Although certain setback forms are typical, Art Deco–styled buildings remain essentially ornamental.

The Streamlined Moderne, on the other hand, is associated in particular with transportation forms and imagery and as a building typology links function with an associational formal language. Streamlined Moderne architecture adopts parallel lines of speed, fluid forms (rounded corners and neon lighting), and progressive and shiny building materials to embody in roadside architecture the streamlining aesthetic evidenced in contemporary industrial design. Product design of the Hoover and Roosevelt years increasingly surplants Art Deco abstractions of the 1920s with streamlining effects of the 1930s, as the works of Kem Weber, Norman Bel Geddes, and Raymond Loewy demonstrate.[6] The application of streamlining to architecture of the 1930s and beyond is evidenced in designs that can thereby no longer be considered Art Deco or International Style Modern. This body of streamlined buildings is functionally and aesthetically linked to transportation and reflects an increasingly pervasive twentieth-century American mobility.

The 1930s Automobile and the 1930s Roadside Building

The most up-to-date (and futuristic) automobiles of the day were advertised as "functionally correct for cleaving through the air . . . and . . . for moving over the uneven surface of the ground." Advertisements described the Chrysler Airflow, for example, as an automobile "balanced like an arrow in flight" and promised riders "a glorious sense of freedom at high speeds."[7] If the 1934 Chrysler Airflow or the 1936 Lincoln Zephyr embodied in their streamlined forms the "lines of least resistance" that marked contemporary economic design, suburban buildings of the Streamlined Moderne, with similar formal features, promised an equally comfortable aesthetic fit for the automobile and the mobile American that these buildings served.

In 1932 Raymond Loewy designed the Hupmobile sedan (1934 showroom model) and annotated his design to emphasize features that would be commonplace in automobile design by the decade's end; such features would be reflected, moreover, in "automobile buildings" during the same period. Loewy's notations draw our attention to the automobile's rounded corners, streamlined lights, and three-sided windshields for better visibility (curved window profiles generally), and these annotations might as readily be describing a streamlined roadside diner as a 1934 Hupmobile. The molded car body, teardrop rear-light housing, or involute wraparound fenders find architectural parallel both in shaped marquees for the roadside diner, depot, or theater, and in decorative arts for modern homes and commercial lighting fixtures for business buildings. Fluid profiles, streamlined shrouds, and dynamic shaping of the automobile body were echoed in building form—both in a building's silhouette and footprint on the landscape. Rounded building corners, plastic entry canopies, metallic architectural facades, neon tubing, curving access ramps, and the streamlining of driveways or streetscapes established a distinctive machine-inspired building typology evidenced in sleek buildings sited along the roadside in the commercial settings of the modern American suburban landscape.

Thus, the buildings of this typology can be easily recognized and enumerated as one considers the changing life of the modern progressive American housewife now using the car to extend her daily activities beyond her immediate pedestrian neighborhood. Further, and most significantly, those businesses existing to serve the mobile American family, the traveling businessman, and the automobile itself help to define the typology. "Roadside buildings" include diners and "fast-food" restaurants, car dealerships, tire retail outlets, auto parts shops and repair garages, gas stations, automatic car washes, suburban schools, suburban theaters, motor hotels (motels), and pioneer shopping centers with off-street parking for the automobile. In addition to such "auto buildings," the Streamlined Moderne building typology is further extended by structures or architectural spaces associated with other transportation machines: bus depots, air terminals, boat marinas, and train station lobbies. This body of architecture reflects more than a period style; it constitutes a building typology linked to function, expressive of the patterns of a mobile society and embodying the progressive ideas of efficiency, economy, and modernity.

Streamlined Moderne buildings are also more suburban than urban. Fundamentally idiosyncratic, these buildings are rarely sited in pairs or groups and are never comfortable if aligned within a row of an urban streetscape. Rather, they carve out corner intersections to shape the flow of traffic off the linear grid of the urban street and into the freer space of suburban parking lots, drive-thrus, or off-street entry ramps. The nineteenth-century commercial row typically aligned flanking storefronts to lot line at the sidewalk and presented itself fundamentally to a walking clientele (or, at best, through a hitching post out front, acknowledged the slow transportation of a horse and buggy). The pedestrian and the wagon had formed the town's streetscape for centuries. The twentieth-century "horseless carriage," with its increasing speed along suburban roads and highways, would by the 1930s begin to be shaped by design theories of streamlining into a modern four-door coupe. Ideals of streamlining and efficient design would be transferred to the new suburban building types linked to these new transportation images. Diners would line the unclogged roads at the edge of the city and frequently resembled railroad dining cars anchored in the landscape along the busy highway. "Automobile streets" at the edge of the city (such as Spring Street in Atlanta) would provide a service street especially *for* automobiles (lined with car dealerships, repair garages, auto parts stores, etc.) and convenient to the residential street (Peachtree Street, Atlanta) nearby. Town and country would be linked by suburban access roads whose intersections were increasingly claimed by high-profile eateries or gas stations[8] and whose roadsides were dotted with Moderne shopping centers, suburban theaters, schools, and motor hotels. Such buildings reflect a new age of transportation machines and illustrate the aesthetic impact of the automobile, in particular, on American life.

Streamlining and the Industrial Designers

Streamlining had emerged from the drawing boards of a new professional: the industrial designer—men such as Raymond Loewy, Walter Dorwin Teague, Henry Dreyfuss, and industrial design's major propagandist, Norman Bel Geddes, who published *Horizons* in 1932. At the end of the decade, the New York World's Fair of 1939–40 provided the "greatest challenge and opportunity" for the industrial designers who found in the fair's theme, "Building the World of Tomorrow," "a perfect vehicle for their imagination."[9] It also made clear by decade's end the impact that the automobile already had made on the American consciousness.

Inside the Perisphere of the New York fair, Henry Dreyfuss created a model city, "Democracity," and a spectacular sound and light production that dramatically proclaimed the progress of humanity in the modern age. Even more popular was

Norman Bel Geddes's "Futurama" display within the General Motors Highways and Horizons exhibit. Breathtaking models of America in 1960 provided a panorama of 35,738 square feet, 500,000 model buildings, and superhighways along which traveled some 50,000 teardrop automobiles, trucks, and buses. Visitors seemed to fly over countryside and townscapes, industrial centers, universities, and experimental farms. The whole finally climaxed at a spectacular model of a metropolis of modern glass and concrete skyscrapers styled by horizontal strips, rounded corners, and rooftop terraces. There could be no clearer evidence of the established and future impact of the automobile on American life than these model highways, streamlined buildings, and transportation machines. Visitors viewed them from moving sidewalks or from seats positioned on conveyor belts on which they experienced an "Aladdin-like flight through time and space."[10] Bel Geddes's 1939 vision of the future world of 1960 today seems extraordinarily clairvoyant.

The Highways and Horizons exhibit was not merely a world of fantasy but reflected an established Streamlined Moderne style of industrial-products design that throughout the preceding decade had influenced commercial architecture and had already created an American roadside aesthetic clearly distinguishable from other architectural manifestations of the Machine Age. The type relied on teardrop forms, parallel horizontal "lines of speed," and rounded corners now applied to or forming buildings functionally linked to transportation and the roadside. It was an architecture of and for the ship, the train, the plane, and the car.

The automobile was one among several transportation machines, therefore, which informed the aesthetic. As the ideal form of a progressive age, the streamlined teardrop represented the true form of least resistance, a symbol of functional efficiency and optimism. The emergance of an architectural style informed by streamlining paralleled design developments in the full range of transportation machines of the period; images of ocean liners, streamlined steam engines for passenger train service, and airplanes and dirigibles repeatedly were presented as symbols of the age. The period dirigible, indeed, might be viewed as the ultimate teardrop, a lasting image of the streamlined age.

When the Wright brothers and their immediate successors piloted "flying machines," the earliest forms of these primitive flight contraptions had more in common with kite construction. By the 1930s, however, streamlined airplanes adopted aerodynamic teardrops for fuselage, wing sections, and other forms. Studies of aerodynamics and hydrodynamics prompted designers, likewise, to streamline the modern ocean liner, and Norman Bel Geddes's designs seem the most futuristic. Wind tunnel experiments encouraged other industrial designers to update traditional steam locomotives. Such a conversion could be accomplished by the simple addition of a streamlined, zephyr-inspired shroud with horizontal ribs, shiny metallic skin, and flashy styling, which seemed to advertise the 100 + mph speed of the newer trains. The Santa Fe El Capitain, the New York Central's Commodore Vanderbilt (1934), the Burlington Zephyr (1934), and Raymond Loewy's 1937–38 S-1 for the Pennsylvania Railroad are among the best known of such streamlined trains.[11]

From Automobile to Architecture

These developments in transportation imagery were immediately reflected in the design of the American automobile. Private wagons and surreys had transported Americans for generations from farm to town and from district to district within the city, and initially the horseless carriage reflected the simple wagon forms. But as Raymond Loewy's evolutionary chart of automobiles illustrates,[12] the successive styling of automobiles progressed from rectilinear to teardrop shapes, culminating in the classic mid-1930s coupe. Indeed, the new reverence for the teardrop was especially evidenced in Normal Bel Geddes's 1931 designs for cars and Buckminster Fuller's Dymaxion cars of the same period. Reduced to the ideal streamlined teardrop, such forms lived the longest in the Volkswagen "Beetle."

The transformation of existing Machine Age architectural forms parallels the evolution toward streamlining observable in the design of the transportation machines themselves, including the automobile as Loewy charted it. To be sure, the architectural borrowings from automobile design extend well beyond William Van Alen's incorporation of automobile hubcaps set within brick tires and mudguards at the thirty-first floor of the Chrysler Building in New York or Richard Neutra's utilization of Ford Model A headlights and rims to light the stairwell of Philip Lovell's "Health" House in Los Angeles.[13]

Among the pluralistic images of the period are noteworthy buildings that reflect the metamorphosis, as streamlining becomes the pervasive aesthetic impulse. Much as the rounded corners, slanted grilles, streamlined rear light, and three-sided sloping windshields of a 1934 Hupmobile or Chrysler Airflow negate the rectilinearity of wagons, surreys, and Model T's, so might rounded-corner windows and kinetic lines begin to streamline the volumetric International Style, the orderly massing of the WPA Classic, and the towered ziggurat forms of the Art

Deco skyscraper tradition.

Airplane, Ship, Bus, and Train . . . and Architecture

The key to our discovery of a Streamlined Moderne typology among the commercial buildings of the 1930s and 1940s, therefore, lies in the very transportation sources of Moderne commercial design and engineering during the period. As the industrial designer's role in the contemporary aesthetics increased, the forms of industry and the aerodynamic lines of transportation emerge as the principal formal determinants of a new building style. In general, Streamlined Moderne architectural design is most often, or at least most effectively, evidenced in the buildings designed to serve the new and updated transportation machines. A novel *dynamic functionalism* styles both building and machine in streamlined streaks, metallic skins, teardrop forms, softened and curved corners, and the fluid contours of a new speed aesthetic.

We may return to these transportation machines and rediscover their architectural equivalents. The impact of airplane design on buildings that serve air transport is illustrated by the modern airport terminal, most especially the small-scale structure of a local airstrip. At the Ramsgate Municipal Airport (published in *Architectural Review* in 1937), an English example presents an almost literal translation of the new air dynamic (figure 2.1); the very plan of the building outlines the spreading wings of a plane, and the airport's control tower is merely the cockpit of the flying machine itself.[14] In Paris, at the 1925 Exposition International des Arts Décoratifs et Industriels Modernes, a similar image characterized the Air Pavilion. As Bel Geddes streamlined his ocean liner designs, river-cruise

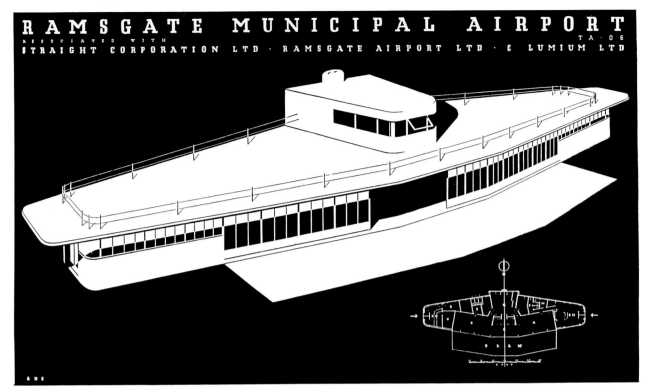

RAMSGATE MUNICIPAL AIRPORT
TA·06
ASSOCIATED WITH
STRAIGHT CORPORATION LTD · RAMSGATE AIRPORT LTD · & LUMIUM LTD

pleasure boats, such as the *Admiral* (still moored today in St. Louis), began to display metallic surfaces and smooth engineered lines of a "machine" for nautical transport—Mark Twain's riverboat or Jerome Kern's "Showboat" as though designed by Vincent Korda for *Things to Come*. The Aquatic Park Casino, now the Maritime Museum of San Francisco, designed in 1935–39 by William Mooser, Jr., provides a literal translation into the new language of Streamlined Moderne architecture.[15] The marine metaphor would appear to reach back to J. C. Loudon's theories of associationism linking image and character, form and function. Once established, the "nautical moderne" would fashion such well-known masterpieces of the style as Robert Derrah's remodeled Coca Cola Bottling Company, moored in downtown Los Angeles since 1937 like a landlocked *Queen Mary*.[16]

2.1. Ramsgate Municipal Airport, Ramsgate, England, D. Pleydell Bouverie, architect, 1937. The spreading wings, overhangs, and "cockpit" control tower (formed almost like the bridge of a ship flanked by ship rails) demonstrate the transference from transportation machines to buildings serving transportation of those formal elements associated with planes, ships, or the automobile. Here the aerodynamic building reflects in plan and elevation the formal language of the airplane designer.

Streamlined trains provided more efficient land transportation for the speed-conscious masses. The very experience in purchasing a train ticket in a chromium-plated, fluorescent lighting–enhanced station lobby provided a foretaste of the modernistic travel a tourist was about to undertake. For the less hearty enthusiast of speed, land transit was possible by such streamlined motorcoaches as the 1940

Greyhound Silversides. And what more appropriate reflection in architecture is there than the Greyhound bus depot of the period (figure 2.2), many of which were designed in appropriate streamlined styling by W. S. Arrasmith?[17] The gleam and glitter of ceramic tile, the continuity of rounded corners, and the "streamlined electricity" of the day—neon light—all reflect the spirit of modern times. The features conspire with the streamlined flow of wall surfaces and building silhouette to impel the motorcoach to ease efficiently out of its berth and to proceed around the corner into the flow of traffic. Beginning its journey through time and space, the Greyhound buses (and depot) were fully imbued with the lines and materials of progressive industrial design, and functionally equipped to "leave the driving to us." Both machine and building are fuelled by the energetic spirit of modern transport, and if the Greyhound Silversides personified the freedom and speed of a leaping greyhound, the aesthetic continuity of the streamlined depot communicated the same message.

The Automobile and Architecture

With these examples, we return to the American automobile as the ultimate symbol of a modern progressive and mobile society. It suffices merely to mention the extensive, indeed pervasive, influence of the automobile on American life from the mid-1920s on and to note the significant role the automobile and related industries continue to play in our national economy. It is relevant to our theme to consider such auto-related industries and to recognize that the streamlined car of the 1930s was as comfortable aesthetically with auto-related architecture as the motorcoach was with its bus terminals.

2.2. Greyhound bus depot, Columbia, South Carolina. Bus depots built across America by Greyhound positioned themselves at roadside as architectural equivalents of the "Silversides" and other streamlined buses. Both bus and depot shared a dynamic, flowing aesthetic of slick skin surfaces, rounded corners, and a sensation of movement.

The gas station, for example, offered opportunities for expressive streamlining appropriate for a building whose sole function was to serve the automobile and its traveling American driver. A noteworthy project in this idiom is the transport-inspired gas station designed about 1935 by students of Kem Weber, a machine for servicing automobiles that is so dynamic that the building appears ready to drive off under its own power (figure 2.3).

The recognizable norm for this vernacular streamlined building type calls for clinically sterile wall surfaces of tile and smoothly rounded corners, often of glass. Some early Gulf Oil stations, as well as Walter Dorwin Teague's prototype designs for Texaco, reflect certain of these typical materials and stylistic elements. Less well known are schemes, never built, proposed by Norman Bel Geddes for Socony Vacuum Oil Company, which became Mobil.[18] Bel Geddes concerned himself with image, visibility, traffic flow, lighting, construction, and road materials, and intended his gas stations to look as efficient as they functioned. At a triangular site in Flushing Meadows, near the 1939–40 New York World's Fair, Bel Geddes proposed three teardrops in a roadside complex that perfectly accommodated the automobile *and* the industrial designer's aerodynamic formal prejudices. Although Bel Geddes's teardrop filling stations were never constructed, Frederick Frost's subsequent curve-fronted Mobil station prototype was ultimately built at intersections across America.[19] In terms of siting, it is not too much to generalize that American gas stations have universally streamlined our urban crossroads by insisting, often, that all four corners of city-street intersections be carved out for service stations. Such sites of maximum visibility would allow automobiles easy access off the street, into the service area, to be refueled by aerodynamic gas pumps.

Streamlining for the architecture of auto-related industries reached beyond the gas station, moreover. Car dealerships began to line early suburban roads of major cities, not only instituting that most typically American pattern of suburban commercial strip architecture but also spreading the rounded corners and machine aesthetic of a streamlined building type along the path. Moreover, tire manufacturers such as Firestone styled their Moderne showrooms and service areas after the other "auto-buildings" (figure 2.4), and soon auto parts outlets and repair garages followed suit.

Roadside cafes operated by uniformed carhops, who would be equally at home as airline stewardesses or movie usherettes, present additional images of the period's Streamlined Moderne architecture. The high visibility of fast-food restaurants and roadside diners, or the novel building forms adopted for hamburger chains such as White Castle (or later, McDonald's), helped to link distant cities together in the minds of the traveling consumer.[20] These earliest prototypes of the now ubiquitous American commercial strip stretched forth across the expanding American suburban land-

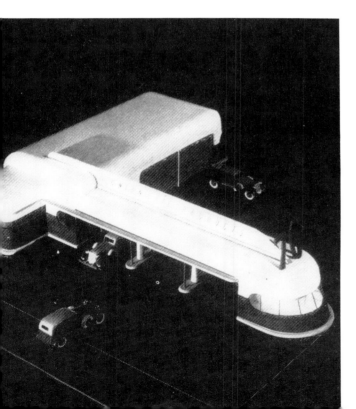

2.3. Gasoline service station project by students of Kem Weber, 1935. With its clinically clean surfaces, aerodynamic lines, soft forms, and a profile clearly inspired by transportation, this gas station would have presented an image so mobile and kinetic that passersby would presume the gas station itself could drive off into the street; here was quite literally a machine for servicing automobiles.

2.4. Firestone Auto Supply and Service Stores, Atlanta, Georgia, Seward D. Legge, architect, 1937–38. As Peachtree Street in Atlanta developed farther and farther northward from downtown, automobile service buildings lined the suburban edge of the city. Auto parts outlets, service stations, car dealerships, and tire stores were among the roadside architecture built to serve the automobile, and the streamlining of their buildings advertised their automobile-oriented function.

scape beyond the Coolidge and Hoover years to Franklin Roosevelt's era. With their bright neon lights or electrified marquees, the drive-in restaurants (figure 2.5) were as recognizable at high speeds on the busy main thoroughfares as were contemporary suburban drive-in theaters or other drive-in commercial outlets. The fast-food eateries were surfaced inside with gleaming tile and polished steel to promote a healthful image (for ease of digestion); at the same time, on the exterior, they seemed to echo the aesthetic of speed associated with the streamlined trains or the new coupes and roadsters of the day (figure 2.6). Designed as machine-inspired, dynamic, streamlined objects of the road, the cafes and diners of the thirties (and later) advertised in their very forms and physical siting their ease of access and efficiency of service.

The impact of streamlining extends to "ordinary" architecture of various other functions as well. Norman Bel Geddes wrote that "just as surely as the artists of the fourteenth century are remembered by their cathedrals, so will those of the twentieth be remembered for their factories and the products of these factories."[21] Factory and commercial buildings often reflected in their forms the Streamlined Moderne aesthetic of the industrial designer, as did the very industrial goods and factory

2.5. The Varsity Restaurant, Atlanta, Georgia, Jules Grey, architect, 1940. The fast-food restaurant presented a streamlined image to advertise its association with the automobile and the roadside. Within a few blocks of this eatery on Atlanta's "automobile street" (Spring Street) were auto parts outlets, service stations, and a Dodge dealership, all adorned in streamlined forms.

products they manufactured or sold. These goods and the services they represented may be viewed as icons and rituals of the efficient and modern "technics" of the period. Perhaps not as literal as the placing of a GE refrigerator atop a local distributor's showroom and office (as at Raymond Hood's Queens and Brooklyn buildings for GE distributor Rex Cole), a streamlined building design for Westinghouse or Sears Roebuck or Frigidaire would be self-evidently progressive during this period. A factory making Hoover vacuum cleaners transferred during the Machine Age the smooth plastic forms of the vacuum's motor shroud to the rounded corners of the building itself. Typically streamlined factory buildings along developing suburban industrial sites advertised in their Moderne forms the progressive machines and appliances fabricated, warehoused, and/or sold inside.[22]

Other buildings, moreover, provided responses in varying ways to the new patterns of the modern, streamlined, American suburban lifestyle. Streamlined elementary schools (such as Tucker and Howell's Morris Brandon School in Atlanta, 1946–47) reflected the shift from neighborhood in-town schools located within walking distance from home to suburban schools accessed by the automobile. Such school driveways were ultimately symbolized by the suburban housewife in her "town and country" station wagon daily depositing a carpool load of children at the streamlined curbside school entry (with hardly the need to slow the automobile).

The motor hotel or motel emerged as a late development in the architecture of streamlining designed for a mobile American society. The progressive motor hotel presented tourists with buildings sporting modern clean lines (advertising clean and comfortable accommodations) and ultimately displaced the "tourist home" industry, whereby travel-

ers rented rooms in private homes. The Coral Court Motel of Marlborough, Missouri (figure 2.7), which is near St. Louis, has recently been discovered by preservationists, who view this object of popular culture as among the city's noteworthy architectural "period works."[23]

The progressive architecture of the modern suburban cinema (such as the De Anza Theater in Riverside, California, or the Alameda Theater in San Antonio [figure 2.8]) reflected the popularity of futuristic film fantasies from Buck Rogers serials to H. G. Wells's *Things to Come* (1936). Such motion-picture houses offered suburban moviegoers streamlined exterior forms and dynamic lobby volumes as a further contribution to the definition of the period aesthetic.

The fin marquee (whether nautical or aerodynamic in inspiration) accented such buildings but advertised other building functions as well. Although it is frequently associated with movie theaters, fin marquees are visible on building types ranging from civic auditoriums to diners and depots. Several finlike design accents adorn the entry of the Pan Pacific Auditorium in Hollywood, Cali-

2.6. The Modern Diner, Pawtucket, Rhode Island (manufactured by Sterling Diners), 1940. The Modern Diner appears to emerge from the brick wall at left like a streamlined railroad engine coming out of a tunnel. The directional slant of the marquee graphics, the shrouded nose of the "engine," and the continuous windows conspire to present a roadside building that is dynamic and both modern and Moderne.

fornia, by Wurdeman and Becket (1935), where the new car designs were yearly introduced at the auto show (figure 2.9).[24] In 1940 the Varsity Restaurant in Atlanta, Georgia, expanded its facility (founded in 1928) and dressed its roadside building in a new Moderne image designed by Jules Grey, complete with a vertical billboard entry marquee (see figure 2.5). Further examples of fin marquees are seen at the numerous bus depots that Greyhound positioned at journey's end throughout the country (see figure 2.2). Such roadside buildings, with their various fin marquees and streamlining, accommodated the automobile aesthetically and functionally.

The most effective examples of streamlined advertisement on buildings employed the period's dynamic graphics of neon-tube calligraphy and lighting. During the 1930s, shoppers began to commute by automobile to suburban centers where collections of shops, drugstores, and theaters awaited a one-stop shopping excursion. Neon dynamically beckoned the traveler off the road into the shopping center. At an early suburban shopping center in Atlanta (1939), George Harwell Bond combined neon lights, strip layout, rounded building corners, glass block, metallic strips, and flowing building lines in a Streamlined Moderne group of retail stores (and movie theater) called Briarcliff Plaza. The sense of motion that neon brings to Plaza Drugs at Briarcliff Plaza directly expresses the role of the roadster in contemporary America (figure 2.10): Briarcliff Plaza was Atlanta's first shopping center designed with off-street parking to accommodate the automobile.

The Streamlined Moderne Housewife

The modern American suburbanite of the late 1930s and 1940s was leading an increasingly efficient lifestyle made more convenient by new household ap-

pliances and especially by the automobile. If Godey ladies playing croquet in the side yard of a Queen Anne house offered the quintessential image of the 1890s, so, for this 1930s era, a new species was emerging. The efficient, modern, suburban house-wife was born in the interwar era, well before her television canonization in the 1950s. She personi-fied an American society that was bursting dynami-cally out of the normalcy and complacency of the Harding, Coolidge, and Hoover years into a pro-gressive, post-Depression era of promise, innova-tion, and modern life-styles. She even employed modern devices (Flexees foundations and stay-free Lastex girdles) to streamline her body so that she could fit into the latest fashions of the day that she found displayed behind the curved-glass storefronts of Streamlined Moderne boutiques and chic dress shops. Indeed, during the 1940s, the streamlined female body was pared down to virtually nothing in an age that revered the lines of least resistance in everything.

2.7. Coral Court Motel, Marlborough (St. Louis), Mis-souri, Adolph L. Struebig, architect, 1941. Glass block and tile are curved around corners to give this modern motel a Moderne look. The dark horizontal bands of tile at the top of the walls, the siting of units amid flowing driveways, and the repeated rounded forms bring the complex a dynamism that static modernist boxes could not have achieved. Among these forms the roadsters and coupes of the day would appear very much at home.

2.8. Alameda Theater, San Antonio, Texas. The dynamic lines of this Moderne theater lobby underlined the mo-tion picture as one of the technical wonders of modern life and provided an appropriate setting for the fantasies and flights of the imagination that Buck Rogers serials and Vincent Korda's sets for *Things to Come* offered moviegoers.

2.9. Pan Pacific Auditorium, Hollywood, California, Walter Wurdeman and Welton Becket, architects, 1935. Streamlining at its best is evidenced at the civic auditorium that annually housed the auto show. This became quite literally Hollywood's automobile building on such occasions, and as a representative image of roadside architecture, its Moderne-ity was exemplary.

2.10. Plaza Drugs, Briarcliff Plaza, Atlanta, Georgia, George Harwell Bond, architect, 1939. Night lighting, including the mercurial light of streamlining (neon), dramatizes the kinetic directional character of this corner unit at Briarcliff Plaza. Plaza Drugs has been an icon of the Moderne era in Atlanta for years.

The progressive ideal touched every aspect of life. The efficient housewife, armed with all new devices for her modern home, and her business-conscious husband populated the garden suburbs of American cities, and if the choice of style for the entire house displayed a slowness to break the "traditional" historicist aesthetic ideals of the American dream house, the kitchen, at least, was to be filled with the most progressive appliances of the day. But when the family spoke of "the machine," they were referring to their new automobile, and by 1930 twenty-six million cars and trucks were registered in America. These car owners were the children of George F. Babbitt; now fully grown and married, they were themselves driven by middle-class values, social and economic competition, and an almost primeval urge to be "au courant." As modern citizens, they eased into the cultural milieu of progressive aesthetics, clockwork routine, and a life

measured by the scales of modernity and futurism. They drove their four-door coupes to corner bake shops, suburban pharmacies, or any of the numerous Moderne emporia that they frequented as they carried on their daily routine of running errands in their automobiles. New modernized storefronts of Vitrolite, stainless steel, or aluminum offered sensual appeal to the modern shopper, and both the suburban roadsides and the downtown central business districts of the period increasingly wore a modern dress. Thus, during the late 1930s and 1940s, a roadside "vernacular" of Streamlined Moderne buildings comprised a modern world of ordinary architectural, commercial Americana. As a new building typology, such buildings especially expressed the new patterns of a mobile society.

Conclusions

This presence of *Moderne*-ity is an increasingly recognized architectural part of our urban, suburban, and rural American landscape, but it has only recently been so. Collectively, these artifacts make up a typology of automobile buildings, a transportation aesthetic not expressed on the theoretical level of Le Corbusier's "a house is a machine for living"[25] but on a populist, egalitarian level of the American Machine Age.[26] Streamlined Moderne buildings share some elements with Art Deco or International Style structures of the day, but the specific link to transportation imagery provides the key distinguishing characteristics.

It may be, in fact, that the period's ultimate artifact is found in the streamlined form where house and automobile transportation finally fuse: the Airstream mobile home (figure 2.11). If the roadside motel sought to provide a home away from home for modern Americans en route, the mobile home

dispensed with all inefficiencies and permitted the home to travel the roadway with us. If the teardrop was the form of least resistance for the Moderne era, then the Airstream was the ultimate fusion of form and function, mobility, and a progressive, modern American way of life. A house may be, to avant garde architects, a "machine for living," but for the 1930s and beyond, a house trailer was an aerodynamic machine for living and moving down the highways of America, past roadside diners, past the sweeping calligraphy of neon lights, and past the commercial strip of the Streamlined Moderne.

But, metaphorically speaking, will the building tradition itself drive off into the sunset and become an extinct typology? The architecture of the Streamlined Moderne tradition is poised precariously in that limbo between the preservationist's views of historic architecture, the aesthete's tastes and views about ordinary building, and the intellectual's notions about noteworthy modern design.[27] All too frequently, the architecture of the Streamlined Moderne has been slipping away unnoticed. Thought to be too ordinary, it was in fact both typically and quintessentially American. It embodied in its forms our changing social habits and reflected our national mobility. It was the architecture of our most representative institution: not the democratic shrines to our Republic based on classical temples of antiquity, not the mansion derived from European palaces, not the parish church reflecting medieval cathedrals. The Streamlined Moderne was the architecture of the automobile, and the automobile had become the central fact of American life. These ordinary buildings, in the end, were, and are, among our most representative cultural expressions.

2.11. Airstream mobile homes, number 1 *(left)* and number 100,000 off the production line. The ultimate fusion of the American home, the road, and the automobile and the expression of America's increasingly mobile society, the Airstream mobile home has changed little since its first Streamlined Moderne expression.

Notes

1. Two recent exhibitions have focused on the aesthetics, machine forms, and culture of the period. "The Machine Age," Brooklyn Museum, October 17, 1986–February 16, 1987 (and thereafter at Carnegie Institute, Pittsburgh; Los Angeles County Museum of Art; and The High Museum of Art, Atlanta, closing February 14, 1988). See Richard Guy Wilson et al., *The Machine Age in America, 1918–1941* (New York: Brooklyn Museum, in association with Harry N. Abrams, 1986). "The Automobile in American Life," permanent exhibit of the Henry Ford Museum, and "Streamlining America," Henry Ford Museum, September 1986–December 1987. See Fannia Weingartner, ed., *Streamlining America* (Dearborn, Mich.: Henry Ford Museum and Greenfield Village, 1986).

2. See Peter Collins, *Changing Ideals in Modern Architecture* (Montreal: McGill Univ. Press, 1967).

3. Robert M. Craig, "Roadside Architecture of the 1930s and 1940s: Evidence for a Distinctive 'Streamlined Moderne' Style of Architecture," paper presented at the Southeastern College Art Conference, Birmingham, Ala., 30 October 1980, abstracted in SECAC *Review* 10 (Spring 1981): 34. An abbreviated version of this preliminary inquiry was published as "The Industrial Designer as Architectural Form-Maker during the 1930s and 1940s" in Donald Harkness, ed., *Design, Pattern Style: Hallmarks of a Developing American Culture* (Proceedings of the Southeastern American Studies Association biennial conference, 7–9 April 1983), 20–26.

4. Donald J. Bush, *The Streamlined Decade* (New York: George Braziller, 1975); Martin Greif, *Depression Modern: The Thirties Style in America* (New York: Universe Books, 1975); Cervin Robinson and Rosemarie Haag Bletter, *Skyscraper Style: Art Deco New York* (New York: Oxford Univ. Press, 1975); and Norman Bel Geddes, *Horizons* (1932; reprint, New York: Dover, 1977).

5. Robinson and Bletter, *Skyscraper Style.*

6. See Raymond Loewy, *Industrial Design* (Woodstock, N.Y.: Overlook Press, 1979), and David Gebhard and Harriette von Breton, *Kem Weber: The Moderne in Southern California, 1920–1941* (Santa Barbara: The Art Galleries, University of California, 1969).

7. Bush, 121.

8. As intrusions into an existing urban fabric, the corner gas station (which emerges during the period) has become the symbolic foe of the urban historic preservationist. See conclusions section.

9. Bush, 154. See also Richard Wurts et al., *The New York World's Fair, 1939/40* (New York: Dover Publications, 1977).

10. Bush, 161.

11. See Bush, chapter 5.

12. The evolutionary charts appear in Loewy, 74–76.

13. Both are illustrated in Wilson et al., 163, 172. In a reversal of the relationship (in which car design borrowed from contemporary Art Deco aesthetics), Maurice Dufrene applied Art Deco zigzags and patterned chevrons to the design of a limousine. Built by H. Levy about 1925, the limousine is illustrated in Bevis Hillier, *Art Deco of the '20s and '30s* (New York: E. P. Dutton, 1968), 156.

14. The Ramsgate terminal is illustrated in *Architectural Review* 82 (July 1937):3–6.

15. The Aquatic Park Casino is illustrated in Bush, 149.

16. See Michael F. Zimny, "Robert Vincent Derrah and the Nautical Moderne" (M.A. thesis, University of Virginia, 1982).

17. Bus depot designs by W. S. Arrasmith are illustrated in Wilson et al., 177, and in Richard J. S. Gutman, "Streamlining the Roadside," in Weingartner, 74.

18. Daniel I. Vieyra, *"Fill 'er up": An Architectural History of America's Gas Stations* (New York: Macmillan, 1979), 67.

19. Vieyra, 68.

20. See Paul Hirshorn and Steven Izenour, *White Towers* (Cambridge: M.I.T. Press, 1979), and Richard Gutman and Elliott Kaufman, *The American Diner* (New York: Harper and Row, 1979).

21. Bel Geddes, 23.

22. Raymond Hood's showrooms in Queens and Brooklyn (1929–33) for General Electric distributor Rex Cole are illustrated in Wilson et al., 161. Outside London on the A-40, the Hoover Factory by Wallis, Gilbert and Partners (1932) offers a polyglot image of streamlining, Deco ornament, and classical modernism. It is illustrated in Dan Klein, *All Colour Book of Art Deco* (London: Octopus Books, 1974), 64–65. The same firm's superb Firestone Building, which was the centerpiece of a range of factories along the M-4 outside London, was brutally demolished in 1980 the day before it was scheduled to be listed (for preservation protection). See Marcus Binney, *Our Vanishing Heritage* (London: Arlington Books, 1984), 251–54.

23. See Thomas W. Sweeney, "Courting Coral: Streamline Style in St. Louis," *Preservation News* (Nov. 1988): 1, 19.

24. A major fire consumed the Pan Pacific Auditorium in May 1989.

25. Le Corbusier, *Towards a New Architecture* (New York: Praeger, 1960), 10.

26. Forrest F. Lisle, Jr., "Chicago's 'Century of Progress' Exposition: The Moderne as Democratic Popular Culture," *Journal of the Society of Architectural Historians* 31 (Oct. 1972): 230. This is an abstract of a paper presented at the twentieth annual meeting of the Society of Architectural Historians, San Francisco, January 26–30, 1972.

27. Preservationists, guided by the "fifty year rule" of the National Register for Historic Places, have only recently come to recognize the historic value and merit of 1930s Moderne roadside architecture. (To be considered historic and worthy of recognition by listing on the National Register of Historic Places—and, frequently, thus "confirmed" as meriting preservation—a building must usually be fifty years old or older. Hence, during the 1980s, year by year, architecture of the 1930s, year by year, was deemed "historic.") Efforts to develop an appreciation for the impact of this body of architecture on the American landscape, and its significance to the mobile American way of life, have been further hampered by perceptions of the deleterious impact buildings of this type have already had on the historic city. Both the gas station and the fast-food eatery have been considered the very causes of repeated preservation losses in our historic cities, as these works of modern commercial building intruded upon our historic streetscapes, destroying, especially, our historic crossroads and major intersections.

Similarly, prejudiced by more academic views of beauty and art, buildings within this architectural typology have not been considered "architecture" at all but mere "building"—ordinary structures of mundane function. At worst, they included automobile repair garages, tire outlets, and auto parts stores—structures whose loss by demolition would hardly be noticed. At another extreme, they incorporated roadside diners that catered to the traveling masses and ordinary folk. Such establishments were rarely, if ever, frequented by the upper crust of society, whose views of landmark architecture were seldom inclusive enough to embrace a streamlined diner and who might even be behind the development interests ready to displace the "greasy spoon" restaurant. Finally, the definition of Modern architecture held by intellectuals and high-style architects has generally reflected more elitist attitudes and has been less populist, and thus exclusive. Bauhaus Modern has been considered superior to Art Deco or Streamlined Moderne. Its architects were the masters of twentieth-century Modernism, while Deco stylists and Moderne builders were relative unknowns. Indeed, the local bus depot, initially a period landmark of the Moderne aesthetic, might be "modernized," as was the downtown Greyhound depot in Atlanta, into a nightmarish travesty in the name of progress.

Technology and Geography in the Emergence of the American Automobile Industry, 1895–1915

CHAPTER 3

PETER J. HUGILL

Before the appearance in 1971 of Automobile Quarterly's *The American Car Since 1775* (henceforth referred to as *American Car*), only Charles W. Boas, compiling data from a wide variety of trade journals, had attempted, in 1961, to address the problem of the geographic origins of the industry. Boas, however, failed to distinguish the different geographies of the different types of automobiles and was concerned more with the industry as a whole. Neil P. Hurley in 1959 and James M. Rubenstein in 1986 followed this concern with location uninformed by technology. In a 1988 publication, I considered technology but not location.[1] Here, I merge the two approaches and analyze location informed by technology for the critical experimental period of automobile manufacture between 1895 and 1915.

I also depend on the notion of normal technology. By this I mean the technology used by all or the vast majority of manufacturers at any one point in time. Thomas S. Kuhn developed the concept of "normal science" in the 1960s, and the aviation historian, Ed Constant, has applied it to aircraft engine technology.[2] Kuhn pointed out that science (and thus technology) does not progress smoothly but as a series of stair steps. Sudden, rapid progress is followed by a plateau of normal science or technology during which one paradigm is paramount. Revolutionaries constantly chip away at that paradigm and, ultimately, overthrow it in another period of sudden, rapid progress. In the following pages, I will analyze the emergence of the first normal technology for U.S. automobile manufacturers in the first decade of this century. A technically successful automobile was not enough. Manufacturers had to be able to sell and service their vehicles as well as produce them. In the experimental period before a normal technology emerged, many manufacturers using a variety of technologies sought to enter the marketplace.

In the twenty-year period between 1895, when the first hesitant experiments in production began, and 1915, when the industry stabilized on one basic type of automobile, four types of automobiles were experimented with, each conforming to one basic mechanical layout and propulsion system. The four technologies that competed between 1895 and 1915 were the Benz-style gas-buggy; the European-style, four-cylinder automobile modelled on the 1901 Mercedes; the high wheeler; and the cyclecar. The normal technology that emerged triumphant by 1915 and was embodied in Ford's Model T was that of the European Mercedes-style, four-cylinder automobile, albeit much modified by the aims of the American manufacturers of high wheelers and cyclecars to produce cheap vehicles for farmers and the urban middle classes.

American Car, compiled by automobile enthusiasts, represents a remarkable attempt to cover the industry completely. Its list of "five thousand marques" gives the names of the companies that entered or claimed to be entering automobile production, the city in which each was located, the years of production, and the types of automobile produced. High wheelers, cyclecars, and automobiles powered by steam or electricity are distinguished with some care. Mercedes-style automobiles were identified by cross-referencing to other sources where questions arose.[3] Before 1904, almost all American manufacturers produced only steam automobiles, electric runabouts, or gas-buggies. Excluding steam and electric automobiles allows the remaining production between 1895 and 1903 to be reasonably regarded as of gas-buggies alone.

The Gas-buggy

The first American automobiles owed their origins to the description of the three-wheeled 1886 German Benz published in 1889 in *Scientific American*.[4] A relatively large number of successful vehicles had been produced in America by the late 1890s. These had four wheels, as did the Benz Velo of 1894, but were all of the Benz gas-buggy type, with a one- or two-cylinder engine under the passenger area, usually just ahead of the driven rear wheels. Charles Duryea of Springfield, Massachusetts, was the first person to set up a company in America "expressly for the purpose of making" and selling gasoline automobiles.[5] In late 1895, a Duryea prototype was one of only two cars to finish the fifty-five mile race sponsored by the *Chicago Times-Herald,* beating a modified Benz Velo. In 1896 Duryea sold thirteen cars.[6] Yet Duryea was out of business by 1898, the year in which Alexander Winton of Cleveland, Ohio, sold the first series-produced gas-buggy. In 1899 Winton's production reached twenty-five vehicles per week.[7] Serious mass production began in 1901 with America's most famous gas-buggy, the "curved-dash" Olds; some 2,100 were sold in 1902. Ford produced his Model A gas-buggy in 1903 and made 1,708 that year.[8]

Gas-buggies were not noted for their power or performance. Despite grandiose claims and some spectacular cross-country and even cross-continent runs by Winton, Olds, and Packard, gas-buggies were essentially urban or suburban vehicles. Their one- or two-cylinder engines lacked the power needed to drag them out of the mud if they left hard-surfaced roads behind, and their cruising speed was rarely over fifteen or twenty miles per hour on the best of roads. Their weight-to-power ratio was abysmal: 157 pounds per horsepower in the curved-dash Olds of 1901. Gas-buggies sat high off the road, and passengers sat high above the engine (figure 3.1), which gave the gas-buggy a high center of gravity, thus poor handling.[9] There was also nothing in the way of weather protection.

Yet gas-buggies introduced Americans to the automobile. One of Winton's less satisfied customers was James Packard, who determined to improve on Winton's vehicle.[10] Ransom E. Olds spun off even more companies when he subcontracted the parts for his 1901 model to Henry Leland (who founded first Cadillac, then Lincoln), the Dodge brothers (who backed Ford, then went on their own), and Fred Fisher (later to merge Fisher Body into General Motors).[11] When Olds's company was merged into General Motors as Oldsmobile, Ransom Olds began a second company, REO. Ford's Model A gas-buggy was his first successful production design.

Gas-buggies also demonstrate that geography is as critical to the success of a new industry as technology. Using data from *American Car,* I have mapped the percentage of total years of potential production in each state (figure 3.2). This data set was generated from companies listed for the years 1895 through 1903 whose names begin with the letters A through E and which are not identified as producing electric- or steam-powered vehicles. Not all these companies would have actually produced vehicles, and many produced only a few, but no figures exist for real production, and even well-known firms kept poor records. Letters A through E account for about one third of the five thousand marques listed. A cutoff in 1903 avoids the transition to the production of Mercedes-style vehicles that was markedly under way by 1904. Gas-buggy companies accounted for 462 years of production potential. The concentration of companies in New York (20.1 percent) and Massachusetts (13.2 percent) was marked. This was a technology imported from Europe, and the East Coast states were the

3.1. Ford's 1903 Model A, a gas-buggy.

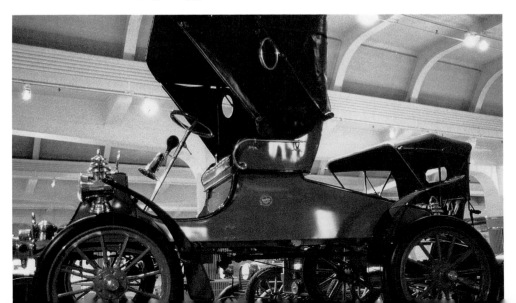

wealthiest. Ohio and Michigan would probably stand out if I could have mapped actual production rather than the number of potential producers. Winton in Ohio and Olds in Michigan were the largest producers by 1903, having both made the decision to pursue series production of a standardized design, but other companies were relatively lacking in those two states. Illinois slightly exceeded Ohio in years of production potential for gas-buggies, and Pennsylvania was between Ohio and Illinois. The industrial states with Atlantic frontage (Connecticut, Massachusetts, New Jersey, New York, Pennsylvania, Rhode Island) accounted for 49.2 percent of production potential. The Great Lakes states (Illinois, Indiana, Michigan, Ohio, Wisconsin) had only 32.3 percent. This implies that the development of series-production technology was more important in the long-term success of the industry than the simple spread of producers. Locational arguments are not totally convincing either, despite the Great Lakes location of the eventually successful states of Michigan and Ohio. New York is also a Great Lakes state, with Buffalo well situated above Niagara Falls to have as good access to Great Lakes iron ore and coal traffic as Cleveland or Detroit. New York had the further advantage of a substantial early lead in gas-buggy production experience. Pennsylvania's access to the Great Lakes at Erie was much poorer than that of New York.

The Mercedes-style, Four-Cylinder Automobile

The automobile that defined the first normal technology of both the world and the American automobile industries was the 1901 Mercedes. The car was a German Daimler built to the requirements of the company's sales agent in Nice, Emile Jellinek,

and named after his daughter to give it a French-sounding name in the critical French market. It had a powerful 35-horsepower, four-cylinder engine mounted just behind the front axle driving the rear wheels. The Mercedes-style automobile had a low, strong frame, only eight or nine inches off the ground, and passengers sat low to the ground behind the engine (figure 3.3). The low center of gravity made for excellent handling. Cruising speeds of fifty miles per hour allowed point-to-point speeds as good as those of crack railroad trains.[12] The Mercedes was first shown in America at the New York Motor Show in January 1902, and it galvanized American manufacturers into a rapid shift to the European-style, four-cylinder automobile. By

1907 the Mercedes was even produced under license in America by the Steinway Company of piano fame. Gas-buggy production was phased out rapidly. Although the curved-dash Olds managed to sell some five thousand copies in 1904, it was almost the last gasp of the gas-buggy. After near collapse in 1905, Olds shifted to the Mercedes-style automobile in 1906, although they held the curved-dash gas-buggy in production for another year or so.[13] Even Henry Ford produced a Mercedes-style automobile in his four-cylinder Model B of 1905 (figure 3.4). He did so reluctantly and only because his backers forced him to, and it was one of several forces that persuaded him to get rid of his backers and strike out alone.

3.2. Gas-buggy manufacturers, percent of total years in production, 1895–1903.

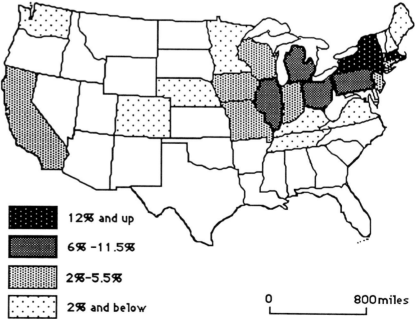

12% and up

6% –11.5%

2% –5.5%

2% and below

0   800 miles

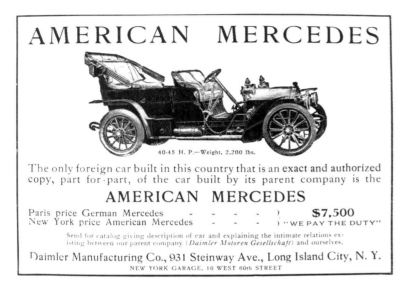

3.3. The Mercedes-style automobile.

3.4. Ford's 1905 Model B.

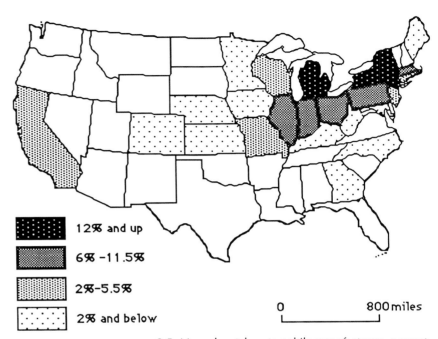

12% and up

6% –11.5%

2%–5.5%

2% and below

0   800 miles

3.5. Mercedes-style automobile manufacturers, percent of total years in production, 1906–10.

In the period 1906–10, during which the gas-buggy was defunct but Ford had not achieved the critical level of production dominance that began in 1911 with the first use of the moving assembly line, the number of production facilities expanded in the Great Lakes states and declined in the Atlantic states. Figure 3.5 maps those companies listed in *American Car* that may reasonably be supposed to have been producing European-style, four-cylinder automobiles of the Mercedes type between 1906 and 1910. The data base is the same as for the gas-buggy. Companies producing Mercedes-style automobiles were listed in production for a total of 518 years. Production potential in Michigan rose to match that of New York exactly, at least on the basis of the number of firms listed for the five-year period. Massachusetts fell from second to sixth place in the ranking. Overall, the combined totals of facilities in the Atlantic and Great Lakes states stayed about the same. But where the Atlantic states accounted for close to 50 percent of gas-buggy production potential, they accounted for only 36.9 percent of companies producing Mercedes-style automobiles. On the other side of the coin, the Great Lakes states accounted for 46.9 percent of Mercedes-style automobile production potential, but only 32.3 percent of that for gas-buggies.

The Mercedes-style automobile was a success for several reasons. It usually had sufficient power to pull itself clear if it bogged down on muddy roads, as well as to maintain a high cruising speed on good roads. It could carry four passengers and their luggage long distances in relative comfort, whereas most gas-buggies were two-seat runabouts best suited to urban use. Although not yet an all-weather vehicle, the Mercedes-style automobile could be used on fine days even in winter since occupants sat inside the vehicle rather than on top of it and could protect themselves reasonably from the cold with appropriate clothing. In the hands of the American elite, it was quickly and enthusiastically adopted for long-distance touring. Many automobile owners in the first decade of this century turned from the joys of the European grand tour to the rediscovery of America. At its best, the Mercedes-style automobile was amazingly competent, as demonstrated by the two great races of the period, the Paris–Peking of 1907 and the twenty-thousand-mile New York–Paris of 1908.[14] No American car was entered for the Paris-Peking, which was won by

an Itala, an Italian car derived from the Mercedes. The most proven of all the American Mercedes-style automobiles was the winner of the New York–Paris race, a Thomas Flyer from Buffalo, New York (figure 3.6). At least one source claims that the original four-cylinder 1906 Flyer was "a carbon copy of the contemporary Richard-Brasier," an "excellent racing design which won the Gordon Bennett Trophy for France in 1904 and 1905."[15] The Richard-Brasier was modelled heavily on the Mercedes.

The drawbacks of these magnificent vehicles were price and the problems of maintenance caused by a wide range of idiosyncratic products emanating from a vast number of factories spread over a wide geographic area, even across the Atlan-

3.6. A Thomas Flyer.

tic. Had they, like gas-buggies, been used only locally, this would have been less important. But the sheer range and competence of the Mercedes-style automobile and its appeal to a wealthy, international elite required far better parts and service availability than any manufacturer realized. In America price was much affected by the 45 percent tariff on imported automobiles.[16] An imported Mercedes listed in New York City in 1904 for $12,450 (without top). By 1907 the Steinway Piano Company was assembling the American Mercedes on Long Island for just $7,000, thus avoiding the tariff. But a fine American copy could be had for much less: $3,500 would buy a Thomas Flyer in 1906, and $4,000 allowed one the choice of a

Packard 24, a Peerless 14, or a Pierce Great Arrow, the great "3 Ps" of American prestige automobiles. A lesser, but still highly competent, Cadillac 30 could be had for $2,500, and an Olds Model S for a little less than that.[17] Ford planned to sell his unsuccessful Model B for $2,000.[18]

Apart from price and service, the Mercedes copies still had some technical problems. They required large engines not only to give good and reliable performance with the poor fuels and oils of the period but also to cope with heavy construction.[19] With relatively poor steels, heavy construction was necessary not only to give chassis strength but also to carry the powerful, heavy engine required to move the vehicle. It was a circular problem: more engine weight required more chassis weight and vice versa. Such vehicles stabilized at a weight-to-power ratio of around 80 pounds per horsepower. The 1906 Olds S had a ratio of 82 pounds per horsepower, the Pierce Great Arrow one of 84:1, and the Peerless 14 one of 87:1. The six-cylinder Thomas Flyer of 1906 was much better, at 64 pounds per horsepower, whereas the Packard 24 was, at 114 pounds per horsepower, much worse. Ford later broke out of the circle by specifying light, high-quality steels for his chassis components, thus reducing the engine power needed. Ford's 1908 Model T, with only 20 horsepower, had a weight-to-power ratio of 80 pounds per horsepower, exactly that of a 1906 Cadillac 30.

The High Wheeler

High wheelers are the only American automobile that can claim to be more American than European in origin, although they clearly owe some of their origins to the gas-buggy. Contemporaries referred to high wheelers as the "Western Buggy Type of Automobile," and indeed they often resembled nothing so much as a motorized farm wagon. Some had centrally mounted engines, others had front-mounted ones, but all had wheels of thirty-six inches or more in diameter (figure 3.7), usually with solid rather than pneumatic rubber tires. All were light enough to be dragged out of mudholes easily, and all were serviceable "by a person of ordinary intelligence, and not easily deranged."[20]

The seeming necessity for high wheelers lay in the fact that roads were appalling away from the wealthy eastern states that had invested large amounts of state bond monies in the "Good Roads" movement at an early date.[21] In the East, hard-packed, gravel-surfaced macadam roads were being built at a cost of ten thousand dollars per mile. By 1911 New York had voted one hundred million dollars in bonds for good roads. Western agricultural states simply could not afford such public spending, and hard-surfaced roads were nonexistent. As a 1906 letter to the editor of *The Horseless Age* had it, midwestern roads "have ruts . . . varying from two to fifteen inches deep. To run a car with a nine-inch clearance over these roads in daylight is exasperating and it is practically impossible after dark."[22] With the gas-buggy departed from the scene as manufacturers switched to the Mercedes-style automobile, western manufacturers picked up the idea of the high wheeler.

3.7. A high wheeler, the 1909 Sears Motor Buggy.

In terms of geographic distribution, high wheeler manufacturers were concentrated in three states: Illinois, Indiana, and Missouri (figure 3.8). Calculated on the basis of a total of 364 years of production potential for *all* manufacturers of high wheelers listed in *American Car,* these three states accounted for 64.5 percent of production potential. The Atlantic states had little to do with high wheelers, accounting for only 7.8 percent of the total years in production. Michigan and Ohio, at 7.1 percent each, were also underrepresented.

High wheelers were aimed primarily at farmers, though also at rural mail carriers, physicians, and drummers. International Harvester clearly had its farm customers in mind when it announced its intention to build high wheelers (figure 3.9), as did Sears, Roebuck and Co. Both companies were in Chicago, as was the third of the four major high wheeler manufacturers, Holsman.[23] This concentration in Chicago seemed to offer the possibility of better distribution of parts, and the involvement of companies with the reputation of International Harvester and Sears offered the promise of reliable service as well. The fourth major manufacturer, Schacht, was in Cincinnati, Ohio, another major midwestern distribution center for farm machinery.

For all its apparent geographic and economic advantages, however, the high wheeler was a failure. It stuck to solid rubber tires on large-diameter wheels in the belief that a wheel that broke through mud to hard ground below would be able to keep its traction. Pneumatic tires spread their load much better and frequently stayed on top of a waterlogged crust when narrow buggy wheels went through. Although clearance was important in such conditions when wheels did break through, pneumatic tires were not the disadvantage they were represented to be by many high wheeler manufacturers.

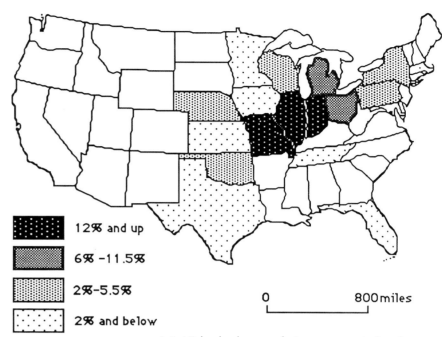

12% and up

6% – 11.5%

2% – 5.5%

2% and below

0   800 miles

3.8. High wheeler manufacturers, percent of total years in production, 1902–16.

3.9. The 1911 International Harvester truck.

Moreover, many high wheelers were as underpowered as the gas-buggies that preceded them, which meant they could not always pull themselves clear when bogged down. Sears's 1910 high wheeler catalog claimed an engine of 14 horsepower and a weight of 1,000 pounds.[24] On the face of it, this promised a reasonable weight-to-power ratio of 71 pounds per horsepower, but performance belied it, with top speed being only 25 miles per hour. Part of the problem was the air-cooled engine, a device common to many high wheelers in the name of simplicity. Such engines were cooled by fans, which routinely robbed an engine of up to a third of its power output. Recalculated on this basis, the Sears weight-to-power ratio would have been close to 110 pounds per horsepower. The catalog is also vague about which model weighed only 1,000 pounds. The Model G lacked the top, fenders, storm front, or side curtains most buyers would have specified, prompting the suspicion that 1,300 to 1,400 pounds would be nearer reality for a vehicle on the road. At such, the weight-to-power ratio would approach 150 pounds per horsepower, about equal to the curved-dash Olds, the performance of which was almost as abysmal.

The Cyclecar

The last of the four vehicle types that characterize the American automobile industry before Ford was the cyclecar. As with the gas-buggy and the Mercedes-style automobile, the cyclecar's origins were entirely European. The first really successful cyclecar was the French-built Bedelia of 1910 (figure 3.10). To keep down weight, this cyclecar mostly used the spoked-wire wheels of the bicycle rather than the heavy wooden artillery wheels common to other automobiles, a plywood body, and a small engine, usually one-cylinder. Only two seats were available. Such vehicles had been common in the early, experimental phase of the industry before 1900. Bicycle technology was critical to the emergence of the first automobiles, since it allowed chassis weight to be kept down to a level where the early, weak engines could do useful work. It was similarly critical to the development of powered flight.[25] Benz used bicycle tubing for his chassis and the light, strong spoked wheels of the bicycle in his pioneering tricycle of 1886. Ford used the same technology in his "quadricycle" as late as 1896. Bicycle technology seemed to offer low weight, but it also meant low durability on the poor roads of the turn of the century, and low engine power meant that the weight of a passenger or two seriously reduced weight-to-power ratios. By 1910, however, roads were better, as least in towns, and the cyclecar seemed ideal as a cheap urban runabout, rarely selling for over five hundred dollars.

3.10. The French-built Bedelia of 1910.

Cyclecar production began in the United States in 1913, when 32 manufacturers entered or at least claimed to enter the marketplace. It peaked in 1914 with 195 manufacturers but collapsed quickly to 41 in 1915, 10 in 1916, and 2 in 1917. The last cyclecar manufacturer closed its doors in 1921, by which time a total of 279 years of production potential had been accumulated by all companies listed in *American Car*. The map of production potential shows how much Michigan had come to dominate the automobile industry in the few years after the turn of the decade (figure 3.11). Michigan alone accounted for close to 23 percent of cyclecar production potential. The Great Lakes states had clearly consolidated their position of automobile-manufacturing dominance with just over 55 percent of production potential, and the Atlantic states were, at 20.8 percent, in severe decline. What is interesting about this map is that it shows a broader geographic spread than the preceding types. Only one more state is represented than for gas-buggies or Mercedes-style automobiles, but the West and the South are far better represented, albeit at the expense of the eastern seaboard.

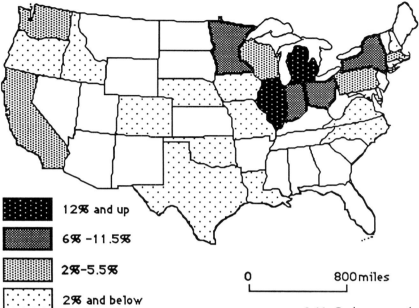

12% and up

6% -11.5%

2%-5.5%

2% and below

0   800miles

3.11. Cyclecar manufacturers, percent of total years in production, 1913–21.

In theory, cyclecars were a reasonable solution to the problems of distribution and service. Since they were essentially unusable away from good roads, they could not normally have been used for cross-country trips, and service and parts would have been instantly accessible if such vehicles were bought where they were built. Yet nearly one-quarter were made in Detroit and Chicago with, respectively, 25 and 22 manufacturers in the banner year of 1914. The geographic advantage lay in having, for example, 10 manufacturers in Minneapolis–St. Paul that same year, or 7 each in New York, Cleveland, and Seattle-Tacoma, 6 in Los Angeles, 5 in Indianapolis, or 4 each in places as far apart as Boston, New Orleans, Philadelphia, and Milwau-

kee. Had cyclecars been reasonably reliable, their low price, coupled with a manufacturing spread greater than any previous type of automobile, might have ensured their success if there had been no competition. But they were not reliable, and there was competition in the form of Ford's Model T.

Model T Confirms the First Normal Technology

The collapse of the brief cyclecar boom in 1915 marked the successful emergence of the first stage of the first normal complex of technologies for automobiles, their production and sale, and their in-

frastructure, not only in the United States but also in the world. In 1915 road conditions were still appalling away from the wealthy eastern states, which had poured considerable state money into road improvement. Outside the East, only California had begun a similar program to correct the problems of a deficient railroad network and to better link farmers to the railheads.[26] Everywhere else, the roads were cleared rights-of-way, baked hard in summer, elongated mudholes in spring and fall.

This was a period of rapid industrialization and equally rapid increase in wealth. The success of bicycles, streetcars, and interurbans indicates a massive demand for better urban, suburban, and regional transportation. The success of the four pioneering types of automobiles indicates the extent to which people were willing to pay for a device with the route and scheduling flexibility of the bicycle but with the range and comfort of the streetcar and interurban.

The four pioneering types of automobiles were all limited in either geographic or economic availability. Although stylish, the Mercedes-style automobiles were too expensive for the rapidly growing classes of white-collar and skilled blue-collar workers. They were also somewhat limited, by virtue of poor ground clearance and high weight, to the relatively good, hard-surfaced roads of the wealthy eastern states. The geography of parts and service availability was usually a problem, given the range and competence of the Mercedes-style automobile. Gas-buggies and high wheelers, though light and cheap, were technologically inept as well as lacking in style. They resembled motorized farm wagons, which many of them were, and held no appeal for an increasingly wealthy urban and suburban population. Farmers bought high wheelers because they promised improved mobility in bad road conditions, but the technical failure of a much poorer weight-to-power ratio than the Mercedes-style automobile worked against them, however good their clearance. The entry of large manufacturers or retailers into the market did, however, offer at least the illusion of good parts and service availability. Cyclecars were also usually underpowered, but given that they were cheap and aimed at urban customers who had mostly good roads at their disposal by 1910, they might have succeeded had they been better made. The geographic spread of manufacturers might have made the parts and service situation acceptable.

Henry Ford combined all of the virtues and few of the faults of these four types of automobile in his brilliant Model T. Mass production guaranteed cheapness even though high-quality raw materials were used. High-quality steels made for a strong, yet light, chassis (figure 3.12). Given a lightweight chassis, a relatively light, economical engine could still give a weight-to-power ratio as good as all but the very best Mercedes-style automobiles, thus ensuring that the Model T could usually pull itself clear of all but the worst mudholes. Ford gave his T almost the ground clearance of a high wheeler and a suspension design that kept the wheels in contact with the road in almost any condition. Both axles were on leaf springs mounted transversely across the vehicle. The front axle was braced back to the rear of the engine by two rods, one from each front wheel, which made a triangle with the axle. The rear axle was braced forward to the rear of the transmission in exactly the same way. The four wheels could thus move easily against the transverse springs in the vertical plane without excessive fore and aft changes in wheelbase length. No suspension dampers were used. There was a price for this flexibility: a high rate of roll.[27] This made the Model

T uncomfortable at speed on good roads, with a tendency for passengers to become seasick. On bad roads, however, or at lower speeds, the Model T was a remarkably capable vehicle.

By 1915 mass production had brought the price of the Model T well below that of the high wheelers or even the cyclecars, let alone the Mercedes-style automobiles. With its excellent weight-to-power ratio, light weight, high ground clearance, and competent suspension, it could be used anywhere. It was only inferior to the Mercedes-style automobile at speed on a good road. It was exactly the right technology for an early twentieth-century America,

where good roads were rare but demand for better transport high. Ford also marketed the Model T far better than any previous automobile company. He recognized the need for good parts and service and moved rapidly to establish a country-wide network of dealers. No previous large-scale producer had come even close to such ubiquity. The potential geographic range of all the Mercedes-style automobiles was usually negated by lack of parts and service any distance away from the factory. Ford's technological and geographic approaches to the problem of the automobile were thus both correct.

Model T characterized the first phase of the first

3.12. Ford's Model T chassis.

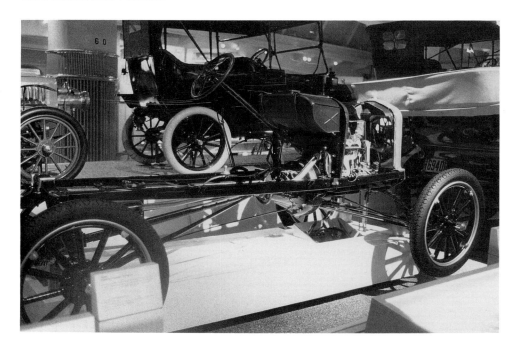

normal technology of the automobile industry. Its decline is as interesting as its rise, since it was brought about by Ford's failure to adjust to a changing geographic reality. In the early 1910s, good roads were rare in America. By the middle twenties, however, the federal government was embarked on a good roads construction program of monumental size.[28] Also by the middle twenties, Ford's ubiquitous parts and service network was being copied by any would-be competitor. Chevrolet was the first to merge the better suspension and handling characteristics on good roads of the earlier Mercedes-style automobiles with the low price and ubiquitous dealer network of the Ford. This merger was achieved in the mid-1920s when the network of hard-surfaced roads had expanded out of all proportion to that of fifteen years earlier. Chevrolet therefore reaped a substantial sales bonanza and forced Ford to imitate the Chevrolet quite closely in the Model A.

None of this failure detracts from Ford's achievement. He merged the strengths of all the four pioneering types of automobile made in America with few of their weaknesses. He sold his Model T at a price almost all could afford, and he established a national marketing network that ensured his customers of ubiquitous parts and service. To copy and improve is always easier than to innovate. Ford's "failure," such as it was, was that he came to believe that he had produced the perfect type of automobile and that he no longer needed to innovate.

Notes

1. Automobile Quarterly, *The American Car Since 1775* (New York, 1971); Charles W. Boas, "Locational Patterns of American Automobile Assembly Plants, 1895–1958," *Economic Geography* 37 (1961):218–30; Neil P. Hurley, "The Automotive Industry: A Study in Industrial Location," *Land Economics* 35 (1959):1–14; James. M. Rubenstein, "The Changing Distribution of the American Automobile Industry," *Geographical Review* 76 (1986):288–300; Peter J. Hugill, "Technology Diffusion in the World Automobile Industry, 1885–1985," in Peter J. Hugill and D. Bruce Dickson, eds., *The Transfer and Transformation of Ideas and Material Culture* (College Station, Tex.: Texas A & M University Press, 1988), 110–42. Other useful but technologically uninformed works include John B. Rae, *The American Automobile: A Brief History* (Chicago: University of Chicago Press, 1965); James J. Flink, *America Adopts the Automobile, 1895–1910* (Cambridge, Mass.: M.I.T. Press, 1970).

2. Thomas S. Kuhn, *The Structure of Scientific Revolution* (Chicago: University of Chicago Press, 1961); Edward W. Constant II, *The Turbojet Revolution* (Baltimore: Johns Hopkins University Press, 1980).

3. Three sources were particularly useful: The Association of Licensed Automobile Manufacturers (A.L.A.M.), *Handbook of Gasoline Automobiles, 1904–1906* (1906; reprint New York, 1969); G. N. Georgano, ed., *The New Encyclopedia of Motorcars, 1885 to the Present*, 3d ed. (New York: Dutton, 1982); and David Burges Wise, *The Illustrated Encyclopedia of Automobiles* (London: Hamlyn, 1979).

4. Flink, *America Adopts the Automobile*, 19.

5. Georgano, *New Encyclopedia of Motorcars*, 214.

6. Flink, *America Adopts the Automobile*, 23–25.

7. Richad Wager, *Golden Wheels: The Story of the Automobiles Made in Cleveland and Northeastern Ohio, 1892–1932* (Cleveland: Western Reserve Historical Society, 1975), 3, 10.

8. Georgano, *New Encyclopedia of Motorcars*, 461, 252.

9. Hugill, "Technology Diffusion," 111.

10. Georgano, *New Encyclopedia of Motorcars*, 471.

11. Ed Cray, *Chrome Colossus: General Motors and Its Times* (New York: McGraw-Hill, 1980), 26.

12. Hugill, "Technology Diffusion," 112–13.

13. Georgano, *New Encyclopedia of Motorcars*, 461; A.L.A.M., *Handbook 1906*, 81.

14. Peter J. Hugill, "The Rediscovery of America: Elite Automobile Touring," *Annals of Tourism Research* 12 (1985):435–47. Firsthand accounts of both races exist: Luigi Barzini, *Peking to Paris in a Motor Car* (London, 1907), and J. J. Mann, *Round the World in a Motor-Car* (London, 1914), the last translated from Antonio Scarfoglio's account in Italian published in 1909. See also T. R. Nicholson, *Adventurer's Road: The Story of the Peking-Paris, 1907 and New York-Paris, 1908* (New York: Rinehart, 1958).

15. Wise, *Illustrated Encyclopedia of Automobiles*, 320, 178.

16. Flink, *America Adopts the Automobile*, 61.

17. A.L.A.M., *Handbook 1904*, 70; *Handbook 1906*, 129, 88, 93, 97, 26, 83.

18. Georgano, *New Encyclopedia of Motorcars*, 252.

19. Hugill, "Technology Diffusion," 117.

20. Beverly Rae Kimes, "High Times, High Rollers—The High Wheeler in America," *Automobile Quarterly* 15 (1977):9.

21. Peter J. Hugill, "Good Roads and the Automobile in the United States, 1880–1929," *Geographical Review* 72 (1982):327–49.

22. Quoted in Kimes, "High Times," 6.

23. Kimes, "High Times," 21.

24. Sears, Roebuck and Co., *Motor Buggy Catalogue, 1909–1912* (Northfield, Ill.: Digest Books, 1973), 8.

25. Georgano, *New Encyclopedia of Motorcars*, 81. Tom D. Crouch, "How the Bicycle Took Wing," *American Heritage of Invention and Technology* 2(1986):11–16.

26. Hugill, "Good Roads," 336. Ben Blow, *California Highways: A Descriptive Record of Road Development by the State and by Such Counties As Have Paved Highways* (San Francisco, 1920).

27. L. J. K. Setright, "Suspension," in Ian Ward, ed., *Anatomy of the Motor Car* (London: Orbis, 1981), 156–65.

28. Hugill, "Good Roads," 342.

Coils of the Commercial Serpent

CHAPTER 4

GERALD T. BLOOMFIELD

A Geography of the Ford Branch Distribution System, 1904–33

When H. L. Arnold and F. L. Faurote considered the success of the Ford Motor Company in their book on Ford factory methods (1915), they used the analogy of a serpent with its tail in its mouth to describe the circular relationships of product, manufacturing methods, distribution, and marketing.[1] The economies of scale brought by the new production methods were balanced by a very extensive distribution network that located the sale and service of automobiles close to the buyers. This process of dispersion of outlets not only fostered the growth of the company but was a key element in the early motorization of America.

In mid-1915, the Highland Park complex was already the center of a very large integrated national system. The Detroit plant supplied finished vehicles and completely knocked-down (c.k.d.) sets to thirty-six branches across the country (twenty-five of these branches also assembled vehicles). In turn these branches served nearly nine thousand dealers with cars and spare parts.[2] By this time, only twelve years after the formation of the Ford Motor Company, the Ford system was almost fully developed. The major change after 1915 would be the quadru-

pling of output from 501,000 units to a peak of 2,011,000 in 1923 (figure 4.1). Having perfected an efficient distribution system for the Model T, Ford's interest then shifted to the development of backward integration, which culminated in the Rouge manufacturing complex.

While Ford's contribution to the development of mass-production methods in very large production centers such as Highland Park and the Rouge is well known, the parallel decentralization of distribution and regional assembly has been almost overlooked. All the standard works on the Ford Motor Company, mass-production methods, and the development of the modern corporation recognize Ford's branch activities but have not commented on or analyzed the magnitude, operations, and geography of the system.[3] The size and complexity of the Ford operations beyond Detroit deserve a similar range of superlatives to those usually lavished on the production complexes.

In developing an integrated distribution system, Ford was following the general American trend of replacing the earlier merchant-dominated systems with marketing channels dominated by manufactur-

ers.[4] By 1900, the distribution of sewing machines, farm implements, petroleum products, cash registers, and other product lines was largely controlled by the manufacturers. National Cash Register had 199 branches across the United States at this time, and the dynamic sales-oriented company served as a visible model to many of the companies entering the new automobile industry.[5] While the early distribution of motor vehicles relied on regional wholesalers, the inadequacies of service and support meant that the manufacturers soon became directly involved in the higher levels of the marketing channels.[6] For Packard, the value of the New York market was so high that in October 1902, the company took over the agency that had been opened only a year earlier.[7]

Development of the Branch System

The success of Ford was based on integration of the many phases of producing, selling, and servicing:

> Thus the commercial serpent of Ford car trade can be seen to have its tail in its mouth, making the

circle complete and endless and, so far as can now be seen, impregnable. The Ford cars are bought by everybody because they are low cost, good and everywhere present; and they are low cost, good and everywhere present because the large sales enable the Ford Company to produce cars cheaply, to make them good and to support thousands of selling agencies scattered over the entire habitable face of the world.[8]

The Ford branch-distribution system evolved through a full life cycle between 1904 and 1933 (table 4.1, figure 4.2). In the first decade, there was a very rapid proliferation of regional sales branches located in virtually every metropolitan city. From 1912 a new policy of regional assembly transformed the sales branches into major centers of production. Within five years, virtually all the cars sold in the United States were being assembled in a network of branch plants. As the adoption of the moving assembly line transformed the production process, a new generation of horizontal assembly

plants was built to replace the earlier multistoried structures. The integrated system of production and marketing was evolved to sell the Model T automobile. Once sales began to falter and this vehicle was replaced by new models, the basis for the branch system was undermined. When the car market collapsed in 1931–32, the Ford management was forced to retrench, and much of the system was permanently closed. Each phase of growth had its own distinctive features that have left lasting traces in the landscape. The artifacts of the Ford Motor Company now provide important physical evidence for the study of twentieth-century industrial and commercial archeology.[9]

The success of Ford branch assembly in the United States prompted similar development in Canada and then overseas. By the early 1930s, there were about thirty-four Ford branch plants outside the United States. The Windsor, Ontario, center not only supplied components to the five branches of the Ford Motor Company of Canada,

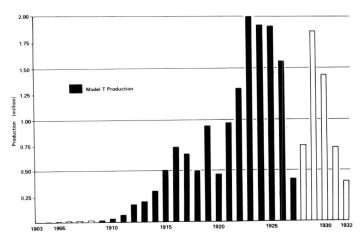

4.1. Ford Motor vehicle production in the United States, 1903–32.

Table 4.1.   Evolution of the integrated Ford system

	Total Ford U.S. motor vehicle output[a]	Other production plants	Central production plants	Branches				Dealers
				Total	Number assembling	Employment[b]		
1904	1,695	...	1 (Piquette Ave)	1	...	...		Very small
1909	17,771	...	1 (Piquette Ave)	11	...	239		859
1914	308,162	...	1 (Highland Park)	27	15	4,217		7,000[c]
1924	1,922,042	11 +[d]	2 (Highland Park, Rouge)	35	30	24,429		9,726
1929	1,862,585	11 +	1 (Rouge)	35	31	47,034		8,275
1932	392,568	11 +	1 (Rouge)	35	31	40,707		na

[a]Allan Nevins and Frank E. Hill, *Ford,* vol. 3 (New York: Scribner's, 1963), app. 1.
[b]Compiled from Ford Archives data.
[c]Nevins and Hill, vol. 1 (1954), 403.
[d]Includes small plants in Detroit area; Green Island, N.Y.; Hamilton, Ohio; Glassmere, Pa. (glass); but not the lumber mills, iron and coal mines.

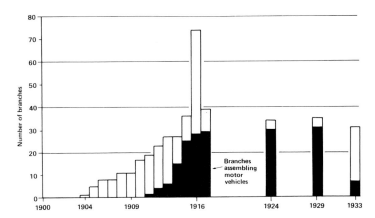

4.2. Ford Motor Company: Branch develoment, 1903–33.

Ltd., but also shipped materials for local assembly in South Africa, India, and Ceylon (four plants), Singapore, Australia (five plants), and New Zealand. In Europe, the mini-Rouge at Dagenham was intended to supply another eight assembly plants across the continent.[10]

Sales Branches and Dealer Networks

The development of the Ford marketing system began in June 1903, at the same time as the incorporation papers for the company were being filed. William Hughson of San Francisco was granted an agency territory covering the entire West Coast together with Alaska and Hawaii.[11] During the following year, James Couzens, Ford's commercial organizer, toured the country, visiting automobile shows and enlisting a network of regional agents and local dealers. Agents varied from bicycle dealers such as Hughson to department-store proprietors such as John Wannamaker, who took agencies for New York and Philadelphia.

As the automobile market began to expand, it became clear that the agency system had major limitations. Most agents were undercapitalized and were reluctant to promote an exclusive line of cars. Few were able to offer after-sales service or could afford extensive stocks of spare parts. John Wannamaker's decision to relinquish his agencies in New York and Philadelphia during 1905 forced Ford into operating direct agencies. Though requiring new capital investment, company-owned branches not only provided a regional base for sales promotion and service to owners but also saved the large discounts that had to be granted to the agents. During late 1905 and the following year, Ford branches were established in Boston, Buffalo, Cleveland, Chicago, St. Louis, and Kansas City. By the fall of

1906, there were nine company branches supervising 450 dealers.[12] The new branches were in modest leased premises usually located on major arterial roads at the edge of the central business district. Ford's early establishments, along with their competitors, became the nucleus of the "automobile rows." The distinctive Ford brand logo, devised as early as 1902, was painted on the agency facades and was soon to be emblazoned on local dealers' premises across the country.

The branches covered only part of the whole national area. While branches at Denver and Seattle extended company-controlled territory to the west by September 1909, there were still large tracks of agency territory covering California, Nevada, Arizona, Minnesota, North and South Dakota, and Nebraska and a huge swathe of the South and Southeast from Texas to Delaware (figure 4.3). At this time, there were eleven branches and 859 dealers. The success of the Model T, introduced in late 1908, impelled the company to look again at the distribution system. From late 1909, Ford began taking over agency territories and established branches in San Francisco, Los Angeles, Dallas, Atlanta, Louisville, and Indianapolis. The last agency territory was acquired in 1912 when the Minneapolis branch was opened.

By 1914 there was a complete national network with twenty-nine branches serving nearly seven thousand dealers. Branch sales rose from 6,429 in the year ending September 1909 to just over 200,000 in the year ending September 1914.[13] Sales handled by the branches amounted to 80 percent of the total sales value. Employment in the branches also increased substantially, from 289 in 1909 to 4,217 five years later. The branches were a key part of the distribution system linking the Detroit production plant with the local dealers. Each branch combined a showroom, service workshop, and stock warehouse for spare parts. The local manager supervised the staff working within the branch building as well as the "road men," the traveling inspectors and service representatives who checked the work of the dealers. Managers were under the close control of the head office at Highland Park. Detailed monthly statistical returns had to be prepared and managers were also on the receiving end of a flood of memoranda from above. Managers also had some role in the distribution of the monthly *Ford Times* magazine. As branch business expanded, their premises were enlarged and changed from leased buildings to new company-owned structures, usually designed by Albert Kahn.

Already by the end of 1912, Ford's local sales

4.3. Ford branch organization, 1909.

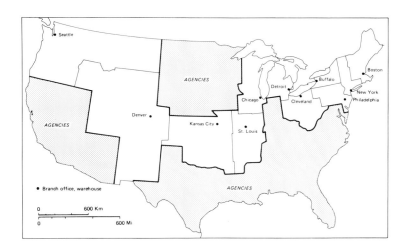

organization covered practically every town in the United States with a population of two thousand or more.[14] Each dealer had an exclusive contract with the company, which specified the precise sales territory. As the branch managers and staff in Highland Park analyzed the sales figures and studied the ledgers and commercial atlases, the dealer territories were subdivided and reassigned. This fine geographical network of dealerships gave Ford an unrivaled basis for sales. By 1914 it was claimed that there were probably more Ford agencies than agencies for the entire rest of the auto industry. Ford's public presence and outreach were probably greater than that of any other manufacturing company.

As the dominance of Ford continued unchallenged, with sales tripling between 1914 and 1917 to slightly over 700,000 units, the branch network was extended still further. The *Ford Times* announced in August 1916 that "in harmony with the policy of promotion, so firmly the faith of the Company," a further thirty-four branches and subbranches had just been opened.[15] Existing branch territories were subdivided as new offices and warehouses were opened in smaller centers. New York State, which had previously been served from Buffalo and Long Island, had new branches at Rochester, Syracuse, Utica, Albany, and Troy (subbranch). Within metropolitan New York, subbranches were opened at Bronx, Brooklyn, Manhattan, and Yonkers. The commercial benefits of this branch extension were limited, however, and numbers were reduced from seventy-four in September 1916 to sixty-seven in April 1917, and cut further to thirty-nine in September 1917. Only a few new places such as Des Moines, Jacksonville, and Salt Lake City remained after the final consolidation. From this time, the branch network was maintained at

about the same size. Retail sales by branches were abandoned in 1916–17, when the volume of direct retail sales had fallen to about 1.5 percent of total sales.

The dealer network that had 6,167 contracts in force in September 1917 fluctuated in size over the next decade, as Ford's marketing policies became more erratic. From a total of about 6,484 dealers in early 1921, the number was increased to 9,724 in December 1924.[16] Henry Ford was very critical of what he called sloppiness and indolence in selling Model T vehicles. A brutally simple "crossroads policy" was devised to punish dealers who were perceived not to be pulling their weight. New dealers were licensed across the road from the original dealer.[17] Many dealers could not survive these tactics and turned to General Motors or Chrysler franchises. Total numbers of Ford dealers fell to about 8,500 in 1927.

Regional Assembly

The rapid growth of business in 1908–9 and the high freight charges on finished automobiles suggested a move towards regional assembly. This innovative policy was approved at the directors' meeting on June 22, 1909, when it was decided that "the officers be and are authorized to purchase approximately 3½ acres of land in Kansas City just north of the Weber Gas Engine plant and located on the Frisco line and MoPac Railway for the sum of $17,500 and to proceed to put thereon an assembly plant to cost $36,000."[18]

4.4. A view of the St. Paul sales and service branch opened in 1915. This building, designed by Albert Kahn, was typical of the company-owned branches that replaced the earlier leased premises. It was closed in mid-1917 during a phase of corporate retrenchment, since the territory was already served by the larger Minneapolis branch.

Assembly of semi-knocked-down (s.k.d.) Model T cars began in the plant during 1910, and a similar operation began in Fargo, North Dakota. There were many advantages to the new policy. In place of the three or four automobiles that could be fitted into a modified boxcar, a standard boxcar could be used for shipping the subassemblies and parts for twelve autos. Savings on shipping costs were translated into additional profit, and delivery times were effectively reduced by lowering congestion on the railway lines around Highland Park. The visible presence of new factories with jobs and more business for local firms made more friends for the company in cities across the United States. The opening of new assembly plants provided free publicity. When the Oklahoma City plant was opened in August 1916, the mayor declared a holiday, and the company and chamber of commerce hosted a luncheon for 5,000 dealers and guests. In the afternoon, a cavalcade of 2,300 Model T's, including 175 assembled that day, paraded through the streets.[19]

During 1911 the directors approved new investment in land and buildings, and Albert Kahn was commissioned to design a new generation of Ford facilities modelled on the Highland Park plant. Long Island City assembled the first Model T's in 1912, and each year new assembly plants were established across the country. As each assembly plant was opened, it replaced the local branch, so that the new multistory buildings incorporated ground-floor showrooms, offices, and parts storage, as well as the space for assembling parts shipped in from Detroit. By September 1914, the fifteen plants assembled 56,365 vehicles at an average cost of $19.92 per vehicle.[20] In the year ending July 1917, the twenty-nine plants assembled 709,029 vehicles. During this period, the proportion of vehicles assembled outside Highland Park increased from about 20 percent in 1913–14 to over 90 percent by 1916–17. The massive building program of 1911–17 cost some $13.4 million and created 5.5 million square feet of building space.[21]

The rapid expansion of the regional assembly system is illustrated in figures 4.6 and 4.7. During the financial year ending September 1914, the average size of an assembly plant was only 3,750 vehicles. Four plants—those in Long Island City, Minneapolis, Kansas City, and Chicago—assembled over 5,000 vehicles. Within the next three years, the network of plants was intensified, especially in the South and the core market areas of the Middle West. The average plant size increased sixfold to 24,450 vehicles during this period. Chicago, the largest plant, was assembling 56,000 units in 1917, and ten other plants assembled over 25,000 vehicles each.

The new branch-assembly buildings were first erected in cities where there was already a substantial local market (New York) or near the boundaries of national freight-rate territories (St. Louis). As Henry Ford recorded in 1926, the saving in freight

4.5. Ford branch organization, 1914.

rates of a fraction of a cent per part often decided the location.[22] Within cities, the plants were generally sited on railroad belt lines (Buffalo), and often where railroad lines crossed major arterial roads (Philadelphia). Such locations also generated publicity by their prominent positions, which were further enhanced by large electric signs. Most of the sites were on the fringe of the central business district rather than being sited in wholly industrial zones.

Ford's pricing policy was always F.O.B. (free on board) Detroit, with a freight charge added for shipment to the customer's final destination. In June 1915, a customer in St. Louis paid $17.40 extra in freight, and the charges increased with distance to $30.90 in Kansas City, $50.50 in Denver, and $75.00 in San Francisco. These rates reflected the railroad rate territories. As Ford shipped parts rather than finished vehicles from Detroit, there were additional profits from the branch-assembly operations. In 1916–17, some $4.1 million profit was made on freight charges.[23] The movement of parts rather than finished vehicles also reduced congestion in the Detroit plant and railways yards.

The Ford assembly and distribution system in 1917 was a highly profitable machine represented in metropolitan cities and with a dealer network in every significant town. Few of the branch structures were more than five years old, and the new reinforced concrete and brick-faced buildings enhanced the cities in which they were located, not only aesthetically but also by stimulating the local economies.

A New Generation of Assembly Plants

As with many other grand schemes built in times of rapid growth and change, the new system was becoming obsolete by the time it was completed. The chain-driven final assembly line, so successfully developed at Highland Park in 1914, was quickly adopted in the branch-assembly plants.[24] Assembly lines at the Pan Pacific Exposition in San Francisco during 1915 and in the Washington, D.C., branch were major tourist attractions. The innovation reduced assembly time very substantially but created new bottlenecks in the loading docks and assembly floors of the multistoried buildings.

4.6. Ford branch assembly plants, 1914.

It soon became clear to the production engineers and Albert Kahn that the new assembly process needed a new generation of buildings designed with horizontal layout. New plans were formulated in the immediate postwar period, and a series of large steel-framed buildings began to replace the earlier reinforced-concrete structures.[25] A new Chicago plant was opened in 1924 with an area of 741,621 square feet all on one floor. This building replaced the 1914 branch, which had 239,000 square feet on six floors. Overall annual assembly capacity was doubled from 60,000 units to 120,000 in the new plant. Between 1923 and 1932, seventeen new Kahn-designed plants entered service. All

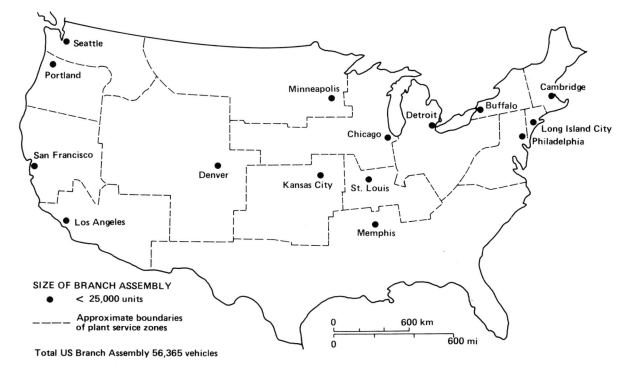

SIZE OF BRANCH ASSEMBLY
●   < 25,000 units

– – – –   Approximate boundaries of plant service zones

0   600 km
0   600 mi

Total US Branch Assembly 56,365 vehicles

were replacements for buildings rarely more than ten to fifteen years old. The floor area of these plants amounted to about eight million square feet.

Figure 4.9 shows the Ford assembly system at its peak output, when the Model T still dominated the market. The average plant size had risen to 66,000 in this year, nearly three times larger than in 1917. Two plants—at Charlotte, North Carolina, and Washington, D.C.—had been closed, and three new ones had been opened. Kearney, New Jersey, which had been built in 1918 as a production plant for the Ford-designed Eagle boats, replaced Long Island City as the assembly plant for metropolitan New York. Des Moines, opened in 1920, was the last of the multistory structures. New Orleans, which went into production in 1923, was the first of the new generation of horizontal plants.

Branch assembly in 1929 (figure 4.10), though very large, failed to reach the 1923 peak of output. Eleven new horizontally designed plants had been opened, mostly to replace buildings of the earlier generation. These were usually on the outer fringes of metropolitan cities, as, for example, the Chester plant, which was several miles downstream of the earlier Philadelphia location. Three new plants—at Norfolk, Virginia; Charlotte, North Carolina; and Jackson, Florida—provided more intensive coverage of the southeastern market area.

This new generation of assembly plants was not only designed on different principles than the first generation but they were also located according to different principles. An edict from Henry Ford in 1917 made a waterside location mandatory for all new plants, so that the materials could be supplied by barge or ship. With the exceptions of Dallas and Charlotte, North Carolina, all the new plants opened after 1924 were located beside navigable waterways so they could be served by vessels of the Ford fleet.

The whole branch-assembly system that had evolved from 1909 was based on the mass production, assembly, and distribution of the Model T vehicle. Although conversion of all plants to Model A assembly was accomplished in 1928, the enormous Ford system had already been undermined by new trends and competition in the industry. Henry Ford's obsession with production, and his emphasis on the Rouge complex in the early 1920s, meant that he and the company he dominated lost touch with the customers. The branches, which in the earlier period had also been listening posts for the central administration, became more subservient to the production ethic of the company. Kuhn's recent critique of the weakness of Ford's strategy and management control in the 1920s helps to explain the demise of the branch system.[26] The commercial serpent's impregnability of a decade earlier had been undermined.

4.7. Ford branch assembly plants, 1917.

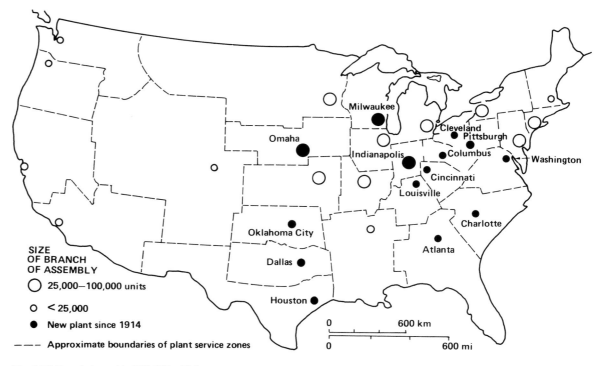

SIZE
OF BRANCH
OF ASSEMBLY

◯ 25,000–100,000 units

o < 25,000

● New plant since 1914

- - - Approximate boundaries of plant service zones

Total US Branch Assembly 709,029 vehicles

4.8. The Seattle branch assembly building (1914–31) exemplifies the first generation of Ford assembly plants erected in most of the metropolitan centers.

The corporate strategy of plant replacement continued after 1929 despite the declining market. Five new plants were opened between 1930 and 1932 (figure 4.12). Edgewater, New Jersey, on the Hudson River, was the largest, with 1,005,000 square feet of floor space. The other four new plants had an average floor area about half that size. As the effects of the Depression and declining car sales began to grip the automobile industry in 1930–31, the extensive Ford branch-assembly network became increasingly and visibly costly. While in 1929 the thirty-one branch plants assembled 1,710,000 vehicles, in 1932 the same number of plants assembled only 334,700 vehicles.[27] The labor force in the branches, which had totalled 47,034 in June 1929, declined only marginally to 40,707 employees in June 1932. The average plant assembly dropped substantially from 53,400 units in 1929 to only 10,450 in 1932.[28] Clearly, substantial retrenchment was needed.

Decisions were made later in 1932 to close most of the plants, and by February 1933 only eight assembly plants were still in operation. Both old and new plants were closed. Seattle's new plant operated just twelve months and assembled only 2,947 vehicles! Though assembly was discontinued at twenty-four plants, most of the buildings were retained as sales offices and regional parts depots. While a few plants were reopened in 1935 to cope with rising sales, Ford's poor overall performance compared with General Motors and Chrysler meant that the full network was never needed again. Sixteen of the thirty-one Ford plants existing in 1932 were never reopened.

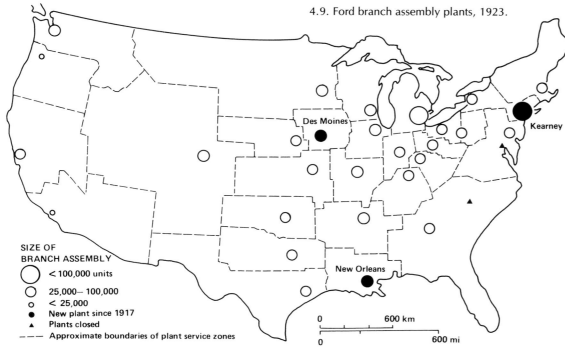

4.9. Ford branch assembly plants, 1923.

SIZE OF
BRANCH ASSEMBLY

◯ < 100,000 units
◯ 25,000– 100,000
◦ < 25,000
● New plant since 1917
▲ Plants closed
– – – Approximate boundaries of plant service zones

Total US Branch Assembly 1,915,485 vehicles

Des Moines

Kearney

New Orleans

0   600 km

0   600 mi

Three men were largely responsible for the successful development of the branch organization.[29] James Couzens established the early agency and dealer network and, as the Ford Motor Company's treasurer until 1915, supervised the corporate finances. Norval Hawkins, an auditor, joined the sales organization in 1907 and played a major role in promoting the company through the *Ford Times*. The concept and economics of branch assembly owed much to Hawkins. William Knudsen came to Ford in 1911, spending much of his time overseeing the building of the assembly plants and working out the logistics of parts movements and assembly operations. While the general strategies were evolved intuitively, the details were costed very carefully. In the growth phase to 1917, the plans worked successfully and very profitably.

Couzens, Hawkins, and Knudsen were acute individuals, well attuned to the market. After they left the company, Ford's direction became increasingly autocratic, and he lost touch with the new market conditions as he continued his obsession with ever larger-scale and lower-cost production of the obsolete Model T. Expansion in the 1920s was haphazard, costly, and often unprofitable. Ford tended to ignore the broad strategy and despised the auditors and planners in his offices. There was little overall coordination. The sales department indicated where plant expansion ought to occur, branch managers picked out possible sites, while the central office used a formula to calculate the size of the building. The simple formula allowed for a space of 3 feet per car per day, and the building proportions were one to three. Thus, for a plant capacity of 400 cars per day, an assembly building would be 400 feet wide and 1,200 feet long.[30] Henry Ford left the broad features to others but spent a great deal of time overseeing the petty de-

tails of construction. He commissioned thousands of photographs showing the brickwork, the choice of floor materials, and every stage of construction from foundations to roof. Little attention was paid to costs and overall operational viability. Branch plant construction in the period 1919 to 1925 appears to have cost about $125 million, a colossal sum at a time when the Model T market was about to collapse.

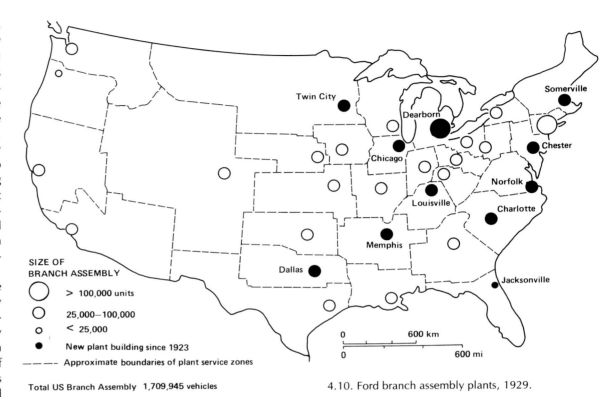

SIZE OF
BRANCH ASSEMBLY

◯ > 100,000 units

○ 25,000–100,000

o < 25,000

● New plant building since 1923

— — — Approximate boundaries of plant service zones

Total US Branch Assembly   1,709,945 vehicles

4.10. Ford branch assembly plants, 1929.

Significance of the Ford Branch System

The massive Ford production and distribution system had a substantial influence on American industrial and commercial organization. As a standardizing force, it was unparalleled; Ford products and the supporting service systems were found everywhere. While Ford was one of many expanding national organizations in the early twentieth century, the pace of its growth, its market dominance, and its visible presence made the company a very significant influence in the new geographical integration of the United States. As John Borchert has explained in relation to the northern heartland states, Ford played a major role in reorganizing the region's work.[31]

The larger automobile companies followed Ford's lead in branch assembly, although on a much smaller scale. During 1915–16, William Durant's Chevrolet company established four strategic assembly branches in Oakland, California; Fort Worth, Texas; St. Louis, Missouri; and Tarrytown, New York. Under the more cautious regime of Du Pont and Alfred Sloan, General Motors established another six plants for Chevrolet in the 1920s and opened three more for the assembly of Buick, Oldsmobile, and Pontiac models in the mid-1930s.[32] As Chrysler grew in the 1930s, the economies of shipping parts in place of built-up vehicles also encouraged the development of some branch-assembly plants away from Detroit. Many other manufacturers of motor-vehicle supplies followed with the establishment of branch plants to serve regional markets. In Los Angeles, for example, Firestone, Goodyear, and Samson built large tire factories to be close to the assembly plants and booming markets.

Ford's integration of the production-distribution system and insistence on high standards of servicing at the local dealer level were gradually followed by all American companies. There were many disciples overseas, such as Tomas Bata, who modelled aspects of his shoe manufacturing and retail empire on Ford's ideas of integration.[33] Volkswagen was a wholehearted adopter of Ford's methods in its development strategy from 1946 to the early 1970s. While the geographical model of the Ford system had universal benefits and wide acceptance, the management model was soon rejected for its inflex-ibility and wasteful expense. Fordism as a production mode now has few supporters.

While the integrated Ford system dissolved fairly rapidly after 1932, many of its features have left a lasting imprint on the American vernacular landscape.[34] In the principal metropolitan cities, most of the fifty or so branch buildings designed by Albert Kahn between 1911 and 1931 are still standing. Their excellent design and high-quality construction have assured their longevity. Although only three of these buildings remain in service as Ford assembly plants (at Chicago, Minneapolis–St. Paul, and Norfolk, Virginia), most have been adapted for other uses. Manufacturing is the most common use, but others have been converted into warehouses, offices, and university laboratories, and one in Cleveland is an art center.

The indirect landscape influences of the dispersed Ford system reached everywhere. Thousands of Ford dealers shaped the development of automobile rows, spawned the beginnings of the commercial strip, and brought new business to isolated villages.[35] The twenty-five million Ford vehicles assembled through 1933 gave Americans a new sense of mobility, which in turn created new perceptions of the country. New infrastructure had to be created for motorized travelers. In place of the concentrations and corridors so vividly depicted in Stilgoe's work on railroads, the automobile had much more widely diffused effects, which not only choked central business district traffic and shaped suburbia but reached to the farthest depths of the rural countryside.[36]

4.11. The Buffalo assembly plant (1931–58), located on Lake Erie waterfront, was one of the last of the second generation plants to be opened. It was about five times larger than the Seattle branch shown in figure 4.8.

The "Fordizing" of the American landscape was already recognized in the early 1920s when Cline described the transformation of Michigan:

> Toward the north there is a great deal of bitterness, not unmingled with envy, at the growing domination of Detroit. Nevertheless the thrill of new vigor shoots into every flaccid limb of Michigan. Highways poke like scalpels into the moribund towns of the timber district and leave garages like new thyroids to give alacrity and bustle. As you come south the cities more and more take on an air of newness, of hardness, of thin varnish, faking up what passes for prettiness, lending themselves to the salesman's glib rehearsal of modern improvements. In Detroit at last you find the consummation of the salesman's ideal.[37]

The coils of the Ford commercial serpent extended much farther than the company's business and were intertwined with the American life and landscape.

4.13. Rural relics of the vast distribution system can be found throughout North America. The Ford logo still remained on this Hickson, Ontario, agency fifty years after it last sold a Model T vehicle.

SIZE OF
BRANCH ASSEMBLY

○   25,000 – 100,000

∘   < 25,000

●   New plant building since 1929

– – –   Approximate boundaries of plant service zones

CONTRACTION OF SYSTEM

◉   Assembly plants closed Feb. 1933

CHESTER   Assembly plants remaining in service

0   600 km

0   600 mi

Total US Branch Assembly 334,703 vehicles

4.12. Ford branch assembly plants, 1932.

Notes

I am very grateful to David Crippen and Betty Jordan at the Ford Archives, Henry Ford Museum, Dearborn, Michigan. They have always provided cheerful assistance and support in finding material on the very complex activities of the company.

Among the many record series consulted in the Ford Archives, the following were used in the compilation of the maps: Figures 4.3 and 4.5 were created from the sales ledgers in Accession 387, "Agents and Contract Ledgers," 1909—Ledgers 1 and 2; 1917—Ledgers 17 and 18. Figures 4.6, 4.7, 4.9, 4.10, and 4.12 were compiled from data in Accession 260, "Monthly Statistical Reports of Branches," and Accession 231, "Production—Body Types 1921–."

More general historical material on the branches was derived from Accession 429, "Branch Histories" (to 1941).

1. Horace L. Arnold and Fay L. Faurote, *Ford Methods and Ford Shops* (New York, 1915; reprint, Arno, 1972), 22.

2. *Ford Times* 8 (June 1915):430.

3. See Allan Nevins and Frank E. Hill, *Ford: The Times, the Man, the Company,* vol. 1 (New York: Scribner's, 1954): *Ford: Expansion and Challenge 1915–1933,* vol. 2 (New York: Scribner's, 1957); *Ford: Decline and Rebirth 1933–1962,* vol. 3 (New York: Scribner's, 1963); David L. Lewis, *The Public Image of Henry Ford* (Detroit: Wayne State Univ. Press, 1976); David A. Hounshell, *From the American System to Mass Production 1800–1932: The Development of Manufacturing Technology in the United States* (Baltimore: Johns Hopkins Univ. Press, 1984); Alfred D. Chandler, *The Visible Hand: The Managerial Revolution in American Business* (Cambridge: Harvard Univ. Press, 1977).

4. Glenn Porter and Harold C. Livesay, *Merchants and Manufacturers: Studies in the Changing Structure of Nineteenth-Century Marketing* (Baltimore: Johns Hopkins Univ. Press, 1971).

5. William Rodgers, *Think: A Biography of the Watsons and IBM* (New York: Stein and Day, 1969).

6. Thomas G. Marx, "The Development of the Franchise Distribution System in the U.S. Automobile Industry," *Business History Review* 59 (Autumn 1985): 465–74.

7. Beverly Rae Kimes, ed., *Packard: A History of the Motor Car and Company* (Princeton: Princeton Publishing, 1978), 71.

8. Arnold and Faurote, 22.

9. Barrie Trinder, *The Making of the Industrial Landscaper* (London: J. M. Dent, 1982), 252–53; Kenneth Hudson, *The Archaeology of the Consumer Society: The Second Industrial Revolution in Britain* (London: Heinemann, 1983).

10. See Mira Wilkins and Frank E. Hill, *American Business Abroad: Ford on Six Continents* (Detroit: Wayne State Univ. Press, 1964).

11. Henry L. Dominguez, *The Ford Agency: A Pictorial History* (Osceola: Motorbooks International, 1981), 12.

12. Nevins and Hill, 1:264–65.

13. Accession 260, Box 3, "Monthly Statistical Accounts," Ford Archives (FA), Henry Ford Museum, Dearborn, Michigan.

14. Nevins and Hill, 1: 471.

15. *Ford Times* 10 (Aug. 1916): 14–15.

16. Accession 260, Boxes 39 and 15, FA.

17. Robert Lacey, *Ford, the Man and the Machine* (Toronto: McClelland and Stewart, 1986), 294–95.

18. Accession 85, Box 1, Minutes of the Board of Directors of the Ford Motor Company of Michigan, 22 June 1909, 151, FA.

19. Lewis, 85.

20. Accession 260, Box 3, FA.

21. Accession 488, Hadas Plant Book, FA.

22. Henry Ford, with Samuel Crowther, *Today and Tomorrow* (Garden City: Doubleday, Page, 1926), 112–13.

23. Accession, 260, FA.

24. Nevins and Hill, 1: 471.

25. Gerald T. Bloomfield, "Albert Kahn and Canadian Industrial Architecture, 1908–1938," *Society for the Study of Architecture in Canada Bulletin* 10 (Dec. 1985):4–10.

26. Arthur J. Kuhn, *GM Passes Ford 1918–1938: Designing the General Motors Performance Control System* (University Park: Pennsylvania State Univ. Press, 1986).

27. Accession 231, "Production—Body Types" (monthly), FA.

28. Accession 118, "Organization Charts—Quarterly Numbers of Employees," FA.

29. See Nevins and Hill, volumes 1 and 2.

30. Frank Hadas Reminiscences, FA.

31. John R. Borchert, *America's Northern Hinterland: An Economic and Historical Geography of the Upper Midwest* (Minneapolis: University of Minnesota Press, 1987), 185.

32. Arthur Pound, *The Turning Wheel* (Garden City: Doubleday, Doran, 1934).

33. A. Cekota, *Entrepreneur Extraordinary: The Biography of Tomas Bata, 1876–1932* (Rome, 1968).

34. John B. Jackson, *Discovering the Vernacular Landscape* (New Haven: Yale Univ. Press, 1984).

35. Chester H. Liebs, *Main Street to Miracle Mile: American Roadside Architecture* (Boston: Little, Brown, 1985).

36. John R. Stilgoe, *Metropolitan Corridor: Railroads and the American Scene* (New Haven: Yale Univ. Press, 1983); Kenneth Y. Jackson, *Crabgrass Frontier: The Suburbanization of the United States* (New York: Oxford Univ. Press, 1985); Reynold M. Wik, *Henry Ford and Grass-Roots America* (Ann Arbor: University of Michigan Press, 1972).

37. Leonard L. Cline, "Michigan: The Fordizing of a Pleasant Peninsula," in Ernest Gruening, ed., *These United States* (New York: Boni and Liveright, 1923), 185–98.

2

ARTS AND
LITERATURE

The Snapshot,
the Automobile,
and *The Americans*

CHAPTER 5

JAMES E. PASTER

The total number of snapshots taken since the introduction of the first Kodak camera in 1888 is unknown. A reasonable estimate would place the number near a trillion. More than fourteen billion will be taken in the United States this year alone.[1] This huge collection of images forms an archive of amazing depth, one that reflects the concerns, obsessions, and aspirations of society.[2] For, although the basic motive of most snapshooters may be simple documentation, snapshots are more than mere documents. Every snapshot is also an assertion, a statement made by the photographer about the world.

Simply stated, a snapshot is a photograph that "has been taken by the photographically untutored, motivated by the simple wish to record and perpetuate their life and times."[3] Although most snapshots look like most other snapshots, they do not look like other kinds of photographs. Snapshots do not follow the "rules." They may have tilted horizons, eccentric framing, blurred subjects, and obscured views. They often contain the shadow of the photographer. They are casually composed, have unglamorous subject matter, and include many details that a more elegant treatment would eliminate. "Once having centered the subject, the snapshooter allows the camera to organize the picture on its own optical, mechanical, and chemical terms. Since the snapshooter interferes least with the photographic process, he tends to produce the most human and visually complex of all photographic images."[4]

Within the huge collection of images, one of the most consistently recurring subjects is the automobile. Since people first began to discover and enjoy the freedom, mobility, and status of the automobile, they have brought their cameras along for the ride. Automobiles have often appeared in photographs made with artistic intentions as well, but as we shall see in the case of Robert Frank's *The Americans,* it was not until art photography started looking to the snapshot for inspiration that the automobile started being used as a deliberate symbol in photography.

The total number of automobile snapshots is vast, but a few types recur over and over. I have found that these types fall into five categories. One large group is comprised of snapshots that have automobiles as their main subject (figure 5.1). It can sometimes be quite difficult to discern the main subject of a snapshot, but in this group there is no question—these are pictures of automobiles. Other details have been cropped out. If there are people in the picture, they appear either in or behind the car, or partially cut off by the frame. The car holds the major place in the composition.

The photographer's decision to emphasize the automobile has several consequences. First, the car is shown as a static thing: big, heavy, immobile, and imposing. Second, context is often excluded—the location is not evident unless the photograph is labeled. This decontextualization denies us knowledge of the role that this particular automobile plays in its surroundings. Is it a new car? Who owns it? What is it doing here? We can't relate it to anything else in the frame: other cars, people, or the neighborhood. In this kind of snapshot, the car becomes a kind of trophy: it is proof of achievement. Where the car is or why it is there is less important than the fact that the car simply *is.* It's as though the photographer were saying, "Look! This is mine!" If there is someone in the driver's seat or standing nearby, the statement made may change from first to third person—"That's Uncle Henry in his Essex!"—but achievement is still the dominant message (figure 5.2). It's *his* Essex. This snapshot shows what Uncle Henry has achieved.

A second group is the go-stand-by-the-car portrait. In these snapshots, people appear in front of the automobile (figure 5.3). In some cases, a large group of people may totally obscure the car. In others, the people and the automobile may share the frame. Some people seem to pose without taking the car into account at all: full face forward, arms crossed, or with their hands in their pockets. When people pose in this manner, the car and the person are often parallel with the film plane. By taking a flat side view of the car, the photographer seems to cast it in the role of backdrop, and the people in the photo seem to agree. Often, only part of the car is included in the frame.

In other snapshots in this category, the people pay more attention to the car. Some simply turn their shoulder in deference toward it. Others may touch the door handle gingerly, while still others may lean comfortably against the car, one elbow resting on the windowsill (figure 5.4). In some cases, the photographer is positioned more toward the front of the car than the side. The decision to frame the car this way does several things. It may cause the people in the photograph to pay more attention to the car by forcing them to include it in their view when they look toward the camera. It also makes it possible for the photographer to include the entire car in the frame. Another effect is to foreshorten the front fender, exaggerating its size in the foreground while diminishing the person, who is usually posed near the door (figure 5.5).

In the snapshots in this category, the automobile serves the same function that the sword and column serve in traditional portraits of kings: the sword and column are symbols of dominance and strength; the automobile is a symbol of social and economic status. The photographer's decision to include the automobile in these snapshots of family and friends tells us more about these people than their portraits alone would. The attributes normally associated with the automobile—status, mobility, freedom—are transferred to the people who pose with it. The automobile is an object that tells us something about who these people are. The car is still a trophy, but now the photograph includes the winning team.

5.1. In one type of snapshot the automobile is the main subject—other details have been cropped out. (1968 photo)

5.2. Even though more details are included in this snapshot, the automobile is still the center of interest. (1951)

5.3. A second type of snapshot is the go-stand-by-the-car portrait. Here the car serves as backdrop. (ca. 1950)

5.4. Some people convey a sense of their relationship to the car. (ca. 1946)

5.5. In some snapshots the photographer's position may cause the car to overshadow the person. (1951)

5.6. Another type of snapshot shows people arriving or departing by car. (1958)

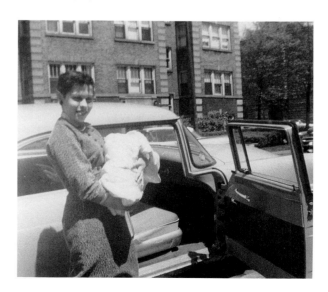

5.7. The composition of this snapshot enhances the sense of imminent departure. (1957)

5.8. Snapshots taken from inside of automobiles comprise a fourth group. (ca. 1950)

5.9. By concentrating on the road ahead instead of looking at the camera, the driver implies that the car is moving even though there are no visible signs of movement. (1953)

In the third group of snapshots, the car changes from a symbol of status to a symbol of mobility. In this group, people are shown either arriving or departing by car: families leaving on vacation, a bride and groom leaving their wedding reception, a mother arriving home with her new baby (figure 5.6). In each case, the car has become essential to the meaning conveyed. Unless we are familiar with the photograph, there is no way of knowing whether the mother and baby are coming home from the hospital or going to visit Grandma, but there is no doubt that they are in transit. The shot of the driver behind the wheel is not so much a picture

5.10. Horizontal blurring implies that the car was in motion when this snapshot was taken. (1946)

of the car and its owner—we can't really see the car—as it is a picture of a person about to drive off (figure 5.7). As in the previous snapshots discussed, the car itself is immobile, but it is no longer monumental. Now it is an instrument, a conveyance, a tool; people in these photographs have one foot in the door, they're loading the trunk, the doors are open. They are not just standing by the car, they are using it, and the car stands ready to serve them. The presence of the automobile is essential to the meaning conveyed in these snapshots. The car here serves as a symbol of potential mobility: these people have either just arrived or are about to leave.

Snapshots taken from inside automobiles form a fourth group. This group includes shots of points of interest along the roadside and pictures of the driver or passengers taken by others in the car. In snapshots like these, the photographer is not so much concerned with the "rules" of good composition as with simply getting the shot. The camera is pointed, and the photography is left to take care of itself. But these photographs also comprise one of the most visually interesting and dynamic groups because they use photography's expressive qualities more fully than other types of snapshots. No longer immobilized, the automobile here is often literally in motion. The theme of mobility continues in this group, but it is taken one step further to indicate freedom. This is expressed not merely by the presence of the automobile but by pictorial convention as well.

By shooting through the windshield at the road ahead, the photographer creates the impression that the photograph was taken while driving, whether the car was actually moving or not (figure 5.8). Shots of the driver taken from the passenger's position imply that the car is moving by showing the driver concentrating on the road rather than looking toward the camera (figure 5.9). Shots directed out the side window also imply motion (figure 5.10). The effect is heightened by horizontal blurring—a photographic convention expressing movement—and by the oblique angles that seem to indicate a "grab shot" taken on the fly.

In these snapshots, the automobile, with all its symbolic connotations, is combined with photographic conventions that indicate motion. The symbol of mobility is shown to actually be *in motion*. Content and form support and elaborate on each other. Sometimes the driver or passengers are shown, sometimes their presence is only implied, but the people in these snapshots are on the move. They are going somewhere. They are free.

Last, there are those snapshots that contain automobiles only incidentally. For example, vacation pictures often include cars simply because huge parking lots are a part of many national parks, monuments, and attractions. Most snapshots taken on city streets will also include automobiles just because they are so hard to avoid. Vacation snapshots become pictures of cars, with motels, campsites, and tourist attractions in the background. A snapshot of Mammoth Cave may show little more than parking lot and automobiles. The U.S. Capitol building may be dwarfed by cars in the foreground. In this group, the automobile conveys not so much status or mobility as car culture itself. They indicate how ubiquitous cars have become; they demonstrate how the landscape has been altered to accommodate the automobile; they show how much we have given up for the freedom that the automobile has delivered.

The majority of automobile snapshots can be placed within one of these categories. The following table summarizes the characteristics of the five types of automobile snapshots.

Type	Subject	Automobile as
1	The automobile alone	Achievement
2	People by the car	Status
3	People arriving and leaving	Potential Mobility
4	Automobiles in motion	Freedom
5	Automobiles in the background	Ubiquitous presence

One of the first art photographers to find inspiration in the snapshot and to use it as a means of personal expression was Robert Frank. Although much has been written about the well-known photographers who may have influenced Frank, there has been little examination of another acknowledged influence: the vernacular snapshot photographer.[5] By examining Frank's work in the light of the previous discussion, it will be possible to demonstrate how, in the service of his artistic vision, he selectively used not only the form and content of the common snapshot but the *types* of snapshots as well.

The Americans is filled with images of car culture—automobiles and gas stations and diners and roads. These images are not made, however, in the studied and pristine style of the art photographers who preceded Frank. These photographs look like snapshots. But the "snapshot aesthetic," as it finally came to be called, did not spring from thin air.[6] It was "in the air" in the form of billions of snapshots when Frank set off on his journey.

In 1955 and 1956, supported by a Guggenheim grant, Frank drove throughout the United States taking the photographs that would be published as *The Americans*. The book marked a turning point in American photography: "Almost every major pictorial style and iconographical concern that will dominate American straight photography in the late sixties and throughout the seventies can be traced back to one or more of the eighty-two photographs in *The Americans*."[7]

Although references to automobiles and automobile culture occur throughout the book, there are two sequences that are concerned specifically with automobiles.[8] The first begins with the photograph entitled "U.S. 91, leaving Blackfoot, Idaho." Taken from the passenger side, it shows two young men staring intently out the windshield. Our assumption, as it is with similar snapshots, is that the car is moving, even though there is nothing in the photograph to indicate movement. This is followed by "St. Petersburg, Florida." In this photograph, a group of elderly people sit with their backs to each other on a bench as a car moves by in the background. This time we know that the car is moving because it is blurred. Perhaps the two young men from the previous shot are driving by these static older people. The third photograph, "Covered car—Long Beach, California," belongs in our first category of snapshots—the car alone—except that the effect is intensified: draped in a shroud, this car is more than immobilized, it is dead. This impression is confirmed by the next photograph in the series, "Car accident—U.S. 66, between Winslow and Flagstaff, Arizona," in which the shrouded car is replaced by a blanket-covered body. In contrast to the movement and vitality of the first photograph, we have come to death and stillness in the fourth. The last photograph in the series, "U.S. 285, New Mexico," puts us back in a car and out on the road. In fact, Frank has put us in the driver's seat.

This juxtaposition of movement and death is continued in the second series. It starts with "Belle Isle, Detroit." A convertible full of children is shown heading right. The cars in the background are

blurred as this car speeds by. In the following photograph, "Detroit," once again we see older people—this time in a car heading left. Movement is implied by their intense forward gaze. They seem anxious as they stare through the windshield, as if they could see the car full of children racing toward them from the previous page. The next photograph, "Chicago," shows a car at rest, and again death is near as the signs on the car warn us that Christ has died for our sins. The last image in the series, "Public park—Ann Arbor, Michigan," returns us once again to youth as teenagers make out in the foreground while the cars that brought them crowd amongst the trees in the background.

When we compare these photographs to the types of snapshots established earlier, a pattern emerges. For example, in "Covered car—Long Beach, California," Frank refers to the "car only" type of snapshot, but the emphasis here is on immobility, not achievement. We can't see the car. He has inverted the usual connotation of this type of snapshot in order to express not achievement, but loss. He associates stasis with death. Not only is the car covered, it is firmly wedged between two palm trees. It is also shot directly from the side to increase the impression of immobility. In fact, seven of the eight cars in these two sequences have been photographed directly from the side or from the back. This makes cars that are not moving appear to be very still indeed.

Frank doesn't present any photographs in *The Americans* that depict people arriving or departing. All of the cars shown are in motion or at a dead stop, and all of the people (except those that stand sullenly by the blanket-covered corpse) are seated quite resolutely in their cars, on a bench, or on the ground. Instead of using their cars, these people seem to be trapped by them. None of these images

imply the possibility of change.

He makes extensive use of the fourth snapshot type—cars in motion (four of the nine photographs fall in this group)—but without the possibility of arriving or departing, the motion depicted becomes perpetual. Again, Frank reverses the connotations we usually associate with this type of snapshot: he shows people in motion but denies them control.

He doesn't present any images that compare with the go-stand-by-the-car type of snapshot. These, as we have seen, are associated with status and pride, and Frank's vision is much darker than that. These automobiles are not status symbols, they are symbols of mobility—or the lack of it.

The final photograph, "Public park—Ann Arbor, Michigan," falls within the "incidental" car category. These cars have brought the teenagers to the park and will carry them home later, but for now they serve as a brooding backdrop for the drama enacted in the foreground. Even the open door of the Packard serves only to frame the bored-looking passenger within—there is no driver.

Frank has suppressed or subverted those aspects of the snapshot that use the automobile to express pride or status or control, and has compressed the full range of iconic possibilities available in automobile snapshots into two opposed notions: continuous movement and complete immobility. He accomplishes this by ignoring some types of snapshots and using the characteristics of other types in uncharacteristic ways. Part of the power of *The Americans* derives from the fact that although these photographs look like familiar snapshots, they don't elicit familiar responses. We are familiar with the type but not with the emotional content that emerges from the familiar form. It is this tension that energizes and transforms the snapshot in Frank's work.

Notes

1. *1986–87 Wolfman Report on the Photographic & Imaging Industry in the United States* (New York: ABC Leisure Magazines, 1987), 38.

2. Access to this "archive" is limited by the fact that it is composed of a vast number of small personal collections. The researcher who attempts to examine these snapshots in a comprehensive way must be prepared to search at the homes of friends and strangers and at garage sales and flea markets. Although public snapshot archives such as the one at the State Historical Society of Wisconsin do exist, the common snapshot is still rarely recognized as being worthy of archival preservation. See Marie Czach, "'At Home': Reconstructing Everyday Life through Photographs and Artifacts," *Afterimage* 5 (Sept. 1977):10–12. For a comprehensive examination of the snapshot, see Richard Chalfen, *Snapshot Versions of Life* (Bowling Green, Ohio: Bowling Green State University Popular Press, 1987), and Graham King, *"Say Cheese"! Looking at Snapshots in a New Way* (New York: Dodd, Mead, 1984). Two books more narrowly concerned with the analysis of snapshots are Julia Hirsch, *Family Photographs: Content, Meaning and Effect* (New York: Oxford University Press, 1981) and Dr. Robert U. Akeret, *Photoanalysis* (New York: Peter H. Wyden, 1973).

3. Brian Coe and Paul Gates, *The Snapshot Photograph: The Rise of Popular Photography 1888–1939* (London: Ash and Grant, 1977), 9.

4. Jonathan Green, *American Photography: A Critical History* (New York: Harry N. Abrams, 1984), 38.

5. See, for example, Tod Papageorge, *Walker Evans and Robert Frank: An Essay on Influence* (New Haven, Conn.: Yale University Art Gallery, 1981); William Stott, "Walker Evans, Robert Frank and the Landscape of Dissociation," *Artscanada* 192 (December 1974):83–89; and Marguerite Welch, "After Evans and before Frank: The New York School of Photography," *Afterimage* 14 (Summer 1986):14–16.

6. For a good overview of the snapshot aesthetic, see *International Center of Photography Encyclopedia of Photography* (New York: Crown Publishers, 1984), s.v. "Snapshot Aesthetic."

7. Green, 92.

8. Robert Frank, *The Americans* (New York: Pantheon Books, 1986), 72–81, 162–69.

The Motorization of Library and Related Services in Rural America, 1912–28

CHAPTER 6

MICHAEL L. BERGER

This essay will explore the hypothesis that the motorization of transportation in the first third of the twentieth century significantly affected the nature and extent of the reading habits of rural America. Comparisons will be made between the reading behavior of farmers and small-town residents before and after the introduction of the motorcar and the bookmobile, with special attention to the impact of the new technology on reading in three social institutions: the public library, the home, and the school.[1]

Although it is difficult to prove a definite statistical correlation between the degree of motorization and the amount of reading in rural areas, there is a wealth of contemporary observations that comment on this relationship. Therefore, this essay will rely heavily on professional and lay writing to explore how and why the car and bookmobile influenced book and periodical reading among rural residents during the years 1912–28.

Availability of Books and Reading Habits before the Automobile

Books, magazines, and recreational reading in general historically played a key role in rural American life, particularly on farms. In open-country areas that were isolated from the social, economic, and political activities of large towns and small cities, reading often provided the sole link with the larger world, a mysterious and different place that nonetheless frequently influenced the lives of rural residents. As historian David L. Cohn correctly notes, "Reading was important before the auto age because there was nothing else to do, and, had there been, no way to get there."[2]

Given the importance of reading, it should come as no surprise that the library was an important institution in rural America. Its location, the extent of the services it offered, and even the individuals who staffed it were significant factors in determining the availability of books and, consequently, the amount of reading that was undertaken.

So great was the realization of the importance of the rural library that in 1914 the U.S. commissioner of education, Dr. P. P. Claxton, conducted a nationwide survey that revealed that libraries in 2,200 counties were so small that their collections numbered less than five thousand volumes. As Claxton observed, this meant that people of "most small towns, of almost all villages, and 90 per cent or more of the people living in the open country have no access to any adequate collection of books."[3]

Compounding this problem for the farmer was the fact that borrowing privileges were sometimes restricted to the residents living within the village or town limits. It was argued that *only* those who supported the library through taxation should be allowed to use it. On occasion, these institutions would permit the farm population to patronize their facilities for a fee. (Such "generosity" was most likely to surface following the realization that bringing farmers into town meant money for local businesses.)[4]

Even in those instances where the libraries were freely available, farmers found it both physically and psychologically difficult to use them. Library facilities were still a considerable distance from their farms, hours of opening were few and often varied from one week to the next, and trips into town were relatively rare in the age of the horse and buggy. The latter was particularly true for women and children, who did not accompany the men on all trips to town, especially those intended solely for business purposes.

It is true, however, that following the introduction of rural free delivery (RFD) in the 1890s, books were available from many libraries by parcel post. This undoubtedly increased circulation, especially during periods of bad weather. However, requesting library books by mail required a degree of knowledge regarding particular volumes and their availability that was often not possessed by the average farmer or small-town resident.

Books could also be secured from some mail-order catalogs, most notably Sears, Roebuck and Co. Unfortunately, there were problems here as well. Farmers and small-town residents were often dependent on catalog descriptions for their knowledge of a book's contents and, probably more importantly, volumes were offered only for sale; i.e., they were not available on loan. Given that farmers usually had relatively little cash to spend, it seems unlikely that significant numbers of them would have purchased books on a regular basis.

Finally, since control and ownership usually rested in the hands of townspeople, farmers often viewed libraries as "alien" institutions that did not cater to their needs. In this regard, a county agent leader in Minnesota cited this bit of advice from his constituents for libraries serious about serving rural areas: "Advertise your books. Take the reading material to the country people; make it easy for them to get books and help them select wisely." Similarly, "Advertise that farmers are welcome at the library and make them *feel* it."[5]

Thus, on the one hand, there was both a need and an interest in books and reading in rural areas. On the other hand, such materials were not as

6.1. Whether borrowed from a public library or purchased from a mail-order company, rural free delivery of books was a regular occurrence after World War I. This scene in York County, Maine, in 1930 could just as easily have taken place a decade earlier.

available as they should have been, forming a part of what was then known as the "country life problem." As Sarah Askew noted in 1916:

> It was evident that country boy and girl, man and woman, to compete with the city boy and girl, man and woman, must have to an extent the same social and educational advantages. Books seemed to be the greatest need. Without them . . . there could be no study clubs, debating societies, reading circles or women's clubs, and civic and social clubs stagnated. Grangers and farmer's institutes needed books in their work [as well].[6]

Furthermore, she observed,

> there was nothing to relieve the monotony of the winter evenings, or to aid parents in giving their children ideals and building up character. Schools were poor and when teachers were taxed with not teaching the use of books and developing a taste for good literature, they answered that they could not teach the use of that which they did not have nor could they build up a love for reading when the only books within reach were textbooks and those not of the best.[7]

The first remedy for this book problem, a pre-automotive one, sought to establish "deposit stations" or traveling libraries at those points where farm people were apt to get together. Thus, collections of books appeared on shelves or in boxes located in country stores, granges, schools, post offices, rural churches, and in some private homes. In Wayne County, Michigan, library centers were located in Pullen's Furniture Store, A. H. Griffin's Home, West's Grocery Store, the Dasher School, Loveland Drug Store, Bentley's General Store, the post office, the village hall, and McCulley's Laundry Service, among others![8]

Such deposit stations or traveling libraries met with a fair degree of success since they were easily accessible from farm by horse and were located in or near buildings that were the scene of social intercourse. Placement of books and magazines there guaranteed a great amount of perusal by farmers, their wives, and their children. This was especially true when bookcases with glass doors were employed. As one observer for the American Library Association noted, under such conditions, "the titles of the books may tempt those who see the bookcase even when the custodian is not there."[9]

Still, circulation of books in the open country was limited by the relatively small selection available and the fact that the initiative under the deposit system was placed on the prospective borrower. There was no trained librarian present to encourage the reading habit, recommend particular volumes, and/or answer related questions. The one exception to this generalization was a traveling library placed in a school, where the teacher acted as a type of librarian's assistant.

In addition, the physical difficulty of delivering books was often a serious obstacle. A traveling librarian with the Monterey (California) County Free Library noted that "it was interesting to watch the supplies for the new Lucia Branch [a deposit station] being deftly packed on the back of 'a submissive mule' [by the rural mail carrier]. A real pioneer experience! The round trip over the trail from Gorda to Lucia is made in a day and the third day the mail carrier returns to Jolon. This is the way all books must come to these two branches on the coast."[10] As a result of such situations, the deposit station was often just that, with little claim to being a true circulating library.

Motorization of Library Services

Into this world of limited rural library service came the motorcar. Though it came slowly at first, after World War I, the automobile entered rural America with a vengeance. Country dwellers found it to be advantageous both economically and socially, as it effectively widened their sphere of contact and influence. Crossroads stores, schools, and churches fell on hard times. As the motorized farmer increasingly bypassed these local institutions to take advantage of the "superior" opportunities in a neighboring town or small city, the deposit stations and traveling libraries suffered accordingly.

While it might have been expected that the farmers would now patronize the town libraries, this was not immediately the case. Municipal control and support continued to deter farm use. Greater mobility for open country residents did little at first to destroy suspicions and hostilities toward town and city people built up over a hundred years or more.

Realizing that it would take time for the farm family to feel at home in town, some librarians began to theorize that it might make sense to use the automobile to bring the books to the people, rather than vice versa. Thus, the very machine that had earlier been seen as a mortal threat to the deposit station movement suddenly became its temporary savior.

The motorcar allowed many of these deposit stations to become full-fledged branch libraries or to be replaced by them. The automobile made possible the organization of county library *systems,* based on the idea that each local community was entitled to, and could benefit by, a library of its own. Although such branches would not have been located in the open country, they did find their way into towns that had been, and still were, too small to support main libraries of their own.

According to Harriet C. Long of the American Library Association, librarians not only secured automobiles for the purpose of visiting country branches and deposit stations but modified the cars as well for their special purpose. "Where a roadster is used," claimed Mrs. Long, "it has been found a great advantage to remove the rear carrying compartment . . . and build in its place a larger carrying compartment with rear doors, which can convey boxes and packages to the branches and stations."[11]

Mobility provided opportunities for rural librarians to do more than merely ride herd on isolated book collections. It allowed for the creation of the position of traveling librarian, a person expected to meet the people face-to-face and spread the good books "gospel." As such, that person had the power to directly influence the reading habits of the residents of rural America. A state library official noted that the responsibilities of such a librarian could be many and varied: "In the morning she meets with school teachers and they talk over 'best books for children,' and the use of books in school. At noon she talks to the managers of a glass factory in a forlorn little glass town. . . . If she has a persuasive tongue they will let her talk to the men. . . . In the afternoon she meets with a mothers' club and they discuss the value of ownership of books, and what constitutes a good book."[12]

The motorcar also provided a means to deliver books directly to patrons on farms or pupils in schools. In a sense, it put the deposit station on wheels, with the addition of a trained librarian. Although the first instance of such a bookmobile involved a horse-drawn wagon in 1905 in Washington County, Maryland, the transformation to mechanical means was so swift (by 1912) that we may consider the real impact of this movement to

6.2. A pioneer motorized home demonstration agent is ready to depart for a meeting in rural Montana (1914). It was not unusual for such agents to carry with them a box of books or other reading matter, similar to those strapped to this car.

6.3. Edward W. Ditto, Jr., poses with the first motorized book "truck" in the United States, placed in operation in 1912 in Washington County, Maryland.

6.4. Members of a Washington County, Maryland, farm family choose volumes from the first bookmobile (ca. 1913).

have been caused by motorized service.

The automobile provided more frequent service than a horse-drawn wagon could, and its radius was wider as well, far beyond that of the traditional "team-haul." Rural residents no longer had to choose their reading for an entire season at one visit, since it became possible to have visits more often than once every four months.

As previously mentioned, many of the early book automobiles were simply touring cars with books in the back seat or in some homemade carrying compartment. However, it should be noted that the first motorized "book truck," built in 1912 by the International Harvester Company for the Washington County [Maryland] Free Library (figure 6.3), was a specially designed vehicle with an integral body. Such vehicles became common in the twenties, as communities purchased both car and truck chassis and had them fitted with custom-made bodies. For example, in Multnomah County, Oregon, the librarian reported that "a Graham truck was chosen with a specially made body fashioned to accommodate six persons and about five hundred books. The entrance is by the front door. Just back of the driver's seat is a small charging desk and in the rear of the car is another seat. Space for magazines is afforded at the top of the car along towards the front. On the inside of the car is a bulletin board which holds notices."[13]

The newness of this library concept was reflected in the variety of names used to describe vehicles that delivered reading matter to rural areas: book auto or book automobile, book bus, bookmobile, book truck, book van, book wagons, and even "bibliobus" were among the terms employed. To some extent, this difference in nomenclature mirrored the fact that these vehicles varied in size and cost, depending on the chassis used and the number of books that could be carried in the body. Typical was a 400-volume book auto made in 1923 on a one-ton Ford truck chassis. The chassis cost $447, the top body an additional $175, and the shelving and special door another $200.[14] While the cost of most bookmobiles in the early and mid-twenties was in the $700-$1,200 range, if a library wanted an all-weather vehicle with space for 1,500 books, the expenditure could be closer to $4,000. Book vans costing as much as $8,000, with room for a librarian's desk and twelve people inside, were also made during this same period.[15] In general, whether a given community had a small book auto or a large book truck was directly related to size and wealth of the library and the community to be served.

Parenthetically, several contemporary accounts note the similarity in appearance of these early bookmobiles and the funeral hearses of the day, and the problems that posed. Writing in 1924, Katherine Tappert observed that "the first book cars were painted darker colors and did not have glass doors, so they usually were taken for the 'dead wagon' and urged to pass on from the door where they had stopped."[16]

The presence of these early bookmobiles, with the name of the local library emblazoned on their sides, did much to maintain and spread the reading habit in rural America during these years. The new means of transportation, combined with its unique literary function, brought knowledge of, and publicity to, the county library on even the most remote farm. The books they provided helped ameliorate the isolation that had so often accompanied life there.

Librarian Mary L. Titcomb of Washington County, Maryland, who is generally credited with being the first to implement the bookmobile idea in 1905, provided a fine summation of its impact on rural Americans. She noted that "no better method has ever been devised for reaching the dweller in the country. The book goes to the man not waiting for the man to come to the book. Psychologically too the wagon [bookmobile] is the thing. As well try to resist the pack of a peddler from the Orient as the shelf full of books when the doors of the wagon are opened . . . at one's gateway."[17]

The Librarian and the Bookmobile

It was never the machine alone that made the bookmobile a success. Contemporary observers were quick to note that it was the trained librarian who accompanied such vehicles that made the difference. "Opinions differ as to the relative value of book-automobile factors," observed Wayne C. Nason in 1928. "A leading official of Jefferson County, Ala., in evaluating these factors and their influence on rural communities in that county, ranks the books two-tenths, the book-automobile one-tenth, and the county librarian seven-tenths."[18] Another observer noted that the person "who drives the automobile at once established a human relationship between the library and the farmer, a thing no deposit station can do."[19] Traveling allowed librarians to determine the likes and needs of the farm family to a degree that had been impossible before the advent of the motorcar. In addition, it allowed them to spread the gospel of good reading habits in highly effective one-to-one conversations. It was not unknown, for instance, for a traveling librarian to spend the night with a farm family, helping with the chores while she talked of the joys and advantages of reading.

As a result of such service, subtle changes in the rural attitude toward books and libraries could be discerned. One visitor, on a tour of rural Minnesota with a "book-bus," wrote: "I fell to wondering why these rural patrons appeared to such advantage in the book-bus, and so devoid of personality when they approached the [town] library desk. It must be that books come to them on their own grounds and terms, and not those of the library. The warm personal interest of the bus librarian no doubt is the means of translating the cold written word to throbbing life to her patrons."[20] Similarly, Katherine Tappert refers to librarians knowing "the psychology of the borrowers" and describes the advantages that brought.[21]

The satisfactions that came with being a traveling librarian were undoubtedly responsible for the positive attitude among those who held such positions. As Lulu M. Miesse, of the Noblesville-Hamilton [Indiana] County Library, observed in 1921: "It is all so different from standing behind a desk loaning books. Here we learn to know our patrons, their homes and surroundings. They are eager for companionship and are so glad to see us with our books, that it compensates us for all the hard work, cold hands and feet, hot and cold weather, and [the] dark looks of a few."[22]

The large number of written accounts by women traveling librarians, and the frequent use of the pronoun *she* in descriptions of the activities of library outreach programs in rural areas, supports an interesting observation. Namely, it appears that the vast majority of librarians who accompanied and drove bookmobiles were female. While elements within American society resisted the idea of women behind the wheel, creating the negative "woman driver" stereotype in the process,[23] motorized female librarians went unopposed. For, like elementary-school teaching, librarianship was increasingly seen as a feminine occupation in the first

6.5. A motorized book truck is on its daily rounds replacing volumes in farm branch libraries in Camden County, New Jersey.

third of the twentieth century. The same "womanly attributes" that were viewed as beneficial in the classroom, especially the nurturing instinct, seemed equally appropriate for traveling library service. When the decision was made in 1912 to replace the original horse-drawn Washington County Free Library book wagon with a motorized one, Mary Titcomb became the mother of a movement that was to become dominated by her sister librarians.

Educational Institutions

Use of the bookmobile was not confined to visits to farmsteads alone. For instance, it was recognized early that this would be an excellent way to augment the meager school libraries then in existence. Bookmobiles could visit country schools every month or so, leaving both children's books to be read for pleasure and text and professional books to be used in class by the teacher.

Two professors at the New York State College of Agriculture, evaluating such a program in the late twenties, noted two fringe benefits. First, the librarians often remained at the school to tell stories and/or kindle an interest in a certain book or collection of books. Second, there developed a system whereby rural schools joined together to purchase books in quantity through the country librarian, thus realizing a considerable financial saving over the previous method of individual purchases.[24]

This school-library cooperation was mirrored to some extent when the traveling librarian allied herself with agricultural extension and home-demonstration agents. One librarian for the California State Library observed as early as 1919 that when such agents went into rural areas, they frequently took the county librarian with them. The latter was often given the opportunity to discuss books with groups that had been assembled primarily to hear the latest word from Washington on scientific agriculture or sanitary food preparation. Thus, by cooperating with other agencies concerned with the education of the farmer, the rural librarian was able to further extend her sphere of influence.

Even when the librarian was not along, the extension agent frequently carried library books and technical volumes intended to assist farmers raise or grow a better product or to help women with their domestic chores. When the agent was not available, some farmers could make use of another new form of technology—the telephone—to request one or more books on a given technical subject to be sent by mail. Unlike general reading, where delivery of books by the postal service never really caught on, this "business" usage proved to be much more successful, probably due to the specificity of the need. A 1928 Farmer's Bulletin claimed that in excess of 600,000 books had circulated by mail in a recently recorded year.[25]

Changes in Reading Habits

Having shown how motorization made reading matter more accessible to rural Americans, a natural question arises: "How did they respond to this opportunity?"

First, it is probably safe to say that the absolute number, though not necessarily the quality, of books and magazines loaned to, or purchased by, residents of rural America increased from 1900 to 1929. As Edward R. Eastman observed in 1927,

> There has been a decrease among farm people in the careful reading of the good books, particularly of the old classics. . . . On the other hand, there

6.6. A Farm Bureau agent pauses to talk to a resident of Malta, Montana (1919). Extension agents often took traveling librarians with them to public gatherings.

is no doubt that the *average* education which comes from reading is higher in country districts than it was a generation ago because many of those of the type who read little or nothing today of the classics do pick up considerable information from current magazines and newspapers.[26]

Such a development was a logical consequence of technological change during this period. The combination of automobility, radio and telephonic communication, and rural free delivery expanded the amount of information available to rural people and generated broader needs and interests in the area of reading.

These technological changes also increased the number and prospects of those individuals who tried to sell magazines in rural areas. Thus, James West [Carl Withers], in his *Plainville, U.S.A.,* a classic sociological study of a midwestern village, observed that "periodicals are sold to farmers by agents who comb the countryside in cars with 'premium offers' which may include magazine combinations, maps, fountain pens, or farm burglary protection service. When farmwives, whom they ordinarily canvass, lack ready cash, payment is taken in eggs, chickens, and other farm produce."[27]

In addition to the magazine merchants, book peddlers became more common and efficient with the automobile. As Katherine Tappert noted, "A half-sister of the book wagon sent out by the county and public libraries is the book shop on wheels."[28] As a result, the number of rural dwellers who could be classified as regular readers increased. An Indiana librarian noted in 1921 that "people will read when the books are brought to their doors that would not come to the library for them."[29]

Second, to the extent that the automobile contributed to the success and greater efficiency of rural free delivery, it affected not just the number but the nature of publications read in rural America. This was probably most obvious in terms of newspaper readership. Whereas farmers, of necessity, previously limited themselves to weeklies, RFD made possible the timely delivery of daily newspapers as well. Since the latter usually were published in large towns and cities, this changed the content of the news that rural residents were reading.

It is important to note, however, that farmers were not substituting one newspaper for the other. Several contemporary sources claimed that RFD and the presence of the more urban dailies stimulated greater newspaper reading and led to increased circulation of the rural *weeklies* as well, though admittedly there were fewer of these latter publications as a result of consolidation and their character changed, with a greater emphasis on local community news.[30]

RFD also brought more and better magazines to the farm door. With a careful eye to the correct adjective, Edward R. Eastman numbered among the mail received by the "up-to-date farm home one or more first class farm papers, high grade magazines, [and] usually a good newspaper."[31] Although farmers subscribed to and read such mass-circulation magazines as *Saturday Evening Post, Ladies' Home Journal,* and *Collier's,* it was the aforementioned farm papers that seem to have had the greatest impact. Contemporary surveys indicated that rural dwellers were much more likely to receive farm journals than general magazines and daily newspapers.[32] Included among the former would be such national publications as *Farm Journal, Progressive Farmer, Successful Farming,* and *Wallace's Farmer.*

The available evidence regarding circulation of books is scarce and often contradictory, especially when one compares different rural communities. Nonetheless, there is one book that ought not to be overlooked, because it probably was second only to the Bible in popularity and may even have been consulted more often, and that was the mail-order catalog. A godsend for people too busy to shop for pleasure and too far away from most stores even if they had the time, the arrival of the catalog via RFD was cause for great rejoicing on the farmstead. Interestingly, the circulation of these "books" was aided by the U.S. Post Office, which allowed them to be sent via the education rate, classifying them as "aids in the dissemination of knowledge."[33]

This policy was not as farfetched as it might appear to be, since these catalogs were indeed intended to be read from cover to cover and to educate their readers. In fact, indices in these early catalogs, especially the one for Sears, Roebuck and Co., were extremely skimpy, providing the reader with little help if he or she hoped to rapidly find a specific item. As Emmet and Jeuck note in their definitive history of Sears, the catalog "was literature in a time when literature was not easily come by and seldom was free. . . . It was recreation in a period when recreational facilities were limited and, in some areas, almost nonexistent."[34]

Third, when one moves beyond the catalog to ascertain which of the more traditional books were read and how reading tastes might have changed as a result of motorization, the evidence, as indicated before, tends to be confusing. On the one hand are people like the Oklahoma postmaster whose observations regarding the reading matter that went into farm homes were as follows: "At least 95 percent of this literature is the light, trashy class, containing the silliest of silly love stories, the adventures of desperadoes, detectives, and outlaws, and that class of reading matter which, to my mind, is degrading, has no inspiration to a higher life, and imparts no information to the reader."[35] On the other hand, a pair of traveling librarians for the Monterey County Free Library, on a 1916 tour of their branch libraries, received requests for books by Shakespeare and Voltaire, and on the following subjects: psychology, bookkeeping, bees, wireless, mechanics, geology, and plant evolution.[36]

The truth regarding what rural residents read is probably an amalgam of the above two observations. In fact, the diversity of the books cited may be indicative of the influence of motorization on the reading tastes of country residents. Like other Americans, those living in rural areas were becoming more eclectic in terms of what they read, evidencing simultaneous interests in the practical, the frivolous, and the educational.

Fourth and finally, contemporary accounts seem to indicate that some of the most significant gains were made in the quantity and variety of reading undertaken by school children. Schools often served as deposit stations or were visited regularly by bookmobiles. As a result, a greater amount of supplementary reading was available for pupils. Teachers were no longer solely dependent on a single set of textbooks, and the school curriculum could be expanded accordingly.

Writing in 1929, agricultural professors Ralph A. Felton and Marjorie Beal observed that

> when the county librarian drives the book truck to a country school, the children and teacher flock out and choose the books they wish to read and to use in the classes. The schools enrich their present libraries with new titles for reading from the county library. The teacher requests special books, which will be sent out to her by parcel post. Enough books are left at each school to satisfy the needs until the county librarian drives in again in one or two months, when new books are left for old.[37]

6.7. Two rural educational institutions are brought closer together for their mutual benefit—the one room schoolhouse and the town library in Hennepin County, Minnesota.

Conclusions

Three broad conclusions seem warranted by this brief exploration of the impact of motorization on the availability of reading matter in rural America: (1) Improvements in vehicular transportation led to increased library service, expanding both the quantity and the nature of books available in rural America. Traveling "literary" salesmen and the maturation of rural free delivery abetted this trend. (2) The number of rural dwellers who could be classified as regular readers increased. As noted, people who rarely visited a a town library were likely to increase the amount of their reading if books were delivered to their door or to a local educational institution or commercial establishment. (3) The increased availability of reading matter improved the quality of rural life. As noted above, reading matter helped ameliorate the terrific isolation that so often accompanied the agricultural existence. It was this isolation that was blamed for such diverse rural problems as "unscientific" farming practices and the frequent psychological depression of farm women.

In 1928, the U.S. Department of Agriculture issued a Farmers' Bulletin that had as its theme the improvement of rural libraries. In a concluding note, the author wrote: "The purposes of this bulletin will be accomplished if rural people, State legislators, local officials, and library agencies, in view of demonstrated accomplishments, cooperate to make rural library service . . . equal, efficient, and complete."[38] As we have seen, rural motorized transport was a powerful force that could be put into service to achieve such equality, efficiency, and completeness.

Notes

1. This essay more fully develops ideas first presented as a "note" entitled "Reading, Roadsters, and Rural America," in the *Journal of Library History* 12 (Winter 1977):42–49, a publication of the University of Texas Press. For a discussion of the automobile's impact on reading in the broader context of education, see the author's *The Devil Wagon in God's Country: The Automobile and Social Change in Rural America, 1893–1929* (Hamden, Conn.: Archon Books, 1979).

2. David L. Cohn, "History Out of a Catalogue," *Saturday Review of Literature,* 9 Mar. 1940, 11.

3. Dr. P. P. Claxton, "Libraries for Rural Communities." *Bulletin of the American Library Association* 8 (July 1914):149.

4. Many of these town libraries had come into existence as a result of "challenge grants" from steel magnate Andrew Carnegie. In the late nineteenth and early twentieth centuries, he volunteered to pay the construction costs for a public library building in any town or city, provided that the locality would finance the operating costs in perpetuity. While this was clearly a beneficial arrangement for small rural towns, it also may have contributed to the antagonism that town residents showed toward allowing library use by the "noncontributing" farmers.

5. F. E. Balmer, "What the Public Library May Do for Its Country Readers," *Library Notes and News* [Minnesota Department of Education] 8 (Sept. 1923):134.

6. Sarah Askew, "Library Work in the Open Country," in "New Possibilities in Education," ed. Ambrose L. Suhrie, *Annals of the American Academy of Political and Social Science* 67 (Sept. 1916):257.

7. Askew, 257.

8. Information gleaned from a photograph of a circular produced by the Wayne County (Mich.) Library, reproduced in Joseph L. Wheeler, *The Library and the Community: Increased Book Service through Library Publicity Based on Community Studies* (Chicago: American Library Assoc. 1924), 382.

9. Harriet C. Long, *County Library Service* (Chicago: American Library Assoc., 1925), 103.

10. Anne Hadden, "Library Trails," *News Notes of California Libraries* 11 (July 1916): 584–85.

11. Long, 164–65.

12. Askew, 259–60.

13. Anne M. Mulherson, "Rural Library Service to Multnomah County, Oregon," *Journal of Rural Education* 4 (Apr. 1925):374.

14. Long, 118.

15. For written descriptions of these larger book trucks or vans, see Ralph A. Felton and Marjorie Beal, *The Library of the Open Road*, Cornell Extension Bulletin no. 188 (Ithaca: New York State College of Agriculture at Cornell University, cooperating with the Library Extension Division of the N.Y. State Department of Education, 1929), 26; and Katherine Tappert, "The Automobile and the Traveling Library: The Book Wagon Service," *Annals of the American Academy of Political and Social Science* 116 (Nov. 1924):67.

16. Tappert, 66.

17. Quoted in Nellie Lee Powell, "A History of the Washington County, Maryland Free Library" (M.L.S. thesis, Catholic University of America, 1966), 21. Given their importance for Washington County and other libraries, Mary L. Titcomb and her book wagon idea play prominent roles in Powell's work.

18. Wayne C. Nason, *Rural Libraries,* U.S. Department of Agriculture Farmers' Bulletin no. 1559 (Washington, D.C.: GPO, Apr. 1928), 45–46.

19. Dalton Wylie, "Taking the Library to the People," *Country Life in America* (Mar. 1913):66.

20. Irma M. Walker, "The Book Peddler Glorified," *Public Libraries* 25 (Feb. 1920):61.

21. Tappert, 68.

22. Lulu M. Miesse, "A Trip on Parnassus," *Indiana Library Occurrent* 6 (July 1921):100.

23. See Michael L. Berger, "Women Drivers! The Emergence of Folklore and Sterotypic Opinions Concerning Feminine Automotive Behavior," *Women's Studies International Forum* 9 (1986):257–63.

24. Felton and Beal, 30, 32.

25. Nason, 5–6.

26. E. R. Eastman, *These Changing Times: A Story of Farm Progress during the First Quarter of the Twentieth Century* (New York: Macmillan, 1927), 24–25.

27. James West [Carl Withers], *Plainville, U.S.A.* (New York: Columbia Univ. Press, 1945), 15. Although West's study was conducted during the period 1939–40, there is little reason to believe that similar opportunities

and operators, though possibly less extensive and numerous, would have existed a decade earlier.

28. Tappert, 67.

29. Miesse, 100.

30. See, for example, Miesse, 93–94; Wayne E. Fuller, *RFD: The Changing Face of Rural America* (Bloomington: Indiana Univ. Press, 1964), 297; Jesse F. Steiner, "The Rural Press," *American Journal of Sociology* 33 (Nov. 1927):414–15; and Frank P. Stockbridge, "Small-Town Papers," *Saturday Evening Post,* 25 Feb. 1928, 42.

31. Eastman, 21.

32. See, for instance, data in E. L. Kirkpatrick, *The Standard of Life in a Typical Section of Diversified Farming,* U.S. Department of Agriculture Bulletin no. 423 (Ithaca, N.Y.: Cornell Univ. Agricultural Experiment Station, July 1923), 29.

33. Louis E. Asher and Edith Heal, *Send No Money* (Chicago: Argus Books, 1942), 39.

34. Boris Emmet and John E. Jeuck, *Catalogues and Counters: A History of Sears, Roebuck and Co.* (Chicago: University of Chicago Press, 1950), 179. However, it should be noted that the Sears catalog had an index system from its very beginning, unlike some of the competition.

35. Quoted in U.S. Department of Agriculture, *Educational Needs of Farm Women,* Report no. 105 (Washington, D.C.: GPO, 1915), 52.

36. Hadden, 588.

37. Felton and Beal, 30, 32.

38. Nason, 50.

On the Road to Adventure

CHAPTER 7

DAVID K. VAUGHAN

The Automobile and American Juvenile Series Fiction, 1900–40

The automobile was one of the most important symbols of American technological achievement in the early twentieth century. It stood for American know-how and inventiveness, and it represented technological prowess. In popular literature generally, but in juvenile series books especially, the automobile represented personal capacity, prowess, and an avenue to excitement and mystery. Imaginatively as well as actually, the automobile provided access to a countryside rich in beauty, adventure, and mystery, a countryside that had previously been largely inaccessible to most Americans. In this regard, as in many others, the automobile significantly affected the American imagination.

The first crossing of the American continent by automobile occurred in the summer of 1903, when Dr. H. Nelson Jackson and his chauffeur, Sewall K. Crocker, drove from San Francisco to New York City in a 1903 Winton Touring Car.[1] That crossing marked a historical turning point: even though the journey had taken sixty-three days across trails, plains, and dirt paths, the automobile had established itself as an important element of American transportation and cultural life. No sooner had it appeared on the roads than the automobile appeared in popular fiction. As early as 1906, youthful American readers were reading of the adventures of the Motor Boys, who traversed the American continent from Massachusetts to Arizona in *The Motor Boys Overland*. The publishers of juvenile series books, always alert to new ways of appealing to younger readers, responded quickly to the advent of the automobile and to other forms of mechanized transport, including motorcycles, powerboats, and flying machines.

Juvenile series publishers integrated these new forms of transportation into their traditional mystery and adventure plots. The automobile proved to be an especially happy development for juvenile fiction books because it provided youthful protagonists with increased mobility and operative powers in their fictional worlds. The young characters in these stories were required to gain an understanding of the principles that made the auto work and to master the techniques of operation. Once they had become proficient in its operation, they found that the auto made possible a renewed appreciation of the American countryside because it provided a means of access to the countryside, where they discovered a setting full of strange characters, unusual events, and physical challenges. These ingredients added a new genre to the traditional forms of juvenile series fiction.

Prior to 1900, the literary fabric of juvenile series books consisted of three primary threads: historical adventures of the Oliver Optic and W. A. Henty type; travel narratives of foreign lands, most typically illustrated in Jacob Abbott's Rollo books; and the recently developed and popular urban adventure series of the Horatio Alger type. Oliver Optic, actually a pseudonym for Walter Adams, specialized in stories of American history—the Civil War, the American frontier—while W. A. Henty primarily described adventures of English historical figures and events. Jacob Abbott's books typically described the activities of Rollo, a young boy, as he traveled to interesting locations in America and abroad. The Horatio Alger books, the most popular reading of younger readers in the years before the turn of the century, described the adventures of hardworking young men, mostly in the large city environments of East Coast America.

While these books offered entertainment and instruction, few of them explored contemporary life in the American rural countryside. One reason for this deficiency may have been the fact that entry into the countryside was limited, physically and imaginatively. The advent of the automobile in the early years of the twentieth century soon made both physical and imaginative access possible in a rapid and dramatic fashion. Even after the novelty waned, the automobile continued to be an important part of the action and impact of juvenile series books.

Early Boys' Series, 1906–25

The first major juvenile series to be based on the theme of the adventure of motor transportation was the Motor Boys series, published by the Stratemeyer Syndicate under the pseudonym of Clarence Young; most of the books were probably written by the prolific Howard Garis. The first book in this series, *The Motor Boys,* appeared early in 1906, less than three years after the first automobile had crossed the continent. The author opened the volume with a short personal note to his readers; "Dear Boys," he said, "The motor-cycle of to-day is fast taking the place of the ordinary bicycle, and the automobile, or auto, as it is commonly called, is taking the place of our horses. This being so, it has occurred to the writer to prepare a line of stories, telling of the doings of a number of lively, up-to-date lads who at first own motor-cycles and later become the proud possessors of a touring car."[2]

The Motor Boys—Ned Slade, Bob Baker, and Jerry Hopkins—begin their adventures in the town of Cresville, Massachusetts, near Boston. Before the final book in the series appears, they have traveled around the world. Typically, the three chums are thwarted in their attempts to assist the more unfortunate of their friends and acquaintances by Noddy Nixon, an envious competitor.

While the initial volume features bicycle and motorcycle races, subsequent volumes dispense with races in favor of mysteries to be solved, in which the automobile provides both the introduction to the mystery and the means of its solution. Because the boys are too young to be setting off on cross-country adventures entirely on their own, they are escorted by an adult, most often Professor Uriah Snodgrass, an eccentric but enthusiastic supporter of their activities. There are a total of twenty-two volumes in the Motor Boys series, the last of which appeared in 1924. The first four volumes (published in 1906–7) described adventures with motorcycles and automobiles, the next four focus on powerboats (1907–9), and the third four involve flying machines (1909–10). The final ten volumes describe a mixture of transportation forms.[3]

The other major series to appear at this time was James Braden's five-volume Auto Boys series, published from 1908 to 1913. All five of Braden's volumes describe the adventures of four boys in automobiles. The Braden series provides more detailed descriptions of automobiles and automobile features than does the Motor Boys books. Most of the boys and girls who are involved in automotive adventures come from families with significant financial resources. In assessing the social status of the characters of the early books (those written before 1925), it is clear that the books describe, and are addressed to, members of the middle class and upper middle class; few citizens could have afforded the kinds of cars described in these adventures.

By 1909 flying machines had gained the attention of the public, and boys' series books soon reflected that interest, most notably in the thirty-eight-volume Tom Swift series, the first volumes of which appeared in 1910. These books were almost certainly written by Howard Garis under the pseudonym of Victor Appleton. In contrast to the Motor Boys series (and probably by Stratemeyer design), the Tom Swift series pays little attention to ground or water transportation (at least initially), focusing instead on aerial travel. In addition, Tom is the main figure of the books, although a variety of youthful companions and adults are involved in his adventures. Tom Swift is characterized as an American inventive genius, whose technological know-how enables him to travel to remote portions of the world. The Motor Boys are resourceful but do not demonstrate a machinery-oriented inventiveness. Tom Swift, on the other hand, is always working on an improved engine component or other technological improvement, a consistent feature of the books even in the final volume, published in 1935.

Early Girls' Series Books, 1910–25

Interestingly, girls' series books made more complete and consistent use of the automobile than boys' series. The first to appear was the Stratemeyer Syndicate's Motor Girls series, which was published in ten volumes from 1910 to 1917.[4] The name of the series author was given as Margaret Penrose, another Stratemeyer house name; Howard Garis's wife, Lillian, probably wrote a number of the Motor Girls books. Like the Motor Boys series, the Motor Girls books describe a variety of forms of motor transportation, including automobiles and boats but not motorcycles or flying machines. The Motor Girls consist of a group of girls who live near New York City, of whom Cora Kimball is the principal figure. A number of boys are also present, probably to provide appeal to boy readers as well as girls, but also to provide male escorts for the girls as they venture out in their groups on the open road. Like the Motor Boys, the Motor Girls pay more attention to the mysteries presented by unusual people and strange events than to the automobiles they operate. In general, the author of the Motor Girls has a much better sense of social interaction and much better control of plot development than the author of the Motor Boys books.

Two other early girls' series are Laura Dent Crane's Automobile Girls, whose six volumes appeared from 1910 through 1913, and Katharine Stokes's six-volume Motor Maids series, which appeared from 1911 through 1917. The Automobile Girls series is much more clearly associated with upper-class social standing and activities, as the titles of the books suggest (*The Automobile Girls in Newport,* for instance, or *The Automobile Girls in Palm Beach*). The Motor Maids series similarly displays characteristics of upper-class social standing and offers the novelty of international travel, as some episodes occur in Japan and Britain.

These three girls' series yielded a total of twenty-two books by 1917; the two boys' series produced twenty-three books by that year, but only about half of those really describe automotive travel. Probably the main reason for the large number of girls' books pertaining to automobile travel was social custom; while it was acceptable for boys to ride motorcycles (which were featured equally with automobiles in the early volumes of the boys' series), girls were not generally allowed to do so. The automobile was the primary form of transportation available to girls, at least in series books. Of course, automobiles were featured widely in other series of the period whose thematic focus was on other areas; these series included the Bobbsey Twins, the Outdoor Girls, and the Bert Wilson and Grace Harlow series.

The Automobile and the Story Line

Initially, the writers of series books felt the need to describe continent-spanning adventures, as indicated in two of the early Motor Boys books, *The Motor Boys Overland,* which describes a trip across the American continent, and *The Motor Boys in Mexico.* Series writers soon realized, however, that more limited locales could offer equally interesting and more comprehensible adventures, as indicated in the titles of the adventures of the Automobile Girls, who visit the Berkshires, Newport, the Hudson River, Chicago, Palm Beach, and Washington. American travelers and readers were more likely to explore limited locales; driving on a coast-to-coast trip would be a rare event. In addition, the writers probably discovered that it was much easier to build a reasonably tight plot for a mystery or adventure story if the action were restricted to a more limited locale. The generally tighter plots of the Motor Girls books seem to be linked to their more limited locales, as opposed to the looser structure and wider range of action of the Motor Boys series.

The automobile provided a new and exciting means of access to the American countryside, actually and imaginatively. For the first time, the pleasures of the country could be visited with relative ease by American citizens and by fictional characters. James Braden's *The Auto Boys' Outing* (1909) contains a good illustration of the sense of exhilaration and escape provided by the automobile:

And now for whole days together the chums were to know no separation from their auto nor from each other. Blessed days and all that they had in store! . . . Summing up these attractions, together with those of the river, there were included . . . the delights of the country generally with its outdoor life of many kinds, and miles and miles of roads, and little towns and villages,—all fertile territory for interesting trips of exploring in the automobile.[5]

Laura Dent Crane's Automobile Girls instructively compare the view north of New York City to those that young readers might have seen in illustrated books depicting the scenic pleasures of Europe:

The crags of the Palisades towered on one side, while on the other were beautiful estates stretching back into the hills, and little villages nestling down on the river front. . . . "Bab," whispered Mollie, awed by the lovely vistas of river and valley, "do you think the Vale of Cashmere could be more exquisite than this? Or the Rhine, or Lake Como, or any other wonderful place we've never seen?"[6]

According to this author, America's scenic views are the equal of those found abroad, but access to American scenery will be obtained primarily through the assistance of the automobile.

In order to appreciate the beauties of nature from an automobile, the young heroes and heroines of the juvenile series stories first have to master the complicated operation of the automobile, a process often described in detail. Mollie Billette, the operator of the automobile in Laura Lee Hope's *The Outdoor Girls in a Motorcar* (1913), demonstrates the proper procedures under the watchful eye of her tutor:

Carefully Mollie threw out the clutch, and slipped in first speed. Then releasing the clutch pedal gradually she felt the car move slowly forward. . . . From first to second gear, and then in another moment to high, was performed by Mollie without a hitch. Then she advanced the spark and gas levers. "Well, so far so good!" spoke Amy, with a sigh of relief. "I knew Mollie could do it," declared Betty. "Look out for that wagon, my dear," she cried, a second later.[7]

The series books strongly implied that with the right kind of preparation and training, young men and women could operate automobiles as well as adults. J. W. Duffield's *Bert Wilson at the Wheel* (1913) describes the excitement generated in the mind of Bert Wilson, the fifteen-year-old central character, at the thought of owning or operating an automobile:

> The huge machine moving so swiftly, so noiselessly, with such a sense of freedom and the sensation of flying, drew him like a magnet. He scarcely dared to dream that one day he might be the actual owner of a motor car, but he did hope that some day or other his hand might be on the wheel, his foot upon the brake, while he steered the flying monster as it sped like a flash across the country.[8]

In *The Motor Girls on the Coast* (1913), a visitor from Chicago, Eline Carlton, asks, "Is it hard to drive a car?"

> "It is, my dear, at first," Cora explained. "Then it all seems to come to you at once. Why you'd never believe it, but first I used to imagine I was going to hit everything on the road. I gave objects such a wide berth that everyone laughed at me. But I did not want to take chances. Now watch!"
>
> She speeded up a little, and turning to one side seemed to be headed straight for a tree.
>
> "Oh!" screamed Eline, and Bess and Belle echoed the cry.
>
> "There!" cried Cora, as she skillfully passed it, far enough for safety, as even the most careful

motorist would admit, but near enough to make an amateur nervous.[9]

These youthful protagonists are required to display significant dexterity and know-how in disengaging their automobiles from ditches and bushes, into which accidents and interruptions often direct them. In one instance, the Auto Boys successfully pull their vehicle out of a mudhole through the use of a block-and-tackle device, a method frequently used by early automobile operators. And it is a part of the special appeal of the girls' series books that the girls are as capable of responding to road emergencies as the boys. In *The Outdoor Girls in a Motorcar*, Mollie Billette extricates her car from some roadside bushes: "Mollie took her place at the wheel, pressed the starting button, and then, with a glance backward to see which way to steer, she slipped in the reverse gear, and let the clutch come into place. Slowly, amid a tearing away of vines and bushes, the car regained the highway."[10]

The automobile provides the necessary means for bringing the youthful characters into contact with unusual occurrences and mysterious events. In *The Motor Boys in Mexico*, the Motor Boys, for instance, witness an amazing attack of a wild animal from the comparative safety of their automobile (figure 7.1). This event is one of many natural hazards they face on their excursion into Mexico.[11] The Automobile Girls outface a gypsy bandit along the banks of the Hudson River (figure 7.2).[12] This encounter in *The Automobile Girls along the Hudson* is the first of a series of mysterious happenings, the meaning of which they eventually discover. In *The Outdoor Girls in a Motorcar*, a young girl falls out of a tree as the Outdoor Girls drive along a country road (figure 7.3), and they attempt to determine her identity and the motives for her unusual behavior.[13]

7.1. "The big beast had a monkey in its mouth." The Motor Boys observe one of the jungle's examples of the survival of the fittest, illustrating the relative comfort in which new and surprising scenes could be witnessed by passengers in automobiles.

7.2. "Drop that knife and run!" A gypsy bandit unsuccessfully confronts the Automobile Girls along a deserted upstate New York road. The automobile provided its operators—including women—with maneuverability and power not previously available.

7.3. "[The girl] toppled from the tree, almost in front of the car." An unknown girl falls into the path of the Outdoor Girls; the early narrow, unimproved roads made such unlikely occurrences believable.

The automobile brings the youthful protagonists into contact with unusual adventures at the same time that it gives them the means of responding appropriately to them.

After the war, owning and operating a vehicle became more commonplace as Henry Ford's revolutionary production line made automobiles available to the greater numbers of middle-class families. As the automobile became an established part of American life, writers of juvenile series books developed an increasingly sophisticated sense of its fictional value, and the challenge of learning to operate the automobile was replaced by the excitement of the mobility it provided and the mental alertness required to operate it in high-pressure situations.

The Later Series, 1925–40

The adventure associated with the automobile in books published after 1925 was not usually in its operation or repair, but in the versatility it offered and in the variety of experiences it could bring to its occupants. It became an extension of the protagonists who used it, a kind of space and time machine that required an understanding of the surrounding life and culture and challenged the mental and physical resources of the youths who drove it. In their automobiles, youthful characters could compete with adults on an equal basis; the automobile offered mobility, speed, protection, and often the opportunity to demonstrate exceptional physical coordination. These aspects of the multifaceted utility of the automobile are repeatedly illustrated in two popular Stratemeyer-produced mystery series, the Franklin W. Dixon *Hardy Boys* series, which began in 1927, and the Carolyn Keene *Nancy Drew* series, which began in 1930. New volumes of these series are still being published today.

The automobile is an important feature of the Hardy Boys books, the early volumes of which were written by Leslie McFarland; the name of the supposed author, Franklin W. Dixon, was a pseudonym. Frank and Joe Hardy would have been able to solve few mysteries had they not had access to their roadster, which brings them into contact with strange individuals and unusual incidents. Although the Hardy Boys begin their careers on motorcycles, they soon graduate to a jointly owned automobile. The frontispiece for the ninth book in the series, *The Great Airport Mystery* (1930), shows an erratically flying aircraft zooming past the Hardy Boys as they swerve off the road to avoid it (figure 7.4). Frank, who is driving the automobile, is require to exercise the skills of a race-car driver to avoid an accident:

> Frank Hardy could scarcely keep the car on the road. He glanced at the speedometer. They were traveling seventy miles an hour. . . . A short distance ahead Frank saw a rough dirt road leading off the highway. . . . Frank slackened speed slightly as he neared the dirt road, bore down on the wheel, and made the turn. The rear wheels skidded wildly, there was a screech of brakes, the car teetered perilously, then righted itself, and shot down the rough lane.[14]

The physical ability of the youthful Frank Hardy is magnified through the technological capacity of the automobile to assist the Hardy Boys in their escape from destruction. In addition, the narrative description of speeding automobiles adds excitement to the adventures in the same way that harrowing car races have become essential ingredients in today's suspense and thriller motion pictures.

Once again, mobile adventure episodes in the later girls' series books matched or even exceeded those of the boys' books, for Nancy Drew also

7.4. "At the same moment the airplane roared past." New technological improvements in autos and other forms of transportation brought with them increasingly exciting episodes; in this scene, the Hardy Boys dodge an erratically flying aircraft.

7.5. "Semitt['s] . . . speeding car crashed into a barb-wire fence." Like the Hardy Boys, Nancy Drew is an above average driver; her small, stylish roadster reflects the latest automotive design.

drove her own "sporty little roadster." Carolyn Keene, the stated name of the author of the Nancy Drew books, is a pseudonym, a Stratemeyer Syndicate house name. The actual writer of the first Nancy Drew books was Mildred Wirt. In *The Sign of the Twisted Candles* (1933), Nancy is called upon to manipulate her automobile in a masterly fashion to avoid being overtaken by an undesirable individual (figure 7.5):

> Nancy ran around the far corner of the house and jumped into her car. A push on the starter made the sturdy motor roar into life. Shifting silently and smoothly, Nancy was already up to a speed of thirty miles an hour as the machine left the exit of The Twisted Candles. The highway was clear, and Nancy darted a glance at her rear-vision mirror to see if anyone were on the road behind. What she saw reflected there caused her to shove the accelerator button to the floor. Frank Semitt's big car had lurched into the road and was roaring after her!

Like the Hardy boys, Nancy escapes her pursuer by turning suddenly on to a side road: "Nancy, calculating her speed and the road with nice precision, almost passed the Smith's Ferry highway; then, with a twist of her wheel, she shot into the fork. The snappy little roadster teetered on two wheels as it made the sharp curve at high speed."[15]

In the boys' and girls' series books of this period, the ability to operate an automobile skillfully is essential to the continuance of the plot and to the characterization of the chief figures, for they are required to display physical as well as mental skills, and the mastery of such a complicated piece of technological equipment as an automobile is sure evidence of those skills. The automobile also conveyed many messages to series-books readers beyond furthering the events of the plot. It suggested

the preferred social status of the protagonists, it conveyed a sense of their power (limited, perhaps, but a power nevertheless), and it suggested a world of adventure with which bicycles and motorcycles could not compete.

In reading the juvenile series books of the 1930s, one can also observe the signs of the transportation evolution. In the early Hardy Boys and Nancy Drew books, there are distinct differences in the quality of main roads and side roads. The main roads are in better repair, although the effects of the weather can disrupt travel. In *The Great Airport Mystery,* the Hardy Boys are forced to detour over rough road: "Fortunately for the Hardy Boys, the detour proved dry. The worst of the holes had been filled with cracked stone, so they got through without much difficulty."[16]

A sudden thunderstorm brings Nancy Drew's roadster to an unscheduled stop: "As she shifted into second gear the motor sputtered warningly. The car lurched, and a sheet of muddy water deluged the windshield as the front wheels sank more than hub-deep into the rain-gouged gutter of the dirt road. With a last cough the engine stopped. 'Oh, pshaw!' Nancy exclaimed in vexation. 'I guess the distributor got wet. We're stuck.'"[17]

The Vanishing Shadow (1932), the first volume of another excellent girls' series, Margaret Sutton's Judy Bolton books, opens with a description of Judy Bolton observing the construction of a new kind of road: "She liked to hear the workmen calling to each other as they busied themselves with shovels and machinery on the new concrete road which, when completed, would bring her . . . nearer town and all the things Judy loved."[18] But both boys and girls continue to display their dexterity at automotive repair. Wet distributor points do not delay Nancy Drew, even in 1933: opening the hood of

her stalled roadster as one of her less mechanically minded friends stands by, she

> jerked the cap off the distributor and began to mop the connections dry. "Look at the spark plugs! They are in perfect wells of water. Throw the flashlight over this way, George."
>
> "Speaking of mysteries," George said, "the insides of an automobile have me baffled. I think you put water in one end and gasoline in the other, but that's as far as my knowledge goes."[19]

By the end of the 1930s, the automobile had become a familiar form of transportation, and although the excitement of owning and operating an automobile was still present, the unique sense of adventure that the automobile represented had largely disappeared. Concrete roads, traffic lights, and automobile accidents had significantly altered the American transportation scene. The new technologies of transportation and communication had transformed the American landscape.

The countryside was no longer an adventure to be experienced through the wonder of automotive travel; it had become an obstacle in the path of direct and rapid movement of cars and trucks, and roadway construction increasingly required the removal of trees or the alteration of hills and streams. Although the countryside might have lost some of the mystery that it had held for readers of juvenile books in the 1920s and 1930s, the sense of achievement represented by mastery of the automobile in the juvenile books of those years remained strong, as the power associated with operating an automobile came to represent a rite of passage universally valued by every youthful driver.

Notes

1. David K. Vaughan, "The First Automobile to Cross the United States," *Strut and Axle* 7 (Winter 1985): 7–13.

2. Clarence Young, *The Motor Boys* (New York: Cupples and Leon, 1906), p. v.

3. Harry K. Hudson, *A Bibliography of Hard-Cover Boys' Books,* rev. ed. (Tampa, Fla.: Data Print, 1977), pp. 145–46. The standard bibliography of boys' juvenile series books.

4. *Girls' Series Books: A Checklist of Hardback Books Published 1900–1975* (Minneapolis: University of Minnesota Libraries, 1978), pp. 3, 58. The standard bibliography of girls' juvenile series books.

5. James Braden, *The Auto Boys' Outing* (Akron, Ohio: Saalfield, 1909), pp. 15–18.

6. Laura Dent Crane, *The Automobile Girls along the Hudson* (Philadelphia: Altemus, 1910), pp. 23–24.

7. Laura Lee Hope, *The Outdoor Girls in a Motorcar* (New York: Grosset and Dunlap, 1913), p. 9.

8. J. W. Duffield, *Bert Wilson at the Wheel* (New York: Sully and Klienteich, 1913), pp. 11–12.

9. Margaret Penrose, *The Motor Girls on the Coast* (New York: Cupples and Leon, 1913), p. 54.

10. Hope, *Outdoor Girls in a Motorcar,* p. 24.

11. Clarence Young, *The Motor Boys in Mexico* (New York: Cupples and Leon, 1906), p. 128.

12. Crane, *Automobile Girls along the Hudson,* pp. 66.

13. Hope, *Outdoor Girls in a Motorcar,* p. 13.

14. Franklin W. Dixon, *The Great Airport Mystery* (New York: Grosset and Dunlap, 1930), p. 8.

15. Carolyn Keene, *The Sign of the Twisted Candles* (New York: Grosset & Dunlap, 1933), pp. 72–73.

16. Dixon, *Great Airport Mystery,* p. 129.

17. Keene, *Sign of the Twisted Candles,* p. 3.

18. Margaret Sutton, *The Vanishing Shadow* (New York: Grosset and Dunlap, 1932), p. 2.

19. Keene, *Sign of the Twisted Candles,* p. 36.

Crossroads

CHAPTER 8

E. L. WIDMER

The Automobile, Rock and Roll, and Democracy

Like music, known as the International Language, design knows no frontier barriers.
R. H. Gurr, *Automobile Design*

Thomas Edison invented the recording cylinder in 1877, only to see it superseded by Emile Berliner's flat phonograph disc in 1895, a year before Henry Ford knocked down the wall of his landlord's barn to push his motorized quadricycle into the street and history.[1] Since that inventive era and the nearly twinned births of automotive and recording technologies, the automobile has exerted a hypnotic hold on the imaginations of popular songwriters, suggesting that a natural harmony exists between their form of expression and this particular theme.

It is inevitable that any twentieth-century art form should delineate cars to some extent, given their dominion over our everyday lives: what is remarkable about American popular music is the *ubiquity* of the automobile's presence. A study of the course of automobile-related music indicates not only that the car has inspired constant subject matter for aspiring minstrels but that this has remained true even as music and transportation have undergone fundamental transformations. Improved technology revolutionized both music and automobiles in the period immediately following World War II, but they remained steadfast to one another, providing an important voice for a rising generation of Americans eager to leave their impress on the national culture. Specifically, the hybrid strains of rock and roll music depended heavily on the independence offered by racy new automobiles in the early 1950s to sound a barbaric yawp over the rooftops of Benny Goodman's America.

Within a decade of the auto's appearance on American streets, Tin Pan Alley was churning out car-related hits with the speed and regularity of the auto industry itself. As early as 1899, a song entitled "Love in an Automobile" indicated how helpful a car might prove to would-be suitors, and at least 120 similar songs were released between 1905 and 1907 alone. As might be expected, levity figured prominently in these early compositions, with titles such as "Fifteen Kisses on a Gallon of Gas," "I'm Going to Park Myself in Your Arms," and "I'd Rather Go Walking with the Man I Love Than Ride in Your Automobile (You Cad)."[2] By far the most successful of these was the 1905 hit, "In My Merry Oldsmobile," which earned a free car for its two songwriters from the grateful manufacturer.

The bonanza following World War II made cars universally affordable and fostered dramatic technological improvements that pushed an already car-crazy nation to the brink of lunacy. This mania expressed itself through all the normal media: film, literature, the fine arts, and, of course, music. No genus of popular expression has celebrated the automobile with more feeling and attention to nuance than "rock and roll." The enormous body of music contained within this ill-defined rubric has been intimately connected with the automobile throughout its brief but mercurial history. Rock performers have not only sung the praises of the car but have traditionally dedicated every sequined fiber of their beings to the pursuit of what we might loosely define as an "auto-mobile" existence, something far broader than the general itinerancy required of musicians. In the rock and roll lexicon, cars have evolved beyond simple instruments of transportation to become the very symbols of the high living and conspicuous consumption sought out by artists and savored by the public.

Easy Rider: Blues and the Automobile

To fully gauge the extent to which this is true, it is useful to compare rock and roll, which by most accounts emerged in the early 1950s, to the simpler blues music that preceded and fostered it. While many genres of music contributed to the gumbo soup that became rock and roll, the blues was arguably its most immediate ancestor, especially for its emphasis on the individual guitar player. The southern black Americans who created the blues legacy understood all too well the nature of long-distance travel. Many were men who went from town to town on a moment's notice to work an odd job or play a low-paying gig. They did this by riding the rails, hitchhiking, or simply walking along the highway, for theirs was anything but a lucrative calling, and transient, black car-owners were few and far between in the 1930s rural South. Honey-boy Edwards recollected his life on the road with the legendary bluesman Robert Johnson, saying,

> There wasn't that many blues players, you know. We would walk through the country with our guitars on our shoulders, stop at peoples' houses, play a little music, walk on. We might decide to go on, say, to Memphis. We could hitchhike, transfer from truck to truck, or if we couldn't catch one of them, we'd go to the trainyard, 'cause the railroad was all through that part of the country then. We'd wait 'till the train was pulling out and jump in.[3]

There was no mention of the automobile whatsoever.

It consequently comes as no surprise that a great many blues songs were about the predicament of the lonely outsider, drifting from place to place. The railroad became a recurring blues motif,

strongly evocative of this transiency and the need to escape the confines of an inhospitable society. When W. C. Handy first heard a blues tune in 1903, he was waiting for a train that was nine hours late in the tiny town of Tutwiler, Mississippi, listening to a ragged stranger sing about "goin' to where the Southern cross the Dog," a slang reference to a nearby train crossing. He called it "the weirdest music I had ever heard."[4] There are so many blues songs about the railroad that it would be well-nigh impossible to catalog them all.[5] Linked to themes of separation and escape, train songs generally suggested the end of relationships, not their beginning, and the railroad's dark power inspired as much despair as admiration.

The highway was also a frequent theme in this music, but only as an ironic commentary, since most blues singers were forced to walk along it, and the overwhelming majority of road songs were written from the pedestrian perspective.[6] One of the most famous of all blues songs, Robert Johnson's "Crossroads" (recorded 27 November 1936), is about the predicament of a black man terrified to be on foot at an unfamiliar highway intersection as the sun is setting.

The automobile was less frequently sung about than the railroad within this musical genre, simply because it embodied a type of unlimited mobility—an *active* as opposed to a *passive* right-of-way—that many American blacks were effectively denied in the South. When it did creep into a songwriter's vocabulary, however, it clearly represented something very different from the anomie linked to train rides and hoboing. As defined in this music, cars were sexy and exciting, one might even say liberating, both for the personal privacy they permitted *and* for the social and financial emancipation they proclaimed. For several reasons, Ford was the make

8.1. The cover of "In My Merry Oldsmobile" songsheet.

of choice among blues singers. Its relative afford-ability was appealing. Furthermore, Henry Ford had been hiring blacks in Detroit since 1914, earlier than his competitors, which lent him a certain pal-atability. Finally, many blacks saw in the durable, hard-working, and monochromatic Model T a crude parallel to their own underappreciated exis-tence.[7] The allegorical songs that sprang from this perception were not only "democratic" in their crit-icism of fancier models but surprisingly racy.

Most of the blues songs treating the car are shocking even today for their unabashed obsession with what Thomas Jefferson delicately phrased the "organs of generation"[8] In 1926, Virginia Liston la-mented that her "Rolls Royce Papa" had a bent pis-ton rod; a year later, Bertha Chippie Hill, in "Sports Model Mama," claimed to receive punctures every day; and in 1929, Cleo Gibson, in what might have proved an effective advertising slogan, belted out "I've Got Ford Engine Movements in My Hips."[9] Male singers were not slow to express similar no-tions. At least three boasted their beds could rock "like a Cadillac car" (Bobby Grant, Leroy Carr and Lonnie Clark), and Washboard Sam complained in "Out with the Wrong Woman" (31 December 1936) that his woman "was built like an automobile, but didn't have no rumble seat."

Other songs stressed economic principles. Sleepy John Estes stated the case succinctly but powerfully: "Well, the T model Ford I say is the poor man's friend" ("Poor Man's Friend," 3 August 1935). Blind Lemon Jefferson announced in "D B Blues" (August 1928) that "a Packard is too expen-sive, Ford will take you where you want to go." Ramblin' Thomas promised, "Some of these days I am going to be like Mr. Henry Ford/Going to have a car and a woman running on every road" ("Hard to Rule Woman Blues," February 1928). One singer

even confused his myths as he lauded the accom-plishments of "John Henry Ford."

Probably the most important car-related song of the period was Robert Johnson's "Terraplane Blues" (Vocalion, 23 November 1936), the first record he released and his best-selling hit. Johnson carried the car-woman metaphor even further, if possible, an-nouncing to his paramour, "I'm gonna hoist your hood, mama, I'm bound to check your oil . . . / I'm gonna get down deep in this connection, keep on tangling with your wires / And when I mash down on your little starter, then your spark gonna give me fire." Johnson's impressive know-how concerning this new make of Hudson never entered into his songs about the railroad, all of which were far less exuberant in comparison (e.g., the lonely "Love in Vain"). Interestingly, Johnson approximated this sexual-mechanical link only in his "Phonograph Blues" (23 November 1936), singing, "I'm gonna wind your little phonograph, just to hear your little engine moan." In Robert Johnson's mind, musical and automotive technologies had generated pow-erful possibilities for alleviating the dreariness of life in the Depression-era Delta, even if he was never to realize them during his abbreviated existence.

Deux Ex Machina: Postwar Innovation

Following victory in World War II, the United States unconditionally surrendered to automania, even in recently impoverished quarters. The war improved the financial climate for all Americans, including blacks who benefited from the manpower shortage in the industrial North. An astonishing 1.6 million blacks left the South between 1940 and 1950, com-pared to 350,000 in the previous decade. As had been the case in World War I, many found work in

Detroit, but even those who did not migrate gained exposure to the automobile with the widespread rise in the standard of living that followed V-E and V-J days.

The influx of money not only made the auto-mobile more affordable than ever but allowed new technologies to develop that rendered it all but ir-resistible to millions of consumers emerging from decades of financial torpor. Simply put, the car was reshaped more dramatically in this brief period than at any time in American history. Wartime technol-ogy had led to the discovery of ductile metals that could be coaxed into exciting new shapes and bright colors. Fenders were phased out as cars were lowered, streamlined, and covered with chrome. The 1948 Cadillac inaugurated tapered tailfins in imitation of P-38 Lockheed Lightning fighter planes, and one-piece "panoramic" windshields followed in 1950. The development of the overhead-valve, high-compression engine (1949) vastly improved performance, and soon cars were introduced that depended almost exclusively on "muscle" for their appeal (i.e., the Corvette, 1953).

At the same time, improved electrical ingenuity resulted in superior car radios and dozens of other accessories. The instrument-panel radio had been pioneered by GM in 1935 and had been much im-proved by elliptical speakers (1940), signal-seeking buttons (1947), foot switches (1950), and "favorite station" buttons (1952). The availability of plastic allowed Chrysler to design a blinking, airplanelike "Jukebox Dashboard" with lots of buttons to satisfy a gimmick-crazed marketplace (its very name hint-ing at the automotive-musical link). The gadgetry paid off handsomely; U.S. annual car production skyrocketed from 83,700 in 1945 to 2,156,000 in 1946, and continued to climb until it peaked at a remarkable 7,942,200 in the banner year of 1955.

For postwar America, the cheapness of raw materials, the scale of production, and the climate of patriotic euphoria allowed, even required, *all* classes of Americans to realistically contemplate car ownership.[11]

Coeval with these developments were rapid advances in recording technology. Just as World War I had initiated a period of intensive radio use, so World War II was followed by a dizzying sequence of technological breakthroughs. The U.S. army discovered the Nazi invention of the magnetic-tape recorder at the end of the war. The defeat of the Japanese also meant that the shellac needed to make records could again be imported from the Pacific regions where it was cultivated, to the great relief of Americans who had been listening to the same crackly 78s for four years. Then in 1948, Columbia Records presented their new long-playing records, which greatly increased the amount of music that could be packaged by spinning at only 33⅓ revolutions per minute. The moribund 78 offered a mere four minutes of playing time to the LP's twenty-five, and the latter's "unbreakable" plastic microgroove discs were also vastly more durable. RCA Victor was quick to follow with the smaller 45-rpm record. Stereo became available in 1954 for tapes and in 1958 for records, and high fidelity was continually improved upon throughout this period. Finally, the portable transistor radio was pioneered in 1954, allowing music to be compressed and taken anywhere. It was in use in cars by 1956.[12]

These innovations soon bore fruit in an efflorescence of musical creativity and also facilitated the means by which this harvest was distributed to the eager consumer. Radio stations proliferated; between 1946 and 1948 the number of AM stations doubled, while FM stations increased from 668 to 1,005.[13] Programming methods also changed, especially as the 45 allowed stations and consumers to focus their attention on single songs that could be made and sold quite cheaply. In 1949, KWOH in Omaha was the first station to convert entirely to a pop-music format, and in 1953 the same station created the idea of a "Top 40" countdown of popular hits.[14]

But perhaps the most important innovation for our purposes was the electrification of the guitar, which had been in the works for years but was not really perfected until the late forties, most notably by Les Paul, who pioneered the solid-body version of the instrument, inspiring the Fender Corporation to issue its famous Stratocaster in 1953. This improvement, seemingly so simple, changed the fundamental sound and rhythm of all guitar music, giving it a faster, louder, and far more voluptuous sound.

Teenagers who were spending their Saturdays fixing up hot rods were eager to absorb the strange new electric sounds coming out of their car radios, for each machine signaled a decisive rupture with older, obsolete models. Suddenly, leisure technology had become universally affordable and comprehensible; taking advantage of it, American youth seized, or rather had thrust upon itself, the cultural means of production. As Tom Wolfe has shown in his essays on the custom-car culture of southern California and stock-car racing in the rural South, the automobile allowed the postwar youth to express himself in ways that no machine had, at least in recent memory.[15] It was hardly accidental that George Barris, the Caravaggio of car customizing, opened his business in 1945, just as millions of battle-weary young Americans needed to shift their attention from the war to less serious matters. As the teenager became a potent economic force, his desires as a consumer were increasingly heeded, and it was to this enormous audience that rock and roll addressed itself, sounding at first every bit as powerful and weird as the blues had to W. C. Handy.

Seeming to suggest the forbidden mysteries of sexuality, both the new music and the new types of automobiles found easy, if not aggressive, acceptance in the concupiscent universe that was 1950s teenage America. Like jazz (and later, funk), the very words *rock and roll* provoked knowing smiles from those who understood the more organic nature of their original slang meaning. It was inevitable that the automobile, as the symbol of the economic arrival of the previously disenfranchised groups constituting the rock and roll audience, would emerge as a central motif in their new form of musical expression. Automobiles offered an easy escape route from restrictive home environments. Appropriately, many of the earliest rock and roll records were directly linked to the automotive experience.

Although there are earlier uses of the off-color phrase "rock and roll," it is generally conceded that the first song to mix the ingredients of modern rock was a tune called "Rocket 88" recorded in Memphis on 5 March 1951 by Jackie Brenston and the Kings of Rhythm (featuring a very young Ike Turner).[16] A paean to the flashy new Oldsmobile model, the song celebrated little beside the joy of being seen riding around in a souped-up vehicle, but apparently this was enough, for it became a number one hit on the rhythm-and-blues charts. Significantly addressed only to women, it invited the listener to go "sporting" with Brenston all over town, then listed the car features (V-8 motor, convertible top, smart design) that made such an invitation irresistible. The generally salacious feel of the song was heightened by the fuzzy tone of the guitar amplifier, which had fallen out of the band's car (appropriately) on the way to the session and was emitting noise like a wounded B-29 bomber.

Sam Phillips, who produced the session for Chess Records, later pinpointed this moment as the birth of rock and roll, and as the man who launched the careers of Elvis Presley, Jerry Lee Lewis, and Carl Perkins, he was in a good position to know. Little Richard acknowledged that "Rocket 88" served as the inspiration for his "Good Golly Miss Molly." Perhaps even more telling is the fact that a white disc jockey in Chester, Pennsylvania, named Bill Haley liked the song so much that he covered it with his country band, the Saddlemen. This showed the crossover appeal of the song. The electricity of the simultaneous black and white influences, to say nothing of the instruments themselves, would soon allow Haley to emerge as the world's first rock and roll star, although he would not enjoy that distinction for long.[17]

The success of "Rocket 88" launched a spate of inferior imitations, including a follow-up number by Brenston himself called "Real Gone Rocket" (July 1951). Before long, the tiny Chess label alone had recorded Billy Love's "Drop Top" (November 1951), Rosco Gordon's "T-Model Boogie" (4 December 1951), Howlin' Wolf's "Cadillac Daddy" (23 January 1952), Johnny London's "Drivin' Slow" (8 March 1952), and Joe Hill Louis's "Automatic Woman" (9 September 1953), which compared his girlfriend favorably to the new GM transmissions being churned out in Detroit. There seemed to be no limit to the poetic inspiration a musically inclined American youth might draw from the national love affair with the automobile.

Après Moi, Le Déluge (Or, 50,000,000 People Can't Be Wrong): Elvis, Chuck Berry, and Their Legacy

The most evocative symbol of this rising generation of musical teenagers and their automotive priorities remains Elvis Presley, the self-styled "King of Rock and Roll" (Little Richard briefly contested the title, until it grew evident he held a stronger claim to another royal moniker). Like many of the black musicians he admired and imitated, Presley had grown up desperately poor in Mississippi during the Depression, until his parents had packed all their possessions in a beat-up 1937 Plymouth and driven along Highway 78 from Tupelo to Memphis in September 1948. When he began singing, Presley was driving trucks for the Crown Electric Company, and his lifetime fascination with automobiles paralleled that of an entire underclass for whom more expensive luxuries, such as large houses (although Presley later acquired plenty of those), were simply impossible to fantasize about. While majoring in shop at Humes High School in Memphis, Elvis announced in his yearbook that his highest ambition in life was to become a Tennessee state highway patrolman.[18]

For Presley, the supreme emblem of his liberation from poverty was a pink Cadillac; at first, just the idea of one, and later, when circumstances permitted, the reality. Although his father had scraped together fifty dollars to buy Elvis a 1942 Lincoln Zephyr coupe for his eighteenth birthday in 1953, Elvis, like most Americans, saw the Cadillac as the quintessence of the social acceptability that had thus far eluded him. In one of his earliest recording sessions (February 1955), again with the ubiquitous Sam Phillips, Elvis covered a sexy song called "Baby, Let's Play House" by Arthur "Hardrock" Gunter, which taunts a respectable society girl into remaining with the singer to attend to some neglected domestic chores. Elvis, however, fiddled with the words and substituted "pink Cadillac" for a reference to her religion, and a large measure of the song's excitement derives from the singer's feeling of triumph over a girl rich enough to drive such a highfalutin vehicle.

Around the same time, Elvis bought the first in what would perhaps become the world's longest succession of fancy cars: a secondhand Cadillac financed by his manager. The night he bought it, he stayed up for hours simply looking at it from his hotel window. Although it was destroyed by fire soon thereafter, Elvis quickly bought another with the insurance money and painted it pink and black, the colors of his performance clothes. As soon as he could afford it, he bought another Cadillac that was entirely new and entirely pink, which he presented to his mother. It is still visible as part of the overwhelming armada of vehicles behind Graceland.

One vehicle especially stands out as a monument to Elvis's Veblenesque fascination with the automobile. When he turned his attention to filmmaking in the late 1950s and early 1960s, Elvis brashly declared, "I don't want anybody in Hollywood to have a better car than mine. A Cadillac puts the world on notice that I have arrived!" Accordingly, he hired George Barris to reshape his limousine. It was inevitable that these two folk heroes, both pauper pretenders to royalty (the King of Rock and Roll and the King of Kustomizing), should meet and collaborate. Perhaps inspired by the ten-thousand-dollar gold suit Elvis was wont to wear on occasion, Barris gold-plated almost every surface of the car, from the headlight rims and hubcaps to the interior accoutrements, which included a television, telephone, record player, bar, ice maker, and the oblig-

atory electric shoe buffer. The enormous back-seat area was called the Center Lounge, with seats arranged in a semicircle and Elvis's gold records lining the ceiling. The floor of the car, if I may call it a car, was covered with white fur, and the exterior was painted with forty coats of a special dust made from crushed diamonds and fish scales flown in from Asia. Barris called it his "most ambitious project," and it garnered so much attention that RCA records sent the car itself on tour, where at one point it attracted forty thousand people to a mall in Houston. If Graceland was Elvis's Versailles, then the Gold Car was his Royal Phaeton, a hillbilly's dream come true. Indeed, the TV sitcom "The Beverly Hillbillies" (which is nothing if not a fable of democracy) was partially inspired by this creation, now resting peacefully in the Country Music Hall of Fame in Nashville. No other material object could symbolize as vividly the values that made Elvis and America great.[19]

As Elvis grew richer, automobiles became a type of personal currency for him and purchasing them a peculiar form of economic self-expression. He bought all different types of cars; he bought many of them, and he bought them often. Like Louis XIV distributing small principalities (this metaphor is inexhaustible), the self-made Sun King offered them freely to his attendants, and these munificent bequests served as informal salaries for his otherwise underpaid minions. There are far too many stories of capricious car purchases during the reign of Elvis to repeat them all here, although my favorite is the night he bought fourteen Cadillacs from a flabbergasted Memphis dealer and offered the last of them to an elderly black woman passing by (perhaps a belated assumption of the debt he owed rhythm-and-blues artists). Throughout his life, his favorite nontoxic form of recreation was racing

8.2. Gilding the lily: Elvis's Gold Car.

8.3. Elvis in one of his Cadillacs.

through the streets of Memphis with his buddies in the wee hours of the morning, and unlike most celebrities, he scoffed at the idea of chauffeurs. Driving was simply too important.[20]

Obviously, cars offered more than simple transportation to Elvis, unless the word is understood to embrace a larger meaning, a social mobility beyond the immediate physical movement they offered. Flashy automobiles did indeed transport him, away from everything that stank of the immobile, inert indigence that had ruled his Depression upbringing. Presley's immense wealth, to say nothing of his *parvenu* urge to gild everything, shocked the nation fully as much as his pelvic thrusts, and his obsession with cars reflected the collective yearnings of an entire generation of formerly underprivileged Americans. His remarkable Cadillacs threw not only sex in the face of Ward Cleaveresque America but a small dose of democracy as well.

Yet another performer who displayed this obsession with the automobile was a former car thief from St. Louis named Charles Edward Berry. Chuck Berry's first song, "Maybellene" (recorded 21 May 1955), reworked a harmless old country tune called "Ida Red" into a sizzling car chase/romance between the singer in his souped-up V-8 Ford and an idealized woman in an elusive Cadillac (what else?). The song cleverly alternates describing the vehicle and the woman, and before long the one becomes a thinly veiled substitute for the other. It begins with the singer leisurely "motorvating" down the road in his V-8 Ford, then spying Maybellene in a Cadillac Coupe De Ville up ahead of him. They engage in a furious car chase with all sorts of sexual undertones until a providential cloudburst cools down our hero's engine sufficiently that he is able to "catch" her at the top of a hill, ending the drama and the song.

"Maybellene" is exciting not only for its original language (neologisms like motorvate) and its mixture of black and white styles (again, the hallmark of early rock and roll) but also for its openly sexual feel and the populistic triumph of the Ford over the Cadillac. Both rhythmically and thematically, this is a far cry from the blues and its general association of travel with despair and escape. In his recently published autobiography, Berry explained the song "was composed from memories of high school and trying to get girls to ride in my 1934 Ford." Interestingly, this was the same year and make of Ford that had transported Bonnie and Clyde away from *their* stagnant southern backgrounds. The Cadillac, Berry confessed, was merely wishful thinking, a "dream De Ville."[21]

Later songs only strengthened the connection he saw between women and automobiles. "Nadine" (4 January 1964) describes another allegorical chase, this time in pursuit of a girl walking toward a "coffee-colored Cadillac." The choice of this wonderfully evocative color could hardly be chimerical, again the car's identity seems to blend with the woman's. Despite another spirited car race and yelling like a "southern diplomat," he can't catch her this time, largely because she moves through traffic like both "a wayward summer breeze" and "a mounted cavalier." Perhaps the most masterful statement of the car/woman conflation occurs in "No Particular Place to Go" (26 March 1964), in which Berry actually has the girl alongside him in his car but sadly cannot undo her protective safety belt. The song is interesting also for its affirmation of Jackie Brenston's philosophy that driving—or, more specifically, "cruising and playing the radio"—is so pleasant in and of itself that destinations have become superfluous.

Yet another Berry opus, "No Money Down" (20

December 1955), says as much as any history book about the economic climate that allowed this expensive exploration of automotive fantasy. The song celebrates the joys of easy car financing, delineating an ideal vehicle remarkably similar to Elvis's Gold Car. Not content to wait, or even ask politely, Berry simply *demands* what he feels to be his prerogative: a yellow Caddy convertible with every option in the book. He continues, calling for power in what almost sounds like a revolutionary pamphlet: "I want power steering and power brakes/I want a powerful motor with jet off-take." Finally, he lists the aristocratic appurtenances that he, like Elvis, can deliciously appreciate as a true *connoisseur* (air conditioning, heat, bed in the back seat, short-wave radio, TV, telephone). Such an optimistic expression of financial and sexual confidence makes it easy to understand why 1955 was not only the year that Berry and Presley struck pay dirt but also the top-selling year for cars in American history.

Like Elvis, Berry fully lived the automotive life he projected in his "oeuvre." His autobiography is full of automobile references. In 1941, at the age of 14, he bought a 1934 V-8 Ford for $35 ($10 down and $5 a month), the same car that inspired "Maybellene." As one of only two students at his school owning a car, his popularity was increased immeasurably. He went on endless joyrides with other "car-crazy" friends, was incarcerated for car theft during one of them, and immediately bought a shiny Buick upon his release from jail. Describing another arrest in 1958, this time for violation of the Mann Act (which seems to have been tailor-made for early rock and roll stars), Berry wrote nonchalantly that the policeman "ordered me to stand aside while he searched the cream-colored Cadillac, which I must admit was attractive." Toward the end of his book, after discussing his children and grandchildren,

Berry summarized a lifetime of achievement by saying, "Up to then I had owned a total of 29 automobiles, most of them purchased new and most of the new ones Cadillacs, which was then the epitome of well-off." In his recent film, *Hail, Hail, Rock and Roll*, one of the most amusing scenes shows Chuck in a garage, surrounded by old Cadillacs, trying to calculate their financial worth, as if this is the only balance sheet that can measure his importance to American culture.[22]

Following the Presley and Berry examples, legions of young rockers in the fifties and early sixties incorporated songs about cars into their repertoires. Little Richard aped car slogans by calling his "Long Tall Sally" "built for speed." Bo Diddley not only adopted a rocket-shaped guitar with two fins (the Gibson Flying V) that imitated contemporaneous car styling, but claimed to be a "Roadrunner" (1960), the "fastest in the land." James Brown, who also did time for car theft, surely would have disputed the claim. In "Not Fade Away," Buddy Holly's love was "bigger than a Cadillac." The Ides of March warbled "I'm Your Vehicle, Baby," while the Playmates sang "Beep Beep," about a little Nash Rambler beating a Cadillac in a race. The Beach Boys and Jan and Dean released dozens of songs that made it difficult to imagine how the state of California had ever existed before Henry Ford came along. Furthermore, many groups, ranging from the famous to the mercifully obscure, took their names from some of the more mellifluous car names floating around, including the Imperials, the Eldorados, the Continentals, the Cadillacs, and yes, even the Edsels.

Cars were so popular that even the grisly deaths they caused received thorough, almost loving attention. In 1956, Nervous Norvus scored a moderate hit with his novelty, "Transfusion," in which an in-jured driver asks for blood by saying "shoot me some juice, Bruce" and "pass the claret, Barrett" over dubbed-in crash sounds. Mark Dinning's "Teen Angel" (1960), Ray Peterson's "Tell Laura I Love Her" (1960), and Jan and Dean's "Dead Man's Curve" (1964) all bespoke the same fascination with death and high-speed car crashes that the Italian Futurists had shown at the beginning of the century.[23] While not a rock star, James Dean immediately entered the teenage Valhalla following a fiery exit on the California desert in 1955. Eddie Cochran's death in a car crash in England in 1960 accomplished a similar deification.

Rock and roll continues to exist and seems to exert an enormous pull on the attentions of adolescents worldwide. It is one of the few art forms that we can call genuinely American in its origin, and the automobile continues to stand out as a pivotal subject, certainly more so than in other types of music. This kinship between theme and form is difficult to explain, but it seems to derive from the fact that both represented a "liberating" principle for the individual, something that has hardly met with resistance in American history. *Automobile*, after all, means "self-moving" in a literal sense, and it is astonishing how many early rockers came from dirt-poor backgrounds, using the music to jack themselves up by their bootstraps. Emerson would surely appreciate this latest form of self-reliance; on a different subject, he wrote, "All language is vehicular and transitive."[24]

Both the automobile and popular music profited from postwar technology to offer an unprecedented amount of personal expression, and each emphasized the importance of the *solitary* performer, away from the watchful eyes of parents and neighbors. Like the automobile, the electric guitar allowed the independently inclined from all back-grounds to stand up and take charge of their own destinies, relegating the more communal forms of railroad travel and big-band music to inferior, antiquated roles in the postwar hierarchy of cultural values. Chuck Berry was one of the first popular musicians of the twentieth century to stand up and perform his own material solo before a national audience, and he remains notorious for his dislike of support bands. Elvis, Little Richard, Jerry Lee Lewis, and the other giants of fifties rock were all individual performers as well. At least in the teenage mind, which feeds on autonomy to begin with, this rebellious and discordant music has always existed in perfect harmony with the escapism afforded by the automobile. Few nations have ever needed a mood of carefree independence as America did after twenty years of depression and war, and fewer still ever created one quite so lasting.

Discussing the changes wrought by the Industrial Revolution in mid-nineteenth-century France, Walter Benjamin noted the arrival of the *flaneur,* the man with enough time and money to do little besides wander along Haussmann's new boulevards and window-shop, trying to be seen as well as look at others.[25] Similarly, in the 1950s, the prosperity of the postwar period trickled down to America's youth and underprivileged sufficiently that for the first time, they were able to act as independent consumers and create their own leisure styles. While Chuck Berry or Elvis may seem a far cry from the *boulevardier* of 1850s Paris, their financial security allowed them to pursue an automotive leisure, not only for themselves but for the millions of fun-starved teenagers living vicariously through them. That the new *boulevardier* was in a pink Cadillac instead of a top hat made little difference. After all, the Chicago Chess label that Brenston, Berry, and other early rockers sang for was originally called

Aristocrat when founded in the 1940s, indicating upward aspiration as clearly as car names like Sedan de Ville, Crown Imperial, and Patrician (a type of Packard introduced in 1951). As Michel Chevalier noted in 1836, observing America's mania for railroads, "The effect of the most perfect system of transportation is to reduce the distance not only between places, but between different classes."[26]

For the teen culture that emerged in the 1950s, the fast car was inextricably linked with the new music hymning its praises. Both relied on new technologies, cared little for past traditions, and shocked older aficionados of travel and music. A souped-up custom car had as little to do with a passenger train as "Maybellene" had to do with "Chattanooga Choo Choo." The availability of cheap, fast, colorful cars made from shiny new materials, and rock and roll records forged in a similar manner, liberated a generation of children emerging from two decades of privation. The new feeling of sexual and economic freedom found its perfect expression in the automobile, and the result was an entirely novel form of musical communication. Together, the automobile and rock and roll proclaimed emancipation for young Americans from all backgrounds, and together they remain vibrant symbols of this not-so-innocent era.

Notes

1. Robert Palmer, *Deep Blues* (New York, 1981), p. 105. See Oliver Read, *From Tin Foil to Stereo* (Indianapolis, 1976) for further details. Palmer gives the disc date as 1897, but Read has it as 1895.

2. Cynthia Golomb Dettelbach, *In the Driver's Seat: The Automobile in American Literature and Popular Culture* (Westport, 1976), p. 58; Stephen W. Sears, *The Automobile in America* (New York, 1977), p. 82; and David L. Lewis, "Sex and the Automobile," in David L. Lewis and Lawrence Goldstein, eds., *The Automobile in American Culture* (Ann Arbor, 1983), p. 125.

3. Palmer, p. 120.

4. Ibid., p. 45.

5. See Norm Cohen, *Long Steel Rail: The Railroad in American Folksong* (Urbana, 1981).

6. See Paul Oliver, *Aspects of the Blues Tradition* (New York, 1970), pp. 21–22, and David Evans, *Big Road Blues* (Berkeley, 1982).

7. See Leroi Jones, *Blues People* (New York, 1963), pp. 97–98.

8. "Notes on the State of Virginia," in Merrill Petersen, ed., *The Portable Thomas Jefferson*, (New York, 1975) p. 93.

9. Paul Oliver, pp. 213–15.

10. This section should not be construed to imply that Robert Johnson was the only bluesman singing car-related songs, although his was perhaps the most interesting voice. Among many other examples are Memphis Minnie's "Garage Fire Blues" (1930), Walter Roland's "T Model Blues" (1933), Sleepy John Estes's "Poor Man's Friend" (1935), Freddie Spruell's "Let's Go Riding" (1935), Little Bill Gaither's "Old Model A Blues" (1938), Blind Boy Fuller's "Worn Out Engine Blues" (1940), Sonny Boy Williamson's "Project Highway" (1937) and "My Little Machine" (1940), Lightning Hopkins's "T-Model Blues" (1947) and "Automobile Blues" (1964), Blind Willie McTell's "Broke Down Engine Blues" (1949), Willie Love's "V-8 Ford Blues" (1951), Brownie McGhee's "Auto Mechanic Blues" (1958), Johnny Shine's "Dynaflow Blues," Lightning Slim's "My Starter Won't Work," Joe McCoy's "One More Greasin'," Charlie McCoy's "Valves Need Grindin'," Willie Borum's "Car Machine Blues," and Sonny Boy Williamson's "Pontiac 88," to name a few.

Most of these link the car with sex, some more explicitly than others. Although the blues tradition continues healthily into the rock-and-roll era, I have largely neglected this corpus of music for organizational reasons. For more information, see Michael Taft's remarkable *Blues Lyric Poetry: A Compendium* (New York, 1984). The "John Henry Ford" reference may be found in vol. 1, p. 751.

11. Richard M. Longworth, ed., *Encyclopedia of American Cars, 1940–1970* (New York, 1980), pp. 47, 48, 102; Jerry Flint, *The Dream Machine* (New York, 1976), pp. 9, 156. For the car-radio information, I am indebted to General Motors and their helpful information staff. .

12. Ed Ward et al., *Rock of Ages* (New York, 1986), pp. 31, 123; *Encyclopedia Americana* (Danbury, 1988) on "Sound Recording and Reproduction"; Oliver Read, *From Tin Foil to Stereo;* and Joseph N. Kane, ed., *Famous First Facts* (New York, 1981).

13. Gilbert Seldes, *The Great Audience* (Westport, 1970), p. 109.

14. Lawrence W. Lichty and Malachi C. Topping, *American Broadcasting* (New York, 1975), p. 400.

15. See especially the title essay and "The Last American Hero" in Tom Wolfe, *The Kandy-Kolored Tangerine-Flake Streamline Baby* (New York, 1963).

16. Earlier uses include the Boswell Sisters' "Rock and Roll" (1934), Buddy Jones's "Rockin' Rollin' Mama" (1939), and Bill Moore's "We're Gonna Rock, We're Gonna Roll" (1947). See Dave Marsh and Kevin Stein, eds., *The Book of Rock Lists* (New York, 1981), p. 186.

17. Palmer, pp. 223–24.

18. Albert Goldman, *Elvis* (New York, 1981), pp. 99, 112.

19. Unless we consider Webb Pierce's 1962 Bonneville, with one thousand silver dollars in the upholstery, ornamental rifles, and carpet made from fetal calfskin (currently on display in the Car Collector's Hall of Fame in Nashville). For the details about the Gold Car, I am indebted to Marge Crumbaker and Gabe Tucker, *Up and Down with Elvis Presley* (New York, 1981), pp. 95–99.

20. Goldman, pp. 641, 162.

21. Chuck Berry, *Chuck Berry· The Autobiography* (New York, 1987), p. 144. For an entertaining and provocative reading of Berry's "Maybellene," see Warren Be-

lasco's "Motivatin' with Chuck Berry and Frederick Jackson Turner," in Lewis and Goldstein, pp. 262—79.

22. Berry, pp. 143, 195, 257.

23. Stephen Bayley, *Sex, Drink and Fast Cars* (London, 1986), p.45.

24. Ralph Waldo Emerson, "The Poet," in *The Complete Essays and Other Writings*, ed. Brooks Atkinson (New York, 1950), p. 336.

25. Walter Benjamin, *Reflections*, trans. Edmund Jephcott (New York, 1978), pp. 146–62.

26. Michel Chevalier, *Society, Manners and Politics in the United States*, trans. T. G. Bradford (Garden City, 1961), p. 204. Anyone dubious of this rather far-reaching comparison should see *Under the Cherry Moon*, a hilariously bad film that portrays Prince as a Proustian dandy wiling his time away on the Riviera.

3

BUILDING
TYPES

Housing the Automobile

CHAPTER 9

JAN JENNINGS

At the turn of the century, automobile ownership offered a profitable opportunity for builders and architects to develop a new building type for the storage of the motorcar. While garage design entailed both aesthetic and functional issues, the aesthetic issues seemed more important to the building industry. In the historical development of garage design, from 1904–30, the industry and its publications, manufacturing companies, and the architects who designed for replication used a variety of design strategies to make the garage appear less like a storage box. The most popular image for the garage was to make it houselike. Coincidentally, with the development of design imagery, the building industry established a market for garages and aggressively sold them to the middle-class homeowner.[1]

Conceptual Image

The key element in resolving residential garage design was the manner in which architects and builders conceptualized the image of the garage. Initially, the usage of the word *house* may have coincided with a conceptual image: the new building type would be a house for the motorcar. From 1904–7, architect's and builder's journals used various meanings of the term *house* to describe buildings that stored motorcars or the act of storage. Typical phrases included the "automobile house," "to house the vehicle," and "housing the motor car."

Americans could have chosen the literal expression "automobile house," but they did not. Its usage was short-lived, giving over to the French word *garage*—"to shelter." After 1910, magazines such as *Carpentry and Building*, *American Carpenter and Builder*, and *Keith's Magazine* abandoned "automobile house" and adopted the word *garage* to describe a separate building, apart from a stable, which was meant to store the motorcar.[2]

The New York publication *Carpentry and Building* was particularly progressive about promoting a separate place solely for the auto. In November 1904, it published a plan, three elevation drawings, and seven detail drawings for an "automobile house" for T. A. Sperry of Cranford, New Jersey. This design represented a conceptual breakthrough. The building was separated from an adjacent car-

riage house and stable, and it was conceived in the form of a small house—a classical temple.[3]

In August 1907, *Keith's Magazine* featured designs for ten auto houses of residential character with full descriptions of building materials and costs.[4] *American Carpenter and Builder*, billed as "the world's greatest building paper," was sluggish about promoting a separate building for the automobile. There is no mention of a garage until 1908, when the magazine published an Oakland, California, building that was a combination house, stable, and garage under one roof.[5] Editor William A. Radford must have considered this a California aberration, because the magazine persisted in publishing designs for "residence barns" or "suburban barns," their terms for city carriage houses and stables. In 1909, when a reader requested drawings for a concrete block garage, *American Carpenter and Builder* complied, and within a few months began to publish garage designs regularly. Radford soon recognized the importance of garages for the building industry, because in 1910 his architectural company produced what may have been the first garage plan book.[6]

9.1. Although William Phillips Comstock expressed the desire that garage designs reflect their function with a simple form, architects Baily and Bassett submitted this elaborately detailed garage with a residential character for *Garage and Motor Boat Houses*.

Garage design offered possibilities that were different from carriage houses. Conceived as miniatures of the big house, carriage houses had been built for the wealthy. But the affordable price and extended use of the automobile made the private garage a possibility for most classes. As early as 1910, builder's journals began to promote garages as a requirement: "A necessary adjunct of every suburban dwelling whose owner is the possessor of a runabout or touring car is a garage of sufficient size to conveniently house the vehicle and provide space for work bench or repair room."[7]

In 1909, when garage design was still in the developmental stages, Ralph de Martin, in an article for *American Homes and Gardens*, pleaded with architects to emphasize the functional aspects of design: "Its design is practically fixed by its form and dimensions, and being strictly utilitarian in purpose calls for no unnecessary artistic features." Even though de Martin spoke against embellishment of the form, he vacillated by stating that the application of trellises to garage walls had advantages and that the "artistic problem of this small structure has yet to be developed."[8]

Two years later, William Phillips Comstock published *Garages and Motor Boat Houses* as an attempt to clarify the problem of designing a building type with which architects and draftsmen had had so little experience. Like de Martin, Comstock also outlined a functional mandate for designers: the garage required a distinctive character of extreme simplicity that could be achieved with common sense. He defined basic principles for garage design: "Absolute protection from fire; an efficient meeting of the needs of the owners; and a convenient arrangement of the various utilities." Although Comstock supported designs with a clean form and the innovative use of modern materials, the architect-contributors submitted designs that were of residential character in scale, elements, and materials—clapboard and shingle cladding; hipped, gable, and gambrel roofs with flared eaves, dormers, gable returns, and gable-end ornamentation; and multipaned windows and doors.[9]

As a substantial investment, the motorcar merited protection from fire, theft, and vandalism for the well-to-do, who purchased luxury vehicles for touring, and for the hundreds of families and businesses that bought Fords to support daily living. The auto deserved housing in direct proportion to its value as an economic possession and a status symbol. No commonplace storage or functional building would do. H. H. Holt expressed it best in a 1907 article that described ten garage designs: "Number three is a little too ordinary in appearance for a man who can afford an automobile. It serves the practical side of an auto house very well, but with very little more expense could be made more sightly."[10]

The practical aspects of storage were subjugated in favor of a less severe image. Builders looked to the house for architectural inspiration because, although early garages were set unobtrusively at the rear of residential lots, they were within visual proximity of the house. Both the trade and popular press endorsed the design of garages as beautiful buildings in their own right. Garages were illustrated standing alone as individual small houses and making their own design statement. They were set on great expanses of green lawn, framed by landscape features such as pergolas and lattice, and protected with plantings. Garages mimicked house effects such as multi-paned windows, multiroof forms, dormers, brackets, and columns. Their interior spaces radiated warmth from natural and electric light.

In 1912 Boston architect Harry Morton Ramsey expressed a common sentiment of the time period: "When completed [the garage] should not convey too strongly . . . at first sight the idea of garage." Garages were made to appear less functional by concealing them or combining them with other uses. An obvious device was to make them into an apartment house since, from the beginning, both one- and two-story garages had been homes to chauffeurs. Although trade journals sometimes referred to these housing arrangements as "pretentious," garages with living quarters ranging from one to five rooms were regularly published. A two-story form, with the garage on the first floor and living quarters above, was the most houselike. Other forms, such as greenhouses, were also annexed to garages in order to break the garage out of its boxlike form and de-emphasize its practical appearance. But perhaps Southern Cypress Manufacturers' Association offered the best example of a garage transformation with their stock plan of the "pergola-garage." In their 1920 advertisement, square columns and a pergola lush with vegetation encased a flat-roofed box (figure 9.3).

Building trade publications humanized the automobile and portrayed garages with homelike qualities in order to increase the market appeal of

9.2. In the first decade of resolving residential garage design, architects avoided the functional aspects of garages and relied on picturesque images of pretty, small houses set on their own site, as in this garage of terra cotta blocks with a plastered exterior.

9.3. Southern Cypress Manufacturers' Association's 1920 advertisement offered an example for enhancing the beauty of the grounds while protecting the car.

9.4. This garage with homelike qualities appeared in *Garages, Country and Suburban* published by the American Architect in 1911.

9.5. In this cover the Southern Pine Association casts an idealized image of the importance of the garage in relation to the automobile and the family.

garages. In figure 9.4, the public is invited to view the motorcar at home in its living room. The cutaway perspective shows a substantial brick house with a large dormered window, a corbeled chimney, and flared tile roof. The spacious interior (large enough for a pair of autos) reveals five windows, including a decorative one centered above a wooden workbench that looks strikingly like a dining room buffet.[12]

During the developmental period of residential garage design, there appears to have been a natural interchange between architects and builders in resolving design issues. Successful examples of garage design were so important, and perhaps rare, that editors Radford, Comstock, and Keith all resorted to borrowing designs from each other or publishing designs that appeared elsewhere. And at least in one case, there is evidence of the source of a design replication: Comstock offered C. H. Wilson's garage in East Orange, New Jersey, "in proof that as far as a small garage is concerned, the architect may be dispensed with." Wilson's garage, which was inspired by "a cut and description published in a magazine," is almost identical to one published in 1907 in *Keith's Magazine*.[13]

Following the logic of dispensing with the architect, the garage was suitable for do-it-yourself building. This approach was taken by the Southern Pine Association. Their cover of a 1926 plan book has a picture of a new garage at the end of a long curving drive (figure 9.5). The garage is the focus of a family's attention. Its motorcar is parked on the lawn beside the garage, indicative of their equality as man-made objects and, perhaps, as investments. The one deserves the other. The car looks little, in need of protection. The father, who seemingly built the garage, has provided a shelter, protecting the car the way he and mother shelter the little girl. She takes care of her wagon and puppy, and in the background, a hen takes care of her chicks.[14] In this picture, the metaphorical use of the French term dominates—the garage is a "shelter."

Architectural Harmony

While during the first decade of this century the garage was most often designed in the image of a small house, by the 1920s it was assumed that the house and garage were to be in architectural harmony with each other. They were to "make a picture." Rarely in the history of the building industry had there been such conviction about a design philosophy. As early as 1907, *Keith's Magazine* endorsed garage design "in keeping with the design of the owner's house. Having the building in harmony adds to the splendor of all."[15] *American Homes and Gardens* discussed the philosophy in terms of design principles: "The best arrangement in planning a garage is to place it where it will harmonize with the general architecture of the buildings to which it is adjacent, thus adding to the beauty and symmetry of the composition line of the assembled outbuildings."[16] There were gentle admonitions from all quarters. The plan book distributed by the Trexler Lumber Company of Allentown, Pennsylvania, stated, "It is desirable to have the garage designed to match the home." Ready-cut building manufacturers like the Aladdin Company of Bay City, Michigan, and Gordon-Van Tine of Davenport, Iowa, produced only a few garage designs. They did not look like any one house type but were meant to be compatible with any of their ready-cut houses. These companies also used the term *match* to describe architectural harmony; Gordon-Van Tine advised customers to buy their "high-quality garages to match your home."[17]

The planning of garage sizes was problematic because builders never knew what size the automobiles would be the following year. Nevertheless, in 1907 H. H. Holt stated that the smallest lot could accommodate a garage "without the owner feeling the loss of room in his backyard." Holt recommended a 14-by-14-foot building with an 8-by-8-foot doorway for an auto to fit comfortably.[18] Although ready-cut manufacturers often named their garages for motorcars—"the Packard," "the Maxwell," "the Buick"—the names did not seem to bear a relationship to the autos themselves. Instead, the descriptive text that accompanied the garage illustration noted what size or, in some cases, type of car the garage would accommodate. In the 1921 Aladdin catalog, *Aladdin Homes*, "the Buick" was available in two standard sizes: the 8-by-14-foot size, which was large enough for a Ford touring car with the top either up or down, and the 10-by-16-foot size, which would admit a car with a 110-inch wheelbase. As early as 1911, William Comstock found it "inadvisable to build a one-car garage. It is absolutely inhospitable, much like building a house wherein no provision is made for an occasional guest. A visiting car cannot be housed in a one-car garage."[19] By the 1920s, two-car garages were advertised as a "fine investment" for owners, who could rent the extra stall.[20] Two-car garages were published frequently because there was more money to be made from their construction and an enlarged form could be manipulated to look less like a garage.

A review of trade journal designs suggests that garages were designed not only with more windows than the carriage house but with full-sized residential windows. Typical of this development is an article in a 1911 *American Carpenter and Builder* featuring "before" and "after" illustrations for a barn converted into a modern garage. The remodeling doubled the window size, increased the number of windows to fourteen, replaced clapboards with stucco, reduced the ramp size, and exposed more foundation.[21] While garages may have required light and ventilation for maintenance and safety, and even added to the cost of the building, it is clear that the use of residential windows in this conversion made the barn look like a house. Windows were also an important architectural detail for the Togan-Stiles Company of Grand Rapids, Michigan, which manufactured factory-built garages that were shipped as almost finished products. Their Togan Garage no. 104 boasted full-sized casement or sliding sash windows "to correspond with the windows in your home or cottage."[22]

Door treatment was an especially troublesome design problem because doors occupied the greater part of one side of the building and, as the largest element, revealed the building to be a garage. One ploy was to conceal the doors with architectural features, such as a projecting portico—as in Radford's design no. G-162, which featured an arched portico with battered piers, or Harry Ramsey's garage and studio with round columns, a pergola treatment, and a balcony (figure 9.6).[23] But after 1915, trade publications gave more attention to the door itself, particularly its operation. And when garage remodeling became a fertile market for designers, garage-door replacement and hardware choices replaced concealment as important design issues.

There were four types of garage doors. The

9.6. For F. M. Archer's Brookline, Massachusetts, garage and studio, architect Harry Ramsey hid the doors to make the garage look like an apartment house. Large swinging doors are concealed by a projecting portico composed of cement columns with a pergola treatment and a balcony. This design was so successful that *Building Age* published it twice.

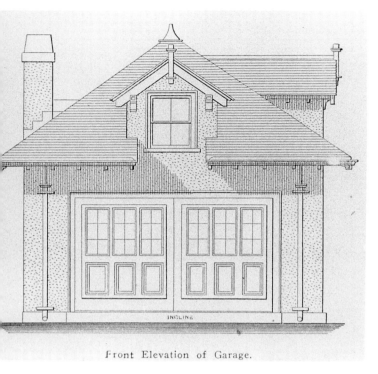

Front Elevation of Garage.

9.7. This substantial cement garage with residential characteristics, by Kendall, Taylor, and Co., appeared in *Building Age* in 1911.

single sliding door, which had been used for a stable door, became the first garage door. In 1910 the single sliding door was a standard item in millwork catalogs, but it was not recommended for an opening wider than 8 feet. Between 1912 and 1925, double doors that rolled to either side (the double sliding door) or swung in or out (the double swinging door) appeared in millwork catalogs. A journal article in 1912 noted that the double sliding doors were the ones most used, because double swinging doors were thought to occupy too much space in their action.[24] By 1915 stock doors that were composed of three to six narrow vertical sections were arranged to fold either in or out, like an accordion. Ideally, folding doors were to stack inside the side wall of the garage. By the 1930s, doors in one section or in horizontal sections were manufactured to slide up against the ceiling. Each door in turn was marketed with aesthetic features in mind: "Its style must be in keeping with the automobile to be housed and its architecture should harmonize with the residence to which it belongs."[25]

Although automobiles were fire hazards and fireproof garages constructed from fire-resistant materials were seen as necessary, maintaining the architectural dignity of the garage was a bigger problem. Popular magazines such as *American Homes and Gardens* were interested in concrete's modern forms and uses. In a 1906 article, concrete construction for country houses and garages was considered the "most engaging topic among the architects of the present day."[26] By 1910 architects were urged to "quickly become familiar with concrete design: in a few years it will be only the cheapest and most flimsy building that will use wooden joists at all."[27]

Concrete, brick, and hollow tile were endorsed by the trade press as appropriate materials for fire-

proof construction. Hollow terra-cotta blocks, faced with brick or cement, were promoted for durability, strength, and lightness. A 1917 advertisement for the Permanent Building Society of Des Moines, Iowa, boasted that a garage built of hollow tile would "last like the pyramids."[28] Concrete garage floors were demanded by insurance companies, as well as the Building Code Committee of the Department of Commerce. Concrete was believed to be durable and maintenance-free. The Atlas Portland Cement Company of New York City offered five methods of construction: reinforced concrete, concrete hollow tile, concrete blocks, pipe frame with wire lath and stucco, and stucco applied to wire lath stapled to a wood-stud frame.

Between 1911 and 1912, *Building Age* gave special attention to cement construction as a fireproofing strategy for private garages, publishing articles about cement garages constructed of hollow tile, concrete, or frame covered with metal lath over which a coat of cement-mortar had been spread.[29] And in 1912, the journal's publisher issued the fifth in its *Building Age* series of designs, *Cement Houses and Private Garages with Constructive Details.* The book featured seven designs of cement-coated garages by various architects that had been previously published in *Building Age.* The garages were expensive, substantial buildings with large roof-forms, multipaned windows and doors, and decorative detailing.

Some architects turned to high-style aesthetics, such as the Prairie style, for fireproof garage design. Stucco and concrete, principal fireproofing materials, were easily adapted to Prairie design. The Prairie style seems to have been ideally matched with the 1911 mandate sought by Comstock for a clean form and the use of innovative materials. Yet in Comstock's *Garages and Motor Boat Houses,* although the majority of garages are constructed with fireproof materials, only one architect designed a Prairie garage. The cover of William A. Radford's 1910 plan book, *Radford's Garages and How to Build Them*, featured a low, one-story building with a low-hipped roof, a large overhang, and some linear wall ornaments (figure 9.8). In the illustration, the garage drive is framed by two stylized lanterns on Prairie piers. Radford described these garages as artistic designs; his was an aesthetic that stressed convenience, practicality, and economy—attributes that were ideal for utilitarian garage design. However, Radford's Prairie-inspired garage designs were not without small-scaled residential effects, such as applied ornamentation, window boxes, and trellised vines. In my review of plan-book designs, there were more designs for Prairie garages than there were for Prairie houses. Perhaps it was less of an architectural risk to design a Prairie garage than it was to design a Prairie house.

Even though trade magazines advocated garage design that harmonized with the parent house, they pictured garages as isolated buildings in an attempt to market garage design and construction as a separate activity. The need for more garages was apparent; from the beginning, private garage construction lagged far behind automobile production. The extended use of the automobile by "all classes" made the private garage so necessary to the new house that by 1921 one trade journal claimed the majority of new, even speculative, houses had the "added attraction" of a garage.[30] The success of the building industry's marketing campaign is evidenced by the variety of businesses that participated. Shares of the garage market were earned by architects who designed garage plan books; by manufacturers of garage doors and garage hardware; by manufacturers of ready-cut and portable garages; and by carpen-

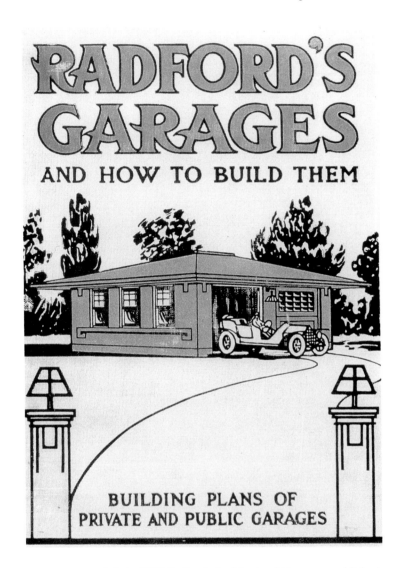

9.8. In 1910 Radford's Architectural Company published the first garage plan book. Several designs in it, including this cover image, evoked Prairie-style characteristics.

9.9. Portable garages were more functional in appearance than architect-designed or even ready-cut garages. This plain, reinforced concrete model of the David Craig Company had portholes instead of residential windows.

9.10. The sun parlor garage was offered as an "artistic" device to conceal the functional aspects of a garage.

ters and builders who erected custom-designed garages, assembled ready-cut buildings, and remodeled carriage houses. Even garage-door and hardware manufacturers, such as the National Manufacturing Company of Sterling, Illinois, distributed garage plan books.

Some builders, such as Gentzen and Company, Garage Builders, of Chicago, declared garage construction as their specialty. E. D. Gentzen advertised once a week in a local Chicago newspaper, displaying a 2-by-4-inch advertisement, stating, "Frame, brick and stucco garages—no down payment." Gentzen's company constructed about five hundred garages a year, "built complete with cement floor, painted, electric lights."[31]

There were also opportunities for garage modernizing and repairs, including the installation of new doors and insulation and the removal of the garage's center post. One trade article suggested that builders create a market for garage improvements by canvassing car owners whose names were obtainable from the state license bureau.[32] Even during the Depression years of 1929 and 1930, garage construction and improvements increased, because the trade journals urged builders to specialize and to aggressively sell their service.

Portable buildings, manufactured nationwide, were promoted for tenants and for those who sought to avoid an architect's fee or construction costs. Most claimed that their design could be "knocked-down" in a few hours and reerected on another location. Many were also fireproof. The David Craig Company of Boston manufactured reinforced-concrete slab walls with tongue and groove joints; the walls were meant to fit together without mortar. The Metal Shelter Company of St. Paul and C. D. Pruden and Company of Baltimore advertised portable sheet-metal garages, which were essentially a metal rectangle topped by a low-pitched gable roof.[33] The majority of portable garages had few windows; one of Craig's 1910 models was reduced to glass portholes (figure 9.9). Although portable garages were designed in the form of a small house, manufacturers made no gestures toward architectural harmony. In general, portable-garage design lived up to the challenge proposed years earlier by Comstock and others who thought that garages should be straightforward and practical. However, even the portable garage companies sometimes compensated a plain form with ornamentation. One of Craig's models offered a spread-wing motif above paneled doors. Some companies pressed decorative patterns into sheet-metal walls or applied stickwork.

The garage's residential character also forced larger-scale design issues. William A. Radford waxed poetic about the garage's responsibility to the neighborhood:

> A man who builds a garage, just as truly as one who is putting up a residence, owes a duty not alone to his family and himself; he is under a moral obligation to the community as well. No man has the moral right to build a structure which will be unworthy of the community in which he lives, or which, by its inappropriateness or utter lack of style, will tend to depreciate the value of property in the neighborhood.[34]

In 1936 W. J. Cameron of the Ford Motor Company reported that the motorcar and its garage had encouraged well-kept alleys. He drew a comparison between the "old-time" alley—unpaved, rutted, littered, with unpainted lean-tos—and the improved 1936 alley—paved, drained, clean, with rows of neat garages. These neat garages boasted houselike attributes; they were well built, painted, doored, glassed, floored, and had electric lights.[35]

Additive Form

In 1920 Charles Alma Byers, writing for *Keith's Magazine,* posed the question, "Why not keep your automobile in the house?"[36] Agreement within the building industry regarded the value of architectural harmony between the house and garage, as well as agreement regarding fireproofing measures, made way for the auto to live inside the house as an added room. As late as 1933, *American Builder* continued to use the humanization of the auto as a marketing ploy—but this time, the building industry was selling attached garages: "The depression has amply demonstrated that the American family will not give up its car. The automobile has become an important member of the family—a place for it must be provided in the house to the same extent that a separate room is provided for other members."[37]

The relationships between the house and the garage occurred in four overlapping design stages. The first was the garage as a separate building, isolated from the main house. It was the most commonly used arrangement, and it avoided fire hazards. But it was expensive, because of the costs incurred in constructing two separate buildings, and it exposed the homeowner to the weather.

An alternative scheme was to connect the main house and garage to the side or the rear with a covered passageway or porch, a design device that continued well into the 1930s and was most often associated with houses of colonial character. This scheme was more convenient in stormy weather. Leila Ross Wilburn, a plan-book architect from Atlanta, favored this design because the garage and connecting porch lengthened the appearance of a small house.[38]

However, trade-journal reports suggest that the second chronological phase of attaching the garage to the house was to place the car beneath the house, in the basement, to be approached from the front, side, or rear.[39] This was economical if the grade of the property was appropriate, but the basement garage was also recommended for narrow lots, even when excavating was necessary.

Finally, the garage was added to the house as an attached room, connected as a wing, most often to the side. This merger occurred at different times regionally, because it was prohibited by some building departments and because of higher insurance rates in some localities. In 1920 *Keith's Magazine* suggested that the attached garage was already popular in Los Angeles and Kansas City.[40] Plan-book architects and builders liked the implications of this design: it was more cheaply constructed than a separate building, it added width to the house, and it had the potential of balancing another one-story wing, such as a sun porch. Considered as an extra room, the attached garage had the convenience of proximity, and it established a passage from inside the house without risking bad weather. Electrical, water, and heating lines could be connected without much additional cost, and the car was less likely to be stolen.

Building Age and the Builder's Journal never discussed outright the design issues involved in attaching the garage to the house; instead, it labeled it the "garage problem" and advised "clever handling."[41] Once again, the related themes of house and garden, which had been responsible in the previous decade for transforming ordinary garages into small houses, were reiterated as a device for attached garages. Perhaps the most imaginative pretense was the "sun parlor garage" (figure 9.10) The "sun parlor" was achieved with multipaned glass doors, sometimes with transoms for additional light. The design resulted in a piercing of the front eleva-

9.11. This garage bungalow could provide temporary
housing.

tion into a window-wall, a residential effect heightened by draped curtains. The only element that revealed the space to be a garage was the driveway,
which led up to the door.

Transformation As a House

"Own your home" was the cry that reverberated
throughout 1920s America. The campaign for home
ownership, aggressively encouraged by the federal
government and the building industry, was executed in the interest of good citizenship, independence, and economic prosperity. Small houses at
moderate cost became the prime focus for builders,
buyers, and lending institutions. But the price of
home ownership was high. One builder's journal
characterized it like this: "After the purchase of a lot
somewhere in one of God's front yards, the family
savings account looks more like thirty cents than
anything like a workable balance!"[42]

One solution for the housing shortage was a
temporary home that could later be incorporated
into a permanent house scheme. Since the garage
was already a small, inexpensive building with residential characteristics, it made an ideal transformation into a new house type—a combined house
and garage. In the 1920s, both trade and popular
presses featured a few designs for house and garage
combinations, appropriately merging the term *bungalow*, a popular house type with homelike connotations, with the word *garage*. The "garage bun-
galo," the "bungarage," and the "garlow" were
offered as a temporary home, adaptable for conversion into a two-car garage. The 1926 Southern Pine
Association's garage plan book also presented a design for a combined house and garage that was
named a "summer home garage," which "proved
popular and profitable for many different purposes."[43]

Two types of garage bungalows were almost square in plan, approximately 23 feet by 21 feet, although Southern Pine's summer home garage was 26 by 18 feet. There were those with a one-car garage and three rooms (living room with a folding bed, kitchen, and bath) under one roof; and those with five rooms (living room, dining room, bedroom, kitchenette, and bathroom) and no space for a car. Some garlows were even promoted as permanent dwellings, composed of five rooms and a two-car garage back-to-back, which doubled the length of the square types. While the garage bungalow was a short-lived phenomenon in the national drive to shake off the landlord's shackles, the design resulted in a house and garage under one roof.

Summary

At the turn of the century, automobile ownership offered a profitable opportunity for builders and architects to develop a new building type for the storage of the motorcar. While trade publications opened the discussion as early as 1904, the years 1910–11 seemed to have signaled a watershed for developing residential garage design. Although it took three decades to resolve the basic issues in residential garage design, the building industry and its publications led the way in developing a design that was residential in character and in marketing garage design to the public.

The image of the garage portrayed by the Southern Pine Association in figure 9.5 foreshadowed the future direction of garage design: automobiles and their storage became so important to American culture that house design was changed irrevocably. Even after 1930, in spite of efforts to integrate the garage more effectively into house design (or even to turn the garage doors away from street view), garages (and their doors) are still the dominant design element in the primary elevation of the contemporary house. In addition, garages affected the placement of houses on their lots and the distribution of houses in subdivisions. Overall, the garage is a powerful indicator of the presence of the automobile culture in American society, due to the consequences of the original concept of making a house for the auto.

Notes

1. For an analysis of the impact of the garage on the house, see Folke T. Kihlstedt's "The Automobile and the Transformation of the American House, 1910–1935," *Michigan Quarterly Review* (Fall 1980/Winter 1981):555–70. See J. B. Jackson, "The Domestication of the Garage," *Landscape* 20 (Winter 1976):10–19, for the cultural aspects of garage design.

2. William A. Radford's publications help pinpoint the dates of usage. In an August 1909 article in the *American Carpenter and Builder*, "Practical Garage Design," both garage and automobile house are used. However, by 1910 when Radford published the plan book, *Radford's Garages and How to Build Them*, he stated that the buildings to store motor vehicles "are known as garages—a term of French origin."

3. "Design for an Automobile House," *Carpentry and Building* (Nov. 1904):309–11.

4. H. H. Holt, "The Garage," *Keith's Magazine* (Aug. 1907):61—64.

5. "Combination House and Garage," *American Carpenter and Builder* (Feb. 1908):597–99.

6. William A. Radford, *Radford's Garages and How to Build Them* (Chicago, 1910).

7. "A Private Garage of Shingled Exterior," *Building Age* (Sept. 1910):401.

8. Ralph de Martin, "A Group of Model Motor Houses for the Small Country Place," *American Homes and Gardens* (Apr. 1909):147.

9. William Phillips Comstock, *Garages and Motor Boat Houses* (New York, 1911), 5–33.

10. Holt, 62.

11. "Arrangement of Sliding Garage Doors," *Building Age* (Nov. 1912):557.

12. The American Architect, *Garages, Country and Suburban: A series of Authoritative Articles on the Structural Features of the Private Garage and Its Equipment* (New York, 1911), 20.

13. Comstock, 9, 10; Holt, 62.

14. Southern Pine Association, *Southern Pine Garages and How to Build Them* (New Orleans, 1926), cover.

15. Holt, 62.

16. Howard Victor Brown, "The Country Dweller

and the Automobile," *American Homes and Gardens* (Nov. 1911):389.

17. Gordon-Van Tine Company, *Gordon-Van Tine Homes* Davenport, Iowa, 1925), 127.

18. Holt, 61.

19. Comstock, 6.

20. Gordon-Van Tine Company, 127.

21. "Garage Building," *American Carpenter and Builder* (May 1911):40–41.

22. Togan-Stiles, *Away from City Cares* (Grand Rapids, Mich., 1921), 23.

23. For design no. G-152, see Radford, 9. For Harry Ramsey's garage and studio design, see "Cement Construction for the Private Garage," *Building Age* (Apr. 1911):217, and "A Garage and Studio Building of Cement Exterior," *Building Age* (Nov. 1912):557–60.

24. J. Gordon Dempsey, "Double Sliding Garage Doors," *Building Age* (Dec. 1912):619.

25. E. J. G. Phillips, "Arrangement of Sliding Garage Doors," *Building Age* (Dec. 1916):57.

26. "The Concrete Garage of Dr. N. B. Van Effen," *American Homes and Gardens* (July 1906):38.

27. "The Use of Cement in the Building of the Suburban House and Garage," *American Homes and Gardens* (May 1910):205.

28. "Cheap and Fireproof" (advertisement), *American Builder* (June 1917):150.

29. See, for instance, "A Few Designs of Cement Garages," *Building Age* (May 1911):275; "A Garage of Terra Cotta Blocks with Cement Exterior," *Building Age* (Sept. 1911): 475–76; and "A Cement-Covered Hollow-Tile Garage," *Building Age* (Oct. 1911): 521–22.

30. "Garages for the Small Home," *Building Age* (July 1921):41.

31. Joseph B. Mason, "Opportunities in Garage Modernizing, Repairs and New Doors," *American Builder* (Sept. 1933):21.

32. Mason, 21.

33. Advertisements from *American Carpenter and Builder* (Apr. 1912): 130 illustrated two portable garage manufacturers with similar names: one for the Prudential portable steel shelter by C. D. Pruden and Co. of Baltimore, and one for the Pruden System by the Metal Shelter Co. of St. Paul, Minn. Both companies claimed to be patentees and sole manufacturers of their system.

34. Radford, 4.

35. W. J. Cameron, "Buildings and Motor Cars," *American Builder* (Feb. 1936):46.

36. Charles Alma Byers, "Keeping the Automobile in the House," *Keith's Magazine* (May 1920):262.

37. "New Styles in Garages and Equipment," *American Builder* (Apr. 1933):30.

38. Leila Ross Wilburn, *Small Low-Cost Homes* (Atlanta, Ga., n.d.), 17.

39. Early mentions of a basement garage in trade journals include "Combination House and Garage," *American Carpenter and Builder* (Feb. 1908):597–99, and Benjamin A. Howes, "Private Automobile Garages," *American Homes and Gardens* (June 1908):245.

40. Byers, 262–63.

41. "The House and Garage Problem," *Building Age and the Builder's Journal* (Aug. 1923):64–65, and "The Attached Garage: Six Ways of Handling the Problem Artistically," *Building Age and the Builder's Journal* (June 1924):80–81.

42. Frank T. Phillips, "The Bungarage," *Building Age and the Builder's Journal* (Apr. 1924):92–93.

43. Plans were published in Phillips, 92–93; Charles Alma Byers, "The Garage Bungalow," *Building Age and the Builder's Journal* (July 1923):51–52; "Garlows, the Modern Type of Temporary Home" and "Garlows as Permanent Dwellings," in *The Home* (n.p., n.d.), 84–85. See also Southern Pine Association for a "summer home garage" (design no. 9).

A Story of Prefabrication

CHAPTER 10

CAROL AHLGREN AND
FRANK EDGERTON MARTIN

*How the Trachte Company Grew
Up with the Roadside*

Now everybody can afford a servicable garage of quality for every one of the rapidly increasing millions of automobiles in the country, and every car can afford the protection it deserves. Every back yard and every vacant lot can now produce a profit by helping to fill that pronounced need for more and more garages. *Order Today!*

"A Quality Steel Garage for $100,"
Trachte Brothers Company brochure, ca. 1927

When George and Arthur Trachte began their tinsmith and furnace repair shop in Madison, Wisconsin, at the turn of the century, they probably never imagined that their company would come to construct more buildings in the region than any single architect. Nor could they possibly have imagined the shape that these buildings would take or how far they would spread. Yet, in the seventy years that followed the creation of their first prefabricated metal garage, the company produced an array of garages, restaurants, warehouses, and gas stations. These distinctive metal buildings evolved with, and even foreshadowed, much of the roadside architecture of our time—including the prefabricated fast-food restaurant, standardized gas station, and most recently the mini-storage warehouse.

In roadside historiography, little recognition has been accorded to small companies such as Trachte that, through producing these structures, grew to have a tremendous impact on the American

automotive environment. Whereas much of roadside study has focused on landmark buildings such as Los Angeles's Brown Derby restaurant, most of today's roadside architecture is neither extraordinary nor unusual; instead, gas stations, car washes, and fast-food restaurants are generally mass-produced. The repetition of such buildings is the essence of their recognizability and contribution to the character of the highway.

In this historical analysis of a significant building company, traditional historical sources such as trade journals, city directories, and company advertising have been supplemented by oral interviews with long-term Trachte Company employees.

The Trachte Story

In 1906 the Trachte company was cited in an early county history as one of Madison's most promising businesses. George and Arthur Trachte, ages nineteen and twenty-one, were two of the city's youngest entrepreneurs.[1] Like many midwestern metal-

building companies, Trachte began as a producer of such agriculture-related products as livestock watering troughs and water tanks for buildings. An early photograph shows George and Arthur Trachte standing in front of their storefront operation on a sidewalk lined with large metal tanks, two blocks from the grounds of the state capitol in Madison. With fewer than a dozen employees, the company also produced a line of "unsinkable" metal fishing and hunting boats during this period.

The key to the young company's success, and the basis for its future endeavors, was a patented "roll form" machine that turned out curved or straight panels of corrugated steel. An early company catalog (ca. 1916) claimed that the tanks were "so corrugated that they will withstand the pressure of water without the aid of braces" and would also withstand any expansion and contraction caused by weather.[2] The corrugated steel panels, mass-produced and available in two types, would be very suitable for walls and roofs.

107

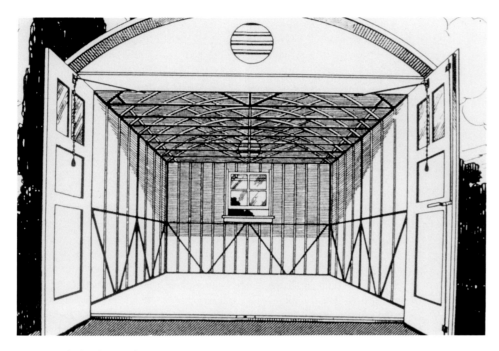

10.1. Ready for the Model T: the original Trachte Model A garage, ca. 1920, as shown in a Trachte brochure.

10.2. Modern, efficient, and easy to assemble: the Model A garage in a picturesque setting, ca. 1920, in a Trachte brochure.

The Trachte Garage

In an interview, Arthur Trachte's son Bob, who is now in his seventies, described the accidental beginnings of the company's involvement with garage production. Bob became company president in the 1960's; when he was young, his father and uncle had put him to work building, repairing, moving, and selling the company's array of metal buildings. The story of The Trachte garage begins with an experimental car shelter at the family cottage in Madison in 1919:

My dad had a brand new Dodge and he'd park it—you know, a new car—so they had the machine that rolled this stuff, they were rolling tanks with it, water tanks—so he rolled some straight panels and some curved panels and bolted it together. It was something to run his car into at night. . . . The wind came and collapsed it because there was nothing, just the sheet metal. . . . But so many people inquired about it that my dad said, "Well—maybe if we put a framework in it. . . ."[3]

The striking novelty of the new garage attracted attention and curiosity from neighbors; most surpris-

ing was the fact that someone wanted to buy it even after it had collapsed. Yet the inquiries persisted. According to Bob, because so many people saw the first structure at the family cottage and asked his mother, "Where can I get a building like that?" she sent them to the family shop.[4] Although the Trachte brothers had not yet begun to produce the garages, they soon developed a structural system that with few modifications would characterize their distinctive metal buildings for the next fifty years.

From this unplanned beginning, the steel garage gained predominance in the array of company products. In towns and cities across the Midwest, the surviving carriage houses and liveries were not specifically suited to shelter the newly emergent automobile. In an age of the assembly line and the mass production of cars, a garage that was itself mass-produced seemed remarkably timely (figure 10.2).

Typical Trachte garages produced in the 1920s and 1930s were humble, visually distinctive buildings because of their rectangular form and barrel-vaulted roofs. The rounded gable end featured a circular vent above the entrance door. The placement of the circle vent, along with flared metal trim that imparted the suggestion of returned cornices, contributed to a symmetry that characterized all early Trachte garages. The basic building unit was suitable for a single car, although the company also produced sizes for two, three, or even six cars.

In the 1920s metal was not yet an accepted building material, and its quality was questioned. Perhaps because of their newness, prefabricated metal buildings were viewed as cheap and impermanent. In his 1922 novel, *Babbitt,* Sinclair Lewis described how a socially aspiring businessman saw his metal garage as a temporary flaw in the complete perfection of his home:

> He looked blurrily out at the yard. It delighted him, as always; it was the neat yard of a successful businessman . . . that is, it was perfection, and made him also perfect. He regarded the corrugated iron garage. For the 365th time in the year he reflected, "no class to that tin shack. Have to build a frame garage. But by golly, it's the only thing on the place that isn't up to date."[5]

In 1927, possibly as a response to negative perceptions of metal structures, the Trachte company produced a brochure that provided ten reasons why metal buildings were not only cleanly efficient but

sound investments: low cost and upkeep, long life, portability, fireproof and lightningproof, attractive appearance, sound investment, enlargement capability, warmer in winter—cooler in summer, and weatherproof.[6]

The company emphasized not only the portability of the new metal buildings but the fact that they were easy to assemble. Provided with each Trachte building was a blueprint with detailed instructions. Although Bob Trachte recalled that the instructions continued to improve and evolve through the years, the company had always emphasized the ease of assembly—that a Trachte garage could almost be put together with nothing more than "a pair of pliers and a screwdriver."[7] The company also encouraged customers to paint their Trachte garages so they would "harmonize with surrounding buildings." Not only would paint help maintain the condition of the metal, it would provide "an attractive decorative feature."[8]

By 1929, after many years of identifying itself in the Madison city directory as a tinsmith shop, sheet-metal works, and a maker of tanks, the primary theme of promotion changed to specify buildings: "Trachte Brothers Company—Manufacturers of PORTABLE STEEL GARAGES." For the first time, the company's advertisement also included a drawing of the distinctive Trachte garage with its vaulted roof and horizontal steel siding.[9] Bob Trachte recalled that through the 1920s, the company was still primarily a metal job shop: "I would say that the buildings were secondary until probably the late 1920s or '30s and then they came into their own."

Trachte Meets the Needs of Roadside Commerce

From the early garages, the Trachte brothers soon

developed an entire prefabricated-steel building system that could span the vast spaces required for airplane hangars and automobile showrooms (figure 10.3). After his 1927 transatlantic flight, Charles Lindbergh visited Madison on a barnstorming tour across the country. An early source of pride in Trachte history was the use made of their first hangar at the old Madison airfield to shelter the renowned *Spirit of St. Louis* (figure 10.4).

Lindbergh's famous airplane was eventually moved to the Smithsonian Institution in Washington, D.C. The anonymous Trachte hangar, indistinguishable from any other Trachte hangar, was moved to another airfield, where it still stands.[11] This capacity for easy portability was a hallmark of the Trachte building system, and one of many distinctive characteristics that set it apart from other metal buildings, such as the Quonset hut, for which Trachte buildings are commonly mistaken. Yet it was the Quonset hut and its pervasive presence in the advertising and imagery surrounding World War II that gave credibility to the concept of a metal building. As Bob Trachte recalled of the World War II era: "Before then it was hard to convince people that you could live or work in a metal building. They'd see them and say 'Oh, they'd be hot in the summer and cold in the winter.'"[12]

Trachte buildings were produced in three types: A, B, and C, referring to length and width of the structural support. The hangar that sheltered the *Spirit of St. Louis* was a type C, the largest available. Type B was suitable for a multicar garage, warehouse, shop, or other commercial venture. The company's advertising reflected the aspirations of those who purchased the buildings for businesses: "Eliminating the necessity of a large capital investment, they make it much easier for the ambitious individual to go into business for himself."[13]

10.3. Suitable for an auto showroom, an early "parapet style" Trachte storefront in Madison, Wisconsin, ca. 1930.

10.4. One of Trachte's proudest moments: the *Spirit of St. Louis* in a Trachte hangar, Madison, Wisconsin, airfield, ca. 1928.

These structures served as a first home to many small businesses, such as drive-ins, shoe-repair shops, and auto-service shops (figure 10.5). In the 1930s and 1940s, the company's building system was sufficiently flexible to meet the booming needs of highway-oriented businesses such as gas stations and restaurants. Unlike the initial barrel-vaulted garages, these Trachte commercial buildings followed new stylistic trends (figure 10.6).

In the late 1930s, the company introduced "modernistic" trim consisting of several bands of metal coursing that concealed the vaulted roof. In keeping with the company's tradition as an innovative family business, the modernistic addition to the product line was designed by Bob's cousin, Florence Trachte, a college student majoring in art. As a design element, this trim generally wrapped around the side of a building to imply a flat-roofed structure (figure 10.7).

The strong horizontality of the molded-metal bands evoked the sleek lines of the Streamlined Moderne style that was popular at the time. According to Bob, the new look was introduced during the Depression, "when there wasn't a whole lot of anything moving"—the modernistic design was a way to "upgrade the look and get people interested."[14] Vernacular expressions of the Moderne style, modernistic Trachte buildings were soon home to businesses such as grocery stores, barber shops, gas stations, and restaurants.

Trachte buildings ranged from the basic round-roof and modernistic units to the extraordinary, a result of the company's willingness to do customized work for individual businesses (figure 10.8) As a company catalog stated: "If you don't see pictured here the exact type of structure you want, write us describing your requirements, and the chances are we will be able to take good care of your demands."[15] One of the most distinctive customized Trachte buildings from this period is an English Tudor–style restaurant still in use in Richland Center, Wisconsin, Frank Lloyd Wright's hometown. Like the modernistic gas stations and stores, this building—with its steeply pitched, symmetrical front-end gables—represented an economical interpretation of a popular architectural style (figure 10.9).

When Bob Trachte became company president in the 1960s, he introduced a new phase to the Trachte building system; the patented round-roof form of the first Trachte buildings was supplemented with buildings having gable roofs, available in three sizes. By this time, metal gable-roofed buildings, commonly referred to as "pole sheds," were becoming a pervasive element in the agricultural landscape. Meanwhile, the company's long-standing experience with customized and "artistic" metalwork, such as the modernistic trim, gave it a strong market position with the emergence of a new roadsde phenomenon: the franchise restaurant.

Trachte Enters the Freeway Era

The company's first work with fast-food architecture began with a profitable venture with the Kentucky Fried Chicken Corporation. The initial buildings the Trachte company built for this chain featured a red-and-white-striped, tentlike roof topped off with a weather vane featuring Colonel Sanders, with his distinctive white suit, cane, and goatee. The buildings may be considered as echoes of the neocolonial style, while the Colonel Sanders weather vane provided a flavor of the Old South. Without mentioning that they were made by the Trachte Company, roadside historian Philip Langdon described these buildings as "pagoda" roofed and "exotic or eccentric"[16] (figure 10.10).

10.5. Small and efficient: a Trachte root beer stand, Madison, Wisconsin, ca. 1940.

10.6. A Trachte canopy-style gas station, ca. 1938.

The Trachte Company constructed a prototype of a Kentucky Fried Chicken building in a partially enclosed courtyard space near their plant on Madison's east side. The model was toured by Kentucky Fried Chicken executives and designers, who critiqued it and suggested changes until it was ready for mass production and distribution. Following the debut of the test building in Madison, Wisconsin, the Trachte Company would construct over 80 percent of the Kentucky Fried Chicken franchises in the United States between 1968 and 1975.[17]

The original Kentucky Fried Chicken buildings, which Bob Trachte claimed never fully "caught on" with the franchisees, nonetheless remained the predominant design for almost ten years—a substantial period in the context of fast-food architecture.[18] In the 1970s, the Trachte Company was responsible for the "image enhancement" of many of these earlier Kentucky Fried Chicken franchises throughout the country. The new buildings were a more modest design: one story with a large, metal mansard roof. Above the entrance, a simplified square "cupola" with red and white stripes carried the image established by the earlier Trachte-made buildings. Although use of the original Trachte siding was not continued in the new buildings, the mansard-roof style was replicated for the company's contracts with other fast-food chains: A & W Rootbeer, Lum's, Shakey's, Dairy Queen, and Wendy's.

In 1974 the company began another lucrative undertaking that reflected its traditions and the increasing mobility of Americans—the production of metal "mini-warehouses" for self-storage. Although the function, roof shape, and siding pattern has changed, the origins of these mini-warehouses can be traced to the multiple-unit garages produced by the Trachte Company in the 1920s. In an interview, an employee stated: "I feel we can honestly say that

10.7. Trachte trademarks: the "modernistic" trim and barrel-vaulted roof of a Trachte storefront in Madison, Wisconsin.

Trachte is the original manufacturer of steel building systems for the mini-storage industry."[19] In a 1988 *New York Times* article, the bright orange Trachte-made doors of a self-storage warehouse in Monona, Wisconsin, were described as typical of this new architectural form.[20]

From the days of its first garage to the era of fast-food and mini-storage, the Trachte Company survived and flourished as a supplier of auto-related buildings because of its ingenuity in finding economical solutions to new design problems and changing economic needs. While the Trachte Company produced few "landmark" buildings, its significance lies in its integration of a keen awareness of visual details and changing fashions with the technology of mass production.

A revealing company anecdote concerns one of Wisconsin's most famous native sons, Frank Lloyd Wright. According to Bob Trachte, Wright, possibly knowing of the company's ability to do customized work, stopped by the Trachte factory in the 1930s to inquire about a special job: metal shingles for a barn at Taliesin. From Wright's perspective as an artist/architect, the idea seemed highly attractive. But the Trachtes saw the difficulty and expense posed by such a project.

During Wright's visit, the Trachtes showed him examples of their new modernistic parapet design. At the end of the visit, according to Bob, a rebuffed Wright "swung his cape around his shoulder and stomped out and said, 'Damn tin buildings!'"[21] While Frank Lloyd Wright gained international fame as an architect, it was his more humble neighbors, the Trachtes, who created more buildings in Wisconsin than all of its architects combined.

10.8. Custom-made by Trachte: a roadside cafe with "modernistic" trim and a "Tudor style" gas station, ca. 1938.

10.9. High-style design for a low cost: the Tudor style restaurant in Richland Center, Wisconsin, ca. 1938.

10.10. A Trachte-produced Kentucky Fried Chicken store with ornamental weather vane, Madison, Wisconsin.

Notes

The authors would like to extend a special thank you to Bob Trachte for his consent to numerous interviews and his loan of company records, brochures, catalogs, and photographs.

1. Western Historical Association, *History of Dane County: Biographical and Genealogical* (Madison, Wis. Western Historical Association, 1906), 915–16.

2. *Catalogue No. 20* (Madison, Wis.: Trachte Bros. Co., ca. 1916), cover page.

3. Bob Trachte, interview with author, Madison, Wis., June 1986.

4. Bob Trachte, interview with author, Madison, Wis., November 1988.

5. Sinclair Lewis, *Babbitt* (New York: Harcourt Brace Jovanovich, 1922), 8.

6. "A Quality Steel Garage for $100" (brochure, Trachte Brothers Company, ca. 1927).

7. Trachte interview, November 1988.

8. *Trachte Portable Steel Garage and Building Catalog* (Madison, Wis.: Trachte Brothers Company, ca. 1927), 10. In my interview with Bob Trachte in November 1988, Bob recalled that the company sold Cemtex paint to customers, made by the Detroit Graphite company. The paint had a Portland cement base and at the time was the best available for galvanized steel.

9. *Madison City Directory, 1929* (Madison, Wis.: Wright City Directory Publishing Co., 1929), 134.

10. Bob Trachte, interview with author, Madison, Wis., September 1986.

11. The Trachte hangar that sheltered the *Spirit of St. Louis* is now obscured by an enormous Shell sign at Madison's Truax Field. The airfield, which is comprised of several WPA-era buildings, along with several Trachte hangars, also has a restaurant in the main terminal that is a "must see" for commercial archeologists, the Jet Room.

12. Trachte interview, June 1986.

13. *Trachte Catalog*, 35.

14. Trachte interview, November 1988.

15. *Trachte Catalog*, 35.

16. Philip Langdon, *Orange Roofs, Golden Arches: The Architecture of American Chain Restaurants* (New York: Alfred A. Knopf, 1986), 100. The development of the Kentucky Fried Chicken Corporation has been further discussed in Phil Patton, *Open Road: A Celebration of the American Highway* (New York: Simon and Schuster, 1986), 178–85, 190, 200–202.

17. Marty Robbins, "A Brief History" (typescript, Trachte Building Systems, 1986).

18. Trachte interview, November 1988.

19. Marty Robbins, interview with author, Sun Prairie, Wis., June 1986.

20. "Self Storage: Success Breeds Changes," *New York Times,* 28 February 1988, sec. 8, p.1.

21. Trachte interview, November 1988.

The Motel in Builder's Literature and Architectural Publications

CHAPTER 11

MARY ANNE BEECHER

An Analysis of Design

With the introduction of the automobile came the public's fascination with touring, and convenient accommodations soon began to develop across the country for this touring public. Called cabin camps or tourist camps in the early state—and later many names, including auto court, tourist court, motor hotel, motor lodge, autel, and, most commonly, motel—the number of roadside accommodations along America's highways increased from six hundred to more than forty thousand between the late 1920s and 1950.[1]

While the aspects of motel evolution that pertain to social history have been substantially documented in works such as *Americans on the Road* by Warren James Belasco, and the operational aspects of motels have been published in guides for motel owners since the 1940s,[2] little information has been published on the physical aspects of motel forms. Therefore, the objectives of this study are (1) to identify general motel design guidelines published for builders, (2) to identify the types of aesthetic treatments used in motel design, (3) to determine a general design typology for the individual units of early motels, and (4) to determine the typical con-figurations into which these units were placed.

These objectives were achieved through the analysis of historic literature that was directed at builders and architects. It was during the period 1930 to 1955 that motel design and construction were most regularly featured in builder's journals and architectural publications. Although vastly outnumbered by domestic designs, both kinds of sources printed plans and photographs of motel units and site plans of their overall organizations with some regularity.[3] These published designs provide a concise sample of the architectural information about motels that would otherwise be unavailable, due to the rarity of unaltered examples.

Of the builder's journals surveyed for this study, *American Carpenter and Builder* (later called *American Builder*), published in Chicago, includes the greatest amount of information about motel design and construction. The information is typically in the form of a one- or two-page article that features the floor plans and photographs of one or two recently constructed motels. Special construction features and innovative design solutions are often highlighted. For example, in 1946 the editors of *Ameri-can Builder* drove 3,500 miles through Washington, Oregon, and California in an effort to gain a better understanding of the current state of motel construction. Featured in the August 1946 issue of *American Builder* was a motel in Albany, California, that was constructed of adobe brick as a way of avoiding the materials shortages that resulted from World War II.[4]

Information on motels was also found in two architectural publications: the *Architectural Record* and the *Architectural Forum*. Articles on motels from these journals are usually several pages long and include a general discussion of the current state of motel design, as well as plans and photographs of new motels. Site plans, perspective and axonometric drawings, and construction details are also commonly found as part of these articles.

This published material provided an initial body of information from which the parts and patterns of composition, both in plan and architectural form, could be derived. The accuracy of the resulting typologies was subsequently assessed through the review of historic postcards of authentic motels. The review of postcards was conducted to determine the level of correlation between the published motel designs and the built environment.

Historic Background

The design of motels must be studied with an understanding of the historic context through which their forms evolved. Free campgrounds, providing a place to park, and community restrooms were the roadside accommodations initially spawned by the advent of auto touring. They were typically operated by the owners of gas stations, grocery stores, or food stands, or by the wives of farmers. The tourists who used these facilities were expected to supply their own provisions. However, owners of the camps soon began to charge tourists from fifty to seventy-five cents per night to encourage use by a higher-class clientele.

Around 1925, low-cost cabins were first constructed on the campgrounds for tourists who wanted more comfort, convenience, and privacy. Although sometimes referred to as the "dog-house era," because the cabins were little more than a wooden shell with a dirt floor, this new concept for roadside accommodations was considered the beginning of the motel industry.[5] Tourists were still expected to supply their own provisions. However, the success of this development caused some camp owners to furnish their cabins with primitive beds and tables in order to justify an increase in their fees.

In the late 1920s, cabin camps began a major movement toward modernization and expansion in the hope that as the quality of the cabin's construction improved, more tourists would utilize camp facilities instead of hotels. This promise of increased economic opportunity caused more and more prospective camp owners to enter the field. However,

because this was a time of general economic depression, many financial incentives to promote the expansion of the cabin-camp industry were developed by lumber and plumbing suppliers. Oil companies and service-station chains, such as the Dutch Mill Service Company, encouraged the addition of cabins to preexisting gas stations. The Dutch Mill Service Company, which built service stations patterned after "the windmills of Holland," operated a chain of five service stations and five tourist-camp stations in Iowa, Nebraska, and Missouri beginning in the late 1920s.[6]

Although the Depression was very destructive to the hotel industry, the motel industry thrived because Americans continued to vacation by automobile. The resulting competition between tourist camps or courts (as they were called by that time, in an effort to better reflect their architectural permanence) helped to raise the industry's overall standards. Cottage construction and modernization was the only growing division of the building industry during the 1930s, according to the *Architectural Record*. The December 1933 issue estimated that more than 400,000 cabins had been constructed since 1929, representing an investment of over sixty million dollars.[7] However, the competition was very stiff, and a number of independent camps were forced out of business.

New motel development leveled off during the early 1940s, as gasoline rationing during World War II limited the number of tourists on the road. However, motels near suburban areas were commonly used as housing for war workers.[8]

Following the war, new construction of small-scale, individually owned motels was again on the rise. It was at that time that motel design was first considered of serious interest to the architect, having left the era of so-called "backyard design."[9] The

motel of the late 1940s was, according to the *Architectural Record*, "asserting a new architectural consciousness."[10]

This postwar boom of individually operated motels was short-lived, however. The 1950s brought the virtual end of individualized motel operations when corporate chains with systematized and centralized operations began to be favored by tourists. The February 1954 issue of *Architectural Forum* stated that many proprietors of small motels were feeling competition from chain operations and super motels (scaled-down hotels), both identified as two relatively new arrivals in the motel field.[11]

Design Guidelines

Several general guidelines regarding the design of motels were provided for builders in their literature. For instance, builders were advised to "let the average home suffer much by comparison with the equipment of the cottages you erect."[12] Exterior appearance was to be made as attractive as possible through landscaping because it was the exterior that first caught the attention of passing tourists. However, the design of the interiors of the motel units was to receive as much attention as the exteriors, in an effort to make travel accommodations superior to the surroundings and equipment left behind by the traveler in the home. The literature focused primarily on the technical aspects of the interiors, discussing desirable surface treatments and devices to be included. There was little discussion of the use of color or styles of decoration. This emphasis on modern equipment provided manufacturers with opportunities to advertise their products in motels' promotional literature, in the hope that tourists using their products on the road would decide to purchase them for their own homes.[13] Postcards boasted "steam heat, box and inner spring mattresses in each cabin, and plenty of warm water" and "a Beauty Rest mattress on every bed" (see figure 11.5).

In the twenty-five-year period studied, the individual motel unit and its relationship to other units underwent some changes, although the key concepts for the design of motels were always variety and flexibility. Variety in design ensured the motel owner's ability to attract the initial interest of the tourist. Within a single motel, the use of landscaping was encouraged to create variety among the units.

Flexibility had more to do with the layout of the individual units. A motel that offered alternative configurations of its units, such as providing single- and multispaced units within a single operation, was thought to be better able to adapt to the needs of the tourist. Planning for expansion, off-season closing of certain units, and making multiple use of common areas were other ways of including flexibility in a motel's design.

Originally, nearly all units were freestanding but were often connected to some sort of covered auto-storage space. The interiors of the early units were single-spaced and small. The interiors were simple and primitive. The furnishings included a single (or sometimes double) bed, a desk, and a closet or wall pegs. With the development of the motel industry, more substantial single- and multispace freestanding units were constructed. Sometimes called "cottages" instead of "cabins," because the word had more permanent and picturesque connotations, these more substantial units were often brick, stucco, or clapboard.

As the exterior designs of motel units became more elaborate and complex over time, the spaces within the units became more complex as well. Multispaced units often included combined living rooms and sleeping rooms, kitchenettes (single-wall units that included a sink, a small refrigerator, and a cooktop), or full kitchens that were large enough to contain dinette sets, as motels began to encourage stays of periods longer than one night.

In the 1950s, the units again became more simplified, due to an increase in the standardization of motels' layouts and architectural forms. The presence of kitchens or kitchenettes in the units was less prominent by this time because of the addition of restaurants in or near most motels.

Aesthetics

The use of aesthetic treatments in motel design was another method of creating variety between motels in the same area. However, aesthetic treatments were rarely discussed in the builder's literature because the importance of constructing motels of good general design was stressed over the construction of motels that might be considered eye-catching or novelties. As with domestic construction of the same period, the motel designs published in the builder's literature were to be, above all else, contemporary. The marketing of the aesthetic aspects of motel design was generally left to hotel, motel, and automobile-related publications. However, although not discussed, the motel designs published in the builder's journals were always given some thematic type of aesthetic treatment, and an analysis of the photographs and drawings published in the articles reveals six specific thematic categories (figure 11.1).

Two of the themes attempted to create images of the familiar. Both featured contemporary design elements and massing. The bungalow theme, which emulated the designs of the small modern suburban houses of the 1940s and 1950s, was the most popular aesthetic approach taken, based on its dominant appearance in the builder's literature (figure 11.2). In its attempt to imitate house design, a gable roof was often used with the gable end facing the road in freestanding units or turned toward the side in linked configurations. Clapboard or brick sidings were most common. The features that were used to create houselike effects during the 1940s and 1950s included overhangs, picture windows, and box plantings; all of which were found in use among the published designs. For instance, one featured motel created the bungalow effect through the use of a 2½-foot planting area, a decorative lamppost, a balcony, a railing over the breezeway, and a surrounding concrete walk.[14]

The modern theme, the second most popular approach, included little or no ornament, similar to the contemporary treatment of most commercial architecture during this period. The form of these motels was plain and boxlike. Their typical features included a smoothly clad, flat facade with no overhang, or a straight flat canopy that projected from the facade at a right angle. The roof was nearly always flat. Rounded corners were sometimes incorporated in an effort to further reduce the architectural details. The earliest modern motels often featured casement windows, and later versions frequently had windows that covered the entire front wall. Few other details were included in the designs of this category, as simplicity and the lack of details were stressed (see figure 2.7).

Based on the prominence of the bungalow and modern themes in the literature, most builders were encouraged to create motels that tourists would find comforting due to the familiarity of their contemporary designs. However, four additional thematic categories (the colonial, the rustic, the southwestern, and the western) focused on creating alternative environments through the interpretive use of vaguely recognizable historic themes. By 1950 the trend of using themes that were recognizably different from the more modern domestic models was discouraged. This accounts for the fact that historic themes were less extensively represented in the builder's literature.

The most popular of the historic themes was the colonial. Unlike the bungalow theme, which focused on creating the image of the modern house, the colonial was heavily endowed with historic, homelike connotations. Steeply pitched gable roofs and white stucco or clapboard siding were typically used for colonial units. Occasionally, a pedimented entry was provided. One of the most prominent features was the use of dark-colored shutters at the windows to define the fenestration and contrast with the light-colored siding. The use of divided-light, double-hung windows further emphasized fenestration that was more domestic than commercial.

The rustic aesthetic was the second most prominently featured historic theme in the builder's literature. Whether freestanding or linked, rustic units were always referred to as "cabins," evoking images of the mythical log cabin of early America. Milled log siding or rough-sawn boards were the typical cladding used, resulting in a prevalence of dark colors. The gable roof and rectangular form was most common. Prominent entrance porches were also often included as part of the rustic designs. The July 1940 issue of *American Builder* speculated about the popularity of the rustic aesthetic, proposing that "when people leave the city or towns where they live, they want a change to country-like surroundings with rustic buildings."[15]

Rustic ■ Natural materials and dark colors ■ Gable roof ■ Porches ■ Log or rough-sawn board siding	
Colonial ■ Home-like and picturesque qualities ■ Gable roof ■ Light-colored clapboard siding ■ Divided-light windows ■ Shutters	
Southwestern ■ Smooth flat surfaces and simple shapes ■ Stucco siding ■ Red tile canopies or roof details	
Western ■ Horizontal lines and natural materials ■ Wide overhang ■ Much landscaping	
Modern ■ Clean horizontal lines ■ Flat facade ■ Large windows ■ Lack of ornament	
Bungalow ■ Imitation of small modern house ■ Picture windows ■ Small details, such as awnings and box plantings	

11.1. Characteristics of the six motel aesthetic systems used for the design of motels between 1930 and 1955.

11.2. The exterior treatment of this Tallahassee, Florida, motel unit typifies the bungalow theme. The low-pitched gable roof is similar to that of the suburban ranch-style, and various porch and pergola forms have been used to articulate entrances. Small-scale details include landscaping with flowering bushes and divided-light windows with trim of a contrasting color.

11.4. Although the rustic theme was often applied to individual units, linked configurations could accommodate it as well. This plan was promoted as being adaptable to single, double, or multiple units.

11.3. The colonial theme is evident in the design of these Miami, Florida, cottages. Two versions of this cottage design were provided to the builders for the purpose of achieving variety in exteriors.

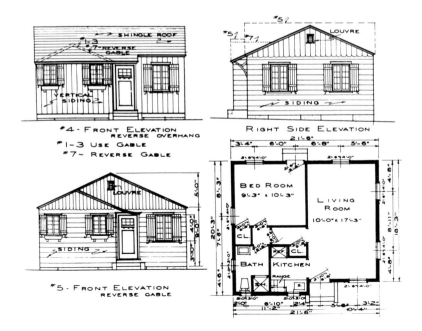

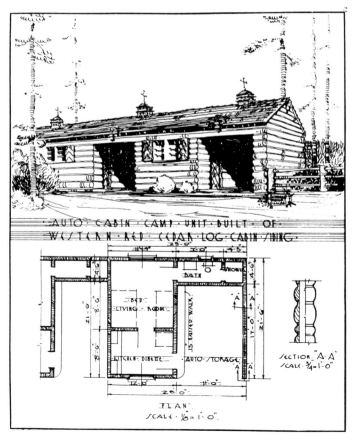

The southwestern aesthetic, which was loosely based on historic adobe architecture, was comparable to the rustic theme in terms of its appearance in the builder's literature. Its major characteristics included stucco cladding, a flat roof with a false front topped by a semicircular or stepped design, or red tile overhangs and roof details. Large-scaled chimneys were often prominently featured in the designs of motel units that included fireplaces. Simple shapes, smooth and flat surfaces, and natural materials were the essentials for creating the southwestern aesthetic.

The least prominent of the historic themes featured in the builder's journals was the western aesthetic. Using the western ranch house as a metaphor, motels of this type featured an emphasis on horizontal line and the use of dark colors and natural materials. Wide overhangs with bracketed supports and large amounts of natural plantings were also used.

All of these aesthetic themes were applied to both freestanding and linked units. Individual themes were not associated with interior aesthetic systems. Instead, differing approaches were taken to the treatment of the interiors of the early motels. The primary differentiation can be made between motels that featured contemporary themes and those that featured historic themes. The modern and bungalow themes most often featured contemporary surface treatments and furnishings. The use of wall-to-wall carpeting, venetian blinds, and exposed concrete was promoted. The furnishings were most often chrome and vinyl in the motels of the 1940s (figure 11.7), and plywood and molded plastic during the early 1950s.

In contrast, the colonial, southwestern, and western motels were more often treated with naturally finished materials, revival-style furnishings,

and an increased use of accessories. Paneling, patterned fabric draperies and upholsteries, and area rugs over hardwood or asphalt floor tiles were typically used (figure 11.8). No information on the interiors of rustic motels was provided in the literature. Because it is the most clearly definable of the themes, greater emphasis was no doubt given to its exterior treatments.

Although some of the historic themes seem to relate to prototypes that are associated with specific regions of the country, no regional relationships were established between the locations of the published motels and their chosen aesthetic treatments. Again, similar to domestic design of the period, the aesthetic treatments were applied nationally.

11.6. The large overhang of the Rancheria Motel of Santa Barbara, California, is a characteristic of the ranch theme. The brick-paved porch increased the living area of the units by including a chair near each entrance.

11.5. Glenora Courts was constructed in the southwestern theme.

GLENORA COURTS
Cafe in Connection

A BEAUTY REST MATTRESS ON EVERY BED - TILE BATHS
AT THE Y LOOP, HI-WAY 81-77 WACO, TEXAS

11.7. The unit interiors of the State Motel in Texas feature wall-to-wall carpeting and streamlined chrome and vinyl furnishings, all of which were promoted as being easy to clean.

11.8. This homey atmosphere was created through the use of Ponderosa pine paneling, a beamed ceiling, a decorative bedspread, and turned or stenciled furnishings.

The Design of Individual Units

A design typology for individual units includes three individual plan types, although a great deal of variety is found in the plans for individual units of cabin camps or tourist courts prior to World War II. During this period, it was not uncommon to find two to four different unit options available in a single court, since tourists were often shown more than one available unit before selecting their accommodations.[16]

Two different plan shapes emerged. The rectangular unit (both one-room and multispaced) was by far the most common shape for unit plans. Rectangular units were often alternated with covered garages in the early courts of the 1930s, because the placement of plumbing in a common wall between two units was not made an issue in the builder's publications until after the war. Even when the units became linked, it was most common to place the bathroom and the closet side by side at the rear of the unit and not back-to-back with the unit next door.

An L-shaped unit was the second alternative, appearing in the literature slightly less often than the rectangular units. The reason for its popularity may have been its ability to interlock with other units or a covered auto-storage space for more economical construction.

After the war, the rectangular and L shapes continued to prevail. However, the introduction of the staggered or zigzag layout, where units were placed at an angle to the road and were set back one from another, created the necessity for a third plan: a rectangle with a wedge-shaped projection. Although it was more expensive to construct, the staggered layout was often used when a single view, such as a beach, was to be seen from every room,

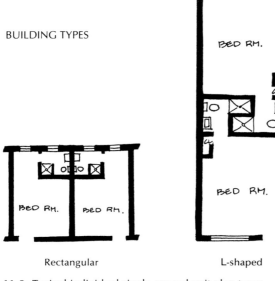

Rectangular   L-shaped

11.9. Typical individual single-spaced unit plan types.

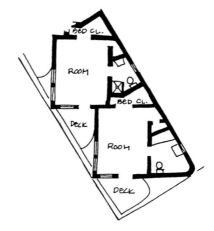

Rectangular with wedge-shaped projections

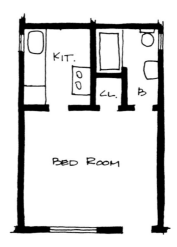

11.10. Typical multispaced unit plan.

or when private outdoor balcony areas were desired.

The first private bathroom (consisting of a toilet, a lavatory, and a shower) was incorporated into the designs in 1938. Prior to that, community shower buildings were generally provided in the courts. During and after 1940, the inclusion of private full bathrooms (usually with showers instead of bathtubs) became the norm.

Multispaced units—usually consisting of a combined living and sleeping space, a kitchen or kitchenette, a private bathroom, and often a second bedroom—were used before and after the war (figure 11.10). However, after World War II, most newly constructed motels included only single-spaced units. The first mention in the literature of including an opening between two units, creating the opportunity for suites, appeared in 1940. This development may have caused the decline in newly constructed multispaced units after 1940, since it was then possible to create multispaced units by combining single-spaced units.

11.11. The linear, enclosed, or clustered unit combinations could take any of these forms, although the number of units provided in each motel was variable.

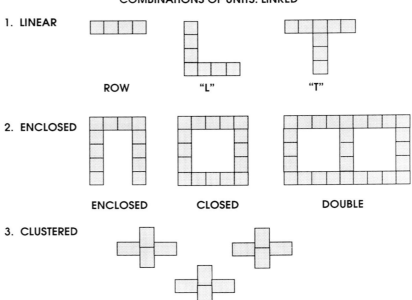

COMBINATIONS OF UNITS: LINKED

1. LINEAR

ROW   "L"   "T"

2. ENCLOSED

ENCLOSED   CLOSED   DOUBLE

3. CLUSTERED

The economical advantages of placing plumbing together were first emphasized after 1945. Both the rectangular and the L-shaped units made it possible to locate the plumbing in common walls. The rectangular unit was less efficient because only two or four bathrooms could be placed together at a time, with all of the plumbing located along an outside wall or in groups of four down the motel's center. With the L-shaped unit, it was also possible to place the plumbing along an outside wall. More popular, however, was the creation of a plumbing core down the center of the motel by interlocking the bathrooms between two units. The rectangle-and-wedge-shaped unit did not allow for the design of common plumbing walls, explaining its added expense.

Combinations of Units

The relationships of the units to each other took two general forms: freestanding units and linked configurations. The freestanding units were placed in both regular and irregular patterns and were considered somewhat unsuitable by the late 1940s when architectural mass was thought more preferable.[17] Undoubtedly, economic factors also led to the freestanding unit's demise.

By contrast, linked configurations were more structured. Three general configurations of links occurred between the units of motels: linear, enclosed, and clustered (figure 11.11). The units in linear links are placed side by side, flush or staggered, in rows. Examples include a single row, a group of single rows, an L-shaped layout, or a T- or Y-shaped configuration. The L- and T-shaped layouts were the most common of the linear configurations.

The enclosed configuration forms courts of at least three sides out of the units. The courts can be open, or U-shaped, or closed, having four sides. Multiple courts, where one court shares a side with at least one other court, were also created. The U-shaped court was by far the most popular type of enclosed motel, although the double court with two courts, open or closed, was a popular alternative. The court arrangement had the advantage of creating a defined community space (unlike the linear and cluster configurations), and this was appealing to the motorist who disliked the ruggedness of the old campground days but yearned for the companionship of fellow travelers.

In clustered configurations, the units were not all connected together. Instead, small groups of linked units were created. Units joined by carports were sometimes combined in clusters of two or four or eight, all of which allowed a covered carport to be near each unit. When multispaced units were used after the war, they most often appeared in clustered layouts as accommodations for tourists needing lodging for several days. Perhaps because of their extended use, a terrace was usually included with each cluster.

Generally speaking, in motels prior to 1940, the units were likely to be freestanding or clustered in groups of two, three, or four. Auto-storage spaces were sometimes used to link the units or clusters together. If linked configurations were used prior to 1940, they were either of the enclosed or cluster type. No linear configurations appeared in the literature up to that time.

During the 1940s and 1950s, all three types of configurations were used, and the layouts ranged from simple to complex. The introduction of multi-level motels and an increase in standardized materials and forms created some simplification of the layouts toward the end of the time period.

Carports or garages were not considered a necessity by 1940, although they continued to be featured occasionally with single- or multispaced linked units. Garages were first alternated between the units. Later, the garages were grouped together. In 1946 the first two-level motel was published. With the advent of this design, garages were commonly located on the ground level of multistory motels, and the units were located above them.[18]

By 1955, literature such as the book *Motels* by Geoffrey Baker and Bruno Funaro discussed the competitive advantages of chain operations, which were subsequently touted as the most advantageous approach to the operation of the modern motel. Most of the motels published in such literature were large-scaled and located in the resort areas of Florida, Texas, and California. The focus in such publications shifted away from the individually operated roadside motel, as it also did in the builder's literature after 1955 and in new motel construction.

Conclusions

Based on a random review of postcards of authentic motels, every category of aesthetic theme and plan configuration established by this study was represented. Only motels that were built as novelties, such as those imitating Indian tepees or Dutch windmills, were found in the postcards but not in the literature. With this exception, the results of this preliminary journal analysis suggests that the built environment has been accurately represented.

The use of postcards for this review had the advantage of occasionally including depictions of interiors as well as exteriors. They were, however, sometimes difficult to date. A more systematic review of postcards or a national architectural survey would more accurately establish the exact distribution of the unit types and plan configurations over time. However, a national survey might also be inconclusive due to a lack of extant intact examples of early motels.

While the unit configurations were easily identified through a review of postcards, the determination of the aesthetic themes was slightly more difficult. The modern, southwestern, rustic, and western aesthetic themes were most easily distinguished. The bungalow and colonial themes were more difficult to distinguish from each other because both are based on domestic designs that bear some similarity. Although the colonial was based on a historic house type, its almost continuous revival in domestic design makes it a familiar, though historic, theme, and one must rely on details such as the use of shutters to determine its presence.

Certain basic differences and general similarities between early and contemporary motels are evident as a result of this study. There seems to be little similarity between the varied configurations of the early motels and the contemporary chain-operated motel. Instead, multilevel, single-row layouts seem to be favored for their economy. In contrast, the basic unit shapes have undergone few changes since the post–World War II era. The use of both rectangular and L-shaped units is evident in contemporary motel design. Convenience and affordability continue to be demanded by the modern tourist. Both characteristics were established for lodging by early motels. Diluted versions of the aesthetic themes that were established prior to 1950 are also applied to contemporary motels, although the themes are more likely to be related to location today, perhaps as an attempt by chains to link themselves with communities to downplay their corporate qualities. Despite these similarities, the popularity of the inde-

pendently constructed and operated motel has become a thing of the past, with few exceptions.

Notes

1. Geoffrey Baker and Bruno Funaro, *Motels* (New York: Reinhold, 1955), 3.

2. For example, see Walter B. Wilkinson, *Profits in Tourist Camps* (Lansing, Mich.: Travel Research, 1940).

3. During the period of 1930–39, the number of published motels was quite low. One or two articles were published per year during the first part of the decade. The mid-1930s provided no information. An interest was again shown in motel design after 1936 when up to three articles per year were published. From 1940–49, there was an increase in the number of published motels, although their appearance was not consistent. The number of articles on motel designs ranged from one to eight during most of the years of this decade. The most consistent publication of motel designs occurred between 1950 and 1955. Publications from each year offered at least one, and as many as ten, motel designs. There was little interest in motel design shown in the publications after 1955.

4. "35 Rental Units in Distinctive Motel," *American Builder* (Aug. 1946):60.

5. Warren James Belasco, *Americans on the Road* (Cambridge, Mass.: MIT Press, 1979), 131.

6. E. L. Barringer, "Tourist Camp Stations Patterned after Dutch Windmills," *National Petroleum News*, 30 April 1930, 105–8.

7. "Roadside Cabins for Tourists," *Architectural Record* (Dec. 1933):457.

8. The March 1942 issue of *American Builder* promoted this alternative use for motels while describing a motor lodge near Hackensack, New Jersey, that was used as temporary housing for persons employed as a result of the expansion of New Jersey's industrial and war work at the beginning of World War II.

9. "Motels Move into the Select Circle," *Architectural Record* (May 1948): 95.

10. Ibid.

11. "Motel Trends," *Architectural Forum* (Feb. 1954): 112.

12. "Grande Vista Tourist Homes," *American Builder* (June 1937): 79.

13. Belsaco, *Americans,* 140.

14. "Here Concrete Helps Solve a Problem," *American Builder* (Mar. 1952):147.

15. "Rustic Cabins and Filling Station," *American Builder* (July 1940):68.

16. E. L. Barringer, "Highway Cabin Camps," *National Petroleum News*, 9 Oct. 1935, 32–34.

17. "Motels," *Architectural Record* (May 1950): 118.

18. "35 Rental Units," 60.

Frank Redford's Wigwam Village Chain

CHAPTER 12

KEITH A. SCULLE

A Link in the Modernization of the American Roadside

The historical process of modernization can explain the development of America's roadside industries. Frank Redford's Wigwam Village motel chain provides a useful case study of modernization. My account of the growth of this chain of visually striking motels relies heavily on oral history and contemporary newspaper accounts, as there are no corporate archives.

Modernization of the Roadside

I use the term *modernization* in this essay to mean the movement toward a way of life resulting from the mass affluence and technologies of the industrial revolution. The contrasting traditional society's essence is a group of small communities, in each of which family and face-to-face communication maintain close cohesion. Modernization results in large-scale relationships of an impersonal nature and has consequences for tourists and businesses that are relevant to roadside industries. Modernization has generated tensions causing tourists to seek collective identities rather than individual autonomy, face-to-face rather than mass communication,

and the unexpected rather than the predictable. For businesses, modernization has led away from small, family-owned operations in local markets toward larger operations, comprised of distinct units managed by a hierarchy of salaried executives, in large geographic markets.

Since the mass consumption of the automobile in the 1920s, automobile tourists have been ambivalent—antimodern in their travel motives, modern in their service demands. The large middle class that swelled the number of auto travelers with the availability of cheap but reliable autos beginning in the 1920s and 1930s had several motives. The most conscious was to escape the tensions of everyday routine, its circumscription to common people, events, and paths at and between home and work. Travel offered an opportunity to break the monotony of modernization's predictability by meeting different people and seeing different places. Escape resulted from the need for individual survival and self-identity in the process of modernization. One unintended benefit of auto travel was the rediscovery of self. Whereas modernization meant specialization in the workplace (resulting from alienation

from the world at large), interaction with residents of the traveler's destination meant interaction with the world and enhanced self-understanding by comparison and contrast with others. Another at first unforeseen benefit of auto travel was the rediscovery of collective identities. Travelers shared their experiences with fellow travelers at their overnight lodging, and family members were thrust together as a unit during their time on the road. And these exchanges were face-to-face, not impersonal products of modernization's mass media. Thus, individuals could overcome their dissatisfactions with the isolation peculiar to modernization by union with a group.[1]

Comfort and convenience, however, were requirements of auto travelers, for which they relied on modern technology. The auto itself was the foremost. The trouble-free, all-weather highway for high-speed auto travel, which required specialized engineering, was another. The comforts of home in the form of hot and cold running water, flush toilets, showers, steam heat, innerspring mattresses, and dependable food completed the traveler's expectations of modern technology at the motel. Roadside

125

entrepreneurs gave their customers what they wanted even in the period of mom-and-pop businesses before the post–World War II era of roadside corporations commissioning sophisticated consumer-satisfaction studies. Consequently, the auto traveler's antimodern quest for adventure was subverted ultimately by his taste for modern comfort and convenience, as previous scholarship has shown.[2]

Redford's Wigwam Villages in Kentucky

Frank A. Redford was born 17 February 1899 in Muncie, Indiana, to a fairly prosperous business family. When he was two, the family moved to rural Hart County, Kentucky. After high-school graduation in Horse Cave, Kentucky, he went to work for the United Fruit Company in Central and South America. He remained with the company for three years and returned home to be with his mother when his father died. Glimpses of his personality derived from rare remarks by several respondents reveal Redford to have been a young boy indulged by his prosperous, single-parent mother, a youth enriched with architectural memories by extensive travel, and an adult who was a loner bearing a vision about his Wigwam Village chain.[3]

Redford began the Wigwam Village in 1933 with the construction of a gas station and lunchroom at Horse Cave, Kentucky, on highway 31E. It was at the heart of Kentucky's cave region, of which Mammoth Cave was the primary attraction. The essence of the tourist destination was nature, not culture. Without conscious intent to make his business a contrasting attraction, Redford nonetheless designed it to have cultural appeal in the 1930s, when many Americans praised pre-industrial life.[4] Redford chose an Indian "tepee" for his lunchroom and gas-station office. In fact, the tepee was a sixty-foot-high steel-reinforced stucco cone. Its sides simulated hide stretched over supporting wooden poles. Its supporting metal rods projected from the apex of the building to simulate extensions of the supporting wooden poles. To capture a sense of Indian design, a zigzag course was painted halfway up the building and repeated on the bottom edge of a cap painted at the tepee's apex. These general lines and form were sufficient to convey the sense of an Indian tepee to the tourist motoring to the cave region. Redford's inspiration derived from popular and folk images, namely, a similarly shaped ice cream shop he saw in Long Beach, California, and authentic tepees he saw on a Sioux reservation in South Dakota.[5]

Customers asked Redford to open a motel at the site. In 1935, he responded by building six smaller tepees (thirty feet high) for cabins or "sleeping rooms," as he preferred to call them. Redford accentuated the setting by flanking the largest original building with men's and women's restrooms in the same stylized Indian motif used for the cabins, and each tepee's entrance was sided in a manner to simulate rolled-back flaps.

Personal satisfaction with the tepee motif most likely explains Redford's persistent use of it, for there were not enough other motels in the area that unusual architecture was necessary to attract business. But Redford's tepees doubtless did arrest the passerby's attention just because they were an unexpected curiosity. They also lured some to stop and lodge there because of their implied message or programmatic value.[6] The tepee's implied message was the promise of simple pleasure. Redford knew it and put up neon signs: Eat and Sleep in a Wigwam (figure 12.1). Many asked if they could do just what the sign invited; and, after their stay, some told the personnel at the motel that they had had fun.[7] Perhaps the fun was in emulating life in another culture, that of the Plains Indian; but this cannot be verified from interviews with those who recall expressions of customer satisfaction when they worked at the Wigwam Villages. An advantage apparent only after taking a cabin for the night was to be experienced in the open, grassy space enclosed between the lunchroom-office and gas pumps on the highway and the cabins in the lot behind them arranged in a semicircle. Here was a suggested community area with an architectural invitation to sit out back and talk with your fellow travelers. Redford was one of those shrewd motel owners who instinctively capitalized on the notion of old-time neighborliness that travelers sought. Like the earlier overnight accommodations that were noted for such comradery, Redford advertised his business as a "camp."[8] He augmented the antimodern setting by displaying Indian artifacts and adding a "trading post." It was a small, four-sided wooden stand added to increase profit through the sale of ice cream, cold drinks, and souvenirs (figure 12.2). In the lunchroom, ten-inch-high menus shaped and decorated like the tepees outside were sold as souvenirs (figure 12.3).[9] Thus, Wigwam Village grew by accretions into an attractive tourist escape (figure 12.4).

Motivated by the modern drive for profit, Redford in 1937 built a second Wigwam Village in a strategic location. It was in Cave City, Kentucky, alongside highway 31W, which the state seemed likely to develop and maintain better than 31E, the alternative access to the cave region beside which Redford had started his chain. Wigwam Village Number 2, as he named it, also was larger: fifteen cabins, a lunchroom seating between twenty and thirty, with flanking male and female tepee restrooms, and gas pumps. These also were arranged in a semicircle around a large grassy area. Instead of a small "trading post," like that at Number 1, Redford built a basement for a large gift shop beneath the lunchroom at Number 2 (figure 12.5). He also used an Indian motif for Number 2's stationery, something that is not documented for Number 1.[10]

12.1. Eat and Sleep in a Wigwam sign at Number 5.

12.2. Isaac Ross in front of trading post at Number 1. The swastika near the top of the teepee was an Indian symbol blotted out in the early 1940s at the Wigwam Villages in Kentucky because of the symbol's adoption by Nazism.

12.3. The inside of Number 1's souvenir menu, which illustrates the extent of the use of the teepee motif.

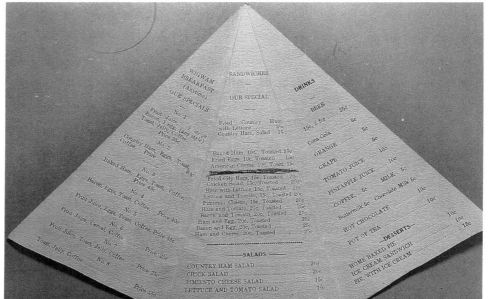

12.4. Oldest known view of Number 1.

12.5. Aerial view of Number 2 on a postcard.

In his two Kentucky businesses, Redford rationalized a system to satisfy the tourist's contradictory yearnings for modern convenience in a traditional setting. Inside insulated cabins with showers, sinks, electricity, and at first gas and then steam heat, Redford contrived an escapist atmosphere. He furnished the cabins with authentic Navajo and Apache rugs and blankets—either bought from catalogs or on trips to Arizona and New Mexico—and hickory furniture, complete with bark, probably from the Columbus Hickory Chair Company in Columbus, Indiana. Hickory furniture, common to western lodges, likely connoted a rustic setting to the tourist. This was accented by knotty pine wall paneling.[11]

Redford also employed Native Americans in authentic costume to clinch the escapist setting. At the Horse Cave location, renamed Wigwam Village Number 1, three young Indian boys were hired to work occasionally before World War II. At Wigwam Village Number 1, Indian dancers from Oklahoma occasionally were employed to perform in the so-called arena, or space encircled by the cabins.[12]

Labor was also used to create the wholesome, modern atmosphere sought by auto travelers. Only the "prettiest, freshest, and brightest, and the most intelligent" lasses in the area were hired to prepare and serve food at both locations. Mrs. Redford successfully recruited the required kind of young woman from reluctant family patriarchs by portraying the propriety of her businesses in contrast to the unsavory local roadhouse image.[13] An unspoken policy of employing young marrieds just out of high school also seems to have been used, perhaps because the young partners' mutual dependence for prosperity assured their industry.

The consequences of these employment practices was a compliant, hardworking, and—in conventional terms—a good-looking group of young adults. Their homogeneity was coupled with the use of uniforms during the early years and must have reinforced subliminally the consumer's assurance of a reliable product (figure 12.6). Perhaps because uniforms are identical, they suggest order. Photographs reveal that men who worked at the gas pumps wore gray Standard Oil uniforms, including caps with visers, shirts, and pants. Other items such as ties and belts were dissimilar and probably came from the men's personal wardrobes. Women wore beige dresses with red decorative rickrack and white aprons and caps. The men were the first permitted to drop these uniforms. By World War II, women at Horse Cave were allowed to replace their stylized Indian garb with conventional white uniforms because poor travel conditions on 31E generated a predominately local trade, which lessened the demand for illusion. The scarcity of appropriate material during World War II also made the uniforms too expensive.[14]

Cleanliness and sobriety, two other elements of modernization, were standards at the Kentucky motels. Mrs. Redford regarded the preparation of food in plain view at Number 2 as certification of its purity. Rooms were kept clean. Drinking was permitted, but not to boisterous excess; and pets were not permitted inside the cabins. These wholesome attributes of Number 2 were published by Duncan Hines, headquartered in nearby Bowling Green, in *Lodging for a Night*. Hines was gratified to find high-quality examples that embodied the high standards he hoped to set for the new mass-automotive travel industry, and Hines and the Redfords became fast friends.[15]

Operation of Redford's Wigwam Village Chain

Redford's Wigwam Village Chain illustrates an intermediate stage of entrepreneurship in the modernization of roadside businesses. Redford's business acumen was more intuitive than rational, never driven by the strongest profit motive, and he responded to public demand. He added a motel to his first roadside business only after others asked for it. He improvised the architectural elements, labor practices, souvenirs, and maintenance standards to convey a special image that suited his taste, not because stiff competition demanded distinction for maximum profit, for there was little competition. It was four years before he patented the exterior design of his tepee (patent D98,617, on 18 February 1936) in response to occasional customers who asked if he might help them start their own Wigwam Villages. Not for three years after acquiring the patent did Redford announce plans to build a chain with other owners.[16] But Redford never promoted his vision. Instead, he waited for prospective owners to approach him.[17] Demand was never great, even discounting the loss of four war years in the patent period that ended in 1950. Only four villages were added by other owners: Number 3 in 1940 in New Orleans, Louisiana; Number 5 in 1940 in Birmingham, Alabama; Number 4 in 1948 in Orlando, Florida; and Number 6 in 1950 in Holbrook, Arizona. Redford himself opened Number 7 in 1947 in San Bernardino, California.

Redford did not pursue infringers, as would be expected of an entrepreneur with visions of a large-scale chain. He reasoned that because he did not sue infringers, he should not collect the annual charge for his patent rights from the chain owners. Apparently, he collected his fee only sporadically.[18]

12.6. Uniformed emloyees of Number 2, including Frank Redford *(second from the right)*.

It is difficult to determine the degree to which the scheme of architecture, labor, maintenance standards, and souvenirs that Redford integrated in Kentucky was implemented throughout the rest of the chain. One must weave a history of Wigwam Village numbers 3 through 7 mostly from interviews with those who opened or are the closest survivors to those who opened them. Some additional facts can be gleaned from newspaper stories and advertisements, street directories, and postcards, but their yield is often irrelevant for investigating the chain.

Redford grasped architecture as the remedy for his customers' modern need for personal communication in escapist surroundings. The one verifiable constant at every Wigwam Village was buildings in the tepee motif enclosing a large grassy area opening to the highway. There were several variations within this layout. Number 4 was arranged in a horseshoe (figure 12.7), and Number 6 was arranged in a rectangle. All others were arranged in a semicircle. Redford himself varied three factors at Number 7. He constructed a large, flat-roofed rear extension to the pivotal office tepee, linked it to the tiny flanking restrooms, situated fireplaces with tables and seats along the edge of the semicircle (figure 12.8), and located four cabins at both highway ends of a second, concentric semicircle (figure 12.9). At every site, the number of cabins varied: three at Number 3, fifteen at Number 5, fifteen at Number 6, nineteen at Number 7, and twenty-seven at Number 4.[19]

An outstanding moral reputation seems to have been the second most important element of Redford's Kentucky operations for the chain. This is clearest in the case of Number 5, on whose owners Redford explicitly impressed the need for clean grounds. Their own sense of propriety was probably a sufficient guarantee to Redford in other regards, for the owners of Number 5 reluctantly sold beer and requested all couples to show their marriage license. It is reasonable to infer from other evidence the demand for conventional moral standards elsewhere in the chain. Number 4 was orderly enough to attract Mr. and Mrs. Elliott Roosevelt, President Roosevelt's son and his wife, as lodgers on 16 November 1951. Number 6's Mormon owners probably satisfied Redford's standards by satisfying their own. Redford probably kept his Kentucky standards at Number 7. The owner of Number 3's dissatisfaction with the decline of standards while he was absent in World War II suggests he may have attempted to enforce Redford's standards during his time.[20]

Redford probably did not believe most other elements of his Kentucky operations to be essential to the chain elsewhere, for no respondent recalls that Redford advocated the pattern he developed in Kentucky for their part of the chain. While it is impossible to determine exactly which aspects of the Indian motif from Kentucky were applied throughout the chain, the following fragmentary reconstruction suggests that no rigid formula was attempted. Whereas all cabins in the chain were furnished with hickory furniture, only Number 4 (figure 12.10) and Number 7 had Indian rugs and blankets. Redford supplied the owner of Number 6 with a mold to make ashtrays in a Wigwam Village design and lamps with a tepee base. Redford apparently used these himself at Number 7. Number 3

12.7. Aerial view of Number 4 on a postcard.

apparently did not use them, and it is not known if Number 4 did. To Number 4, he supplied miniature plaster tepees, which he sold at Number 7. One of the owners of Number 5 recalls that Redford did not urge strongly the need to retain the Indian motif in perishable items. Nor was labor recruited as it had been in Kentucky. Native Americans were not employed outside Kentucky. It is unknown whether the chain owners sought the characteristics Redford did. As for stylized Indian uniforms for waitresses, they were used at Number 3 before World War II. Number 5's waitresses wore a headband with a vertical feather but plain white uniforms from a local supplier. Souvenirs complementing the Indian motif were sold by some members of the chain but not by

others. Miniature ceramic tepees were supplied by Redford to the owners of Number 5, who also used tepee menus like those at Number 1 and stationery like that at Number 2. Napkins with the tepee motif were used at Number 5, but it is not certain if they were used elsewhere.[21]

Demise of Redford's Wigwam Village Chain

Before World War II, Frank Redford significantly helped modernize the American roadside. He was among the first roadside entrepreneurs to discover that the most profitable business was one with an

arresting visual image and wholesome reputation. By 1937 he had integrated the usually separate elements of roadside businesses—architecture, labor, maintenance, and souvenirs—into memorable images at his two Kentucky gas station–motel-restaurants. He also realized that the centrally located communal areas of their settings were therapeutic attractions for the tourist. For this clever but also creative marketing strategy, Redford drew on his own inspiration. Paul L. Young was the only other owner in the chain who approached Redford's comprehension and creativity for marketing an otherwise ordinary set of services as a highly memorable visual ensemble. Young, who owned both Wigwam Villages in Kentucky immediately after Redford (1944–46) and Number 1 again (1946–57), was a traveling salesman of advertising novelties. He introduced handbills that simulated checks, matchbooks, and ashtrays with the tepee motif, which customers were invited to carry away as advertisements for the chain.[22]

As a creative rather than an adaptive entrepreneur, Redford's talents lay in marketing design, not in finance.[23] His purchase of commodities in bulk for distribution to the chain can be substantiated in only two cases.[24] Not only were his chain's owners required to pay a relatively small annual amount, but he did not even collect that consistently. He had faith in voluntary business relationships. His was a referral chain, a voluntary agreement between owners to recommend others in the chain to travelers. Referral chains grew beginning in the later 1930s with organizations like the United Motor Courts, of which Redford's chain was a member of the eastern division.[25] Redford was only one among many to participate in this early trend. The strength of his business relations was in personal and informal relationships. In the serious and hardworking owners

12.8. The campfire facility shown in this postcard view was a variation at Number 7 that emphasized the communal arena.

12.9. Aerial view of Number 7 on a postcard.

12.10. Interior view of Number 4 on a 1948 postcard.

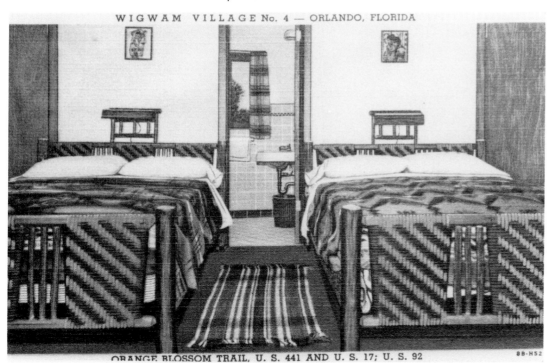

of Number 5 and Number 6, Redford found kindred spirits with whom he became close personal friends. And when Redford grew too sick to manage Number 7, he called his friend Paul Young from Kentucky to carry on.[26] But no corporate structure was established to insure the chain would persist without key individuals. When Paul Young was killed in a holdup at Number 7 in 1961, not entrepreneurs but managers remained as owners.

At this time, further modernization significantly restructured roadside businesses. Huge corporate chains with resort-motels supplanted small-scale operations with antimodern settings like Redford's. Travelers were more diversified. Those seeking to escape modernization did not go on vacations serviced by roadside businesses. To increase their earnings, motels sought travelers who expected modernization's latest indoor comforts, including plush suites, air conditioning, free TV, and swimming pools. They were not content to fraternize with fellow travelers before a night's rest in a tepee. Nor was their satisfaction left to opinions randomly offered by word of mouth to occasionally attentive owners. Instead, mass surveys of consumer opinion became a common means to determine what to offer.[27] Without a corporate structure to respond to the new conditions for successful competition, the Wigwam Village chain went out of business.

Today only three of the seven Wigwam Villages survive. Number 7 remains in business but will be razed shortly because it is no longer profitable. Long-abandoned Number 6 is scheduled for rejuvenation by the family that started it. Presently, Number 2 is the only one with a thriving business.[28] Regardless of their condition, all three have attracted the attention of historic preservationists and architectural proponents of the vernacular as an antidote for modernism. Number 2 was recently listed in the National Register of Historic Places. If James Marston Fitch is correct that historic preservation is a reaction to the alienation resulting from modernization, then historic preservationists' concern for surviving Wigwam Villages helps verify the chain's latest phase in the modernization process.[29]

Notes

1. For further discussion, see Warren James Belasco, *Americans on the Road: From Autocamp to Motel, 1910–1945* (Cambridge, Mass.: MIT Press, 1981), 67–69 and 133; Richard D. Brown, *Modernization: The Transformation of American Life, 1600–1885* (New York: Hill and Wang, 1976), 3–22; Alfred D. Chandler, *The Visible Hand: The Managerial Revolution in American Business* (Cambridge, Mass.: Belknap Press, 1977), 1–12; John A. Jakle, *The Tourist: Travel in Twentieth-Century North America* (Lincoln: University of Nebraska Press, 1985), 2 and 153–54; Philip L. Pearce, *The Social Psychology of Tourist Behavior* (Oxford: Pergamon Press, 1982), 62; and George Ritzer, "The 'McDonaldization,' of Society," *Journal of American Culture* 6 (1983):100–107.

2. Belasco, *Americans,* 173; Warren James Belasco, "Toward a Culinary Common Denominator: The Rise of Howard Johnson's, 1925–1940," *Journal of American Culture* 2 (1979):514–15; Daniel J. Boorstin, *The Image or What Happened to the American Dream* (New York: Atheneum, 1962), 91–92; and Jakle, 185 and 195.

3. Warren I. Susman, *Culture As History: The Transformation of American Society in the Twentieth Century* (New York: Pantheon Books, 1973), 176.

4. Raymond Branstetter (at Number 1, general employee, 1936–42; manager, 1942–45), interview with author, 11 Jan. 1986; Mrs. L. H. Lindsey, Jr., interview with author, 20 Nov. 1986; and Ellis Jones (Cave City resident since 1919 and local historian), interview with author, 2 Aug.1986.

5. Vetra Long (Redford's wife), interview with author, 30 Dec. 1985; *Glasgow Times,* 8 Dec. 1938, sec. 5, p. 2, cols. 1–6. The lunch stand in Long Beach was on the corner of Covina and Fifty-second Place from sometime in the 1920s until it was razed in 1950, according to the Long Beach Historical Society (Loretta Berner, letter to author, Feb. 1986). Several details of the tepee-shaped lunch stand stuck in Redford's memory and were copied by him for the Wigwam Village, namely, rolled "flaps" at the entrance, red zigzag decoration, and small "tepees" as restrooms on either side of the lunch stand. Redford's first roadside business in Horse Cave was a tepee-shaped ice cream shop he opened and briefly operated.

6. Jim Heimann and Rip Georges, *California Crazy: Roadside Vernacular Architecture* (San Francisco: Chronicle Books, 1980), 13.

7. Mrs. Roger Proffitt (co-owner of Number 2, 1953–present), interview with author, 23 Dec. 1985; J. H. Taylor (co-owner of Number 2, 1946–53), interview with author, 26 Dec. 1985; Mae Isenberg (manager of Number 1, 1963–78), interview with author, 29 Dec. 1985; Mrs. L. H. Lindsey, Jr. (co-owner of Number 5, 1940–45), interview with author, 6 Nov. 1986. Mrs. Lindsey recalled the same questions of disbelief by customers at Number 5.

8. Belasco, *Americans,* 137 and 159; *Hart County News,* 26 Nov. 1936, p. 8, col. 7.

9. Long interview; Mary Lois Lockett (waitress, 1941–43), interview with author, 3 Jan. 1986; *Glasgow Times,* 7 June 1934, p. 1, col. 2.

10. The fortunes of 31E versus 31W raged in local politics from the time Redford started his first Wigwam Village. At various times, threats included making only W route 31 and putting a superhighway on W, not E (*Glasgow Times,* 20 Sept. 1934, p. 1, col. 4, and 22 Nov. 1934, p. 1, col. 1). Joe Richardson, the local newspaper editor and publisher, regularly railed against the state highway department for discrimination in favor of 31W and against 31E in maintenance plans (*Glasgow Times,* 26 Nov. 1935, p. 1, col. 8). To lobby for 31E, a group of citizens and merchants along 31E formed the Jackson Highway Association in early 1939 (*Glasgow Times,* 6 April 1939, p. 1, col. 3; *Hart County News,* 21 Sept. 1939, p. 1, col. 1). Information about the stationery is from the interview with Vetra Long.

11. Long interview; *Glasgow Times,* 8 Dec. 1938, sec. 6, p. 2, cols. 3–4.

12. Chief Eagle was the first Indian to work for Redford. He was in charge of the service station and garage (*Glasgow Times,* 9 Aug. 1934, p. 1, col. 2). Chief Whitehorse (*Glasgow Times,* 4 April 1935, p. 1, col. 6), also called Charlie Whitehorse (Vetra Long, letter to author, 26 Jan. 1986), was the next, and he was a service-station attendant. After an illness in Kentucky, he returned for treatment to North Carolina, near his home, but died of pneumonia in early 1935. Several years passed before the third and last Indian boy worked at Number 1. He was Isaac Ross, about seventeen years old, a full-blooded Cherokee from North Carolina, who worked at the "trading post"

before he went into military service in World War II. He was killed in the war (Branstetter, interview; Vetra Long, interview with author, 22 Jan. 1986; and Ruby Gordon Roberts—waitress at Number 1 during the summers of 1938 and 1939—interview with author, 29 Mar. 1986). Information about Indian performances at Number 1 is from Long interview, 22 Jan. 1986; *Glasgow Times*, 27 April 1938, p. 1, col. 8; and 4 May 1939, p. 1, col. 8.

13. Vetra Long, interview with author, 5 Mar. 1986. Joe Richardson, editor and publisher of the *Glasgow Times*, strongly endorsed Redford's management in an editorial, 5 June 1941:

> Frank Redford's Wigwam Villages on US 31-E and US 31-W are fine examples of what good management and good order can do for a business. But, best of all, it demonstrates the fact that a tourist camp can be operated orderly and without those disagreeable things generally associated with tourist camps—that a camp can do this and be a success. Mr. Redford's camps are a model of decency, of cleanliness and of fine service. He will not tolerate misconduct or anything that smacks of indecency at either of his two places of business. And these rules, more than anything else, have contributed to the very deserving success he is making of the Villages. Ladies and gentlemen are always welcome and they can always feel perfectly at home in a Wigwam Village (p. 1, col. 2).

The reputation of two roadside types, the roadhouse and tourist court, as places of sin, including sex, gambling, drunkenness, brawling, and occasional murder, was widely held in Barren and Hart counties, where Redford operated (e.g., *Glasgow Times*, 14 July 1938, p. 7, col. 3; and 18 Aug. 1938, p. 1, col. 3). The opinion was shared enough throughout Kentucky that the state enacted a law in 1938 for county circuit courts to license only law-abiding roadhouses and tourist camps (*Glasgow Times*, 14 April 1938, p. 1, col. 6). Local enforcement lagged. Beginning in May 1939, Joe Richardson regularly editorialized against the failure to enforce the law (e.g., 11 Aug. 1939, p. 1, col. 5; and 17 Aug. 1939, p. 1, col. 3); but

not until ministers and voters united in November 1942 to elect a reform judge were the noncomplying roadside businesses closed in Barren County (*Glasgow Times*, 12 July 1945, p. 6, cols. 4–7; and 21 July 1949, p. 8, cols. 1–8).

Redford's local reputation for decency persisted despite one questionable event, the carbon monoxide poisoning in July 1942 at Number 2 of a newlywed couple by gasoline-powered heaters (*Glasgow Times*, 17 Dec. 1942, p. 2, col. 4). An earlier murder at Number 1 in December of 1935, also did not flaw Redford's reputation (*Glasgow Times*, 19 Dec. 1935, p. 1, col. 7; and 30 Jan. 1936, p. 1, col. 7).

14. Raymond Branstetter, interview with author, 13 Mar. 1986. According to Paul Young's sister, Frances Young Jones, Number 1 became "the social center of the neighborhood." As confirmation, she cited the recollection of a local resident, R. E. Palmore, Jr., that Number 1 was used nightly for croquet contests between neighbors on the grassy area surrounded by the cabins (Frances Young Jones, letter to author, 20 Oct. 1986). Leona P. Young (Paul Young's wife), interview with author, 13 Mar. 1986.

15. *Lodging for a Night,* 4th ed. (Bowling Green, Ky.: Adventures in Good Eating, 1941), v–xi and 122; Long interview, 22 Jan. 1986. Advertisements for beer sales at Number 2 contradict the recollection that Redford prohibited drinking altogether, but he kept a careful watch. (For Number 2, see *Glasgow Times*, 8 July 1937, p. 3, cols. 1–2; and for Number 1, see *Glasgow Times*, 20 Aug. 1942, p. 2, cols. 1–3.) For example, when two customers waiting for dinner at the restaurant talked about their enjoyment of alcohol, Redford refused their order (A. P. Young, Jr., Paul Young's brother, interview with author, 23 Dec. 1986).

16. In return for building specifications for the "tepees," which were beyond the capacity of most contractors, and the provision not to open a Wigwam Village within one hundred miles of another, a Wigwam Village owner annually was to give Redford one-half of one percent of the profits from food, lodging, and souvenirs, co-operate with other owners in the chain, advise customers to patronize other places in the chain, and keep their places in an "exceedingly sanitary and high class manner" (*Glasgow Times*, 17 Aug. 1939, p. 1, cols. 4–5).

17. This is confirmed for Number 3 by its first owner (Frederick O. Rudesill, interview with author, 23 May 1986); for Number 5, by one of its first co-owners, Mrs. Lindsey (6 Nov. 1986 interview); and for Number 6, by the wife of the first owner (Mary A. Lewis, interview with author, 25 April 1986). No one was available to interview about the inception of Number 4.

Two other members of the chain were considered but never built. The earliest would have been in 1939 with Paul F. Miller of Luray, Virginia (*Glasgow Times*, 17 Aug. 1939, p. 1, col. 3), and the last would have been in 1946 with Paul L. Young in Portland, Oregon (Leona P. Young, letter to author, 15 Feb. 1986).

18. The annual fee was never collected for Number 3 (Rudesill interview). One-half of one percent was collected from the owners of Number 5 during their ownership, 1940–45 (Lindsey interview, 6 Nov. 1986). The fee for Number 6 was supposed to come from coin-operated radios in the cabins, but this was not collected because too little was earned from the radios (Lewis interview). Two surviving letters by Redford to Lewis, however, suggest that Lewis may have paid some fee (Redford, letters to Chester Lewis, 5 July 1955, and 4 April 1956). No one was available to interview about payments for Number 4.

According to the Redfords, infringers would have included The Wigwam Lodge in Tempe, Arizona (see J. J. C. Andrews, *The Well-Built Elephant and Other Roadside Attractions* [New York: Congdon and Weed, 1984], 12–13), and another motel in either Virginia or West Virginia (Long interview, 30 Dec. 1985). The DLD Tepee Motel in Hastings, Nebraska, was copied from the Wigwam Village in Holbrook, Arizona, in 1953, after expiration of Redford's patent. See Keith A. Sculle, "Nebraska Notes," *Society for Commercial Archeology News Journal* 3 (Spring 1986):12.

19. More were intended at Number 3, but the owner's recall to military service in August 1940 interrupted construction. After World War II, the additional cabins were not built because business was bad (Frederick O. Rudesill, interview with author, 6 April 1986).

20. Lindsey interview, 6 Nov. 1986; *Orlando Sentinel,* 16 Nov. 1951; Lewis interview; and Rudesill interview, 23 May 1986.

21. Redford apparently did not recommend to the owners of Numbers 3 and 6 that the Indian motif be kept

(Rudesill interview, 23 May 1986, and Lewis interview). However, he did advocate the motif be kept by the owners of Number 5 (Lindsey interview, 20 Nov. 1986).

The Indian furnishings are verified in Numbers 4 and 7 by postcards—Curt Teich 88-H529 and Tichnor Brothers 85686, respectively. Other aspects of the Indian motif are discussed in the Lewis interview; Rudesill interview, 23 May 1986; Allan B. Waggener, postcard to Frank Redford, 10 Dec. 1948; Lindsey interview, 20 Nov. 1986; and *The Carbuilder* (Aug. 1944):22.

22. Leona P. Young, interviews with author, 1 Feb. and 13 Mar. 1985.

23. For distinctions between types of entrepreneur, see C. Joseph Pusateri, *A History of American Business* (Arlington Heights, Ill.: Harlan Davidson, 1984), 6–7.

24. Redford furnished Indian jewelry from Cherokee, North Carolina, for Number 5 (Lindsey interview, 20, Nov. 1986) and Ivory soap with the chain's name for Number 6 (Frank Redford, letter to Chester Lewis, 21 Feb. 1950).

25. *Glasgow Times,* 19 May 1938, p. 1, col. 6; Chester H. Liebs, *Main Street to Miracle Mile: American Roadside Architecture* (Boston: Little, Brown, 1985), 185.

26. Leona P. Young, interview with author, 1 Feb. 1986; and letter to author, 15 Feb. 1986.

27. Belasco, *Americans,* 170–73; John A. Jakle, "Motel by the Roadside: America's Room for the Night," *Journal of Cultural Geography* 1 (Fall/Winter 1980):43–46; Jakle, *Tourist,* 195; and Liebs, 186–88. For an example of the trend to consumer surveys, see Herbert K. Witzky, *Modern Hotel-Motel Management Methods,* 2d rev. ed. (Rochelle Park, N.J.: Hayden Book Co., 1976), 224–42.

28. Number 3 was the first to go out of business. That happened in 1954 (Collin B. Hamer, Jr., head of the Louisiana division of the City of New Orleans Public Library, letter to author, 18 Feb. 1986). Number 5 went out of business in 1964, the year of its last listing in *Polk's Birmingham City Directory* (Richmond, Va.: R. Polk and Co., 1965), 228 and 1,243. Number 4 was razed in 1974 (Jeff Kunerth, "Mileposts in Memory," *Orlando Sentinel,* 29 July 1986, sec. E, p. 4). Number 6 closed for business in 1974 but was left standing (Lewis interview). Number 1 was razed in 1981 (Mae Isenberg, interview with author, 2 Aug. 1986).

29. Advocacy of the Wigwam Village as part of the general vernacular critique of modernism is exemplified by Andrews, xii. Roger A. Brevoort (architectural historian, State Historic Preservation Office, Arizona), in a letter to Mary A. Lewis, 26 April 1988, and David L. Morgan (state historic preservation officer, Kentucky), in a letter to the author, 11 April 1988, illustrate the commitment of official state historic preservationists to their state's parts of the chain. James Marston Fitch, *Historic Preservation: Curtorial Management of the Built Environment* (New York: McGraw-Hill, 1981), 404.

Of Motorcars and Movies

CHAPTER 13

MAGGIE VALENTINE

*The Architecture of
S. Charles Lee*

Richard Hollingshead, the inventor of the drive-in theater, declared that the two things Americans would give up last were the automobile and the movies. Both were products and symbols of the Machine Age, and the relationship between them is both physical and symbolic. Each offered escape from the pressures of urban life, one literally and the other figuratively. The architecture of the motion picture theater in the first half of the twentieth century reflected this relationship and was in part shaped by automobile consciousness. This is best exemplified in the work of S. Charles Lee, one of the most prolific and creative motion picture theater architects of the 1920s, 1930s, and 1940s. His work celebrated and embraced the automobile by accommodating, imitating, and finally incorporating it into the design of the building. His cinemas adopted a dashing modern style and character in response to the primacy of the car, utilizing the lines and materials of the automobile. Parking lots were included as a part of the architecture, and both the graphics and the building were directed toward motorists instead of pedestrians. He also experimented with drive-through and drive-in theaters, which in-

vited the automobile itself into the theater.

S. Charles Lee was born in Chicago in 1899, the son of a traveling salesman, who taught him a respect for entrepreneurship.[1] He developed his artistic and mechanical talents at a vocational high school and in his bedroom workshop. At Armour Institute (later Illinois Institute of Technology), he studied art, architecture, and engineering, receiving an education shaped by an Ecole des Beaux Arts approach to all three disciplines. After graduation, Lee found employment with the Chicago architectural firm of Rapp and Rapp, who specialized in elaborate movie palaces.

Lee left Chicago in 1921, the year he received his architectural license, to travel to California in a car he built in his parents' apartment. He decided to stay in Los Angeles, a city in large part shaped by both the automobile and the movies, and opened a general architecture practice downtown. He spent the next several years acquiring modest commissions and important connections, his early work devoted primarily to single-family residences and hotel-apartment buildings throughout the city, always with a theatrical flair. By 1927 he was also

designing movie theaters.

Like the first automobiles, the first movie theaters had been boxy, black, and built to house a function previously unknown and hardly imaginable prior to its creation. Only after automobiles and motion pictures had reached a state of technical maturity did design become a conscious marketing feature, as both car manufacturers and theater operators discovered that product distinction through style was a marketable commodity. In the 1910s and 1920s, architects designed increasingly elaborate movie palaces of two thousand to six thousand seats. They employed elaborate exaggerations of neoclassical and exotic motifs that recalled cultural landmarks and fantasies of Europe, Egypt, and the Orient. These were places most Americans had read about but never seen. Now their glamor, previously available only to kings and potentates, could be experienced firsthand in a democratic setting. Described as "an acre of seats in a garden of dreams,"[2] each theater competed in opulence with the last in an effort to attract customers. Concurrent with 1920s automobile design, plain, monotonous Model T–type theaters gave way to styled Model A's and culminated in the grand, flamboyant Cadillacs of movie palaces and cathedrals.[3]

Flamboyance was a key principle of the Depression-era movie palace. For example, in 1927 Lee designed the Tower Theatre in Los Angeles (figure 13.1), a nine hundred–seat movie palace squeezed onto a fifty-foot lot. The elegant sculpture, painted ceiling, and stained glass windows were designed to give the movies the connotation of upper-class culture and to make such opulence and culture accessible to all classes. As with most movie palaces, its period revival style drew on historicist references and focused on intricate detail and ornament, which gave the building a static, staccato rhythm, best understood on a pedestrian scale. Located on a main shopping thoroughfare, which served as a theater district for the city, the detailing invited close attention and careful viewing. It slowed and delighted the eye, luring the customers inside to the lobby, where a graceful staircase and crystal chandeliers imitating Garnier's Paris Opera awaited them.

While Lee always considered himself a modernist, he also freely "borrowed from the church"[4] to combine art and entertainment in a format otherwise available only to the wealthy. The reigning style for commercial architecture during the 1920s was period revival, and movie-theater owners capitalized on fashion. Lee's philosophy was that the architecture should be a part of the entertainment. It should please the customers and, in turn, serve the client by returning a profit on the investment. Period revival style was for Lee a means, not an end; it was an applied decoration. Even Art Deco, considered modernistic, was applied with the traditional gusto and heavy-handedness of the period revivals. It was a modern ornament that replaced Renaissance motifs with an abstract geometric vo-

13.1. The Tower Theatre was typical of downtown movie palaces in its staccato rhythm, intricate detailing, and dark, small marquee oriented toward the pedestrian. Automobiles of the 1920s matched the bulky, boxy buildings in this rendering by S. Charles Lee.

13.2. Black and silver dominated the Art Deco interior of the Fox Wilshire Theatre as theatre owners competed with one another for the most fashionable and modernistic look.

cabulary, as seen in the interior of the Fox Wilshire Theatre (Beverly Hills, 1929) in figure 13.2. Motion picture theaters always sported the newest, most fashionable designs. They evolved from complex period revivals to sleek Deco and Streamlined Moderne but were never without ornament. Theatricality required decoration, but it was increasingly integral to the structural lines and less an applied motif. At the same time, however, Lee was rethinking the configuration of interior spaces and adding innovations, including air conditioning, restaurants and nurseries, and substantial ground-floor space to be leased to commercial businesses.

Movie palaces were downtown showcases for first-run movies, as downtown was traditionally the center of the city and cultural events. However, parking became a serious problem with the increased reliance on personal transportation in the 1920s. The studios began to commission first-run theaters in the newly developing suburban residential neighborhoods of the late 1920s, served by private automobiles rather than public transportation. This new link between the automobile and the theater was quickly exploited by creative architects. The West Coast, which ranked highest in cars per capita, was one of the first areas to adopt large park-

ing lots adjacent to the theater.[5] Ample parking, a major marketing advantage of the suburban theater over its downtown counterpart, was advertised in lights along with the latest feature.

Film production companies had begun acquiring theaters in the 1920s, establishing theater chains that carried the name of the studio that was the parent company. Each theater in the chain would only show movies produced by that studio, establishing exclusive first-run policies. Fox West Coast, a subsidiary of Fox Film Corporation, commissioned Lee to design a number of suburban movie houses in the 1930s, including the Fox Florence Theater (Los Angeles, 1931).[6] Stylistically, this theater embodied many of the characteristics of a movie palace, but certain innovations distinguished it from its predecessors. The pedestrian entrance to this Spanish Colonial Revival theater led to a courtyard surrounding a tiled fountain, while another arched entry covered a driveway that led past the patio to free auto parking in the rear (figure 13.3). Providing convenient access to safe parking encouraged drivers to go to the movies on impulse and certainly lessened the chance of losing potential customers who could not find a place to park. The Fox Florence marked the beginning of Lee's "drive-through" theater designs, which invited the patrons into the building even before leaving their cars.

The marquee was always the most important and distinctive part of any movie theater. The Bruin Theater (Los Angeles, 1937) marquee in figures 13.4 and 13.5 proclaims, "This is a movie theater; this is the Bruin Theater; and we are currently showing *Tucker*." The name frequently described the location as well, in this case adjacent to the University of California at Los Angeles campus. It also created a visual landmark, extending outward from the facade so that the building stood out physically

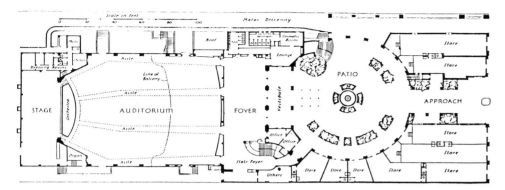

13.3. In Lee's design, drivers entered the Fox Florence through a porte cochere and drove past the central fountain and courtyard, where they could deposit passengers, to a parking lot at the rear of the building.

13.4. By the mid-1930s the marquee had evolved from a dark, square sign attached to the building into an integral architectural element, large and colorful, aimed at the motorist instead of the pedestrian, as seen in the Bruin Theater.

13.5. The Bruin Theater marquee, which wrapped around the corner of the building, was the facade, especially at night with its patterns of flashing lights. The message became the architecture, defining the form and purpose of the building.

and aesthetically from all the others on the street. In the 1910s and 1920s, marquees were dark, flat, delicately decorated sources of detailed information (see figure 13.1), but during the 1930s, designers and showmen transformed them into what Ben Hall has called "electric tiaras."[7] They were bold and bright, outlined in moving lights known as "flashers" and "chasers" that danced in windshield reflections. A comparison of figures 13.4 and 13.5 demonstrates how the marquee redefined the building at night through light and shadow instead of mass and volume.

What started as a mere sign to announce the film had grown to envelop the entire facade. The horizontal band of light that wrapped around the corner of the Bruin Theater recalled a chrome bumper and headlights, and could be seen from approaching streets in four directions. Located in a busy theater district, the sign made the building stand out from its competition as a thousand square feet of coordinated colored lights blinked in harmony. The message constituted the architecture; the walls had virtually disappeared. Lee capitalized on the value of this huge "billboard" as an advertising medium, realizing that it far exceeded that of newspapers in attracting customers.[8]

13.6. The Lyceum Theater, a typical period revival theatre when it was built about 1920, looked dated a decade and a half later before remodeling. The marquee, set at a right angle to the facade, with its small letters on a dark background could only be read up close.

13.7. Lee designed a modern box office and marquee for the Lyceum Theater in 1936, making the otherwise unretouched building look modern in a typical Depession-era, low-budget remodeling. The large marquee angled toward the street used larger graphics on a light background so that it could be read from moving vehicles.

During the Depression, Lee was commissioned to modernize many older theaters, often on a very limited budget. The Lyceum Theater (San Francisco, ca. 1920) appeared to have a new, modern facade after it was remodeled by Lee in 1936. In fact, the only changes were a new box office and marquee (figures 13.6 and 13.7). The marquee was angled toward the street instead of the sidewalk, making its backlit letters and shorter messages easier to read from a moving car.

The importance of visibility and publicity was extended to include the vertical sign as well. Neon-outlined beacons announcing the name of the theater were discernible up to ten miles away. The 130-foot tower of the Academy Theatre (Inglewood, California, 1939) featured a neon spiral (figure 13.8), described by Lee as a "traveling lightning bolt," that could be seen from airplanes landing at Los Angeles International Airport. Neon block letters spelled out "Academy" on one side and "Preview" on the other. These alternating messages were visible only at night when unveiled by a descending streamer of neon that slid down to the marquee.

In the mid-thirties, movie theaters borrowed a design ethic known as streamlining from automobiles and other transportation machines, including ocean liners, railroads, and airplanes. Lee received his pilot's license in 1933, and his interest in aerodynamics fed his search for new and original architectural images (figure 13.9). Streamlining, introduced by engineers and industrial designers, permeated the Depression decade. Wind tunnel studies showed that a parabolic curve offered the least resistance to a solid moving through air or water, thereby increasing its speed and efficiency. The Chrysler Airflow, introduced in 1934, was the first mass-produced streamlined automobile. The technique was applied by industrial designers in the 1930s to every conceivable kind of product, including those that did not require wind tunnel resistance, such as pencil sharpeners and radios, but desired the status associated with speed, efficiency, and modernism.

Lee applied this style to movie theaters, such as the Academy with its curved line and spiral motif. It was a visually dynamic aesthetic that attracted the attention of passersby, especially motorists. Interestingly, the streamlined car was less successful than the streamlined theater, which had no practical use for speed. Automobile designers and historians have suggested that the Airflow's styling was too extreme to be popular.[9] It violated industrial designer Raymond Loewy's MAYA principle—giving the public the "Most Advanced Yet Acceptable." Chrysler projected people into the future instead of previewing it at a level of acceptable risk. But at the movie theater, one could borrow from the future and escape for an afternoon without making an embarrassing, permanent investment.

13.8. As the neon light slid down the spiral of the tower, it spelled out the name of the Academy Theatre. The smooth, flowing lines of this streamlined theater contrasted with the period revival movie palaces of the 1920s.

13.9. Lee stands next to his streamlined Beach Craft airplane. Architects borrowed the streamlining motif developed for transportation machinery by industrial designers in the 1930s, and with it, the promise of progress represented by such twentieth-century technology.

The style's swooping lines, horizontal emphasis, and sleek veneer projected the image of modernism, the promise of the twentieth century. "Speed lines"—the horizontal bands of thin parallel lines, like the trail left by a speeding object in comic strips, seen on the wheel guards in figure 13.9 and on the De Anza Theater (Riverside, 1939) in figure 13.10—added to the illusion of movement. Automobiles and cinemas even used the same machine-made industrial materials of steel, glass, and chrome tubing—hard, shiny, slick surfaces that were novel and modern. Streamlining was a new conception of integrated design, in which the outer shell was a sleek line that incorporated all of its parts into a deliberately designed object. This was in contrast to the previous functional approach, in which the accidental shape was the sum of its necessary parts attached where they needed to be and then decorated with applied ornamentation. (Compare the smooth lines of both the buildings and the automobiles in the 1927 rendering of the Tower Theatre [figure 13.1] with the angled lines of both in the 1939 photo of the De Anza Theater [figure 13.10]).

13.10. Streamlining was applied by Lee to the design of the De Anza Theater in the rounded corners, horizontal band of windows, and the lack of applied ornament on the sleek, curving facade. The style connoted the speed, efficiency, and modernism associated with automobile, airplane, and ship designs in the 1930s.

13.11. Streamlining was used on the interior of the Tower Theatre. Curved seats, rounded walls, and chrome tubing framing the smart, etched-glass mural gently pull the customer toward the auditorium. Rather than announcing the entry, they create a sleek set design in which the ticket-holder is an actor, not just a witness.

Streamlined Moderne styling also was used for interiors. The sleek lines and undulating walls as well as the etched-glass mural in the Tower Theatre (Fresno, 1939) suggest a set from a Fred Astaire and Ginger Rogers musical (figure 13.11). The movie-goer literally enters this fantasy world, extending the romance and escape from the screen to the lobby.

Vertical theater signs, heretofore separate metal attachments that hung on the front of period revival or classical facades, evolved into pylons of neon, stucco, or Vitrolite that flowed "naturally," if obtrusively, out of the lines of the building's structure, like the automobile tailfins of the late 1950s (figure 13.12). Round porthole windows, glass block walls, and spirals provided images of speed, cleanliness, and modernity. Designs were increasingly futuristic and sports car–like. Even the box offices were symbols of the experience, not just ticket booths, although they resembled transportation vehicles more likely found in the pages of science fiction (figure 13.13).

Everything about these buildings expressed modernism and elegance. The image of speed and efficiency was a common thread in the 1920s and 1930s that linked people's optimistic hopes and belief in the future with their contemporary experiences. Streamlined movie theaters were concrete and steel symbols of an elegant life-style unavailable to previous generations and limited in the rest of life to those people who were on the other side of the movie screen.

Lee had continued to refine the drive-through feature first used in the Fox Florence Theater until it was perfectly and functionally integrated into the marquee (figure 13.14). The marquee formed a porte cochere that covered the parking entrance and the box office. Motorists purchased tickets from

13.12. The vertical sign of Lee's 1942 Fremont Theatre in San Luis Obispo, California, was a stucco and neon pylon that emerged from the facade.

13.13. Box offices, such as this designed by Lee in glass and aluminum for the Academy Theatre, were architectural gems. They captured in miniature the uniqueness, glamor, escape, and futuristic imagery of the theater itself.

their cars, and passengers exited directly into the lobby. The driver then parked the car free in a well-lit lot next to the building. Lee recognized and designed to accommodate an essential truth of the twentieth century: that the automobile was an extension of the driver, not merely a means of transportation. The American automobile was a symbol of leisure and affluence, and motoring was an end in itself. Like the drive-in, the drive-through acknowledged the importance of the motoring experience as pleasure, not necessity, and allowed for the smooth transfer of amusement without having to reject one for the other.

The drive-in theater was introduced by Richard Hollingshead in 1933 in Camden, New Jersey, but reached its peak of popularity by the mid-fifties. In 1944 *Motion Picture Herald,* a trade magazine for theater owners, accurately predicted a construction boom, anticipating the following postwar conditions:

1. The joy of being released from gasoline rationing.
2. The availability of all-beef hot dogs.
3. Resumption of normal restrictions upon the amorous impulses of youth.
4. Need for fresh air after years of propaganda.

13.14. With the 1947 Arden Theater in Lynwood, California, Lee incorporated the automobile into the architecture with his drive-through marquee.

13.15. At drive-ins, including the Edwards, the automobile was recognized as both customer and architecture. Motoring and movies were no longer in competition as leisure activities.

. . . The drive-in will grow, some—but as a social phenomenon reflecting the average American's inability to decide which he likes better, the movies or automobile riding. A drive-in theatre permits him, at one and the same time, to get a little of each.[10]

These reasons reflect an attitude shaped by wartime conditions rather than the postwar perspective of building families and suburban neighborhoods, but the magazine was right about the growth of drive-ins. They multiplied in the United States from 102 in 1945 to over 4,000 a decade later.[11]

Lee designed several drive-ins, including the Edwards Drive-In Theatre (Arcadia, California, 1948) in figure 13.15. The screen formed a windswept parallelogram angled away from the street, making it easier to read as a signboard, while the marquee formed an acute angle toward the street, reaching out to passing traffic. Both gave the illusion of speed and movement. Lee's rendering of the Ventura Drive-In (ca. 1949) indicated the futuristic direction of both the automobile and the life-style it engendered, as predicted by the architect (figure 13.16).

The drive-in theater was the ultimate automobile architecture. Motorists no longer needed to leave their cars at all; the parking lot replaced the building in importance. The cars themselves became the form, providing the shape, color, line, and structure of the space. Traditional architectural ornamentation was reduced to an overscaled hood ornament, found on the back of the screen and in the box office. Its primary purpose, however, was still to pull customers in from the highway and give the theater definition and distinction.

The drive-in was a social phenomenon as well as a business. It successfully combined public and private life during a period in American history that

13.16. In his sketch of the Ventura Drive-In, Lee emphasized speed and clean, modern lines. A comparison of the role of automobiles in this sketch with that of pedestrians in figure 13.1 suggests the change that had taken place from the late twenties to the late forties.

was trying to strengthen both. Families could watch movies together and talk, fight, sleep, or kiss without disturbing others. But at the same time, they were interacting with other people in their cars. Nostalgia in the 1980s for the rapidly disappearing drive-ins produced the American Classics Drive-In in a converted warehouse in Manhattan—probably the world's first walk-in drive-in. Customers arrived on foot or by cab, paid $5.00 per person ($7.50 on weekends), and parked themselves in thirty-six vintage convertibles to watch movies from the fifties.[12]

In the early 1950s, Lee retired from architecture to pursue a career as a developer when he foresaw

major changes in film exhibition techniques. Television began to cut into box office receipts and became the new, modern entertainment medium. In 1948 the Supreme Court had ruled that the movie studios' ownership of movie theaters constituted an illegal monopoly. As the studios divested themselves of their theater chains and monopoly on first-run movies, the demand for flagship theaters vanished. Independent exhibitors discovered that the real money in movie exhibition was to be made in selling popcorn. To increase candy sales, designers focused on getting people *out* of the theater, eventually eliminating any amenities that encouraged them to linger. The economy car–approach resulted in stark and efficient multiscreen theaters usually swallowed up by shopping malls. The theater facade disappeared entirely; its only remaining vestige was a plastic, backlit sign—which could hardly be called a marquee—listing the names of up to eighteen movies to be found inside the mall.

Lee's architecture summarizes an important sequence in the evolution of the American motion picture theater as a distinct building type. His signature trademarks and innovations—including terrazzo sidewalks, use of light as an element of design, exotic box offices, and expressive ornament—became characteristic of all motion picture theaters by the 1950s. His spatial manipulation created a sense of wonder that invited exploration and gave the ticket buyer a feeling of power and elegance. His concept of design, motivated by the psychology of entertainment, produced urban stage sets that included the user as a part of the architectural experience.

Lee successfully merged commerce with art and engineering with architecture to produce a unique product that defined its era. His lasting contribution can be found in how his work served the client, the customer, and the city. He stayed within budget and saw the commission as an investment that demanded a return. Customers, treated to convenience, comfort, and glamor, thus returned on a regular basis. The city skyline was enhanced with graceful, sculptural pieces that created visual and social landmarks.

From 1920 to 1950, when Lee was designing movie theaters, automobile ownership in the United States increased fivefold, from 8.1 million to 40.3 million.[13] Automobiles symbolized personal freedom and bestowed on their owners independence and status. At first glance, they would appear to have been in conflict with the movies as a medium of entertainment. But Lee and other movie-theater architects minimized the conflict by adapting theater design to complement the car. Like the automobile, the movie theater embodied the essence of twentieth-century values: technology, speed, efficiency, and newness.

Notes

The author gratefully acknowledges the cooperation of the staff of the Department of Special Collections, University Research Library, UCLA, which houses the Lee Collection, and Mr. Lee, whose generous and candid conversations made this project possible.

1. Biographical information from conversations with author and from Maggie Valentine, *The Show Starts on the Sidewalk: An Oral History with S. Charles Lee* (University of California at Los Angeles Oral History Library, 1986).
2. Ben Hall, *The Best Remaining Seats: The Story of the Golden Age of the Movie Palace* (New York: Bramhall House, 1961), 93.
3. A definitive history of the motion picture theater as a building type from the arcade parlor to the multiplex has not been published, but pieces of the story have been told. See "Film Spaces," *Design Quarterly* 93 (Minneapolis: Walker Art Center, 1974), and David Naylor, *Great American Movie Theaters* (Washington, D.C.: Preservation Press, 1987).
4. Conversation with author, 14 Feb. 1984.
5. Helen M. Stote, ed., *The Motion Picture Theater: Planning; Upkeep* (New York: Society of Motion Picture Engineers, 1948), 38.
6. Fox West Coast Theaters Corporation became a subsidiary of Fox Film Corporation in 1925, reorganized in 1935 as Twentieth Century Fox. By the 1930s, Twentieth Century Fox was one of the "Big Five," an oligopoly that controlled production, distribution, and exhibition. In 1948, the Justice Department ordered the breakup of these vertical organizations, declaring that the integration of the three levels of the movie industry violated antitrust laws.
7. Ben Hall, "The Crown Jewels," *Marquee* (June-August 1970):6.
8. Valentine, *Oral History*, 65.
9. See Walter J. Boyne, *Power Behind the Wheel: Creativity and the Evolution of the Automobile* (New York: Stewart, Tabori and Chang, 1988), 119; Donald J. Bush, *The Streamlined Decade* (New York: George Braziller, 1975), 118.
10. "Post-War Growth of Drive-In's," *Motion Picture Herald Better Theatres*, 1 April 1944, 71.
11. *Film Daily Yearbook*, 1946, 1956.
12. Kelli Pryor, "A Night at the Drive-In," *New York*, 9 May 1988, 35.
13. John B. Rae, *The American Automobile: A Brief History* (Chicago: University of Chicago Press, 1985), 238.

4

ROAD AND
STREET

The Death of the Street

CHAPTER 14

RICHARD INGERSOLL

The Automobile and Houston

During the 1920s, the presence of 24 million automobiles in the American urban environment had social and spatial consequences so drastic they would redefine the concept of human freedom. The right to mobility became a national preoccupation and appears to have superceded previous concerns for the right to assembly guaranteed by the First Amendment. The figural space of the traditional street, which for hundreds of years had been the locus of public life and the theater for human ritual, was brutally disfigured by the congestion, noise, and pollution of the automobile. The appalling statistic of 32,500 auto-related deaths per year, reported in 1930, was a clear indication that the street was no longer a safe place for community activities.[1] Equally shocking was the aggressive demeanor of traffic and the anxious competition for parking, which led to rapid mutations in the form of the street. The gutting of the urban core for increased traffic and parking, along with the sprawling expansion of suburban residential districts that could now be reached by the automobile, led to the radical atomization of urban space. The traditional street was literally driven to its death by the prepossessing ambitions of the automobile.

Since that time, American consciousness has been saturated by two verbs, the Ur-words of daily life, *to drive* and *to park;* they have replaced the primary gestures of social intercourse that once gave identity to urban streets. Driving may indeed have become the key to American existence, as our principal form of identification is the driver's license. Parking, while not as specifically ontological, does challenge our being, not just because it is so difficult to find a parking space in the city but because it presents a semantic paradox. Although the origins of the term refer to leaving one's vehicle in the park, the current meaning connotes the negation of the park, as trees have been uprooted to make on-street parking and areas that might have been better saved as green spaces have been paved over as parking lots.

Planners and city officials, pressured by the demands of the automobile, and usually complicit with its conquest of the city, acquiesced during the 1920s to a new creed, "the city practical rather than the city beautiful."[2] Although some of their utilitarian adjustments were enhancements to the street, such as traffic signals, crosswalks, and efficient illumination, the general trend was to lose sight of individual urban spaces in the effort to conceive of a greater whole governed by the imperative of circulation. The street was even suppressed from the language of planning in favor of the sort of biologically inspired vocabulary used by nineteenth-century engineers that spoke of urban spines, arteries, and lungs. Design interventions were thus described as surgery rather than art.

One of the greatest would-be surgeons of the city was the French architect and automobile enthusiast, Le Corbusier. Recognizing in the mid-1920s that automobiles had made the Parisian streets unsafe for the pedestrian and that traffic congestion had made it impossible to get anywhere on time, Le Corbusier pronounced one of his famous jeremiads: "Il faut tuer la rue corridor" ("We must kill the corridor street").[3] This typically uncompromising solution, a brazen call for urban euthanasia, was accompanied by an alternative vision of the city, with elevated superhighways, high-speed interchanges, and freestanding skyscrapers set at great distances from each other in parkland. The Ville Radieuse, as

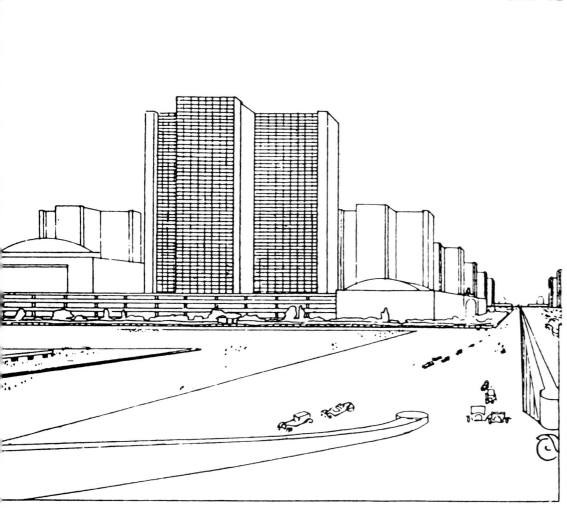

14.1. Detail of Le Corbusier's "Contemporary City for Three Milion Inhabitants" (1922) matched with a view of Houston's freeway 610 loop at the Post Oak–Galleria area. Ironically, Le Corbusier's vision for a highly planned city without corridor streets was realized in Houston, a city that developed without coordinated planning or zoning.

he renamed his ideal city in 1935, was totally planned and totally zoned, using the automobile as the lowest common denominator of human need. Le Corbusier's utopian vision, while unacceptable in its authoritarian premise, was not so far removed from the mentality of pragmatic American planners and businessmen and was a prescient scenario of what unfortunately occurred in most American cities after World War II.

The shredding and loosening of the urban fabric, in which the percentage of paved surfaces came to outnumber greatly that of built-on or green spaces, has transpired both with and without the help of urban planning. To blame the wholesale destruction of American downtowns during the urban renewal of the 1950s and 1960s on Le Corbusier, however, is to give him far too much credit. An extreme example of eviscerated urban space can be found in Houston, Texas, where a zoning code has never been enacted and municipal planning has been inconsequential.[4] This adventure in environmental anarchy has had the de facto regulation of two technological dictators: the automobile and air-conditioning. The issues of mobility and controlling interior space have had clear precedence over those of architecture and urban space. The gaping pattern of the rebuilt and newly built parts of the city presents such porous fabric that it is hard to imagine that there had ever been corridor streets in Houston. For the history of urbanism, it constitutes a significant watershed, comparable to the straight streets of papal Rome or Haussmann's boulevards in Paris: Houston is the first major city without streets. It has loops, freeways, feeder roads, parkways, super blocks, and residential blocks, but little that approximates the enclosed urban spaces of the traditional street. The uncanny resemblance of parts of Houston to Le Corbusier's Ville Radieuse has been fre-

quently noted,[5] the irony being that instead of issuing from an authoritarian planning agency, it has occurred nearly spontaneously, the Darwinian adaptation of motorized humanity.

Although Houston is commonly portrayed as the shameless product of free-enterprise greed and absent civic intentions, there is no denying that the quality of life, the ease of parking, and the efficiency of circulation are higher than in other cities of its size. Nor is Houston uninteresting from an aesthetic point of view: it has a great many buildings of distinction, especially from the last two decades; it hosts an effulgent growth of live oaks and subtropical flora; and, in its sudden juxtapositions of scale, use, and type, it has invited a fantastic surrealist undercurrent that dazzles one with constant surprises. Regardless of what it looks like, the success of Houston, which rose from a small city at the beginning of the century to become the fourth largest in the nation in the 1970s, is evidence supporting the contention that freedom of mobility has become more important than freedom of assembly.

Current efforts around the country to salvage existing streets, or to revive the form of traditional streets, have been inspired by aesthetic and social motives. In reaction to Modernist visions of architecture as freestanding sculpture, a new appreciation for congruency with the urban context has been bred among architects by the treatises of Robert Venturi, Rob and Leon Krier, and Colin Rowe. The results in practice can be found from coast to coast, from Jon Jerde's pop-medieval fantasy at Horton Plaza in San Diego (1984) to the pseudo-Venetian canal walk at Las Colinas near Dallas (Harwood K. Smith Associates, 1984) to the promenades of Rowe's Wharf in Boston by Skidmore Owings and Merrill (1988). At Johnson and Burgee's PPG Place in Pittsburgh (1984), the human

14.2. Las Colinas (near Dallas, Texas), the canal walk (1984). A simulated Venetian canal created a pedestrian zone between vehicular roads and ordinary parking structures.

scale of the piazza and the arcades are accompanied by the willingness to adjust the volumes of the project to the scale of neighboring structures. The attempt to render parking lots more figural by using paved paths and sensitive planting is a positive step to putting the park back into parking. In Baltimore, the Fells Point district has been established as a preservation zone, and the central boulevard lined with restored Victorian facades has been revived as a thriving market square. Seaside, Florida, a new town built around the idea of the traditional nineteenth-century town to the plans of Elizabeth Plater-Zybeck and Andreas Duany, is a further demonstration of what these designers have termed the "conservative revolution" in urban design.[6] This change in sensibility was heralded by Jane Jacobs's convincing argument in the early 1960s that vital street life was the key to community security. With few exceptions, however, both the preserved street and the revived street have been marketed with intense nostalgia, resulting in disappointing simulations of the pre-automobile city rather than genuine expressions of modern community. The contradiction of these preindustrial images for postindustrial occupants is that they do not usually comprehend the transcending value of mobility; no matter how folksy we pretend to be, the automobile still rules.

If we are to accuse the automobile for the death of the street, we should make some effort to identify the victim. The concept of the street as a designed entity was first recognized—or more properly, rediscovered—in the urban statutes of such twelfth- and thirteenth-century mercantile republics as Bruges in northern Europe and Siena in the south. Codes for the design and maintenance of paved areas and facades served to protect public space from the obstructions of balconies and external stairs, while encouraging fire safety and hygiene; the codes also promoted an urban aesthetic. At the end of the fourteenth century, the partial widening of via Calzaioli in Florence, with its stone-revetted elevations and regular arches, shows a clear application of these codes.[7]

In papal Rome, which inherited Tuscan planning practices, the cultural identity of the street also became an instrument of policy for the state. New straight streets, such as via Alessandrina in 1500 and via Guilia in 1508, required substantial demolitions and expropriations. By carrying the name of their respective patrons (to be followed by Leonina, Clementina, Paola, Gregoriana, and Sistina), they celebrated papal authority while supplying public utility. The width of these streets never exceeded thirty feet—quite wide when compared with the average ten-foot widths of medieval streets, but insubstantial when compared with Houston's original 1836 grid of seventy- to eighty-foot widths. Circulation, an obvious criterion for the military control of the city, was usually mentioned in terms of ritual purposes. The greater declared purpose of the straight street was as a structuring device for palace architecture, providing a new sense of order, decorum, and well-being. The continuous elevations of Renaissance streets gave them a three-dimensional formal unity, or figural coherence, recapitulated in the perspective stage-set designs of Peruzzi and Serlio. When, in the late sixteenth century, new streets were planned for unsettled territory within the Aurelian walls of Rome, they were required to have high-perimeter walls, even if the site was unbuilt, to give the street a clear sense of bounded, figural definition.[8]

Although the cultural unity of the street might have been used to promote a regime, it could also pose a threat to the security of the state. The Parisian revolutions of 1830, 1848, and 1871 were fought on barricades built through neighborhood solidarity. Baron Haussmann's system of boulevards, begun in 1852 and averaging two hundred–foot widths, were the engineer's solution to circulation, hygiene, and building speculation—they were also the politician's antidote to barricades.[9] The Parisian boulevard, while unquestionably an excellent place for a promenade and an aesthetic triumph as landscaping, constituted the first major threat to the life of the street as a figural and social unit; the bold, broad strokes broke down the scale of the street, producing spaces that were too open for community appropriation. As Rimbaud commented, Haussmann's Paris had become the locus for "these millions of men who do not need to know one another."[10]

Paris at the turn of the century, due to the advanced state of its bourgeoisie and the superior conditions of its roads, was the prime market for the nascent automobile industry.[11] Thus, with the drastic example of Haussmann behind it and the future traffic congestion ahead of it, Paris was ripe for being rethought in relation to the automobile. The first great urban theorist to accept the automobile as the new module of modern life was Eugène Hénard, the urbanistic progenitor of Le Corbusier. Hénard was the architect for the city of Paris and published his spatial and architectural prognostications during the first decade of this century. His city of the future called for the separation of pedestrians from vehicles and included complex traffic interchanges, layered roads, and subterranean garages, along with various ways to break up perimeter facades and bring more light into apartment buildings. His architectural recommendations for jogging frontage lines, while respectful of the scale of Paris, would have contributed to the erosion of the spatial unity of the street. Lacking the power of Haussmann, however, his ideas remained at the level of polemics.[12]

When, in 1907, the United States surpassed France and all other nations in automobile production and consumption, it also inherited the mantle of urgent traffic management. The automobile contributed to a wider range of housing locations, but the subsequent decentralization of the urban population led to greater vehicular congestion in the center. The Ford revolution in production and marketing of automobiles between the years 1908 and 1914 was the single most important factor in intensifying traffic. Automation brought the price of the Model T down from $950 in 1910 to $350 in 1917: sales increased 1,000 percent to 350,000 per year.[13] It is quite clear that the success of Ford in making the automobile a mass-consumer item was the greatest single cause of the street's demise, as it allowed most classes of the population the option of private transportation.

In New York City by the 1920s, traffic had reached alarming proportions. In conjunction with the Regional Plan Association, the Manhattanist architects—in particular, Raymond Hood, Harvey Wiley Corbett, and Hugh Ferris—proposed alternative urban patterns to accommodate, as Rem Koolhaas has so brilliantly phrased it, "a culture of congestion."[14] Hood's "City of Towers" (1927) called for skinny, freestanding skyscrapers with increased setback space at their bases, eventually leading to the erosion of continuous street elevations. Corbett's schemes showed a complex layering of traffic, with pedestrians sent to open arcades on the top level, slower traffic on the middle level, and faster traffic at the bottom level. His vision, a version of which was realized in full scale by Norman Bel Geddes for the General Motors Futurama of 1939, was for a "very modernized Venice, a city

of arcades, piazzas and bridges, with canals for streets, only the canals will not be filled with water but with freely flowing motor traffic, the sun glittering on the black tops of the cars and the buildings reflected in the waving flood of rapidly rolling vehicles."[15] While defending the figural aspect of the street in the most romantic terms, the split-level solution continued the erosion of street space in the vertical dimension. In opposition to the densifying schemes of the Manhattanists, another group, led by Clarence Stein and Lewis Mumford and calling itself equivocally the Regional Planning Association of America, promulgated a decentralized solution derived from Ebenezer Howard's Garden Cities. The Manhattanists accomplished their ideal of multiple levels and increased density, along with significant production of figural space, at Rockefeller Center; the garden-city group achieved their streetless utopia in 1927, at Radburn, New Jersey, sixteen miles from Manhattan.

Radburn became known as "the town for the Motor Age" and has had an immense impact on subsequent suburban layouts. The guiding principle was to create a place where nuclear families could raise children away from the horrors of the urban environment. Subdivided into three superblocks, with the fast traffic confined to its perimeters, the houses were placed on internal cul-de-sacs. The principal facade of each house was on the rear of the building facing the greensward, a communicating backyard, with paths extending the length of the superblock. Children were kept away from the dangers of the streets by eliminating the streets altogether. Underpasses carried the children from green space to green space without them ever having to cross the road. This wilful elimination of the street also coincided with a curtailing of political rights: Radburn was not an incorporated city but was gov-

erned by a board of directors that did not include residents. Though intended as an independent, low-density, mixed-income town, Radburn quickly became an affluent suburb, with 87 percent of its residents in 1933 commuting.[16] It is yet another bit of evidence for the thesis that mobility gained priority in the scheme of democratic rights.

During the 1930s, transportation in the region of New York City was reorganized to facilitate automobile egress mostly through the organizing skills of Robert Moses. Over the course of forty years, this tyrannical planner implemented a series of parkways, high-speed interchanges, and outer beltways that became the model for the rest of the world, replacing models of public transit. The traffic artery became a thing unto itself, an independent design type, free of the confining walls of the traditional street. Along with the skyscraper, the concrete and steel structures of the highways are America's most original contribution to architectural history.[17]

Houston, which in 1929 had a greater proportion of automobiles to people than New York City, faced similarly egregious problems for circulation and parking. Unlike the island of Manhattan, where street life is still quite viable, Houston, which is not geographically confined, has met with little resistance to the domination of urban space by the automobile. Like Los Angeles, Houston had an extensive network of streetcar lines, which allowed residents before the advent of the automobile to live within a five-mile radius of downtown; since the completion of the freeways (1942–72), the radius has been multiplied by five, and the city's territory is currently equal to about 550 square miles.[18] Main Street was once the focus for civic ritual, shopping, and entertainment. During the 1920s, it also became the chief funnel for traffic and the site of the first electric traffic signals and of the first parking

154

14.3. Houston's Main Street, ca. 1920. The streets were shaded with arcades and deep awnings for the comfort of pedestrians; street cars served areas within a five mile radius of downtown.

14.4. The ABC Store (1928). This early shopping facility on the edge of downtown Houston was much admired for its ample parking lot.

restrictions. While new automobile-oriented building types such as the parking garage and the gas station began to gnaw at the continuity of downtown streetscapes, retail businesses were beginning to relocate to the edge of downtown. The ABC store (a grocery "stoa," 1928) by the distinguished architect William Ward Watkin was located at a distance of one mile from the center of downtown and was clearly denied any engagement with the street. It was generally admired for the size of its parking lot.[19] Other shopping centers were located near the new suburban developments: the River Oaks residential tract, planned by Herbert A. Kipp in 1923, after the success of Country Club Estates in Kansas City, had a small adjacent shopping area (since demolished) bordered by a double row of drive-up parking. During the next four decades, most of the downtown retail outlets either relocated or went out of business; only Foley's, which built its own garage in 1949, remains.[20] In 1951 there were over one hundred shopping strip centers, and since the opening of Gulfgate in 1956, a dozen regional shopping malls at the major freeway intersections have followed, including the Galleria. The Galleria was developed as a luxury shopping district by Gerald D. Hines from 1967 until the present. Its air-conditioned interior mall, roughly half a mile in length, has absorbed many of the functions of Main Street, having a higher concentration of shopping, entertainment, hotels, and restaurants than anywhere else in the city. In some ways, this privately owned, climate-controlled concourse is like the traditional street, but it completely lacks the unpredictable interchanges of the street, not least to mention the exercise of First Amendment rights.

Houston's downtown was left strictly for big business, government, and official culture, such as the opera. The new pattern that emerged with the

Cullen Center of 1963 was for high-rise complexes to be built as insular enclaves set back from the street with their own parking structures and connected to other buildings either by underground tunnels or elevated walkways. Thus the street elevations have either disappeared with the setbacks of the high-rises or have become opaque with the impermeable walls of parking structures. Instead of entering a building from the street, one is now delivered into its core from the garage or the tunnel. Retailing and all of the elements that contributed to the formal and social continuity of the traditional street have been introverted in Houston, and people's paths have either been relegated below grade or into the air, where they can be airconditioned.

The automobile killed the life of the streets that existed in downtown Houston and elsewhere, and in its quest for speed and good parking prevented the reproduction of the traditional street type as the city expanded. With it has perished the setting for community life and the sense of *civitas,* or civic responsibility. In an age when less than 50 percent of the citizens vote in national elections, and even fewer in local elections, we should not be surprised that the right to assemble and exercise First Amendment rights is such a low priority. It is only hopeless romantics prompted by nostalgia who seek the revival of the human-scaled street; their simulations of urban space are addressed to the consumer as sanitized versions of the past, bereft of real public life. While the form of the traditional street may be successfully evoked as an aesthetic construct, the reality of such a street will not materialize until people have outgrown their dependence on the automobile and the great desire for privacy and individual gratification it supplies. And there are some clear signs of such a change of heart: referenda for

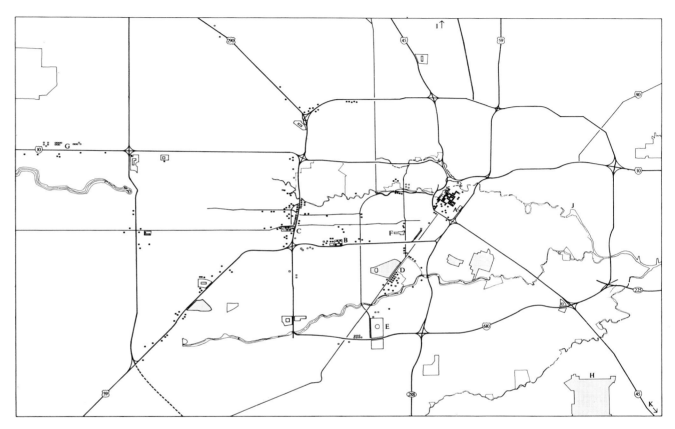

14.5. Map of Houston (1989), showing how widely major commercial development has ranged. The black squares represent buildings of over ten stories; A is the downtown, C is the Post Oak–Galleria area.

light-rail mass transit in both Los Angeles and Houston have been approved by the voters and are awaiting implementation.

As the automobile killed the street, we drivers experienced a kind of *omertá* (the refusal to bear witness): we can't really blame the automobile since we want and need to drive it ourselves, and in many cases we have no alternative. Ultimately, how we decide to live is a question of political consciousness: if and when mobility ever becomes as much a drag as voting currently is, we can begin to project the true revival of the street.

Notes

1. Mark Foster, *From Streetcar to Superhighway: American City Planners and Urban Transportation, 1900–1940* (Philadelphia, 1981), 101–11. In a recent article in *Time* (12 Sept. 1988, 52–60), Stephen Koepp reports there are 181 million automobiles in the U.S.A.

2. Mark Foster, "City Planners and Urban Transportation: The American Response, 1900–1940," *Journal of Urban History* 5 (May 1979):379.

3. Le Corbusier, *Précisions sur un état présent de l'architecture et de l'urbanisme* (Paris, 1929), 169.

4. Peter C. Pappademetriou, *Transportation and Urban Development in Houston, 1830–1980* (Houston, 1982). A comprehensive city plan was commissioned from Arthur C. Comey in 1913, with some minor results; the activity of a city planning office has been erratic ever since, and currently, privately funded groups, such as Central Houston Inc., are having more of an influence than government planners. In 1929 the first zoning proposal was made; this and all successive zoning legislation has been defeated. Only in 1986 were timid setback laws affecting commercial properties instituted as the first step to zoning.

5. John Kaliski and Peter Jay Zweig, "Houston: How and Why?" *Texas Architect* (Sept.-Oct. 1984):42. In the same breath, most observers also liken Houston to Wright's Broadacre City.

6. Philip Langdon, "A Good Place to Live," *Atlantic Monthly,* March 1988, 39–45; Benjamin Forgey, "Harking Back to Our Town," *Washington Post,* 11 June 1988, p. C4.

7. Giovanni Fanelli, *Firenze, Architettura e Città,* vol. 1 (Florence, 1973), 93.

8. Richard Ingersoll, "The Ritual Use of Public Space in Renaissance Rome" (Ph.D. diss., Univ. of Calif. at Berkeley, 1985), 64–83.

9. Anthony Vidler, "The Scenes of the Street: Transformations in Ideal and Reality, 1750–1871," in *On Streets,* ed. Stanford Anderson, 29–111.

10. Quoted in T. J. Clark, *The Painting of Modern Life* (Princeton, 1984):23.

11. James Laux et al., *The Automobile Revolution: The Impact of an Industry* (Chapel Hill, N.C., 1982), 3–15.

12. Eugène Hénard, *Études sur les transformations de Paris* (1903–1909), ed. Jean Louis Cohen (Paris, 1982). Excerpts published in English in *The American City* 4 (Jan. 1911):27–31.

13. Laux, 54.

14. Rem Koolhaas, *Delirious New York* (New York, 1978).

15. R. A. M. Stern et al., *New York 1930* (New York, 1987), 39. Folke T. Kihlstedt, "Utopia Realized: The World's Fairs of the 1930s," in *Imagining Tomorrow,* ed. Joseph J. Corn (Cambridge, 1986), 107. Kihlstedt discusses Bel Geddes's revival of Corbett's model.

16. Carol A. Christensen, *The American City and the New Towns Movement* (Ann Arbor, 1986), 58–67.

17. Marshall Berman, *All That Is Solid Melts Into Air: The Experience of Modernity* (New York, 1982), 290–312.

18. Pappademetriou, *Transportation.* For the 2.8 million population in 1980, there were 2 million automobiles.

19. Katherine Pollard, "Houston Provides for Shopping on Wheels, in *Civics for Houston,* Jan. 1929, 6.

20. Peter Pappademetriou, *Houston: an Architectural Guide* (Houston, 1972), 14. In 1940 70 percent of doctors, 76 percent of engineers, and 30 percent of architects had offices downtown; in 1963 14 percent of doctors, 24 percent of engineers, and 10 percent of architects were located downtown.

Chicago Architects and the Automobile, 1906–26

CHAPTER 15

R. STEPHEN SENNOTT

Adaptations in Horizontal and Vertical Space

In 1908 the Ford Motor Company introduced the Model T, "a car for the multitude" that transformed the fundamental requirements of American urban streets and their contiguous buildings.[1] The Model T was mass-produced between 1908 and 1927, when commerce and population in Chicago quickly multiplied, and when the city's business streets were increasingly burdened by too many tall buildings and too many vehicles.[2] Yet early photographs of Chicago School skyscrapers, showing empty business-district streets, neglect to show how automobiles and other forms of urban transportation clogged urban streets and created critical spatial problems.[3] These views also neglect to reveal how the automobile and it spatial consequences directed some Chicago architects to reorganize horizontal and vertical spaces to accommodate the automobile. Between 1906, when the Merchants Club (later the Commercial Club) commissioned the Chicago Plan, and 1926, when Wacker Drive and the adjoining Jewelers Building were completed, Chicago's architects and engineers were commissioned to provide practical solutions to the remarkable spatial and circulation requirements of the automobile.

Their remarkable solutions appeared early in the nascent automobile culture, and their design schemes have ever since affected Chicago's buildings and streets. In particular, architects in Chicago proposed new and effective concepts for street design that addressed circulation requirements for thousands of automobiles; more importantly for the history of buildings, they adjusted interior plans to permit established building types to function in new ways to satisfy the automobile driver.[4]

To integrate the automobile within the urban spatial framework, architects reformulated the existing relationship between the building and the street. Whether street or building, each had to be sympathetic to the practical necessities of the other to serve the automobile. Addressing simultaneously the large scale of the urban grid and the situated scale of the individual building, Chicago architects designed across horizontal planes that defined interior space and directed streets, as well as along the vertical axis that defined multistory buildings or bi-level street systems. Overcrowded streets, traffic congestion, and a severe lack of parking space threatened to outweigh the automobile's benefits.

These drawbacks required urban planners to modify systems of streets and bridges, electrical and mechanical engineers to design new machines, and professional architects to modify the interior spaces of established building types. As architects and urban planners were asked to merge the needs of automobile drivers with conventional street design and established building programs, they frequently discovered that revised planning strategies provided effective solutions. These strategies were exhibited in comprehensive civic plans and private building programs.

Chicago's business leaders, civic planners, and architects were frustrated and fascinated by the unprecedented spatial and social consequences that accompanied motorcars over the Chicago River into the congested business district. In response, the Commercial Club in 1906 commissioned architects Daniel Burnham's and Edward Bennett's Plan of Chicago, a comprehensive scheme designed to incorporate civic buildings, open parks, and public transportation systems.[5] In the years following the Plan's 1909 publication, clients often hired architects to design traditional urban building types, which conformed to conventions of scale and image established in the Plan or earlier. Thus, buildings designed during the early years of the automobile often appeared unaltered from the outside. But when these conventional building types were required to accommodate the automobile, clients and architects decided to alter interior plans and programs, often radically. Similarly, as architects reshaped interior spaces to accommodate automobiles, developers selected commercial sites made more profitable by their borders adjacent to primary automobile thoroughfares. It seems to me that what emerges from this complex design response of architects and clients to the automobile are two patterns of use that significantly determined Chicago's automobile culture and its related architectural and urban landscape. Denoted by the private automobile club, one purpose appears restrictive and private, available to a select group; denoted by the Michigan Avenue bridge, another purpose appears unrestrictive and accessible, available to a diverse urban community.

Automobiles shaped social and spatial meaning as early as the 1890s, beginning in Chicago with Germany's demonstration of a Daimler motorized road carriage at the World's Columbian Exposition in 1893. But Transportation Day at the Exposition[6] excluded the motorcar from a parade that began with mules and ended with carriages and bicycles; nonetheless, by 1900 Chicago's small but exclusive group of motorists had promoted America's first automobile race,[7] established in 1895 America's first automobile club (the American Motor League), initiated the magazine *Motocycle,* and hosted several annual automobile exhibitions over the next decade. From 1895 to 1910, Chicago's central business district changed drastically in density as population, vertical office space, and automobile use increased.

What did not keep pace with this expansion was the available horizontal space in the business district. Initially, Chicago's business leaders believed motorized vehicles improved commerce and commuting, but restricted horizontal space soon made preexisting street systems and building types wholly inadequate.

15.1. View looking north at State and Madison streets in Chicago's central business district, about 1911. In cities like Chicago, hundreds and then thousands of mass-produced automobiles filled streets originally planned for smaller numbers of horse-drawn carriages and streetcars.

Across Chicago's architectural and automobile grid in the years around 1900, patterns of automobile use first emerged as private and inaccessible. This exclusivity was expressed in the private automobile clubhouse.[8] Chicago's early automobile owners were frequently the socially prominent and wealthy families who purchased motorcars for pleasure, social prestige, sport, or reliable private transportation. Late in 1899, Chicago's wealthy motorcar owners were numerous enough to establish a separate association, the Chicago Automobile Club (CAC). Described as a "social organization," the Chicago Automobile Club in 1902 set out to sponsor reliability runs, help secure reasonable legislation for automobile use, and promote highway improvement.[9] Before 1908, bankers and industrialists often perceived motoring as a sport, listing "automobiling" as a recreational activity alongside golf and tennis in Chicago's social directories.[10] In the same pages, a citizen's prestige was measured by memberships with the fashionable private clubs, including the Calumet Club, Union League Club, or the Chicago Athletic Club. Acknowledging the social meaning tied to club memberships, Chicago Automobile Club officers selected two buildings for their club that they believed would convey the exclusivity associated in the early 1900s with automobile ownership. Paralleling the automobile's evolving prestige, they chose in 1902 an existing mansion converted to a hotel. In 1906, when their exclusive identity was more widely recognized, they commissioned an architect to design their own fashionable club.

The Chicago Automobile Club was located first in a four-story Italianate mansion and former hotel situated along South Michigan Avenue (figure 15.2), a wide public thoroughfare favored by motorists for its straight and unimpeded road surface.[11]

Although the club was formed in 1900, low membership and ineffective leadership prevented significant growth. But apathy ended in 1902 when members refurbished this domestic building as a club that "probably excels all others in the world." In less than six months, membership had more than doubled, due to the appeal of the club's impressive facade and luxurious interior rooms. Still, the club's domestic image, made explicit outside by the dormers and veranda, did not quite match in unparalleled splendor the wealthier and more exclusive urban clubhouses of Chicago, such as the 1893 Calumet Club.[12] In short, the CAC's building appeared more like a house than a club. Lower floors

included a billiard room and dining rooms to suit the club's social needs, and upper floors contained bedrooms for resident members. The clubhouse's small automobile repair shop and storage station were attached at the rear and indicated the club's initially small number of devotees. The automobile had not yet become a necessity for transportation, but it certainly was associated with private wealth and exclusivity. Because the automobile, still relatively expensive in 1902, so instantly granted social status to its owner, Chicago motorists soon wished to acquire the appropriate architectural status symbol: a private clubhouse.

15.2. Architect unknown, 243 South Michigan Avenue, the location of the Chicago Automobile Club in 1902. With a front veranda and mansard roof, this mansion more closely resembled domestic structures than other elegant and private clubs in Chicago.

CLUB HOUSE AND STORAGE STATION - REPAIR SHOP IN REAR.

15.3. Marshall and Fox, Chicago Automobile Club, 321 Plymouth Court, Chicago. The colonial facade and classical ornament evoked the prestige and exclusivity associated with private clubhouses in New York.

The automobile's prestige in Chicago was marked in 1907 when, as a result of increased membership, the Chicago Automobile Club moved into its newly completed and exclusive clubhouse (figure 15.3).[13] The elegant building was commissioned in 1906 from one of the club's members and second vice presidents, Chicago architect Benjamin Marshall (1874–1945), in partnership at the time with Charles Fox (1870–1926).[14] Located away from Michigan Avenue in the midst of Chicago's private club district, Marshall and Fox's colonial-style, redbrick building, in its fenestration and materials, resembled several prestigious Chicago residential apartments and hotels designed by the firm. The automobile club's symmetrical facade and classical detailing reflected the lasting impact of the Columbian Exposition as well as Marshall and Fox's preference for inventive classical ornament. Resembling a preestablished private clubhouse type, the automobile club's colonial facade also paralleled in elegance and proportion several clubs and urban residences designed in New York by the well-known architectural firm of McKim, Mead, and White.[15]

However closely in exterior image and scale the club conformed to conventional standards for private clubhouses, Marshall and Fox's automobile club was fundamentally altered in program and interior plan (figure 15.4). The clubhouse had six floors, each with interior spaces set aside specifically for automobile service or storage. At street level, club members asked for two entrances, one for pedestrians and one for automobiles. Above first-floor storefronts, the architects arranged a lounge with a balcony overlooking the street, a kitchen with men's and women's cafes, and sleeping chambers with closets. Adopting the clubhouse to automobile owners like themselves, Marshall

and Fox laid out interior spaces at the rear of each floor for automobile use, combining automobile garage and social functions in one interior space. Laid out specifically to allow for automobile storage and repair, these interior spaces included a small wash rack and abundant garage space, the latter equipped with a lift and turntable for directing vehicles. Inside, the plan accommodated the automobile; outside, the facade was, like the automobiles within, a "blatant crier of surplus wealth"[16] and expressed the club's restrictive and elite pattern of automobile use. Yet in Chicago and other American cities, this elitism was short-lived.

By 1908, Ford, Olds, and others were manufacturing and selling thousands of affordable and reliable automobiles and making the private automobile available to a larger public. Concurrently, however, these growing numbers threatened to strangle the efficiency of major business districts.[17] In Chicago, where rapid growth had already led to overcrowding and congested traffic, Daniel Burnham and Edward Bennett were commissioned in 1906 by Chicago's influential business leaders to restore and improve their city's business functions and express Chicago's civic achievements. The Chicago Plan was finished in 1909. The Plan's colored renderings were exhibited internationally and were published with an informative text, written by the architects and distributed by the Commercial Club.[18] Assimilating architectural programs with street plans, the Commercial Club's comprehensive plan was designed to improve commercial facilities, ease transportation of people and commercial goods, correct acute traffic circulation problems, and reestablish order and convenience in the central business district. In their plans, the architects wished to expand the metropolitan park system, restructure the city's railroad terminals and tracks, improve commercial and transportation facilities along the lakefront and the Chicago River, provide a coordinated system of streets and highways within the city and out to the suburbs, and finally, promote coherent architecture that was sensitive to key sites along major avenues or waterways. Within these broad guidelines, the architects specifically addressed perceived current and future requirements of the automobile, such as convenient circulation, sufficient parking space, and a diversified system of streets, so that "the city may be made an efficient instrument for providing all its people with the best possible conditions for living." The comprehensive civic plan addressed public needs of access rather than private needs of a few motorists. Not surprisingly, many sponsors of Burnham's plan were also Chicago Automobile Club members who commuted daily by automobile. Due to its supporters, the Plan inspired or guided nearly every large-scale civic building, public park, or transportation project well into the 1920s. But traffic congestion only grew worse.[19]

Assuming Chicago would only expand, Burnham and Bennett provided a spacious and accessible scheme dedicated to a public pattern of use. Modeling their civic ideals in part after plans for European cities, the architects were dedicated to classical traditions of symmetrical planning, monumental scale, and coherence of parts. For automobile owners, in particular, the Commercial Club and their architects recommended a large and coherent system of modern bridges, streets, and parking facilities; a system of encircling highways to unite suburbs with the city center; and an ordered arrangement of streets within the city limits to improve traffic flow. Streets and the bordering buildings were nearly inseparable. For Chicago's architects and building interests, the Plan provided

inspiring images of modern buildings, harmonious in design, scale, and proportions, and unified along broad avenues and boulevards (figure 15.5). From the end of World War I to the late 1920s, Chicago's commercial district was transformed by a sustained building boom. Several architects accommodated their designs to Burnham's and Bennett's recommendations for public streets and bridges, private office blocks, and railroad terminals. Fortunately, Bennett served from 1913 to 1930 as chairman and chief consulting architect for the Chicago Plan Commission, a power-packed group of politicians and businessmen who promoted Chicago's new program of civic and commercial development.[20] Bennett's influential position helped to assure that the city's subsequent architecture and streets were consolidated under the Plan's recommendations.

Because railroads continued to contribute so significantly to Chicago's strength as a commercial and transportation center, Burnham and Bennett recommended several new railroad terminals at strategic points along the boundary of the central business district. But by 1909, the siting of a modern railroad terminal would necessarily incorporate planning criteria for easy access by auto, truck, and taxi traffic. In 1914 Graham, Burnham, and Company began planning Chicago's Union Station (figure 15.6), a complex, multilevel passenger station that originally consisted of two separate buildings: a spacious passenger waiting area and a train concourse, which were connected by a passage beneath Canal Street. The train terminal serviced two separate sets of tracks, one running north and the other running south. Passengers reached modern communication and transport facilities by means of a coherent system of graded streets, ramps, and distinct spaces. Opened in 1925, the station remained unmatched for passenger convenience and efficient

handling of baggage, due in part to the multilevel arrangement along horizontal and vertical planes of separate passenger and train service areas (figure 15.7).

15.4. Chicago Automobile Club, first floor interior plan. Members could drive their automobile directly through the building to a garage and lift in the rear.

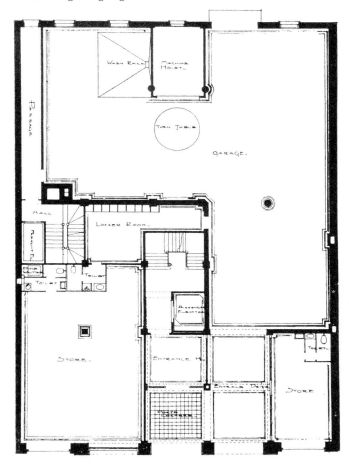

First Floor

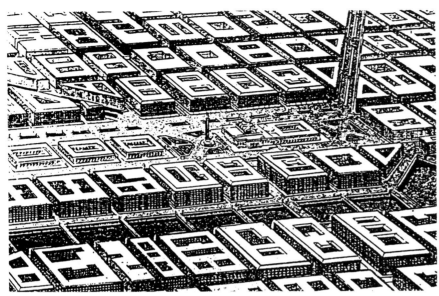

Probably modeled in image, scale, and expression after McKim, Mead, and White's 1911 Pennsylvania Station, Union Station was adapted specifically in plan to the requirements of automobiles. Whereas the preexisting terminal building type served passengers and trains, a modified type, significantly altered in plan, was required to serve the automobile culture as well. To accommodate hundreds of taxicab drivers and private chauffeurs that daily arrived and departed with thousands of train passengers and their baggage, the architects in Chicago incorporated features of the street within the terminal's plan in order to alleviate heavy traffic and make the building serviceable to automobiles and the surrounding streets (figure 15.8). The architects designed ample interior ramps and driveways, located behind the terminal's north and south walls,

15.5. Detail from "Railway Station Scheme West of the River Between Canal and Clinton Streets, Showing the Relation with the Civic Center." The Civic Center, not shown in this detail, was located southwest of the proposed railway station. The arrangement of broad boulevards and streets was intended to reduce traffic congestion around the railway station.

15.6. Graham, Burnham and Company, Union Station, Chicago, 1914–25, exterior view. From the outside, the conventions of the established building type disguise the inventive interior plans that incorporated heavy automobile traffic and often kept the streets as unclogged as they appear in this 1924 photo.

that exited at the Clinton Street corners. Automobiles or taxicabs could enter or exit the station along vehicle ramps that descended below street level; at the entrance to the main waiting room, drivers could stop to load or unload passengers; farther along the ramp, luggage was unloaded and forwarded to the train terminal. This system was arranged to allow motorists to service passengers and baggage inside the station and off the street, thus freeing curb space and easing circulation around the station. Located on the site proposed in the Chicago Plan, Union Station was situated west of the river and business district to relieve traffic congestion and encourage commercial development further to the west. Burnham and Bennett also recommended a new Chicago Post Office as part of this west-side development.[21]

Another congested commercial district addressed by the Chicago Plan extended along the Chicago River, where six north-south streets and their bridges defined northern entry points to the established central business district. When Burnham died in 1912, the city had already begun to widen the city's major north-south thoroughfare, Michigan Avenue, which Burnham and Bennett believed was "destined to carry the heaviest movement of any street in the world." To ease heavy downtown traffic and inaugurate a more systematic arrangement of streets, avenues, and boulevards, the architects had proposed redesigning Michigan Avenue and several other major axes as double-level boulevards. Employing multiple street planes on a vertical axis, these designs surpassed the limited results of widened streets. In addition, to disperse traffic and

commercial development to areas north of the Chicago River, Burnham and Bennett had recommended a wide, bi-level Michigan Avenue bridge (figure 15.9). Designed by Bennett, the 1920 double-decked bridge carried slower freight traffic on a lower level to serve the riverfront wharves; the upper level carried faster automobile traffic, thereby facilitating traffic circulation between the cramped city center and expanding business and residential districts north of the river. The consequences of this bridge were immediate and long lasting, particularly because the bridge helped to disperse traffic from the congested central business district. Additional northbound traffic would also stimulate real estate interests to take advantage of undeveloped commercial sites, thus expanding the commercial district along Michigan Avenue.

During the early 1920s, when automobiles had become a widespread necessity for city transportation, Chicago attracted international attention for the famous 1922 Chicago Tribune competition. The chosen site was located along the east side of Michigan Avenue and along the north edge of the Chicago River, just north of the 1920 bridge designed by Bennett. Despite Howells and Hood's first-prize design, the second-prize entry submitted by Finnish architect and urban planner Eliel Saarinen attracted widespread praise from critics and architects alike. One year later, Saarinen attracted attention when he designed a comprehensive development project for the Chicago lakefront, one motivated significantly by the automobile.[22] Saarinen had praised Burnham's and Bennett's Chicago Plan; his lakefront project incorporated several urban-planning concepts addressed by the Chicago architects. If constructed, Saarinen's sprawling project would have extended the business district north past the Chicago River and past the site of the Chicago Trib-

15.7. Union Station, cross section. The architects carefully staged horizontal and vertical planes to handle baggage, passengers, trains, and automobiles in an efficient and highly successful design.

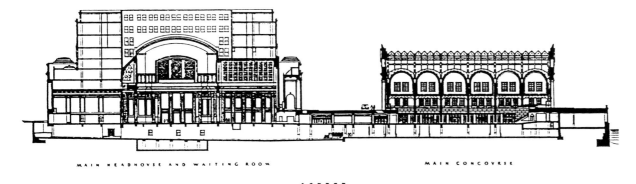

MAIN HEADHOUSE AND WAITING ROOM

MAIN CONCOURSE

SCALE IN FEET

une Building. Like Burnham, Saarinen confronted heavy automobile traffic on the horizontal plane, attempting to link important sites by means of long avenues and boulevards. In the center of the commercial district, and in response to traffic movement, Saarinen designed a gigantic, multilevel parking structure beneath Grant Park that would serve as a "terminal" for thousands of automobiles. Although not built, the comprehensive plan's images must have inspired architects and engineers who were grappling in Chicago with large volumes of automobile and truck traffic.

The only double-decked street completed in accordance with the Chicago Plan was named after Charles Wacker, the first chairman of the Chicago Plan Commission.[23] Completed in 1926 after designs by Bennett, Wacker Drive replaced produce markets and a narrow South Water Street to form a major, new east-west thoroughfare that would divert through-traffic from the north around the central business district. With an increase from one to six bridges, the region's northbound traffic out of the city would be more efficiently dispersed. Important to developers, the improved traffic and accompanying freight-handling facilities would raise property values along the riverfront. Important to motorists, the bi-level road surface accommodated general automobile traffic above, thereby easing the increased business and pleasure traffic along the drive. Slower freight traffic below could shuttle more easily between proposed rail and boat terminals at the lakefront and industrial sites further inland along the river. The multilevel road surfaces would permit more traffic to move horizontally across the city's streets, thus reducing congestion.

Bennett and the Chicago Plan Commission also addressed the severe shortage of parking spaces in the central business district when they designed Wacker Drive. By 1920, nineteenth-century streets were totally unable to carry efficiently the increased numbers of people, trucks, trolleys, and automobiles. Wacker Drive provided one lower bay for auto storage to lessen parking problems along the business-district streets. Able to carry eight thousand vehicles each way in an eight-hour day, Wacker Drive was designed in part to profit private business, ease transportation, and benefit commercial interests, yet the advantages of reduced traffic congestion and separated traffic contributed to an unrestricted and public pattern of use.[24]

By virtue of its steady traffic and beautiful lakefront location, Michigan Avenue had previously induced developers and architects to build spectacular skyscrapers overlooking the lake and parks. When Wacker Drive was completed in 1926, developers and architects immediately recognized the advantages of locating modern office blocks along the prestigious mile-long riverfront, which some compared for its beauty and civic significance with London's Thames River.

Completed the same year as Wacker Drive, the Jewelers Building was situated specifically to capitalize on the riverside location and the business district's improved automobile circulation (figure 15.10). In a promotional brochure,[25] the owners pointed out how their building represented one of "the finest buildings in harmony with the Chicago Beautiful Plan," particularly on account of its location and its proximity to the celebrated Michigan Avenue Bridge. Furthermore, the owners predicted that a second bi-level traffic bridge for Wabash Avenue, combined with the traffic generated by the new Wacker Drive, would bring ever-increasing amounts of traffic past their building on two sides. Aware of how a building's site and potential revenues could be enhanced by their close relationship

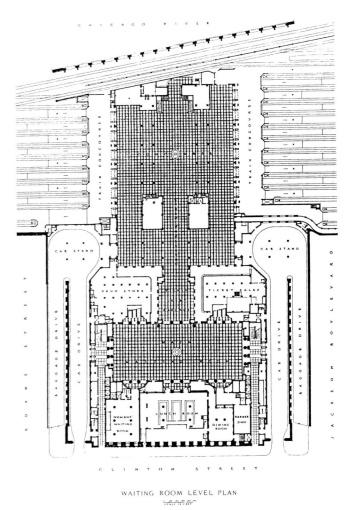

WAITING ROOM LEVEL PLAN

15.8. Union Station, interior floor plan. The plan shows how the street has been brought within the terminal's walls to facilitate the terminal's key function, collecting and dispersing thousands of passengers by train and taxi every day.

to major automobile thoroughfares, the developers claimed that "the unexcelled approach by automobile over Michigan Boulevard and the broad Wacker Drive make the Jewelers Building location unrivalled for access." Although the building's outward monumental scale, symmetrical design, and classicizing Renaissance ornament resembled architectural renderings from the Chicago Plan, the building's interior planning and site were adapted to the automobile on an unprecedented scale.

Designed by the firm of Giaver and Dinkleberg, with the firm of Thielbar and Fugard, the forty-story office building—the tallest west of New York City—was topped by a sixteen-story office tower that contained an observation room, a dining hall, and an open-air terrace at the tower's base. The developers boasted of the building's security; direct access to the street; beautiful river, lake, and skyline views; and central location near railroad terminals and other transportation systems. Accessed by ten passenger elevators, the rentable offices were arranged along exterior walls, thus taking advantage of the site's abundant light and making the standard interior-light court unnecessary (figure 15.11). Insofar as the offices were arranged in plan to provide ample light, fresh air, and the greatest amount of rentable interior commercial and office space, the Jewelers Building conformed to the established planning conventions of the tall office-building type made famous by the previous generation of Chicago architects. But the architects experimented radically with interior planning when they sought to accommodate the needs of automobile drivers and to protect the jewelry clients.

Addressing the downtown's acute parking and circulation problems, the architects of the Jewelers Building radically adjusted the typical skyscraper floor plan to incorporate a separate interior auto-

mobile elevator, the Ruth Safety Garage (figure 15.12). This exclusive feature, designed to accommodate 550 automobiles in one building, was possible because the interior-court area of the plan was not required to provide light to the offices. In place of a central light court, usually a required feature in conventional skyscrapers, the architects installed

15.9. Edward H. Bennett, with Thomas G. Pihlfeldt and Hugh E. Young, engineers; Michigan Avenue Bridge, designed and built 1912–20. The wide bi-level bridge carried faster automobile traffic at street level. While not clear in this 1920s photograph, slower truck traffic was conveyed on a second plane, carried below street level, that connected freight arteries located beneath street level on both sides of the river. (© 1989 The Art Institute of Chicago. All rights reserved.)

15.10. Thielbar and Fugard, with Giaver and Dinkel-berg, Jewelers Building, Chicago, 1926. Photograph shows building and adjacent Wacker Drive under construction, exposing the interdependence of building and street when the automobile had become accessible to thousands of drivers.

four elevators that serviced an automobile garage extending vertically from below street level to the twenty-third floor. Importantly, this interior garage and elevator was designed to protect the building's imagined clients, the city's jewelers, who would be carrying valuable diamonds, precious stones, and metals to their places of business. Entering below street level, jewelers would not need to exit their autos until they were safely within the building's walls and protected from robbery. As if to underscore the interior garage and the building's extraordinary design accommodations for the automobile, continuous exterior molding and arched windows indicate how high the building's interior parking floors and automobile elevators were stacked.

Automobile owners and jewelers entered the building's secure and private garage through an entrance approached from the lower level of Wabash Avenue and made available by Wacker Avenue ramps (figure 15.13). The driver left the car with an attendant, and the car was hoisted to upper-garage floors and rolled into parking areas automatically by means of several electrically operated ramps. The developers no doubt believed that self-contained automobile facilities would attract businesses to rent offices in the Jewelers Building for reasons of safety, convenience, and beauty. Clients would have direct access to the street or to the building's garage, eliminating the frustration of traffic jams and inadequate parking space. As one of the earliest buildings with self-contained parking facilities, the Jewelers Building marked a significant shift in how architects conceived of the relationship between buildings and the street. In this case, both the building and its adjacent street (Wacker Drive) were designed as an integral and functioning unit, constructed at the same time. Indeed, the building seems to have brought together the exclusive pattern of use associated with private-office spaces and the accessible pattern of use associated with public thoroughfares. Ironically, this ingenious skyscraper garage operated until 1940, when automobiles had become too wide to fit in the elevators. Above street level, the owners filled the garage and elevator shafts with storage space and rentable office space. Yet the Jewelers Building was not the last Chicago building where architects were to attach street and automobile needs closely to the planning of a tall building.

15.11. Jewelers Building, second floor plan. Ten passenger elevators and four automobile elevators transported businessmen and their automobiles upwards, providing parking for 550 automobiles that otherwise would clog streets below.

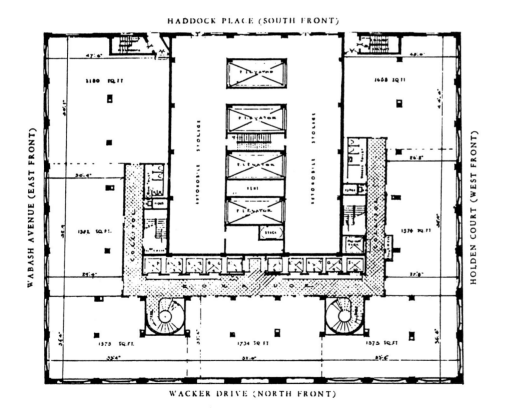

15.12. Ruth Safety Garage, Jewelers Building, cross section. The entire system was automatic, carrying individual automobiles safely from the entrance below street level to one of twenty-three interior parking levels above.

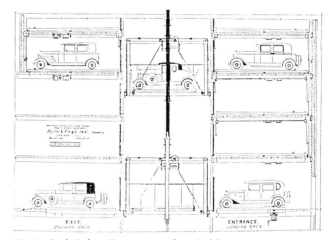

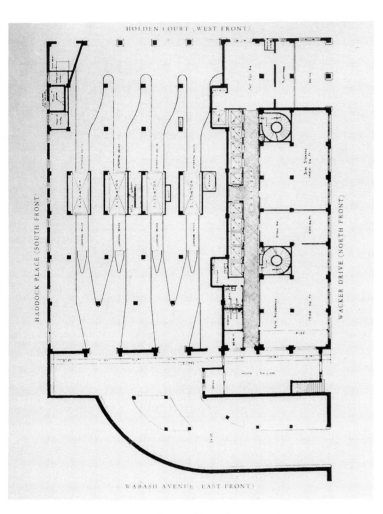

15.13. Jewelers Building, basement floor plan. Privileged occupants could drive their automobiles directly from the street into the building's garage, eliminating frustration, saving time, and providing security to the jewelers.

As any urban dweller who owns an automobile knows, the difficult relationship between buildings, the street, and automobiles remains problematic. More automobiles and more buildings crowd downtown streets and contribute to slow circulation and limited parking. At the same time, however, a tandem design program combining automobile and building needs has stimulated architects, still cognizant of Burnham's and Bennett's Chicago Plan, to experiment with vigorously arranged horizontal and vertical planes that define how the street relates to its adjacent buildings, as well as how the automobile and its inhabitants are to move within those spaces. Since the 1920s, various solutions have both benefited and cost the city's inhabitants. Some architects and planners agreed that to solve the related problems of circulation and parking, city planners should tear down buildings to create parking lots, solitary horizontal planes that severed any design link between automobiles and urban buildings. As a result, much of Chicago's historic architecture was sacrificed to automobile needs. However, the city currently is experiencing another major building boom like in the 1920s. As rental space and automobile volume density increase, architects are faced with nearly identical design issues that confronted Chicago architects in the 1920s who wished to reconcile streets and buildings. Now more strictly guided by municipal building codes that answer in part to automobile necessities, architects are designing new buildings, both residential and commercial, that incorporate in their interior plans specific space for interior parking and that respond directly to automobile density in the city. As building plans address automobile necessities, new bi-level bridges and streets at the core of the business district, near the Chicago River, echo Wacker Drive and revive Burnham's plans in helping to increase circulation and reduce congestion. For example, Columbus Drive joins a bi-level system of streets in the region of Wacker Drive and also provides drivers with direct access to interior parking garages beneath tall office blocks, just as the Jewelers Building did in 1926. But none of the parking garages thrust directly far upward through the interior office spaces; instead, parking facilities are kept just above or below street level.

Radical interior planning strategies conceived during the first decades of automobile transportation might have prompted architects in Chicago and other metropolitan centers to conceive of the automobile as a peculiar kind of building client, an inhabitant. As a permanent and highly influential unit moving within the urban network of vertical and horizontal planes, the automobile and owner bring peculiar functions and needs that must be addressed in any new building design at least as carefully as the peculiar functions and needs of human inhabitants who work, consume, and play within. As such, the automobile as inhabitant signifies a theoretical tie between buildings and the street that may have only been a source of fantasy for Chicago architects and urban planners between 1906 and 1926.

Notes

The author gratefully acknowledges the suggestions and advice of Dennis Doordan (University of Illinois at Chicago); Reinhold Heller (University of Chicago); Jan Jennings (Iowa State University), editor; Richard Longstreth (George Washington University), session chair; and Katherine Taylor (University of Chicago).

1. Quoted in James J. Flink, *The Automobile Age* (Cambridge: MIT Press, 1988), 37–38. Other histories of the American automobile culture consulted were Scott L. Bottles, *Los Angeles and the Automobile: The Making of the Modern City* (Berkeley: Univ. of California Press, 1987); John B. Rae, *The Road and the Car in American Life* (Cambridge: MIT Press, 1971); and James J. Flink, *America Adopts the Automobile, 1895–1910* (Cambridge: MIT Press, 1970).

2. Chicago architecture and the automobile evolved in association with public policy, real estate, economic and political issues discussed in Paul Barrett, *The Automobile and Urban Transit: The Formation of Public Policy in Chicago 1900–1930* (Philadelphia: Temple Univ. Press, 1979); Harold M. Mayer and Richard C. Wade, *Chicago: Growth of a Metropolis* (Chicago: Univ. of Chicago Press, 1969).

3. See, for example, Sigfried Giedion, *Space, Time and Architecture* (Cambridge: Harvard Univ. Press, 1940), and Carl Condit, *The Chicago School of Architecture: A History of Commercial and Public Building in the Chicago Area 1875–1925* (Chicago: Univ. of Chicago Press, 1964).

4. Some American architects were automobile owners who designed buildings with interior spaces reserved for automobiles. For example, New York architect Ernest Flagg designed his own residence that featured an auto entrance and garage. See "A New Type of City House," *Architectural Record* 22(Sept. 1907):177–94; "House of Mjr. Ernest Flagg, Architect," *American Architect and Building News* 89(12 May 1906):163–64. Flagg also designed the Automobile Club of America in New York, published in "The Automobile Club of America," *American Architect and Building News* 91(4 May 1907):187.

5. Daniel H. Burnham and Edward H. Bennett, *Plan of Chicago* (Chicago, 1909). For recent studies, see John Zukowsky, ed., *The Plan of Chicago: 1909–1979* (Chicago: Art Institute, 1979); Joan Draper, "Paris By the Lake: Sources of Burnham's Plan of Chicago," in John Zukowsky, ed., *Chicago Architecture, 1872–1922: Birth of a Metropolis* (Munich: Prestel-Verlag, 1987), 107–19.

6. Rossiter Johnson, ed., *A History of the World's Columbian Exposition* (New York, 1897–98), III: 236. Transportation Day is described and illustrated in vol. I, p. 441.

7. Russell H. Anderson, "The First Automobile Race in America," *Illinois State Historical Society Journal* 47(Winter 1954):343–59.

8. The early significance of the automobile club in American cities is shown by a competition sponsored by the Department of Architecture at Washington University in St. Louis in 1904. The winning automobile club design was published in *Architectural Review* 11(Feb. 1904):124.

9. For a list of officers, bylaws, and the club's constitution, see the annual yearbook, *Chicago Automobile Club* (1902).

10. Albert N. Marquis, ed., *The Book of Chicagoans* (Chicago, 1911), 144. An early president of the Chicago Automobile Club, Ira M. Cobe, was also a member of the Chicago Athletic Club and the South Shore Country Club; he listed "motoring" as his recreation.

11. Unless stated otherwise, quotes are from "The Chicago Automobile Club," *Motor Age* 2(20 Nov. 1902):1–3.

12. Charles Frost's 1893 Calumet Club is illustrated in Zukowsky, *Chicago Architecture*, 377.

13. See *The Inland Architect and News Record* 50(Aug. 1907):24, and *Architectural Record* 22(Sept. 1907):214. The clubhouse was demolished in December 1989.

14. Carroll William Westfall, "Benjamin Henry Marshall of Chicago," *Chicago Architectural Journal* 2(1982):8–27. I wish to thank John Zukowsky, curator, Department of Architecture, Art Institute of Chicago, for sharing their Marshall and Fox files.

15. Leland Roth, *McKim, Mead & White, Architects* (New York: Harper and Row, 1983).

16. Herbert Ladd Towle, "The Automobile of To-Morrow," *Scribner's Magazine* 42(Jan.–June 1908):581.

17. Carl Condit, *Chicago 1910–29: Building, Planning, and Urban Technology* (Chicago: Univ. of Chicago Press, 1973), 301–21. Between 1890 and 1910, Chicago's architects and developers had increased by a factor of nearly five the total office space in the Loop. Between 1900 and 1910, Chicago's population density increased by over 25 percent, yet the city's area had increased by only one-half square mile. When automobile registration in Chicago jumped from 5,500 in 1908 to nearly 10,000 only two years later, automobiles seemed nearly to overwhelm an urban center already oppressed by expanding population density and office space.

18. Unless otherwise noted, all quotes are from Burnham and Bennett, *Plan of Chicago*.

19. Condit, *Chicago 1910–29*, 301–21. Between 1908 and 1920, the number of automobiles in Chicago had expanded from 5,500 to 86,500; in the 1920s, when automobiles were even less expensive and more reliable, the number of motorcars in the city would quadruple. In 1916, 27,000 passenger and commercial vehicles entered the city from the north; in 1926, the city's total approached 100,000 vehicles.

20. Joan Draper, *Edward H. Bennett: Architect and City Planner, 1874–1954* (Chicago: Art Institute, 1982), 14–15, 17.

21. Although not finished until 1932, Graham Anderson, Probst, and White's post office is famous today for the building's highly unusual plan. The architects left a wide central opening at the base, along the Congress Street axis suggested by the Chicago Plan, which eventually permitted motorists of the 1950s to drive through the building on an expressway to western suburbs.

22. See Eliel Saarinen, "Project for Lakefront Development of the City of Chicago," *American Architect* 124(1923):487–514.

23. Mayer and Wade, 312.

24. See "Chicago Double Deck Street for Congested District," *Engineering News-Record* 85(22 July 1920):173–75; and Draper, 17–19.

25. Unless otherwise stated, text is quoted from a copy of *The Jewelers Building* (Chicago: Poole Bros., n.d.) made available by John Zukowsky. Thanks also to Patrick Heatherly and John Miner of 35 East Wacker for permission to examine their clippings file and the building's blueprints.

Roadside Blight and the Reform of Commercial Architecture

DANIEL M. BLUESTONE

Roadside commercial architecture is not generally recognized for its subtlety or understatement. Attempts to catch the eyes and dollars of passing motorists led twentieth-century owners of gas stations, restaurants, tourists' accomodations, and other businesses to proclaim loudly their merchandise and services from the edge of the right-of-way (figure 16.1). Roadside proprietors gave unambiguous commercial appeals a drama, scale, and power that eclipsed most earlier forms of American retail architecture (figure 16.2). Today the enthusiasts of commercial form revel in what they view as the vitality and flash of historic roadside architecture, while critics are appalled by what they see as its tawdry vulgarity, crudity, and lack of aesthetic refinement. Such sharp divergences of opinion have always characterized aesthetic views of this architecture. In this essay I explore the early twentieth-century battles between roadside proprietors and roadside reformers. The reform movement emerged during the 1920s with the rise of mass automobiling and still persists today. I am interested in the initial creation of the concept of roadside "blight," or "linear slum." Early reformers viewed

16.1. In roadside architecture, signs in their number and scale often eclipsed the buildings themselves in the effort to catch the eyes of passing motorists.

CLUBB'S NUT SHOP, ON ROUTE 17, FOUR MILES NORTH OF BRUNSWICK, GEORGIA commercialism as the agent of blight where it "ob-trude[d] . . . to an undue extent . . . along a route attractively rural or scenic in character" where "a straggling ribbon of commercial structures de-stroy[ed] the pleasure of driving over an otherwise unspoiled . . . country road."[1] Scrutinizing the his-tory of blight in the 1920s and 1930s leads to the unexpected conclusion that the struggle between proprietors and reformers actually pushed Ameri-can roadside design toward subtlety and understate-ment and strongly influenced subsequent plans for commercial architecture.

At the heart of the struggle between roadside proprietors and reformers stood fundamental differ-ences over the extent to which the rural American countryside would be commercialized. During the second half of the nineteenth century, many urban Americans enthusiastically sought out nature in places as diverse as landscaped parks, mountain spas, and seaside resorts. These settings provided strong counterpoints to cities; most importantly, they were viewed as noncommercialized places where harried urban residents could gather and briefly set aside the everyday preoccupations of lives spent in the narrow pursuit of Mammon. The automobile, for all its complex technology and ex-pense, promised many wealthy Americans much greater range in getting to the countryside. Cars and countryside would, it was hoped, help enervated city people transcend the urban and commercial context of their lives. However, the idealized urban view of the countryside as morally pure and non-commercial conflicted with the countryside resi-dents' view of the automobiling public as present-ing an opportunity for commerce that had long eluded many rural regions caught in sharp agricul-tural decline. Campaigns to eradicate roadside blight were promoted by middle- and upper-class

16.2. Beyond signs, some designs for roadside architec-ture adopted unusual building forms and the open dis-play of merchandise to attract the attention and patron-age of motorists.

urban interests at the expense of poorer rural pro-prietors, who desperately wanted to profit from the auto-borne commerce unleashed in their regions (figure 16.3).

The roadside reform movement encompassed many of the same reform interests that had sup-ported the City Beautiful movement in the early twentieth century. Most importantly, roadside re-formers drew upon the aesthetic and political views of the antibillboard campaigns that had been an im-portant part of the City Beautiful ideal.[2] Between

the 1920s and the 1950s, Elizabeth Boyd Lawton led the roadside reform movement. She helped transfer the City Beautiful's antibillboard efforts from the city to the country. An 1895 graduate of Vassar College, an educator, and a lifelong resident of Glens Falls, New York, Lawton founded the Na-tional Committee for the Restriction of Outdoor Ad-vertising in 1923. She was joined in her efforts by J. Horace McFarland, president of the American Civic Association and an important early leader of the City Beautiful movement. Joseph Pennell, the artist, and Anna Maxwell Jones, of the New York State Federation of Women's Clubs, also helped found the organization. From a small group of dedicated activists, Lawton built her organization into a national institution. In the late 1920s, Lawton changed its name to the National Council for the Protection of Roadside Beauty. Although still committed to antibillboard programs, Lawton's organization increasingly directed its efforts toward reining in commerce and effecting aesthetic improvement along the roadside. Within a decade, the organization had chartered twenty state councils and had established affiliations with sixteen national and fifty-six state organizations. A broad coalition of reformers in the American Civic Association, the American Nature Association, the American City Planning Institute, the General Federation of Women's Clubs, the Garden Club of America, the National Society of Colonial Dames, the National Grange, the Woman's National Farm and Garden Association, the National Highway Beautification Council, the National Council for Protection of Roadside Beauty, the American Automobile Association, and hundreds of committees of local chambers of commerce, rotary clubs, garden clubs, town councils, and state legislatures supported the effort to reform roadside architecture. The membership of the organizations that contributed to roadside-reform efforts numbered over three million people.[3]

Reformers viewed roadside commercial development as a threat to their ability to escape urban commerce by driving into the countryside (figure 16.4). Elizabeth Lawton asserted in 1926:

> We all realize that today [outdoor] beauty is threatened in America by commercialism. The great stream of automobile traffic, increasing at a rate almost incredible, is trailing the commerce of the cities out along every country road, and the quiet beauty of our rural roads is fast giving way to the sordid ugliness of cheap commerce. . . . We go on living our daily life in more or less ugliness, and when we escape to the country seeking relief, we find that the ugliness is coming there too.[4]

She complained that "hot dog stands, filling stations and billboards spring up like magic with no regard for the appearance of the roadside or its immediate vicinity. . . . The new highway, designed to open up the beauty of the state, has become in itself a thing of ugliness"[5] (figure 16.5).

16.3. "On Such a Highway, With Such a Public, the Selling Possibilities of Certain Commodities Is Limited Only by the Blue-Sky Vault Overhead." Upper-class urban tourists sought out the supposed benefits of natural and rural scenes made accessible by the automobile, while poorer residents of the countryside hoped to tap the market presented by passing motorists. The *Saturday Evening Post* recognized the new possibilities implicit in the encounters between tourists and rural residents.

In 1930 Stuart Chase, a regional planning advocate, echoed Lawton's sentiments. He declared, "Slums and slum behavior are to be expected in American cities, for a long tradition lies back of them. . . . What is new, hardly a scant decade old . . . is the *extension* of the metropolitan slum over most of rural America. Where highways run, where the motor car goes . . . [there is] an acneous eruption of filling stations, hot-dog stands, Tumble Inns, garages, vegetable booths, scarifying field and forest for rods around."[6] In 1928 Anne O'Hagan described some of the frustration of people seeking countryside beauty. She reported that the

> Hot Dog Trail has stretched its vulgar, desecrating length over hill and valley, beach and cliff, until the most permanent memory of what the automobile associations optimistically call "ideal tours" is the memory of a string of Eddie's Red Hot Eats, of Charlie's Campers' Cottages, of Gus's Free Air and Water, not forgetting Ye Olde-Tyme Gyfte Shoppes. . . . Whole communities ha[ve] been thoroughly grounded in the practice of regarding "nature" as a background for mercantile information. And Aunt Jane with her coffee and waffles, Hot Dog Ike with his sustaining packers' products, Jeff with his filling station and Si with his lodgings-for-a-night knew exactly what to do to advertise their wares.[7]

Roadside reformers worried about more than their inability to preserve natural settings that stood apart from the modern forms of the urban commercial world. They felt that roadside commercialism threatened their ability to travel through time, visiting landscapes associated with a simpler and morally edifying preindustrial past. The "unique charms" of New England's village greens represented one such repository of older, more communal, less commercial values. Roadside reformers

16.4. During the 1920s and 1930s Herbert Johnson provided roadside reformers with a number of important cartoon images of the problem of roadside blight. Here Mother Nature's beauty is defiled by roadside commercialism.

16.5. Roadside reformers viewed such haphazard rows of businesses with their disordered assemblages of merchandise and signs as an intrusion on their pursuit of morally invigorating natural and rural scenes.

16.6. Artist John B. Allison joined the roadside reform movement out of a sense of indignation over the commercialization of the landscape. When this painting, *American Landscapes,* was placed on view at the Montross Gallery in 1930 a critic for the *New York Times* (28 Dec. 1930) viewed it as "disarmingly gay" and wondered whether it would "bring about anything very sensational in the way of actual landscape reform."

declared that the "tourist wants to see countrysides and village greens like those pictured in the folders sent him by the publicity bureaus. . . . But many times he finds the village green marred by one hideous stand plastered with signs, or the whole effect of his shore and mountain pictures spoiled by unsightly roadside development."[8] In North Carolina, roadside reformers sought to restrict commercialism in the hopes of bringing tourists closer to another image of the preindustrial past—the dubiously romanticized life of the antebellum slave plantation. In 1930 they declared, "The highways are the windows of the State. When you travel over the roads you want to look out upon the fields, the tobacco crops, the cotton pickers, the old mammy at her tubs, the darkie cabins, the woodlands and the hills. You want to see North Carolina, or any other state, in its natural way."[9] Roadside reformers looked alternately to both nature and historic landscapes to buttress reassuring images of "simpler times," images clearly threatened by a burgeoning commercial culture and economy and by modern technologies embodied by the automobile itself.

Roadside reformers were not fundamentally opposed to commerce and its attendant display. They were generally men and women who had prospered in the urban commercial world, people who could afford a car and a vacation in the countryside away from the business of making ends meet, people who were prosperous enough to worry about the moral challenge presented by wealth and to seek architectural and landscape forms that suggested a certain refinement and even gentility in regards to commercial pursuits. They sought to reform the aesthetics of roadside businesses along the lines of modern urban commercial establishments. Many builders of nineteenth- and early twentieth-century department stores, theaters, office buildings, banks, and arcades had promoted a commercial style that suggested that engaging in commercial exchange did not necessarily preclude refined attainments. In 1908 Richard Watson Gilder, the editor of *Century Magazine,* reflected on the difference between high-style commercial architecture and cruder vernacular forms. He wrote that he felt admiration when he passed a new white-marble bank building designed in classical style; he viewed it as a "noble and restful structure." He also felt pain and anger at seeing in the same sight an enormous billboard advertising liquor; Gilder wondered, "What is the use of building exquisite structures, if any tasteless and remorseless trader can come along with his glaring dominating appeals for your money, and utterly spoil the effect? It is as if at a symphony concert, venders of soap should be allowed to go up and down the aisles and bawl their wares."[10] White marble and refined classical forms apparently blinded Gilder to the fact that bank buildings, like billboards or the hot dog stands, were designed as "appeals for your money." On the roadside, where automobile people moved more quickly than Gilder did on his urban walking tours, the husk of refinement was often removed from the kernel of commerce in order to promote sales—therein lay the challenge to the roadside reformer.

Prosperous urban vacationers and roadside beautifiers viewed the proprietors of Eddie's Eats, Charlie's Cottages, Gus's Gas, or Aunt Jane's Waffles as just so many uncouth vendors "bawling their wares" at the symphony. Indeed it can be surmised that these early roadside proprietors were operating at both the margin of the road and the margin of the economy. Anne O'Hagan identified the agents of blight as the people of the countryside (figure 16.7). Just as what she called the "save-the-scenery societies" were making headway against billboard ad-

16.7. This nineteenth-century residence near Cumberland, Maryland, was converted in the twentieth century to serve as a tourist house, restaurant, campground, store, and gas station for passing motorists.

vertising, "there issued from every farm house and every seaside cabin a son or daughter of the soil with something to sell—gasoline or eggs, or grandmother's set of pink lustre, or coffee and doughnuts, or beds for transients—and proclaimed the fact as garishly as possible."[11] Jesse Merl Bennett's 1936 *Roadsides: The Front Yard of the Nation* characterized the roadside's "Shacks and Fantasies" as "a mushroom growth, as for the most part they are temporary, being established overnight in the hope of gleaning at least a wage income from motorists who are more concerned with traveling than stopping. As a consequence, all sorts of means are used to attract attention, from grotesque building designs to signs actually commanding everyone to stop."[12]

These early proprietors were no doubt uncertain about the possibilities of winning a "wage from motorists" and avoided investing in substantial new buildings. They adapted existing structures—houses, barns, outbuildings—or they built simple vernacular shelters and shacks to house their businesses. Eschewing the more subtle aesthetics of urban commerce, they proclaimed their wares loudly with an array of hand-painted signs. They plastered their buildings with the small metal "snipe" signs advertising the national brands that they carried. The assemblage of signs created a commercial aesthetic obscuring the meager architecture; the forms and designs aimed to convey quickly a sense of plenty—to promise a far-flung range of commodities enticing to the appetites of passing motorists. The burgeoning use of snipe signs provided ramshackle quarters with the higher associational qualities of popular national brands, and proprietors apparently viewed them as improvements to their property (figure 16.8). Roadside beautifiers thought otherwise and set out along the roadsides to promote a less glaring commercial aesthetic.

Reformers also crusaded against encampments of roadside merchants who simply set up along the right-of-way without any buildings at all. In attempting to rid the roads of truck markets, reformers followed the nineteenth and early twentieth centuries' municipal campaigns that attempted to move street hucksters and pushcart vendors off of the street and into orderly, regulated public markets. Advocates of roadside control sought to ban completely market selling from trucks. In Michigan in the early 1930s, for example, roadside reformers complained that "near the cities, especially on holidays you will find [hucksters] lined up close to the pavement, selling their wares which are many and varied—from produce, soft drinks, wicker baskets,

caps, ferns, ice cream, pop corn, angle worms, home made furniture, etc. etc." They proposed that commerce be restricted to buildings in established commercial zones and limited to the sale of items absolutely necessary for use by the traveler while on route.[13]

Recognizing that motorists needed convenient places to purchase gasoline and food, reformers made concerted efforts to refine the architectural designs of Eddie, Charlie, Gus, Aunt Jane, and other proprietors of roadside businesses. The most notable educational effort came with the initiation in 1927 of a series of national design contests for roadside stands and gas stations sponsored by Mrs. John D. Rockefeller, Jr., the Adolf Gobel Company (a New York manufacturer of hot dogs and other meat products), the American Civic Association, and the Art Center of New York. The initial contests awarded prizes for the most attractive existing wayside refreshment stands and the best architectural plans of refreshment stands and gasoline stations. Subsequent contests rewarded proprietors who constructed new stands from the prizewinning architects' plans. Awards were also given for the best maintenance and upkeep of individual stands. Under the title "Elevating the Standing of the 'Hot Dog Kennel'," *American City* magazine insisted that the contests were "a far-reaching effort to clean up the miscellaneous hodgepodge of unsightly hot dog stands and the accompanying riffraff of roadside markets."[14]

Norma Bamman, the proprietor of Pinkie's Pantry—located on the road between Plainfield and Metuchen, New Jersey—took first prize from the seven hundred entries that poured in from forty-six states to the wayside-stand competition (figure 16.9). Succinctly expressing the ideals of the roadside beautifiers, the judges declared, "It has great

charm and picturesqueness. It was remarkably neat and orderly. Its display was most temptingly arranged. . . . Its sanitary conditions were well handled. It was most conveniently and economically planned and, most fortunately, it preserved and featured a beautiful roadside tree that most stand owners would stupidly have cut down." The judges clearly did not object to construction and operation of roadside stands. Rather, they wished to promote and reward stands that stood aloof from the glaring commercialism that prevailed on the roadside. They applauded the fact that Pinkie's Pantry "looked like a roadside stand and nothing else;" it was advertised with only two small signs, charm outweighed commercial appeals, and the preserved tree provided a model for the reform of the entire countryside where nature would dominate and determine the lines of commerce.[15]

The judges' enthusiasm for the architecture of Pinkie's Pantry also spread to Norma Bamman herself; she was pictured as something of a country innocent, for whom commerce was almost a secondary consideration. Her "reddish hair and pink cheeks and fondness for frocks of rose color" were noted prominently in reports of Pinkie's contest victory. She had built her business in the front yard of her mother's house after observing the dearth of "nice places" where people on the road could get a nice meal. She had hunted in secondhand lumber yards for materials and had adapted a discarded glassed-in porch for her stand. After a first successful season, she expanded by adding on an old hot-dog stand, which she painted with two coats of shining white paint. There was certainly enterprise and by all accounts deliciously baked breads, pies, and cakes at Pinkie's Pantry, but there was little of the commercialism of other roadside establishments, which is precisely what the judges and roadside reformers sought.[16] Similarly, George A. Parker's second-prize-winning "Bee Hive" establishment in Hoosick Falls, New York, impressively showed "restraint and taste in the exhibition of advertising signs. Even the gasoline sign is an interesting feature in the general composition."[17] Parker's picturesque log-building design was associated with the natural beauties of the region. Henry Ives Cobb, Jr., took first prize among the six hundred entries in the architectural competition, an entry that the judges lauded for the "sheer charm" of its "delightfully simple" design. Cobb designed a pitched-gable, wood-cottage refreshment stand with a cozy bay window, a large veranda, and two simple hanging signs. Malcolm Cameron received second prize for his "particularly good use of Spanish mission architecture"[18] (figure 16.10).

The design ideals approved in the wayside-stand competitions received broad publicity in newspapers and magazines. In March 1929, Rockefeller and the Arts Center of New York started the monthly publication of the *Wayside Stand Review* to promote directly the educational goals of the competition. The first issue published the prize-winning designs; the second issue featured ideal wayside stands and filling stations that were available in prefabricated form. Filled with pictures, articles, and business information, the *Review* was intended to reach the operators of all wayside stands and filling stations in the United States with the message that "the surest way in which to attract attention and tempt business is to abandon sign-plastered, bill boarded shacks and replace them with neat, clean, attractive structures."[19] In the face of what were thought to be aesthetically superior models, the lively commercial vernacular was supposed to give way to quiet charm and a controlled, noncommercial picturesque attractiveness.

16.8. The snipe signs advertising national brands and the custom signs of this particular establishment are stretched out along the road to alert passing motorists of the abundance and plenty on the vernacular roadside, ca. 1935.

16.9. Pinkie's Pantry's tidy appearance and white paint, the stepping of the building around a tree, letting naure dominate over commerce, and the modest scale of the two signs helped Norma Bamman, the proprietor, win the 1928 roadside-stand contest.

16.10. Malcolm P. Cameron's rendering suggested that his 1928 prize-winning roadside stand and gasoline station would nestle into the landscape and foster images of a romantic past; the arcade helped physically separate but aesthetically harmonize the gasoline station and the restaurant.

In 1929 the American Automobile Association reported that the influence of the wayside-stand competitions was evident throughout the country, where unsightly stands were being torn down and replaced with more artistic ones. Nevertheless, the association noted the enormity of the problem when it estimated that there were fifty-nine thousand stands in operation.[20] The aesthetic reform of lower-class roadside proprietors could prove a time-consuming and difficult process. To spur continued reform, the National Association for the Protection of Roadside Beauty undertook a series of state roadside surveys. Surveys had been the hallmark of various reform campaigns in the early twentieth century and were aimed at providing "scien-

tific" support for the reformers' conclusions. In the case of roadside reform, surveyors traveled over thousands of miles of highways, compiling data on the amount of blight per mile. They also gathered a copious photographic record, usually made up of glaring examples of local roadside blight. Reformers insisted that the surveys put their campaigns on "a practical basis" and inspired proposals "founded upon irrefutable facts carefully gathered and considered."[21] In the early 1930s, often with the sponsorship of state civic associations, Elizabeth Lawton and her organization undertook surveys of North Carolina, South Carolina, Washington, D. C., Oregon, Washington State, California, Illinois, Michigan, Georgia, Connecticut, Maine, New Jersey, and

parts of New York and Virginia.

Beyond contests, surveys, and educational campaigns, roadside reformers looked hopefully to the emergence of large corporations that would embrace reform ideals and replace the unrefined roadside independents. Standard Oil of California, for example, came to be seen as an agent of roadside beauty. Standard Oil was lionized in reform circles in March 1924 when its board of directors resolved to remove the company's advertising billboards from the highways of the West. The board members reported that they had become "convinced that highway advertising signs detract from the natural beauty of the great routes of travel of the Pacific Coast," and they ordered the immediate removal of twelve hundred distinctive circular billboards advertising Red Crown Gasoline (figure 16.11). Expecting some public approval and "scattered applause," the company received a national "ovation" as newspapers and civic groups spread word of its good deed.[22]

The Standard Oil of California sign removal came a decade after the company had undertaken a campaign to beautify its retail gasoline stations. The company created a model station consisting of a gable-roofed station house with large glass windows and an overhanging canopy. Standard insisted that "these stations represent the best that science and the resources and experience of the Standard Oil Company can produce. The buildings, equipment, and grounds are designed and maintained as attractive spots of utilitarian beauty."[23] Stations were extensively landscaped and designed to minimize their physical intrusion on urban neighborhoods and rural scenery. By adapting domestic, regional vernacular, or high-style models, Standard, Atlantic Richfield, and other major oil companies hoped to blunt public criticism, build a reputation for civic mindedness, and head off restrictive zoning that would interfere with their distribution strategies[24] (figure 16.12).

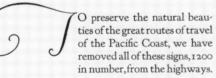

TO preserve the natural beauties of the great routes of travel of the Pacific Coast, we have removed all of these signs, 1200 in number, from the highways.

STANDARD OIL COMPANY
(CALIFORNIA)

16.11. Despite the rendering's suggestion that their advertising signs were actually benign elements in the natural landscape, Standard Oil of California had covered the western states with these signs, which were 12 to 15 feet in diameter and painted in bright red. They commercialized the landscape and their removal was presented as evidence of corporate virtue and reform.

16.12. In 1923, hoping to blunt public the criticism that gasoline stations blighted residential districts, Standard Oil of California entered these floats into a civic celebration and asserted that their stations could actually contribute to neighborhood improvement.

Standard Oil of California followed up its decision to tear down its billboards with its own contest aimed at promoting roadside beauty. In 1929 over ten thousand people entered the company's "Scenic or Sign-ic Contest." They competed for cash prizes with essays on how to end the erection of "objectionable advertising signs along highways" and on why signs that obscured scenic beauty should be removed. They also submitted photographs showing the defacement of natural beauty and slogans that would stir public action, such as "Why Sign Away Beauty?," "A Sign Removed is a Scene Improved," "Landmarks—Not Trademarks," and "Roadside Beauty—A Roadside Duty."[25] These various initiatives endeared the company to roadside beautifiers and led them to insist that corporations could actually assume the lead in reforming and beautifying the American roadside. Surveyors in North Carolina observed in 1930 that "a marked improvement in filling stations has come within the last five years, due mainly to the leading oil companies. North Carolina has many fine stations, company-owned, which illustrate this point. The Country stations, however, are largely privately-owned, and do not show th[is] improvement."[26] In 1931 a highway engineer in Westchester County, New York, reported that the "crudely improvised filling stations of earlier years . . . [built in] the bizarre and garish tradition of the roadside sign-board . . . have been improved somewhat by the application of better design and neater maintenance at stations built by the large oil companies and chain distributors."[27] In 1930 the road surveyors touring Washington, D. C., reported that "nowhere in the country are there more ugly sign-plastered stations than many which stand today on the approaches to Washington." They hoped that "large oil companies could be persuaded to establish company owned stations on the immediate approaches to Washington, or at least to establish some control over the stations selling their gas."[28]

Roadside beautifiers hoped that contests and educational campaigns and the example of Standard Oil and other corporate models would reform the aesthetic tastes and building designs of the country's roadside proprietors. However, the alliance between roadside reformers and roadside corporate interests in the campaign for beautification could get the job done in another way—by driving roadside proprietors who failed to emulate the new, refined commercial aesthetic out of business. For reformers, this promised a more refined roadside; for corporate interests, this would reduce competition and increase the corporate share of roadside business. Arthur Torrey, the editor of the *Wayside Stand Review,* put the issue quite succinctly in 1929.

> Wayside merchandising is more and more taking on the caliber of big business, and . . . good merchants and good restaurant men are on the verge of entering the field with attractive, well-built chains of wayside stands. When this idea is developed . . . only the neat efficient operator with a tidy, well-managed stand can survive; for the slovenly operator will have nothing to do but watch the cars go by—an occupation in which there is little if any nourishment.[29]

Reformers urged motorists to patronize corporate chains or the establishments that evidenced the charm of understated commerce. These more substantial designs were increasingly codified by local building and sanitary codes, which undermined the viability of the vernacular assemblages occupied by independent proprietors. The bawlers of soap at the symphony would be evicted from the hall.

In addition to corporate efforts and educational campaigns, roadside reformers also hoped to enlist the legal powers of the state in their cause. In the mid-1930s, Abigail Rockefeller funded a study by the American Planning and Civic Association for "legal research to determine the possibilities under existing laws, and types of new laws needed, to improve roadside conditions." Flavel Shurtleff, a pioneer of the American planning movement and the author of the roadside study, focused upon zoning legislation that would restrict roadside development to specific, limited zones. In addition to zoning restriction, the study endorsed public ownership of the entire roadside, which would give the state the power to enforce roadside reform ideals.[30] Increasingly, these ideals aimed to promote modern road forms, the parkway and the limited-access highway, which would banish all commercial development to areas beyond the margin of the roadway. Reformers felt limited-access highways with no roadside development (figure 16.3) would be a contribution to the "preservation of natural scenic beauty; banishment of the unsightly clutter of billboards and the stands that shut off beautiful views, order instead of disorder; roadside improvement, not roadside disfigurement."[31]

As product promotion converged with the readily identifiable architecture of specific corporations, roadsides took on a quieter, more homogenized appearance (figure 16.14). They would be less jarring to the reformer because their buildings would be familiar from travel along other, similar roads. Many enthusiasts of the commercial roadside celebrate the architecture for its dynamic vitality, its powerful direct appeals to the imagination and the pocketbook. What should perhaps be apparent in the standardization of our contemporary commercial strips is the extent to which roadside forms have been refined and tempered through long years of continuous confrontations and collaboration between reformers and corporate interests.

A brief survey of other forms of commercial architecture beyond the roadside reveals that development interests made creative use of the reformers' roadside critiques to promote their own forms for commerce. In the 1920s, Jesse Clyde Nichols developed Kansas City's County Club Plaza, which provided an influential model for the planned, automotive-oriented shopping district.[32] In promoting the plaza, Nichols adopted the rhetoric and ideals of contemporary roadside reformers. He was quite hostile to prevailing forms of roadside commerce, which he termed the "ugliest, most unsightly and disorderly spots of the entire city. . . . Buildings of every color, size, shape, and design are being huddled and mixed together in a most unpresentable manner. A mixture of glaring billboards, unsightly rubbish dumps, hideous rears, unkempt alleys, dirty loading docks, unrelated uncongenial mixtures of every type and use, with no relation to one another."[33]

Nichols hoped to capture the local auto-borne commercial market for his own development. He built, on land he owned, a profitable middle- and upper-class retail shopping district for people living in his residential development, the Country Club District. Working closely with his architects, Edward Buehler Delk and Edward W. Tanner, Nichols built the Country Club Plaza's shops in a unified Spanish revival style, which reinforced the domestic images of retreat, stability, and refinement that pervaded the area's residential architecture. He carefully weighed the impact of the commercial area on the aesthetic sensibilities of his middle- and upper-class residents. He proposed that shops be grouped in a square or circular center with interior alleys so that the unadorned workaday sides, rears,

and loading areas of his structures would not offend the domestic tranquility of the surrounding areas. The coordinated design of the "center" was conceived in opposition to the linear strips of automotive blight. Nichols undertook an ambitious program of civic sculpture, fountains and landscape design that buttressed the plaza's aesthetic of understated commerce. When it came to commercial advertising, Nichols enforced the ideals of roadside reformers on the Country Club Plaza proprietors; he insisted on "reasonable regulations as to the placing of billboards, of dangerous and unsightly overhanging signs, [and the] elimination of screaming advertising lettering across . . . otherwise pleasing store front[s] or plate glass window[s]. . . . The general good to any new shopping center preventing such unsightly, ugly appearance will give far greater value to each unit in the center than any sacrifice suffered by a merchant."[34] The ideals and models of roadside reformers were easily and profitably adapted by Nichols at Country Club Plaza.

In the 1930s, Jesse Bennett had insisted that the new buildings take the place of the roadside's "Shacks and Fantasies . . . should conform to the ideas of a competent architect." He also concluded that "substantial buildings having a conservative yet desirable appearance are, of course, to be preferred."[35] The expression of such views could be seen in the individual designs of roadside businesses, in planned centers such as Country Club Plaza, and would find its broadest application in the postwar designs of regional shopping centers. In the 1950s, architect Victor Gruen's theories of shopping-center design emerged from a critique of roadside commerce. Gruen, the most prominent and prolific shopping-center designer, argued that "we pass through the avenues of horror, stretching for endless miles through the suburban areas,

16.13. Visions of roadside reform, New England Regional Planning Commission, 1939. In the early automobile development of "yesterday," horseless carriages and gasoline sales blended into older patterns of country store commerce. Reformers viewed the roadside of "today" as a confused, life-threatening world of commercial chaos and blight. The modern limited-access highways of "tomorrow" would be devoid of commerce.

flanked by the greatest collection of vulgarity—bill-boards, motels, gas stations, shanties, car lots, miscellaneous industrial equipment, hot dog stands, wayside stores—ever collected by mankind."[36]

Gruen's early shopping-center designs—for Detroit's Northland Center in 1954 and the Southdale Center, near Minneapolis, in 1956—clustered shops around landscaped pedestrian plazas ringed by large parking lots.[37] At Northland, the plazas were open to air; at Southdale, Gruen established the important modern precedent of placing the pedestrian area in a climate-controlled, enclosed court. As in the Country Club Plaza, an abundance of art, landscaping, and "public" gathering spaces obscured the commercial nature of the design (figure 16.15). These civic features complemented the tight controls placed on storefront design and advertising to foster an atmosphere of understated commerce. The shopping centers' pedestrian scale permitted the designers to eschew the lively vernacular of the commercial roadside.

By concentrating retail establishments and providing parking areas, Nichols's, and later Gruen's, various shopping-center clients were able to expand automotive retail commercial land from roadside lots of a few hundred square feet into massive centers covering vast tracts of land. To attack the designs of commercial competitors as a form of "blight" was to draw upon the older alliance between corporate promotion and roadside reform. For Gruen, who built a thriving architectural practice on shopping malls, the critique of automotive blight represented a classic exercise of the expert's imperialism in design and planning. Shopping centers were promoted by expert planners, architects, and their corporate patrons. They were meant to replace the vernacular roadside created primarily by builders rather than architects and operated by in-

dependent proprietors rather than corporations. The class-based distinction between the roadside's "cheap commerce" and the roadside's refined aesthetic pervaded the creation of the automobile shopping mall. Here the pretence of community and civic gathering, the understated signs and graphics, the water fountains and sculpture tended to obscure the centrality of commodities and cash in the entire organization of the form. Despite the assertion that planned neighborhood shopping centers and regional malls eclipsed the blight and bad planning of the roadside, there were rather obvious debts owed. The gesture toward refined, understated commerce had been overtaking the roadside under the aegis of the beautifiers and the corporate reformers. Most tellingly, Gruen prided himself on the fact that the Southdale shopping center hosted the annual fund-raising ball for the Minneapolis Symphony.

16.14. A 1927 gasoline station in Randolph, Massachusetts, adopted forms of regional domestic architecture from the Colonial and Federal periods and reinforced the interest of automobile tourists in traveling, by automobile and through time, to scenes of a simpler pre-industrial past.

16.15. Victor Gruen's Southdale Shopping Center, Edina, Minnesota, the first enclosed modern automobile shopping mall, permitted shoppers to buy in a quiet setting of refined aesthetics, sheltered from weather and from the supposed vulgarity of the commercial roadside, 1957.

Notes

1. New England Regional Planning Commission, *The Problem of the Roadside* (Boston: National Resources Committee, 1939), 8

2. William H. Wilson, "The Billboard, Bane of the City Beautiful," *Journal of Urban History* 13(August 1987): 394–425.

3. Elizabeth Boyd Lawton, *Progress in Roadside Control and the Next Step* [*Address before the National Conference on Roadsides in New York City, November 16, 1938*] (New York: National Roadside Council, 1938); National Roadside Council, *National Roadside Council, What It Is—What It Does* (New York, 1938).

4. Elizabeth Lawton, "Regulation of Outdoor Advertising," in *Planning Problems of Town, City and Region: Papers and Discussions at the Eighteenth National Conference on City Planning* (Philadelphia: Wm. F. Fell, 1926), 87.

5. Elizabeth Lawton and W. L. Lawton, *The Roadsides of North Carolina* Washington, D. C. (1930), quoted in *Roadside Bulletin* 1(1930): 7. Elizabeth Boyd Lawton and the National Council for the Protection of Roadside Beauty started publishing the *Roadside Bulletin* in New York in 1930, "dedicated to public education with relation to the problems and progress of roadside beautification in the United States." It was published at irregular intervals from 1930 to 1950, with each number ranging from 12 to 44 pages. The illustrated journal, 10.5 inches by 7.75 inches, reported news items from around the country concerning the activities of reformers, state legislatures, and corporations as they related to roadside improvement.

6. Stuart Chase, "The Mad Hatter's Dirty Teacup," *Harper's Magazine* 160(April 1930): 580–86.

7. Anne O'Hagan, "The Hot Dog Trail," *Woman's Journal* 13(May 1928):12–13.

8. New England Regional Planning Commission, *Roadside*, 6–7.

9. National Council for the Protection of Roadside Beauty, *The Roadsides of North Carolina* (Washington, D. C.: American Nature Association, 1930), 6.

10. Quoted in Clinton Rogers Woodruff, *The Billboard Nuisance* (Salem, Mass.: American Civic Association, 1908), 8.

11. O'Hagan, "Hot Dog Trail," 13.

12. Jesse Merl Bennett, *Roadsides: The Front Yard of the Nation* (Boston: Stratford, 1936), 162.

13. "Michigan," *Roadside Bulletin* 2(1933):14.

14. "Elevating the Standing of the 'Hot Dog Kennel'," *American City* 38(May 1928):99–100.

15. "Standing of the 'Hot Dog Kennel'," 99.

16. Helen Christine Bennett, "'Pinkie's Pantry' Took the Cake," *American Magazine* (June 1928):65–66.

17. "Standing of the 'Hot Dog Kennel'," 99.

18. "Standing of the 'Hot Dog Kennel'," 99.

19. See Kenneth L. Roberts, "Pests," *Saturday Evening Post* 30 November 1929, 71.

20. *New York Times,* 12 May 1929.

21. "More About Roadsides," *Nature Magazine* 15(February 1930):116.

22. "Down They Come," *Standard Oil Bulletin* 11(March 1924):3; "Back to Nature," *Standard Oil Bulletin* 11(April 1924):1. Standard Oil Company of California published the *Standard Oil Bulletin* in San Francisco from May 1913 to June 1942. The illustrated journal chronicled the economic and personnel activities of the company. There were periodic articles on the design and organization of company gasoline stations.

23. Advertisement, *Standard Oil Bulletin* 10 (January 1923):back cover.

24. John A. Jakle, "The American Gasoline Station," *Journal of American Culture* 1(Fall 1978):525; John A Jakle and Richard L. Mattson, "The Evolution of a Commercial Strip," *Journal of Cultural Geography* 1 (Spring/Summer 1981):12–25. Thomas J. Schlereth, *U.S. 40: A Roadscape of the American Experience* (Indianapolis: Indiana Historical Society, 1985), 44; Chester H. Liebs, *Main Street to Miracle Mile: American Roadside Architecture* (Boston: Little Brown 1985), 95–115; J. F. Kuntz, "Greek Architecture and Gasoline Service Stations," *American City* 27(August 1922):123–24; William B. Rhoads, "Roadside Colonial: Early American Design for the Automobile Age, 1900–1940," *Winterthur Portfolio* 21(Summer/Autumn, 1986); 133–52.

25. "Scenic or Sign-ic?" *Standard Oil Bulletin* 17(September 1929): 14–16.

26. "Filling Stations and Food Stands Are Real Problems," *Roadside Bulletin* 1(1930):7.

27. "Engineer Deplores 'Countryside Slums' along Rural Roads," *Roadside Bulletin* 1(April 1931):15–16.

28. National Council for the Protection of Roadside Beauty, *Highway Entrances to Washington—The Federal City:A Survey* (Washington, D. C.: American Nature Association, 1930), 36–38.

29. Quoted in Roberts, "Pests," 71. The *Wayside Stand Review* appears to have ceased publication after only a short run.

30. See Flavel Shurtleff, "Roadside Improvement," *Planning and Civic Comment* 4(October-December 1938):1–24.

31. New England Regional Planning Commission, *The Problem of the Roadside* (Boston:National Resources Committee, 1939), 2–3.

32. Richard Longstreth, "J. C. Nichols: the Country Club Plaza and Notions of Modernity," *Harvard Architecture Review* 5(1986):121–35.

33. J. C. Nichols, "Planning Shopping Centers," *National Real Estate Journal* 22 March 1926, 47–49.

34. J. C. Nichols, "The Development of Outlying Shopping Centers," *Planning Problems of Town, City and Region: Papers and Discussions at the Twenty-First National Conference on City Planning* (Philadelphia: Wm. F. Fell, 1929), 16–31.

35. Bennett, *Roadsides*, 167.

36. Victor Gruen, "Introverted Architecture," *Progressive Architecture* 38(May 1957):204–8.

37. Howard Gillette, Jr., "The Evolution of the Planned Shopping Center in Suburb and City," *American Planning Association Journal* 51(Autumn 1985):421–44.

CHAPTER 17

Fifty Years of Parkway Construction in and around the Nation's Capital

Sara Amy Leach

When the automobile accelerated to prominence as a democratically affordable machine for travel during the first decade of the twentieth century, its impact was directly felt in the realization that America had a new priority: roads. Coupled with—and fueling—the domestic rage for state and national parks as a leisure-time destination, the scenic byway was born. "It is the informal landscape parks of all sizes, and in the parkways," insisted landscape architect Charles W. Eliot II, "that the automobile has notably changed the situation."[1] The nation's most dramatic parkways were established as predominantly rural, traversing hundreds of scenic miles—notably the Blue Ridge Parkway and Natchez Trace. But in urban centers such as Washington, D.C., and Greater New York City, parkways were installed as pleasure roads that quickly assumed the added responsibility of commuter routes. This contradictory function is uniquely evident in the nation's capital, where ceremonial and military needs, as well as a demand for rush-hour arteries, have shaped fifty years of urban parkway design that reflect the evolution of the meandering scenic road into an efficient freeway.

Although this type of thoroughfare is the twentieth-century outgrowth of suburban development, ironically, Washington's citywide network of pathways was developed in keeping with the eighteenth-century city plan of Major Pierre L'Enfant. This plan was resurrected by the McMillan Commission of 1901; the parkways were built over the years and today exist, preserved, under the auspices of the National Park Service.

Charles Eliot, a longtime influence on Washington's many park projects, believed parkways serve three purposes: to provide "agreeable routes" between parks, as in the Rock Creek and Potomac Parkway; to connect parks with cities, as does the Mount Vernon Memorial Parkway; and to connect "the suburbs and countryside with the congested districts," accomplished by the Baltimore-Washington Parkway. This last, in particular, was "a recognition of the changed methods of travel introduced with the automobile," first evidenced in New York's Westchester County system.[2]

Historically, a parkway's foremost task has been to separate traffic into two groups: pleasure and commercial motorists. During the early decades of automobility, most use was devoted to recreation, with new and improved highways increasing "manyfold the patronage of scenic and recreation areas."[3] During the late 1930s, President Franklin D. Roosevelt created the U.S. Tourist Bureau as part of the U.S. Department of the Interior because he felt "touring is fundamentally recreational," when in fact the emphasis was already shifting from "getting there" to simply "arriving."[4] So, too, changed road design.

Design professionals offered guidelines and definitions, but it was always the speed of the motorized vehicle that lent itself to new aesthetic and technical needs: bold and simple landscape enjoyable from afar rather than in detail at a meandering pace, and safe highways unencumbered by roadside clutter. Frederick Law Olmsted, Jr., cites only two criteria to serve as a design guide—controlling purposes and local physical conditions—from which four parkway models emerge. These include an elongated park, a glorified and ornamental street, and a boulevard or similar road that in some way provides enhanced driving conditions. Last is something "intermediate and transitional between the first and third" type, a stream-valley park characterized by a road to one side of a green space and local waterway. These informal thoroughfares, which "do not possess extraordinary scenic qualities . . . but prevent uninterrupted built-up areas," are prevalent in the Washington, D.C., region—in Sligo Creek, for instance.[5]

Legally, a parkway was defined simply as "an attenuated park with a road through it," but the federal government's first codification of parkway guidelines, the "Regulations and Procedures to Govern the Acquisition of Rights-of-Way for Parkways," was approved by the Secretary of the Interior in 1935.[6] Three years later, the Bureau of Public Roads (today's Federal Highway Administration) issued similar design recommendations, including advisement that "the collaboration of landscape architect and engineer should be fundamental from the start of the planning . . . to fit present needs and future possible demands in an attractive manner."[7] These were the foundation for a set of eight characteristics intended to differentiate parkways from ordinary highways—criteria that represent the lessons of a quarter-century of modern parkway planning: a limit to noncommercial traffic; a ban on unsightly roadside developments and signage; wider right-of-way buffer; no private frontage or access rights; development on a previously unbuilt site; best access of native scenery; elimination of major grade crossings; and well-distanced entrance and exit points.[8]

Despite these in-house guidelines and several completed parkways to its credit in the capital and vicinity, in 1944 the Department of the Interior complained that "to date, Congress has not defined parkways. Legislation pertaining to parkways is piecemeal and lacks uniformity."[9] Yet today, Washington's auto-oriented infrastructure includes four major parkways and miles of ancillary stream-valley parks that depict the evolution of this road type during the first half of the twentieth century—along the way retaining fundamental parkway design features while adopting characteristics of modern, high-speed motorways.

17.1. William T. Partridge, design of the Federal City, site plan of the city of Washington showing part of the radial avenue system, 1926. This scheme incorporates the design elements of Major L'Enfant's 1791 plan of the city with its demarked outroads and city entrance, as well as wide, radiating avenues.

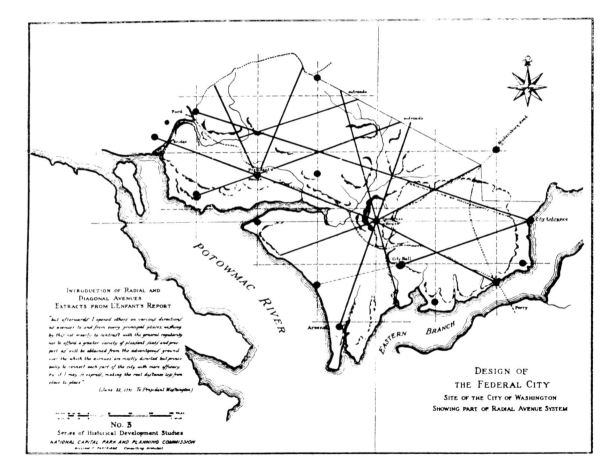

Foundations of the National Capital Parkway System

Major L'Enfant anticipated ceremonial entry points, parks, and monumental landscaped avenues in his 1791 plan of the Federal City, which remains the foundation of the complex street system in place today. While he surely could not have anticipated the national capital nearly two hundred years hence, the elements to his plan beyond the sites for the president's house and capitol building include wide, tree-lined avenues with an eye toward natural and urban vistas. "Outroads" and a "city entrance" identified on William T. Partridge's 1926 study (figure 17.1) of plans by L'Enfant and his successor, William Ellicott, allude to the major avenues that enter the modern city. The notion of appropriately formal inroads was stressed by early twentieth-century city planners as well as idealized in the Mount Vernon Memorial Highway; and Partridge's city entrance on the Potomac River is the approximate area where the Baltimore-Washington Parkway egress exists today. Little of L'Enfant's or Ellicott's designs were accomplished in the remaining years of that century, however, and they were largely ignored during ensuing nineteenth-century urban development.

The District of Columbia's Division of Trees and Parking, established in 1871, was "one of the first public bodies to regard street-tree planting as a public function," but at the turn of century, the city trailed behind others in the establishment of urban green space.[10] "There has been candid admission in Congress," reported a local newspaper, "that the park system of the National Capital is not what it should be," for which the poor economies of recent years were blamed.[11] The first attempt to revive the dormant ideas of L'Enfant came in the 1890s as mu-

nicipal growth began to extend beyond the diamond-shaped capital city. Successive legislation for the 1893 and 1898 highway acts both proved ineffectual, however, because they did not incorporate the park elements—"reservations" in the shape of squares and circles containing fountains and statuary—that are the heart of the eighteenth-century plan.

Several nationwide movements contributed to the swelling tide of critics calling for the aesthetic improvement of Washington, D.C.: the success of the 1893 World's Columbian Exposition in Chicago inspired designs of formally integrated city plans with a generous landscape component, the essence of the City Beautiful movement; the rising popularity and affordability of the automobile, which resulted in the betterment of roads; and a decline in urban living conditions, which rendered the out-of-doors a popular recreation destination.

A trio of local events further drew attention to the city. "A small group of the country's best-known designers" assembled to coordinate the centennial celebration of the "removal of government" to Washington; the American Institute of Architects addressed sculpture, landscape, and public-building design at its convention there in 1900; and Senator James McMillan of Michigan orchestrated the creation of the Senate Park Commission. This highly influential McMillan Commission, as it was commonly known, in turn advised the formation of a team of professionals "eminent in their professions, who shall consider the subject of the location and grouping of public buildings and monuments to be erected in the District of Columbia and development of the entire park system."[12]

Commission members included Charles Moore, layman assistant to McMillan who went on to serve on the city's Commission of Fine Arts for

twenty-seven years; Charles W. Eliot II, son of the designer of Boston's comprehensive park system, formerly of the Olmsted Brothers firm and seven years a planner with the National Capital Park and Planning Commission; Frederick Law Olmsted, Jr., a principal in the Olmsted Brothers firm and head of the nation's first landscape-architecture curriculum at Harvard University; preeminent architects Charles F. McKim and Daniel Burnham, both of whom worked on the Columbian Exposition; and sculptor August Saint-Gaudens, who joined the team later.

In addition to other projects, the commission recommended a series of drives and park connections around the city: in Virginia along the Potomac River from Mount Vernon to Great Falls, and in the District of Columbia and Maryland up to Great Falls; Fort Drive, "a great circumferential parkway" (figure 17.2), to connect the sites of forty or so historic Civil War fortifications; and the improvement of Rock Creek Park.[13] Credit for this regionwide foresight belongs to New York and its precedent-setting system of parkways, in particular Riverside Drive, the scenic drive that winds along upper Manhattan's west side and the Grant's Tomb monument—in principal akin to the Mount Vernon Memorial Highway. Thus, in keeping with L'Enfant's vision, "the City Beautiful movement in Washington was . . . swept along to include city entrances, parkways boulevards, monumental bridges, and entire streets."[14]

Washington did have a token scenic road in its own "riverside drive," built in 1904. This muddy carriage path, which wound along the perimeter of the Tidal Basin well before the Federal Mall took on its monumental and marbleized appearance, represented a figurative and literal prologue to the forthcoming era of parkway design. Recreating traf-

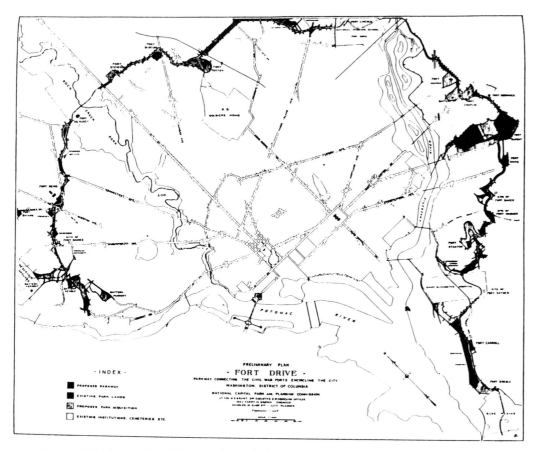

17.2. National Capital Park and Planning Commission, preliminary plan for Fort Drive, a parkway connecting the Civil War forts encircling the city of Washington, D.C., 1927. This ambitious plan was never realized because development along the route had progressed so far that land prices made acquisition prohibitive, if it would have been possible at all.

fic dared this rutted dirt road to partake of the river view and developing mall for slow-paced enjoyment. Still in its foundling, nineteenth-century form of curvaceous carriage path, the riverside drive established in Washington the tradition of pleasure driving along the Potomac shore; meandering up to the base of Twenty-sixth Street to merge with the regular city grid, the route ended about where the Rock Creek and Potomac Parkway begins today.

Planning for regional parkways by necessity became a regional concern, one jointly addressed by the National Capital Park and Planning Commission (NCP&PC), created in 1926, and the Maryland–National Capital Park and Planning Commission (MNCP&PC), created the following year. Symbolic undertakings such as the demarcation and embellishment of portals at Sixteenth Street and Connecticut Avenue—city entries found on L'Enfant's scheme—as well as the protection of Rock Creek's watershed and construction of the Mount Vernon Memorial Parkway were immediate concerns of the respective jurisdictions, which considered themselves part of a much larger conservation effort that encompassed the area between Washington and Baltimore. But "to inspire the District's neighbors to substantive action, the carrot of federal aid was deemed necessary."[15]

The critical vehicle to implement expansion of the park and parkway system was the Capper-Cramton Act, approved 29 May 1930. This legislation provided $33 million for the development of parkways along both shores of the Potomac River and the extension of Rock Creek Park into Maryland, as well as protection of part of the historic Chesapeake and Ohio Canal, three forts, and the river gorge of Great Falls, under the blanket auspices of the acquisition of lands in the District of Columbia, Maryland, and Virginia for the national capital's comprehensive park, parkway, and playground system.[16]

As a result of these formative groups and their efforts, today the national capital system includes four important parkways, constructed from 1913 to 1954, approximately seventy miles of roadway that exemplifies design ideals driven by the evolution of the car and motoring public itself—from meandering parkway proper to destination-oriented freeway. They are Rock Creek and Potomac Parkway, connecting Rock Creek Park in and north of the city to the East and West Potomac parks along the river; an incomplete collection of protective neighborhood stream-valley parks, slivers of green relief threaded among the urban sprawl; the Mount Vernon Memorial Highway, linking the presidential estate and capital city via the Potomac's western shore, and its evolution northward into the George Washington Memorial Parkway; Suitland Parkway, a defense highway from Washington, D.C., to Andrews Air Force Base; and the Baltimore-Washington Parkway, an intercity thoroughfare that serves as a primary commuter and defense route among the two cities and several federal installations (table 17.1).

Some elements of the fully idealized system remain unbuilt—among them, the Fort Drive to have encircled the city and the George Washington Memorial Parkway along the east bank of the Potomac running south to Fort Washington. But despite these absences, the half-century of parkway construction in Greater Washington has produced a largely complete and elegant network of much-appreciated scenic drives.

Rock Creek and Potomac Parkway: 1913–35

The Rock Creek and Potomac Parkway (figure 17.3), legislated as a short two-and-one-half-mile connector between the river at Virginia Avenue northwest to Rock Creek Park, has historically leaned toward service as an efficient yet pleasurable thruway in the larger context of preserving Washington's largest urban park. Established in 1890, Rock Creek Park is a rustic "open valley" of streams and forest accessible from only twenty or so neighborhood streets, which the parkway preserves through its limited access.

The parkway's enabling legislation, signed in March 1913 by President William H. Taft, cites the goals of "preventing the pollution and obstruction of Rock Creek and of connecting Potomac Park with the Zoological Park and Rock Creek Park."[17] The same goals of conservation and transportation were the basis of the New York bill of 1906 that paved the way for the extensive Westchester County system. The Rock Creek bill also stipulated that the cost of more than $1 million was to be split by District and federal governments. Landscape architect James L. Langdon of the city's Office of Public Buildings and Grounds completed the essential design, with modifications made by NCP&PC landscape architects.[18] Land was acquired starting in the teens, and by 1923 the Rock Creek and Potomac Parkway Commission had amassed most of the sought-after acreage; a few troublesome parcels were acquired through boundary adjustments and property condemnations. Segments of the parkway were already built by this time, but title disputes and private ownership prevented a continuous thoroughfare until 1935, when the final leg of the road between K and P streets was opened to traffic.[19]

Table 17.1.   Washington, D.C.'s major parkways

	Rock Creek and Potomac Parkway	Mount Vernon Memorial Highway	George Washington Memorial Parkway	Suitland Parkway	Baltimore-Washington Parkway
Location	D.C.	Va.	Va., Md.	D.C., Md.	Md.
Built	1913–35	1928–32	1930–65	1943–44	1942–54
Function/ justification	Conservation, commuting	Commemoration	Commuting, conservation	Defense, commuting	Defense, commuting
Length	2.5 miles	15.2 miles	32.6 miles[a]	9.5 miles	29 miles
Acreage	174	518	7,146[a]	88	1,353
Designers	James Langdon, F. L. Olmsted, Jr., James Greenleaf	Gilmore Clarke, Wilbur Simonson, Jay Downer	Gilmore Clarke	Gilmore Clarke, T. C. Jeffers	Gilmore Clarke, T. C. Jeffers
Scenic highlights	Superb natural topography	Memorials, natural and historic sites	Natural and historic sites	Modest natural topography	Modest natural topography
Original speed limit	22–30 mph	35 mph	ca. 50 mph	55–60 mph	75 mph

[a]Includes Mount Vernon Memorial Highway statistics.

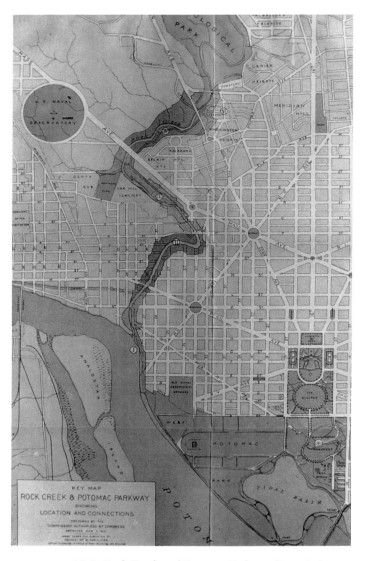

17.3. Rock Creek and Potomac Parkway Commission, Rock Creek and Potomac Parkway showing locations and connectors, 1929. The 2.5-mile parkway that snakes from the Potomac River parks up to Rock Creek Park and the zoo was designed to protect the creek and provide a limited-access commuter entrance into the city in the morning and out at night.

Amid its construction, concern for the parkway's influence remained an issue. It was challenged by the difficult role of conserving the park by directing automobile traffic quickly through the valley, or it could contribute to its demise by leading traffic right up to the park boundary. Frederick Olmsted believed there should be a distinction between the upper and lower portions of the Rock Creek valley. The bulk of it—above the zoo—remains a natural park, while the parkway snakes through the narrowest, southerly right-of-way. "You must be careful not to ruin that valley if it is to be all one," he warned. "The valley of Rock Creek should not be turned into that kind of thoroughfare and ruin the stream and park character."[20]

The newly formed NCP&PC echoed Olmsted's concern for distinguishing between functional and scenic roads: "There are and should be in the development of plans . . . a number of things which may be called parkways, to serve as lines of pleasure traffic; but in another sense [they are] part of the thoroughfare system of the District. There is overlapping there of the two types of functions. We need to be careful . . . that it does not extend too far."[21] The isolated nature of the resultant parkway is retained by the sharp turns it takes along the bottom of the rugged park gorge, beginning at the river's edge as a single four-lane route; heading north, the road divides into one-way ribbonlike roadways that undulate with the natural hillocks, pulling apart laterally as well as into higher and lower grades. The motorist's vision is confined to the medians and bordering buffer, highlighted by natural rock outcroppings, forest, native foliage, and grassy open space (figure 17.4). Rough-faced stone culverts and retaining walls protect the now-ebbing creek, picturesque details best seen from the foot and bicycle paths alongside the road. Overhead, the mammoth

scale and eclectic styling of the arched masonry crossing bridges include romantic corbelled arches and sculpted Indian visages; these carry the irregular avenues and streets across the valley in a manner reminiscent of lofty, gigantic aqueducts.

Although parkway traffic was initially "intended to be pleasure driving," use increased drastically and the one-way rush-hour orientation for commuters traveling into the central city in the morning and out at night has been in place since 1937.[22] Within the park itself is a sparse maze of narrow two-lane roads, collectively named Beach Drive, which access picnic areas and historic sites. On weekends, auto traffic is banned from many of these routes, perhaps in an effort to balance the ever-increasing use of the Rock Creek and Potomac Parkway as a commuter-oriented thruway.

Stream Valley Parks

Ancillary to Rock Creek and the Potomac and Anacostia rivers are a number of stream-valley parks that occupy the floodplain of local tributaries and park-related topography. One estimate cites more than 11,500 such publicly owned acres by the late 1930s, with as many more slated for preservation, a use that proved sensible because the valley floors were subject to flooding and the abutting rocky hillsides were unsuitable for house construction. "Stream valley parks form the backbone and major portion of the District of Columbia and Metropolitan Park System," stressed one official. "Their value as routes for passenger-car traffic, augmenting the city street system, cannot be overestimated. One of their primary values which is often overlooked is the conversation of small wildlife, woodland and water."[23]

Sligo Branch Parkway, one of the MNCP&PC's first independent efforts at developing the regional park system, with its first mile completed in 1931, is today the single longest stream-valley park in the region (figure 17.5).[24] Descending about ten miles from Wheaton to Hyattsville in Maryland, this two-lane, undivided road winds alongside Sligo Creek, where numerous picnic and parking spots are provided within the wooded setting, although access to the parkway from adjacent neighborhoods is limited. Little has changed in the fifty years since it was "designed as a pleasure drive with an 18-foot waterbound macadam surface. . . . All construction has been planned to blend with the landscape as much as possible. The stream is bordered by large weatherbeaten boulders, and the almost precipitous hillside and occasionally level bottoms are covered with a fine stand of large oaks, beeches, tulip poplars, and sycamores."[25] Modern motorists find the scene largely unchanged, despite occasional encroaching development on the side of the road opposite the stream itself.

During the 1930s, Maryland accepted donations of land for this purpose, eighty to one hundred feet wide, with a total of forty-six miles anticipated upon completion. Projects in Maryland to be implemented with Capper-Cramton enabling legislation included valleys—and roads—of the Cabin John River, Rock Creek, Sligo Creek, Northeast Branch, and Anacostia River.

Other similar stream-valley parks exist throughout Greater Washington, such as Piney Branch and Pinehurst parkways, both associated with Rock Creek Park, as well as the Glover-Archibold Park, Arizona Parkway, and Little Falls Parkway. Collectively, and in relation to their respective neighborhoods, these natural respites fulfill important transportation and conservation functions. At the local

17.4. View of Rock Creek and Potomac Parkway today. In the recreational spirit of the earliest parkways, the twisting roadway has been augmented with adjacent bicycle/jogging paths whose travelers are dwarfed by the massive, rustic-styled bridges that loom overhead.

17.5. Irving C. Root, Sligo Creek Parkway—Colesville Road to Carroll Avenue, ca. 1931. Today this parkway is one of many thoroughfares that preserve local floodplains, wildlife, and woodland.

level, they are most like the Rock Creek and Potomac Parkway, gently preserving an interior watershed region while facilitating automobile travel.

Mount Vernon Memorial Highway: 1928–32

The Mount Vernon Memorial Highway (figure 17.6)
was built to commemorate the bicentennial of
George Washington's birth, and in doing so marks
the route he frequented from the estate through the
historic port town of Alexandria to the site of Arlington Memorial Bridge. Based on an idea that dates
back to an 1886 citizens group, the highway was
legislated on 23 May 1928.[26] In 1930 Congress had
the foresight to approve extending the parkway
north to Great Falls—the site of Washington's ill-
fated Potowmack Canal—on both shores, and
south to Fort Washington; and two years later, all
existing and future components were renamed the
George Washington Memorial Parkway. Its role as a
commuter route was originally of secondary importance to that of linking the many parks, recreational
areas, Civil War–era sites, and presidential memo-
rials. Today that function is largely limited to week-
end and tourist traffic.

Gilmore Clarke, chairman of the Fine Arts
Commission for many years, was the consulting
landscape architect on the Mount Vernon Memorial
Highway. He, too, looked for a precedent to New
York's thirteen-mile Bronx River Parkway of 1923,
which was designed exclusively for pleasure motoring: "I doubt whether the Mount Vernon Memorial
Highway would have been built in the manner in
which it was, had those in charge not seen and profited by the work of the Westchester County Park
Commission. And so Washington has one example
of the type of motorway that should . . . extend out
from every portal of the city."[27]

Clarke, who was responsible for the parkway's
uniformly rustic and low-slung bridges (figure
17.7), headed a design team made up largely of
Westchester County Parkway Commission alumni.
It included himself, engineer Jay Downer, horticul-
turist Henry Nye, and Wilbur Simonson, landscape
architect with the Bureau of Public Roads. As a consequence, the site and structures of both parkways
are similar in appearance.

The Bureau of Public Roads built the highway
in a phenomenal four years as an early fast-track
project—aspects of construction such as clearing,
grading, paving, and planting overlapped one another—as opposed to designating work contracts in
succession, as was common practice. It was also
one of the first roads designed using aerial photography, which afforded much-improved topographi-
cal detail, a novelty that generated a more sinuous
and irregular layout than that attainable with traditional tangential curves.[28]

Along the southern portion, from the Mount
Vernon estate and its dramatic circular terminus to
Alexandria, the motorist enjoys a four-lane undivided road that winds in tight curves along a re-
claimed and cultivated shoreline of buffer forest and
marsh; occasional overlooks, parking areas, and
picnicking points offer views to Fort Washington
across the river. The sites are historic as well as natural: in Alexandria, Christ Episcopal Church, where
the Washingtons worshipped, and Gadsby's Tavern,
where he reviewed the troops for the final time, as
well as remains of Civil War fortifications. In contrast, the route from Alexandria to the bridge (figure
17.8) is divided by a narrow median and features
long, linear curves and short dips. The mown borders are maintained with groves of native trees and
beds of colorful daffodils, tulips, and other seasonal
flowers—the backdrop to which is the magnificent

Washington skyline. This segment of the parkway
also contains formal monuments: the Columbia Island Circle at Memorial Bridge, the "waves and
gulls" Navy–Merchant Marine Memorial, and the
Lyndon Baines Johnson Memorial Grove, the only
"living" memorial to a president.

The construction of Washington National Airport in 1941 caused some disruption of the parkway
site plan, but otherwise federal acquisition of land
and construction continued northward to Great
Falls from the 1930s. The entirety of the George
Washington Memorial Parkway was not completed
until 1956. As a later conception, its emphasis lies
in natural, scenic vistas, with less-strident buffering
against encroaching development on the west, and
the establishment of a commuter link with the beltway.[29] In all, however, the George Washington Memorial Parkway is maintained with as much natural
landscape as it has been developed with roads,
pavement, and lawn; about three hundred acres of
scenic easements further protect the integrity of this
largely ornamental byway. Yet it succeeds in its
ceremonial functions as well as it provides hurried
motorists a direct access into Washington. Today it
is considered the most comprehensive, complete,
and formal means of entering the capital city, fulfill-
ing the expectations of L'Enfant, the McMillan
Commission, and Clarke.

Suitland Parkway: 1943–44

By the late 1930s, parkways and highways took on
new and more exacting connotations. The lagging
economy and impending war demanded that speed
and efficiency take precedent over aesthetics, and
parkways could no longer be developed from a
strictly recreational standpoint:

By the 1930s especially express highways [were promoted] with a view toward rescuing their cities. As urbanites moved to the suburbs of deteriorating and contested cities, planners insisted that an accelerated road program would hasten traffic flow and boost morale and economic development. . . . Highway building was a form of social and economic therapy.[30]

With World War II came a modern and new justification for a type of road that combined parkway principles with freeway proficiency—its model was the high-speed German autobahn. The Defense Highway Act of 1941 appropriated $10 million in federal funds to this end, to be matched with state monies. Beginning that year, FDR called for a priority on roads "essential to national defense," which included access roads to military installations, defense plants, airports, and ports.[31]

Suitland exemplifies such a defense highway, and as such is the watershed between the genuine parkways of prewar years and the highways of the future. Nevertheless, the origins of it and the later Baltimore-Washington Parkway also lie with the turn-of-the-century McMillan Commission plans.[32] The parkway begins amid the tangle of modern freeway connections at South Capital Street in Washington and leads to Andrews Air Force Base in Maryland, with a southerly connector to Bolling Field, also in the District—both military installations.

Despite a well-packaged justification as a military road, Suitland "was so designed and construction so executed that the roadway system could be ultimately developed into a fully landscaped parkway."[33] At the west end, it succeeds as a winding, somewhat natural setting. About half its secondary "B" roadway is graded but unpaved, so traffic briefly shares a single, undivided twenty-four foot lane. Other recognizable parkway standards include semi-maintained buffer plantings and a varied-width median of up to two hundred feet, but these features are overshadowed by aesthetic vio-

17.6. National Capital Park and Planning Commission, Lower Potomac Park Project, Mount Vernon and Fort Washington parkways, 1929. Had the complete network of shoreline parkways been fully carried out, the Mount Vernon Memorial Highway would exist on Virginia's western shore as it does today, matched by the Fort Washington Parkway on the opposite Maryland bank.

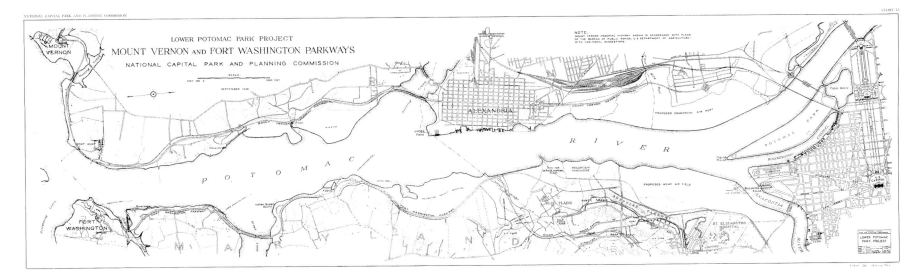

lations that include at-grade intersections, with their clutter of signals and signage, and its interrupted state. Unfinished in 1945, when it became the responsibility of the National Park Service, its continued haphazard appearance may stem from its manipulated function as a parkway and its relative obsolescence upon construction, making it fail the definitions of either highway or byway.

One function of a defense highway was to be impervious to air attack. Hypothetical images demonstrate the impact of aerial bombardment on a slash-cut, or straight, roadway as compared to typical parkway siting, fitted to the natural contours of the landscape. The latter provides a "detour and scatter" area, with vegetation that offers camouflage to vehicles seeking concealment. The limited access of parkways and defense highways also shared the advantage of easy closure to nonmilitary traffic in times of emergency. While the sleek autobahn did enhance safety and boost speeds, it failed as a defensible avenue because, noted one Bureau of Public Roads administrator, "I recall how effectively these direct and highly conspicuous arteries . . . can be used to guide hostile air attacks to its important objectives."[34] With parallels to military maneuvers rather than characteristics of beauty, the role of the parkway shifted considerably. Henceforth, scenic attributes would be viewed as bonus design components as the era of anonymous highway construction got under way.

Construction of Suitland Parkway was pushed through as a War Department measure, part of building Camp Springs Airport (Camp Springs was later renamed Andrews AFB).[35] But there was a hiatus on nonmilitary projects until "September 6, 1945, when Harry S Truman dropped war-time controls [and] normal state and federal road construction got under way."[36] Washington, like other

17.7. Construction of Mount Vernon Memorial Parkway showing bridge and grading, ca. 1930. Gilmore D. Clark, who worked on the precedent-setting Westchester County, New York, parkway system, designed the bridges and other architectural elements of this parkway, which closely resemble those of its model.

17.8. View of Mount Vernon Memorial Highway today. Looking north from the historic port town of Alexandria where the parkway briefly becomes "Main Street," the Washington Monument obelisk stands as the visul terminus of the artery designed to commemorate the one followed by George Washington en route from his estate to the Federal City.

automobile-oriented cities, suffered greatly from the postponement of road building. According to Wilbur Simonson, "This deferrment of normal construction programs has resulted in a huge backlog of needed highway facilities, which is most serious near cities where traffic congestion is our country's No. 1 post-war highway problem."[37]

It is not surprising, then, that between 1946 and 1950, officials of local, state, and federal agencies spent $8.4 billion on highway development, more than any previous five-year period in history.[38] In this hurried context, landscape architects continued to assert that even the most sensible road could be enhanced at no extra cost through preliminary inclusion of traditional parkway features such as grade differentials and native plantings. "Most of these practices have been dictated . . . by the criterion of beauty," asserted one critic, "yet time has proved not only their popularity, but also their promotion of safety, comfort, and speed with respect to traffic, and efficiency with respect to maintenance and operation."[39]

With the new priority on high speed, national defense, and city-to-city regional growth, the elements were in place for the Baltimore-Washington Parkway, the last of the capital's full-fledged parkways and its first modern highway.

Baltimore-Washington Parkway: 1942–54

The Baltimore-Washington Parkway stretches twenty-nine miles from the capital northeast to Baltimore, an historic north-south route during the preceding two centuries: the northern ten miles were built and are maintained by the state of Maryland, the southern nineteen miles by the federal government (figure 17.9). Although completed after mid-century, a Baltimore-to-Washington route was studied and promoted from the 1920s on as a proper entrance to the capital and a safer option to the near-parallel U.S. Route 1, unanimously proclaimed one of the deadliest stretches of road in the nation. Had the road been built when proposed, it might have been a true parkway, more elaborate and part of an expansive conservation project some advocates hoped to establish between Baltimore, Washington, and the eastern shore. As construction took place decades later, however, the Baltimore-Washington route represents the final gasp of parkway policy imposed on a tardy regional road-development plan.

17.9. Site plan, Baltimore-Washington Parkway showing federal- and state-built portions, ca. 1930s. Although such a connection between the two cities was theorized in the early twentieth century as an alternative to the dangerous Route 1, the parkway was not completed until after mid-century and as such derives some of its characteristics from contemporary freeway design.

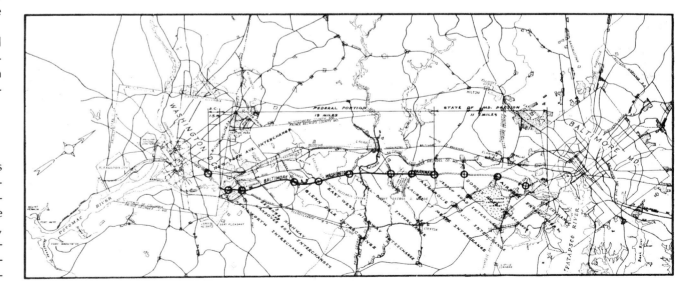

Like Suitland, era and function are reflected in a design that blends parkway principles with post-war austerity. The route accesses Fort Meade, the Agricultural Research Center, and the then-model Greenbelt garden community, as well as other federal installations that abut more than half its course.

Despite the lack of any outstanding scenic or historic features, the parkway's forested buffer, medians, and modest natural topography are much-suited to high-speed appreciation (figure 17.10). This simple background may or may not have been the vision of landscape architect T. C. Jeffers, whose experience also included six years in the Olmsted Brothers office and, ultimately, twenty-six years with the NCP&PC.[40] Design of the land and architectural elements—such as the twenty-two bridges—fell to the National Park Service, while the Bureau of Public Roads was responsible for construction.

The parkway was never technically completed with a comprehensive landscape-planting plan, but it features a generous four hundred- to eight hundred-foot right-of-way and a median that widens and fluctuates to include mature foliage and grassy open space. The dual roadways accommodate two lanes, with space historically and fortuitously slated for a third lane, in keeping with traffic demands. Like the modest attention to landscape details, the bridge designs also indicate a concession to economy. The low-slung, arched crossings over, and visible from, the parkway are clad in the rough-faded stone associated with structures of the 1920s and 1930s, nearly identical to those Clarke designed for the Westchester system, while bridges carrying the main line roadway are largely unadorned concrete with perfunctory rustic detailing, and generally have a modern appearance.

A $2 million appropriation in 1942 took the Baltimore-Washington Parkway as far as land acquisition and piecemeal grading, which was followed by eight years of general delay caused by discussion over design, funding, and purpose. Although the war threat had passed, the thoroughfare was finally justified, as was Suitland Parkway: "If it is not a national-defense road from here to Fort Meade and the other Federal reservations, it would be difficult to point one out," testified one congressman in 1950 public-works hearings.[41] Unlike Suitland, which fails at many levels, the southern two-thirds of the Baltimore-Washington route succeeds as a late-model parkway. Today that federal-owned portion of the parkway retains its scenic qualities and serves as the primary intercity commuter route in the region. Had designers instead followed the loose dictates of contemporary highway design, it might resemble the Maryland-owned counterpart, which has devolved into a widened expressway marred by excessive lighting, signage, exits, and abutting commercial development—the complete antithesis of parkway design and philosophy.

Parkways of the national capital were conceived during the first half of the twentieth century, modeled most immediately on New York's successful scenic highway system. They were the cooperative effort of federal agencies, including the Bureau of Public Roads and National Park Service, as well as regional planning and design-control commissions. These entities were in large part guided by a handful of nationally known and visionary landscape architects who possessed an expansive vision for the nation's capital, an image founded on the ideals of Washington's first planner, Pierre L'Enfant. Design and implementation of each parkway reflects the priority of transportation, for it was the automobile that spurred the need for adequate roads. The unique situation of Washington, D.C., however—with the resident federal government burgeoning in the 1930s and 1940s—necessitated the incorporation of other functions. Conservation, recreation, commemoration, and military defense developed as diminishing, and often overlapping, secondary justifications that evolved up to midcentury. After World War II, creative parkway development in Washington, as everywhere, was for all practical purposes eclipsed by modern highway construction.

17.10. View of Baltimore-Washington Parkway today. Justified after World War II as a military highway accessing federal reservations such as Greenbelt and Fort Meade, the twenty-nine-mile thoroughfare boasts a simple landscape and gentle gradient with no dramatic scenic features—the last gasp of parkway construction in the nation's capital.

Notes

1. Charles W. Eliot II, "The Influence of the Automobile on the Design of Park Roads," *Landscape Architecture* (October 1922):27.

2. Eliot, 36.

3. National Park Service, *1937 Yearbook: Park and Recreation Progress* (Washington, D.C.: Government Printing Office, 1938), 37.

4. *1937 Yearbook,* 33–34.

5. Frederick Law Olsmted, Jr., "Memorandum as to 'Border Roads' for Parkways and Parks" (25 September 1925), 1–3; Maryland–National Capital Park and Planning Commission, "Regional Planning Report IV: Baltimore-Washington-Annapolis Area" (November 1937), 2, 34. By definition, stream-valley parks are synonymous with "strip parks" and "border roads."

6. National Capital Park and Planning Commission, "Comments on Report of Maryland State Planning Commission on State Recreational Areas" (1938?), cited in Jere Krakow, "Historic Resource Study: Baltimore-Washington Parkway" (U.S. Department of the Interior, National Park Service, 1987, draft), 28; Memorandum to A. E. Demaray, Appendix A, Minutes of the NCP&PC, 16–17 March 1944, 2, RG 328, National Archives Collection, Washington, D.C.

7. *Washington Star,* 5 June 1938, cited in Jere Krakow, "Historic Resource Study: Rock Creek and Potomac Parkway" (U.S. Department of the Interior, National Park Service, 1988, draft), 32, 41.

8. Harlan D. Unrau and G. Frank Williss, *Administrative History: Expansion of the National Park Service in the 1930s* (Washington, D.C.: Denver Service Center, 1983), 146; ASLA fellow Laurie Cox identified the same standards in "Appearance: Essential Element in Superhighway Plans," *Landscape Architecture* (January 1942): 56.

9. Memorandum to Demaray, 1.

10. Wilbur Simonson, "Roadside Planting," *Landscape Architecture* (July 1936):167.

11. Bill Price, "A Great National Park along the Potomac," *Washington Times,* 18 April 1922.

12. Cited in Frederick Gutheim, *Worthy of a Nation: The History of Planning for the National Capital* (Washington, D.C.: Smithsonian Institution, 1977), 113, 116.

13. Charles W. Eliot II, "Planning Washington and Its Environs," *City Planning* (July 1927): 181.

14. Gutheim, 135.

15. Irving Root, "Planning Progress in Maryland-Washington Metropolitan District," *City Planning* (January 1931): 7; Barry Mackintosh, *Rock Creek Park: An Administrative History* (Washington, D.C.: NPS History Division, 1985), 67.

16. Public law no. 284, *United States Statutes at Large, 71st Congress, 1929–1931,* vol. 46, pt. 1 (Washington, D.C.: GPO, 1931), 482–85.

17. Public law no. 432, *United States Statutes at Large, 62d Congress, 1911–1913,* vol. 37, pt. 1 (Washington, D.C., 1913), 866–90.

18. Cited in Krakow, "Rock Creek and Potomac Parkway," 17.

19. Mackintosh, 61, 63.

20. Minutes of the NCP&PC, 16–18 September 1927, 15, National Archives Collection, Washington, D.C.

21. Minutes of NCP&PC, 16–18 September 1927, 15.

22. Cammerer to Delano, 8 June 1936, RG 79, Box 2835, National Archives, Washington, D.C.; cited in Krakow, "Rock Creek and Potomac Parkway," 25.

23. Max S. Wehrly, "Stream Valley Parks in the District of Columbia and Metropolitan Area," 12 October 1939, RG 328, National Archives Collection, Washington, D.C.

24. Roland W. Rogers, "A Park System for the Maryland-Washington Metropolitan District," *City Planning* (January 1931):17–18.

25. Rogers, 18.

26. Public law no. 493, *United States Statutes at Large, 70th Congress, 1927–1929,* vol. 45, pt. 1 (Washington, D.C.: GPO, 1929), 721–22.

27. Gilmore Clarke, "D.C. in Need of Modern Parkway Cited by Fine Arts Chairman," *Sunday (Washington) Star,* 5 June 1938.

28. U.S. Department of Transportation, *America's Highways, 1776–1976* (Washington, D.C.: Government Printing Office, 1976), 329, 396.

29. Discussion of the portions of the George Washington Memorial Parkway built later than the 1928–32 Mount Vernon Memorial Highway is not undertaken here because they do not represent new designs, techniques, or justifications for parkways.

30. Mark Rose, *Interstate: Express Highway Politics 1941–1956* (Lawrence: Regents Press for Kansas, 1979), 5.

31. Rose, 12.

32. U.S. Congress, Senate Committee on Public Works, *Providing for the Development, Administration, and Maintenance of the Suitland Parkway in the State of Maryland as an Extension of the Park System of the District of Columbia and Its Environs by the Secretary of the Interior,* 81st Cong., 1st sess., 1949, Rept. 747 (Washington, D.C.: GPO, 1949).

33. D. G. White to T. S. Settle, 22 April 1948, RG 328, National Archives Collection, Washington, D.C.

34. H. S. Fairbank, "Military Highway," *Proceedings of the 27th Annual Highway Conference* (24 July 1941): 37.

35. Cited in Jere Krakow, "Historic Resource Study: Suitland Parkway" (U.S. Department of the Interior, National Park Service, 1988, draft), 19.

36. Rose, 12.

37. Wilbur Simonson, "Advanced Designs for Post-War Highway Needs," *Landscape Architecture* (July 1943):130.

38. Rose, 29, 31.

39. Cox, 55–56.

40. "Thomas C. Jeffers, Sr.: A Biographical Minute," *Landscape Architecture* (July 1952):173.

41. U.S. Congress, House Committee on Public Works, *Baltimore-Washington Parkway,* 81st Cong., 2d sess., 1950 (Washington, D.C.: GPO, 1950). *Congressional Record,* 81st Cong., 2d sess., 1950, vol. 96, no. 103:7131.

Mapping Route 66

CHAPTER 18

ARTHUR KRIM

A Cultural Cartography

Route 66 was more than an official U.S. highway number, it was the symbolic river of America moving west in the auto age of the twentieth century. Along its course flowed American migration from the Midwest to California. In the process, it became an icon of free-spirited independence linking the United States across the Rocky Mountain divide to the Pacific Ocean. Yet whatever the symbolic bond that drew Americans to Route 66, the actual highway occupied a precise location in time and space. It is this convergence between the cartography of description and the mapping of symbolic location that will be the focus of this essay. Original period road maps, highway atlases, and illustrations will give a sense of Route 66 in time and space.

Historically Route 66 reached from Chicago over 2,200 miles to Los Angeles by way of St. Louis, Tulsa, Oklahoma City, Amarillo, Albuquerque, Flagstaff, San Bernardino, and Pasadena. It crossed diagonally southwest through Illinois, Missouri, and a corner of Kansas, turning directly west across Oklahoma, the Texas panhandle, central New Mexico, and northern Arizona into southern California

(figure 18.1) In official records, Route 66 was designated as a U.S. highway in 1926 and was adjusted with more direct routings over the next fifty years until it was replaced by the Interstate Highway Program and deactivated as a U.S. route number in 1985. This official resume makes the often complex detail of locational change and the symbolic role Route 66 created in American highway culture.

Oklahoma Origins

While the origins of U.S. Route 66 appear at first to be straightforward, the genesis of the numbering and its initial location are matters of some question. In actual fact, the original Route 66 location was designated as U.S. Highway Number 60 in 1925 by the Bureau of Public Roads under the Department of Agriculture. The numbering change from Route 60 to 66 is a sequence recently documented by Quinta Scott and Susan Croce Kelley in their history of Route 66.[1] The genesis of a national highway from Chicago to Los Angeles is credited to the efforts of Cyrus W. Avery, a Tulsa, Oklahoma, highway commissioner who proposed the route as a

means of linking Tulsa into a regional network.[2] This system of nationally numbered routes had been suggested by E. W. James of the Bureau of Public Roads in conjunction with the American Association of State Highway Officials in 1924 as a means of regulating the confusion of privately marked motor trails, like the Lincoln Highway that had developed before the First World War.[3] By 1925 James had devised a national route-numbering system and had suggested a shield sign to mark the new U.S.–sponsored highways in standard signage. With colleagues from Missouri and Illinois, Avery proposed that the transcontinental route from Chicago to Los Angeles be designated as number 60, following sections of the Ozark Trails and National Old Trails to California.[4] The new national highway map published in November 1925 by the Department of Agriculture clearly showed the Route 60 designation from Chicago to Los Angeles.[5] Indeed, the Rand McNally *Road Atlas of the United States* of 1926 was the first national highway atlas to show the new Route 60 shield markers with the National Old Trails label across California to Arizona (figure 18.2).

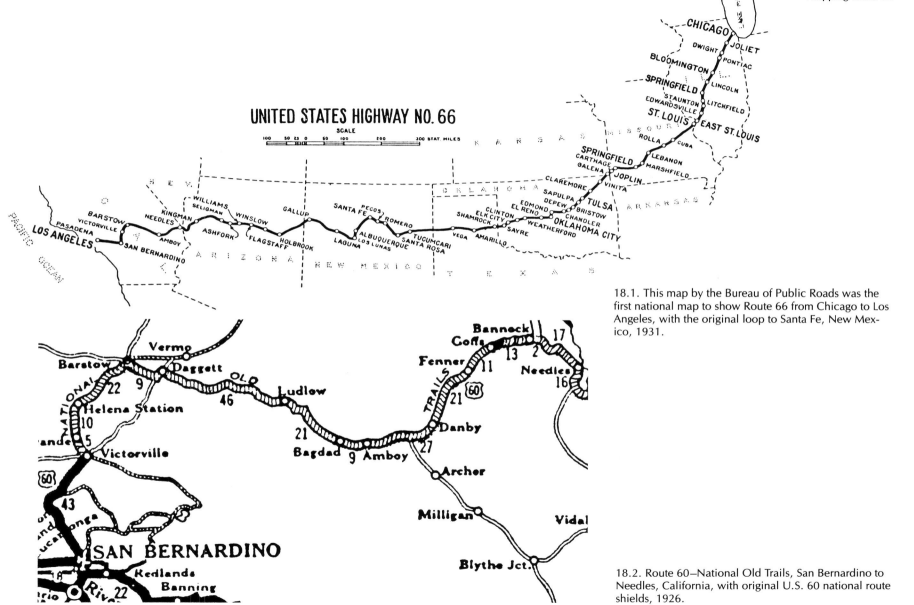

UNITED STATES HIGHWAY NO. 66

SCALE

100   50 25 0   50   100   200   300 STAT. MILES

18.1. This map by the Bureau of Public Roads was the first national map to show Route 66 from Chicago to Los Angeles, with the original loop to Santa Fe, New Mexico, 1931.

18.2. Route 60–National Old Trails, San Bernardino to Needles, California, with original U.S. 60 national route shields, 1926.

Immediate objections to the use of the transcontinental Route 60 designation were raised by Governor Field of Kentucky, who wanted to maintain the Midland Trail as a national route number from Virginia.[6] Considerable debate emerged concerning the use of number 60, with Public Roads officials in Washington mediating between the Oklahoma and Kentucky factions during the spring of 1926. Cyrus Avery and his ally, B. H. Piepmeier of Missouri, were given optional choices of numbers 62, 66, and possibly 68 as compromise solutions in March.[7] At this point, either Peipmeier made the decision of number 66 for Avery, or as Scott and Kelly relate, Avery's superintendent highway engineer in Oklahoma, J. R. Page, selected number 66 as the best possible choice in the national highway network.[8] Whoever made the final selection, route number 60 was given to Kentucky and number 66 was given to the Chicago–Los Angeles route in July 1926, when Avery received a confirming letter from E. W. James of the Bureau of Public Roads. Avery responded that "U.S. 66 will be a road through Oklahoma that the U.S. Government will be proud of."[9] By October 1926, the Arizona Highway Department had adopted the new Route 66 shield markers for their state map, among the earliest published examples of the bold graphics created by the double-digit sixes (figure 18.3).

Whatever the actual sequence of decisions that created Route 66, the selection of the double sixes was soon recognized for its alliterative power and symbolic suggestion of speed. This was first acknowledged in 1927, when the Phillips Petroleum Company of Bartlesville, Oklahoma, adopted the "66" as a signet of their new high-octane gasoline (figure 18.4). The traditional accounts in company histories recall a testing of the new gasoline on a section of Route 66 east of Tulsa before the Bartles-

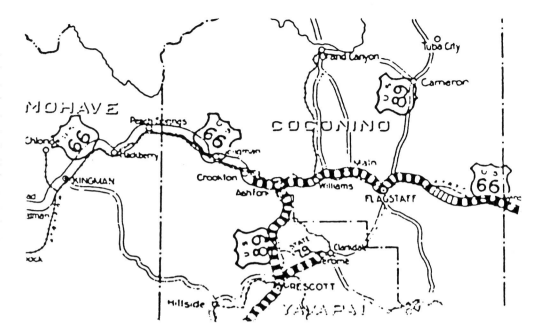

18.3. U.S. 66 across northern Arizona on the first state map to show the Route 66 shield sign for national numbering, October 1926.

ville turn, with company officials declaring the speed at "sixty-six" to match the highway number.[10] At the same time in Tulsa, Cyrus Avery also recognized the newly designated signage as a commercial product and helped form the U.S. Highway 66 Association in February 1927 to promote tourist travel along the highway through Oklahoma and the Southwest.[11] Thus, within a year of its designation, Route 66 had entered the national vocabulary as a special American road.

18.4. Evolution of the Phillips 66 shield logo. Initial design of the disk-shaped shield from 1927 (left) was transformed in 1928 by simply using the numeral "66" (right) and was further modernized in 1930 by changing to a shape that was similar to the U.S. Route 66 shield (bottom).

Dust Bowl Depictions

Tracing Route 66 during this early period is rather simple from an overview of national maps. Examples such as the Department of Agriculture sectional for June 1931 show the full extent of United States Highway No. 66 from Chicago to Los Angeles, with the original route in New Mexico north to Santa Fe (see figure 18.1). Detailed government maps of the actual route location are less available for this early period, although occasional U.S. Geological Survey topographic sheets will show red-lined U.S. 66 locations.[12] More frequent and more readily available to the public, are the oil-company road maps of the period that were distributed for free at highway filling stations.[13] A fine regional example is the 1934 Marathon Oil Company road map of Missouri, Oklahoma, and Texas, where bold, pencil lines probably drawn by a gas-station attendant to highlight the highway for an inquiring tourist mark the Route 66 corridor from St. Louis to the Kansas border; it is a true piece of folk cartography of the auto age (figure 18.5). Such personalized maps are valuable resources of the early highway period, ephemera that deserve preservation as authentic documents of the roadside culture.

Beyond the free road maps of the oil companies, the most valuable cartographic portraits of Route 66 in the early years are the privately published *Sectional Road Maps* of the Automobile Club of Southern California at Los Angeles. These maps were compiled in regional strip books and show a variety of roadside features and town details for the highway traveler. Originally commissioned by the Auto Club to advertise the 1932 Olympics in Los Angeles, later editions revised road conditions and alternative routes to Chicago, Kansas City, Denver, and New York.[14] A section of the 1937 series be-

tween Needles, California, and Kingman, Arizona, shows Route 66 through Oatman and the difficult Sitgreaves Pass of the gold country (figure 18.6). Clearly drawn are the twisting loops of the grade, roadside camps, and springwater locations as the highway crests the Black Mountain divide, the final westward barrier before facing the Mojave Desert. The experience was immortalized by John Steinbeck in *The Grapes of Wrath*, written about the Dust Bowl immigrants from Oklahoma during 1938 and published the next year.[15] Steinbeck had traveled west on Route 66 in the late summer of 1937, re-

cording the details of his highway journey on a personal road map.[16] The Oatman section is specifically described in Chapter 18 as the Joad family make their exodus along Highway 66:

> They drove all night, and came to the mountains in the night. And they crawled the jagged ramparts in the night, and their dim lights flickered on the pale stone walls of the road. They passed the summit in the dark and came slowly down in the late night, through the shattered stone debris of Oatman; and when daylight came they saw the Colorado River before them.[17]

18.5. Marathon Oil Company road map, *Arkansas-Kansas, Missouri-Oklahoma*, 1934, with Route 66 marked in pencil from Springfield to Joplin, Missouri.

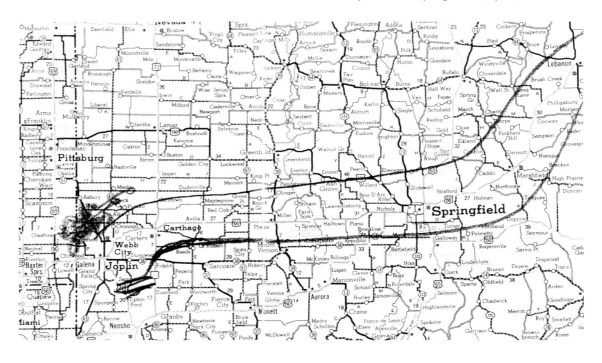

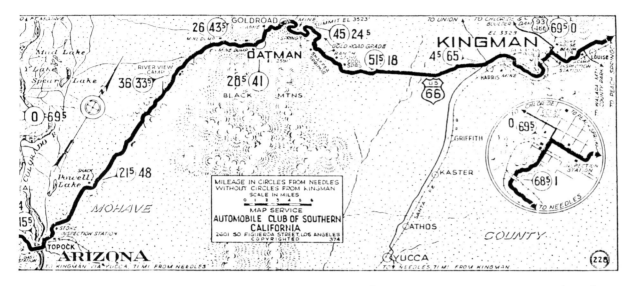

18.6. Oatman to Kingman, Arizona, *Sectional Road Map (36)*, section of the Automobile Club of Southern California's detailed strip map, 1937.

While *The Grapes of Wrath* captured the drama of the Dust Bowl exodus, surprisingly few documentary photographers of the period actually recorded location shots along Route 66. Only two dated photos by the Farm Security Administration (FSA) have come to light. Both are in central Oklahoma, one by Dorothea Lange taken near Weatherford in August 1938, and the other by Russell Lee near Warwick in July 1939.[18] These photos show families by the side of Highway 66 seeking respite from their journey out of the Dust Bowl, isolating the sense of migrant despair.[19] Perhaps the most convincing FSA imagery of Route 66 was the map of the origins of migrants to California in *An American Exodus* by Dorothea Lange and Paul Taylor (figure 18.7), where thick black lines funnel from the Dust Bowl states across Texas, New Mexico, and Arizona, following the path of Highway 66.[20] Steinbeck defines the vital role served by the road in the Depression years:

> Highway 66 is the main migrant road. 66—the long concrete path across the country, waving gently up and down on the map, from the Mississippi to Bakersfield—over the red lands and gray lands, twisting up into the mountains, crossing the Divide and down into the bright and terrible desert, and across the desert to the mountains again, and into the rich valleys of California.[21]

ORIGINS OF MIGRANTS TO CALIFORNIA

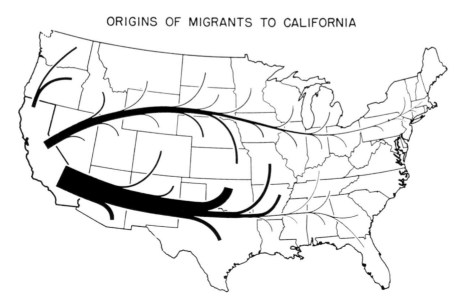

18.7. Published in *An American Exodus* in 1939, this map shows the percentage, by state, of the total number reported in Farm Security Administration and California Department of Agriculture data on 210,268 migrants.

The publishing success of *The Grapes of Wrath* encouraged producer Darryl Zanuck of Twentieth Century–Fox studios to rush a movie version of the Steinbeck novel during the summer of 1939. A midwestern native, Zanuck was inspired by Steinbeck's documentary style and hired John Ford to direct the film version under the working title of *Highway 66*.[22] Actual location shots were made on Route 66 by cameraman Gregg Toland to match with FSA photographs. Footage was taken at Bridgeport, Oklahoma, near Weatherford; and at the border station between Arizona and New Mexico. Full dramatic scenes were shot at the Colorado River bridge at Needles, California, where actor Henry Fonda played the film's hero, Tom Joad.[23] Released in January 1940, the movie captured the drama of the Dust Bowl migration and stands as a valuable cinematographic record of Route 66 in its historic period. Indeed, the journey of the California imagists—Steinbeck, Hader, Lange, Toland, and Taylor—following Route 66 and back into Oklahoma provides an important document of the highway for a folk migration that otherwise left little visual trace. In retrospect, *The Grapes of Wrath* and the FSA photographers hold a crucial moment in the symbolic mapping of Route 66, for the outbreak of the Second World War in 1939 soon diverted public attention away from the Dust Bowl exodus and the rural trek along Highway 66.[24]

Superhighway Segments

As Route 66 served as the migrant road from the Dust Bowl west to California, so in contrast, the highway had a more modern complexion in the confines of the key cities it connected. St. Louis was perhaps the most congested city to navigate on Route 66, and by 1932 the suburban county had

constructed an advanced system of superhighways.[25] U.S. 66 was looped around the western rim of St. Louis County on an innovative beltway named for Charles Lindbergh and had full cloverleaf interchanges (figure 18.8). A similar system of superhighways was constructed into Chicago before the Second World War, bypassing Joliet, Bloomington, and Springfield with Route 66 projects.[26] Los Angeles likewise developed early express-highway segments for Route 66 locations; the Arroyo Seco Parkway carried U.S. 66 from Pasadena on the first metropolitan freeway in 1941.[27]

18.8. *St. Louis and Vicinity,* Phillips 66 road map, ca. 1948. Detail of Kirkwood suburbs shows the U.S. 66 beltway cosntructed with superhighway interchanges in 1932.

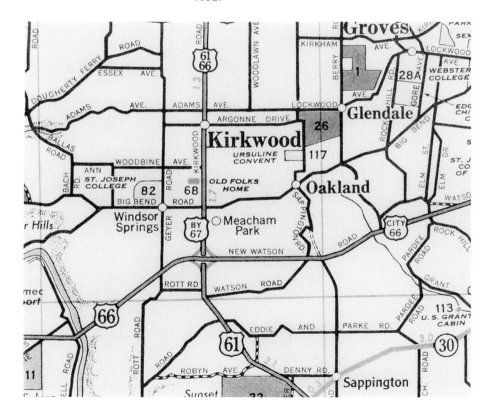

Postwar Interstates

After the Second World War, Route 66 was gradually improved from the superhighway segments around the major cities to long distance expressroad projects. Perhaps the most telling sign of this postwar change was the construction of the Turner Turnpike between Oklahoma City and Tulsa, which opened as a state toll road in 1953.[28] The Rand McNally *Road Atlas* of that year shows the new toll road in bold red lines bypassing Route 66 entirely, the first programmed discard of the original highway by a regional expressway. Such bypassing of Route 66 was formalized by the creation of the Interstate Highway Program for a national system of regional freeways with a new national numbering system that was designated in 1957.[29] Considerable opposition emerged when it was realized that Route 66 had been completely discarded as a through-numbered interstate from Chicago to Los Angeles, especially by the Highway 66 Association, which had pioneered the original road thirty years before.[30] Route 66 was thus divided into five major interstates: from Chicago to St. Louis as I-55, from St. Louis to Oklahoma City as I-44, and from Oklahoma City to Los Angeles as I-40 (Barstow), I-15 (San Bernardino), and I-10 (Santa Monica). Evidence of the new interstate bypassing of Route 66 is seen in the 1960 Rand McNally *Road Atlas* for the Albuquerque area. In figure 18.9 segments of Route 66 have been upgraded to Interstate 40, while others remain as four-lane portions of postwar design and an original remnant of the early U.S. 66 loops south along the Rio Grande as New Mexico Highway 6. Such complexity was common to Route 66 in the early interstate period and creates a challenge for accurate reconstruction of postwar highway locations.

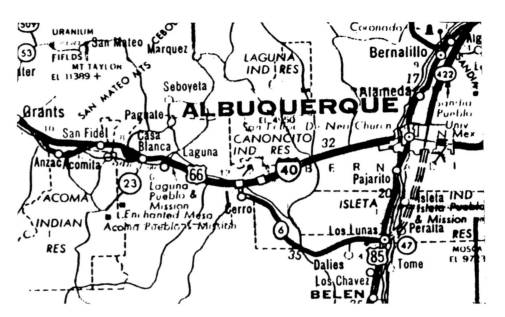

18.9. Albuquerque, New Mexico, Rand McNally *Road Atlas,* 1960. Detail of section to Grants, New Mexico, shows newly designated I-40 with U.S. 66 sections.

With the advent of the Interstate Highway Program, Route 66 became the subject of increasing popular interest. High-speed travel made U.S. 66 more accessible for cross-country tourism, and postwar prosperity linked Route 66 to the youth culture of Southern California. Signets of this fascination can be seen in the "Route 66" television series, first broadcast on CBS in October 1960 and running four full seasons to 1964.[31] Produced for Screen Gems in Los Angeles and conceived by Sterling Silliphant and Bert Leonard, the series used California location shots of Route 66 with a white Corvette to give authentic setting to the stories of its two popular heros, played by George Maharis and Martin Milner.[32] Also from the highway culture of Los Angeles was pop artist Edward Ruscha, who used Route 66 as an anonymous setting for his underground classic book *Twentysix Gasoline Stations* (Hollywood, 1962).[33] Ruscha photographed a random selection of roadside stations from Los Angeles back to his hometown of Oklahoma City, a valuable record of commercial architecture from the pre-interstate period. Of the group, the Standard station in Amarillo became his own icon of international fame for the pop art of Route 66.[34]

As the interstates gradually bypassed Route 66, the Highway 66 Association continued to function as a business group for motel and service-station operators along the road. By 1970, however, the effects of bypassing and rerouting had taken their toll, and the Highway 66 Association was disbanded shortly thereafter.[35] The removal of U.S. 66 shield signs from interstate sections in California, Illinois, and Missouri in 1976 signaled the official dissolution of the highway as a continuous numbered route.[36] The only signed sections of the road remained in Arizona, New Mexico, Oklahoma, and Texas, and even these were replaced by interstates as soon as feasible. Indeed, by this time Route 66 had entered the realm of nostalgic recreation. Along the highway west of Amarillo, Texas, the Cadillac Ranch was implanted in 1974 with a series of classic tail fins burrowed in the prairie. This sculptural monument to Route 66 was conceived by local benefactor Stanley Marsh III and designed by Chip Lord and Hudson Marquez of the California Ant Farm collective.[37] In 1976, director Hal Ashby resurrected wooden U.S. 66 shield signs for scenic identity in *Bound for Glory,* the film biography of Oklahoma folksinger Woody Guthrie, who used "66 Highway" lyrics in several of his early Dust Bowl ballads.[38] Such conscious reverence for Route 66 marked the beginnings of serious preservation of the highway as an American cultural symbol.

Historic Preservation

As the final section of Route 66 was replaced by Interstate 40 at Williams, Arizona, in October 1984, historic interest in the highway became noticeably overt in the national media.[39] Articles in regional publications such as *Arizona Highways* and Phillips Petroleum's *Shield* matched those in such popular magazines as *Life* in documenting surviving sections through photographs and interviews with notable personalities associated with the highway's history.[40] Systematic collection of oral narratives from living memory have proved a valuable resource in the preservation of Route 66 experiences. Especially notable are those by Tom Teague, from his news-journal articles in Illinois, and by Quinta Scott and Susan Croce Kelly in *Route 66: The Highway and Its People,*[41] which contains important original research and documentary photography of the highway from period sources and marks the scholarly study of Route 66 as a crucial era in recent American history.

Precise documentation of Route 66 on historic road maps has proved elusive. In part, this is due to the continuous rerouting of the highway over the course of its sixty-year history, particularly the direct overlap of interstate locations with original U.S. 66 segments. The most informative attempt at historic reconstruction of Route 66 has been the series of recent articles in *Hot Rod* magazine, surveyed with Tom Snyder of the Route 66 Association.[42] The series followed original roadbeds of the "Old 66," as feasible driving would allow, especially in abandoned sections such as the Oatman grade in Arizona. Other local efforts have formed Route 66 preservation groups, with published guides and maps from the Historic Route 66 Association of Kingman, Arizona; Kathrine Hilleson's *Route Sixty-six Revisited,* a guide to Route 66 in New Mexico; and the reprinting of Jack Rittenhouse's 1946 *A Guide Book to Highway 66.*[43]

Since no systematic map exists for historic Route 66 locations, the best available source for original sections are the two-mile 1:250,000 topographic sheets of the U.S. Geological Survey. These maps indicate local features, with elevation contours, streambeds, and settlement patterns in reasonable detail overlaid with modern highway data. Examples, such as the sheet for "Clinton, Oklahoma" of 1969, show Route 66 and Interstate 40 entwined with the regional railroads across the rolling prairie lands of the Dust Bowl era (figure 18.10). Clinton is of particular significance as the home of the original Highway 66 Association and the location shots for filming *The Grapes of Wrath.* Twenty-four such government sheets cover the entire length of Route 66 during the interstate transition period from 1962–78, although not all are of the same survey date or have the same quality of detail.[44] For recent surveys, the best available maps are either detailed topographic sheets at half-mile scale of 1:24,000 or revised editions of national road atlases, such as those published by Rand McNally or Gousha. When all such original Route 66 locations are compiled on a single national base map, a general historic pattern of surviving sections may be seen (figure 18.11). Obvious surviving sections of the original Route 66 can be found in Arizona, California, and Oklahoma as state highways numbered 66. In New Mexico and Missouri, original portions survive again as state highways 6 and 66, along with St. Louis County 366.[45] In Illinois, bypass segments remain unnumbered, as do several sections in Oklahoma, California, and Arizona of secondary paved roads. While original Route 66 can still be located from national atlases, often specific segments of historic locations need direct archaeological site surveys. This has been demonstrated by the recent National Park nomination in Williams, Arizona, by Teri Cleeland, who has used aerial photographs to locate the 1922 National Old Trails Road that became U.S. 66.[46] By using such detailed surveys, with the California Auto Club maps and the *Hot Rod* articles, a reasonable reconstruction of historic Route 66 can be made.

Lyric Mapping

One road map of Route 66 has been postponed for final review. It is a map in the most abstract sense, yet it served a direct cartographic need for many highway travelers. This map, of course, is the famous Bobby Troup song, "Route 66." Written in 1946, the hit was first recorded in jazz piano–blues style by the Nat King Cole Trio in Los Angeles for Capitol Records on March 16 of that year.[47] The genesis of the song, which lists stopover towns from "Chicago to L.A.," is credited to Troup's first wife, Cynthia, who originated the rhyming signet "Get your kicks on Route Sixty-six" as the couple traveled west from Pennsylvania to the West Coast in February 1946.[48] Troup stated that he rhymed city names from a road map, approximating a day's drive from Chicago to St. Louis, to Joplin, Missouri, to Oklahoma City, to Amarillo, to Gallup, New Mexico, to Flagstaff, Arizona (and Winona), to Kingman, Barstow, and San Bernardino, into "L.A."[49] Indeed, Troup has remarked that the song was used as a mental road map by motorists for navigation of Route 66, as a cartographic ballad in the oral tradition of a Homeric legend where the unknown world is given geographic identity through repeated song.[50] The original "Song Map," with the lyric city names circled in pencil, was framed as a momento of the Route 66 trip by Cynthia Troup (figure 18.12).

As a song, "Route 66" has outlived the highway and has been repeated in the popular music charts with each new generation, from the Andrews Sisters and Bing Crosby, to Chuck Berry and the Rolling Stones, and most recently to Manhattan Transfer and Depeche Mode.[51] Perhaps most importantly, the song's continued popularity has helped establish the eastern pronunciation of Route 66 as "rewte sixty-six" over the original Midwest description of the road as "Highway 66," which had prevailed before the Second World War.[52] The song clearly projected Route 66 into the national consciousness and has helped maintain its historic memory as a living highway of American imagination.

Symbolic Synthesis

In retrospect, Route 66 has become an icon of the auto age because it encompassed both the real geography of westward migration and the abstract need to symbolize the independence of the American road. As a practical geography, Route 66 linked the expanding frontier of the Southwest with two vital cities of the twentieth century, Chicago and Los Angeles, which was Avery's original vision for a transcontinental highway. Route 66 thus pioneered a new trail west through a region made accessible by the mobility of the automobile. It was a continuing course of migration, from Dust Bowl despair to postwar prosperity. In this regard, it was a river of travel, and like the Mississippi of Mark Twain, Route 66 continually shifted its course to meet the volume of traffic between its roadside banks. Former loops and meanders are now abandoned, cut-off by interstate relocations. Thus, mapping early Route 66 locations is akin to retracing the sloughs of an ancient river bed. The result is a modern archaeology of Route 66 with relic sections proposed as national historic landmarks.

In an abstract sense, Route 66 was a highway that linked the rural culture of the Midwest to the free-spirited horizons of Southern California across a travail of deserts and mountains in the Southwest. Its path was biblical, leading the hopeful from the confines of an Eastern culture to the promised land of the unlimited West. This was the intent of Steinbeck's prose and Troup's lyrical rhyme—to capture the meaning of Route 66 as a metaphor of democratic determination on the open highway. Most importantly, Route 66 served as a suspended bridge between the East and the West. It offered the frontier to those in the center of Oklahoma and Missouri and provided the expressive mode of images for those in Hollywood, California. As the Joads traveled west, Dorothea Lange traveled east to document their Dust Bowl experience; and as Bobby Troup traveled west, his song was broadcast east by Nat King Cole and overseas to Europe as an icon of the American highway. This cultural cartography of Route 66 went well beyond the practical needs Avery had mapped for his new Oklahoma national highway in 1925, and it has proved more powerful than the limited rationale to discard Route 66 from the federal interstate network in 1985. This is why Route 66 has always been more than a mere highway number and why its cartographic history has transcended the road maps that marked its diagonal line across American space.

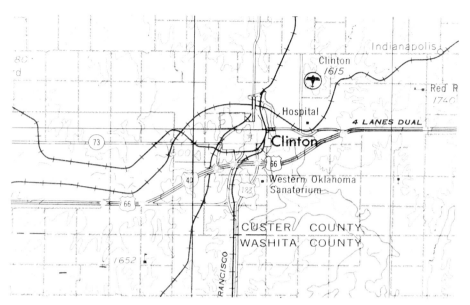

18.10. "Clinton, Oklahoma," *U.S. Geological Survey,*
1969. Detail of a two-mile scale series shows overlap of
U.S. 66 and I-40 across historic Dust Bowl counties.
Such maps are useful for reconstructing original Route 66
locations within the interstate system.

18.12. *"Route 66"* song map by Cynthia Troup and
Bobby Troup, "February 7–15, 1946." Map section
shows lyric names circled from Flagstaff to Los Angeles.
The snapshot is of Cynthia Troup at U.S. 66 sign in Cali-
fornia. The piano score of her verse "Get your kicks on
Route Sixty-six!" was composed by Bobby Troup for the
Nat King Cole Trio.

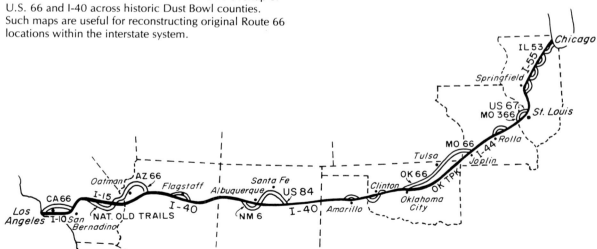

18.11. Surviving sections of Route 66, 1988. A sche-
matic map shows modern interstates and historic Highway 66 segments that are still active as state routes.

Notes

Development of Route 66 research is owed to many supportive individuals. I would like to thank Michael Jackson of the Society for Commercial Archeology for his original invitation of the project and his creative advice over many months; Richard Weingroff of the Federal Highway Administration for his careful critique and many useful articles; Tom Snyder of the Highway 66 Association for his ideas and enthusiasm; Quinta Scott and Susan Kelly of the Oklahoma University Press for their timely suggestions and contact addresses; Ron Phillips of the Phillips Petroleum Company for his early material; Janice Vandeventer of the Automobile Club of Southern California for her cartographic consultation; Bobby Troup for his generous conversation; and the Boston Architectural Center for their media services.

1. Quinta Scott and Susan Croce Kelly, *Route 66: The Highway and Its People* (Norman, Okla., 1988), 3–17.

2. Ibid., 7–12.

3. E. W. James, "Making and Unmaking a National System of Marked Routes," *American Highways* 11 (Oct. 1933): 16–18; Drake Hokanson, *The Lincoln Highway* (Iowa City, 1988).

4. Scott and Kelly, 14.

5. *Report of the Joint Board of Interstate Highways* (Washington, D.C., 18 Nov. 1925), 48–60.

6. "Ky. Will Ignore Road Named by US as Highways," *Frankfort (Kentucky) Journal*, 8 Dec. 1925.

7. Scott and Kelly, 15; *Report of Joint Board*, 54.

8. Scott and Kelly, 17.

9. Ibid.

10. Michael Wallis, *Oil Man: Frank Phillips and Phillips Petroleum* (New York, 1988), 244–47.

11. Scott and Kelly, 23–24; "Route 66," *Shield* 7 (1982): 17–21.

12. "Edmund, Okla.," U.S. Geological Survey map (1:62,500, 1935).

13. Douglas A. Yorke, Jr., "Blazed Trails: A Pictohistory of the Oil Company Road Map." Paper at conference, *Americans and the Automobile*, 5 Nov. 1988, at the Henry Ford Museum in Dearborn, Michigan.

14. Automobile Club of Southern Calif., *Sectional Road Maps* (Los Angeles, 1937), nos. 36, 49, 51–53.

15. Nelson Valjean, *John Steinbeck* (San Francisco, 1975), 164–65; Jackson J. Benson, *The True Adventures of John Steinbeck* (New York, 1984), 385–90.

16. Harry Thornton Moore, *The Novels of John Steinbeck* (New York, 1939), 54; Robert DeMott, ed., *Steinbeck's Working Days: Journals of the Grapes of Wrath* (New York, 1989), 45, 152.

17. John Steinbeck, *The Grapes of Wrath* (New York, 1939), 275.

18. Scott and Kelly, 58–60.

19. Jefferson Hunter, *Image and Word* (Cambridge, Mass., 1987), 101–2; Jack Hurley, *Russell Lee* (Dobbs Ferry, N.Y., 1978), 50.

20. Dorothea Lange and Paul Taylor, *An American Exodus* (New York, 1939), 68, 104.

21. Steinbeck, 160.

22. Warren French, *Filmguide to The Grapes of Wrath* (Bloomington, Ind., 1973); 16–20; Benson, 109.

23. Howard Teichmann, *Fonda: My Life* (New York, 1981), 136–37; Scott and Kelly, 62.

24. Milton Meltzer, *Dorothea Lange* (New York, 1978), 229.

25. "Highway Grade at Kirkwood," *Missouri Motor News*, February 1932.

26. "An Interregional Highway Developed from a Two-lane Road," *Concrete Highways and Public Improvements* 32 (Winter 1944): 12–17.

27. H. Marshall Goodwin, Jr., "The Arroyo Seco" *Southern California Quarterly* 47 (1965): 73–102.

28. Kent Ruth, ed., *Oklahoma* (Norman, Okla., 1957), 233.

29. "Interstate Route Marker Selected and Numerology Map Approved," *American Highways* 35 (Oct. 1957): 1, 21–22.

30. "Chop U.S. 66 into Five Interstate Markings?" *Daily Oklahoman* (Oklahoma City), 28 June 1962; Scott and Kelly, 181–84.

31. Alexander McNeil, *Total Television* (New York, 1984), 554–55.

32. Michael Seiler, "Route 66," *Los Angeles Times*, 24 July 1977; Drew Greenland, "Route 66," *Life* 6 (June 1983): 76.

33. Minneapolis Institute of Arts, *Edward Ruscha (Ed-Werd Rew-Shay)* (Minneapolis, 1972).

34. Christopher French, *Pop Art* (London, 1968), 133.

35. Michael Wallis, "Route 66," *Oklahoma Today* (Sept./Oct. 1984): 22–23.

36. Seiler; Scott and Kelly, 186.

37. Gordon Chaplin, "Stanley Marsh Plays with His Money," *Esquire* 82 (Dec. 1974): 168–69, 240–41; Chip Lord, letter to author, 10 July 1989.

38. *Bound for Glory* (Los Angeles, 1976), original motion-picture score record sleeve, UA LA 695-H; Joe Klein, *Woody Guthrie* (New York, 1981), 70.

39. "The Road Ends for Route 66," *AASHTO News*, 27 June 1985.

40. Don Dedera, "Old U.S. 66," *Arizona Highways*, 57 (July 1981): 15–16; "Route 66," *Shield*, 14–23; Greenland, 70–78; Wallis, 14–23.

41. Tom Teague, "Route 66," *Reader* (Chicago), 27 September 1985, 1, 18–40; Scott and Kelly, 199–202.

42. "Route 66," *Hot Rod* 40–41 (Dec. 1987–Mar. 1988), 4 part sequel.

43. Patricia Buckley, *Route 66: Remnants* (Historic Route 66 Assoc. of Ariz., 1989); Kathrine Hilleson, *Route Sixty-Six Revisited* (Albuquerque, 1988); Jack Rittenhouse, *A Guide Book to Highway 66* (Albuquerque, 1989).

44. U.S. Geological Survey, *National Topographic Maps, 1:250:000 Scale Series*, January 1980, index.

45. Rand McNally, *Road Atlas* (Chicago, 1988), 64th ed.

46. Teri A. Cleeland, "Historic Route 66 in Arizona," Nat. Register of Historic Places, Nat. Park Serv., 1988.

47. Don Dedera, "Route 66, The Lyric Lingers On," *Arizona Highways* 57 (July 1981): 11; James Haskins and Kathleen Benson, *Nat King Cole* (New York, 1984), 46.

48. Dedera, "Route 66," 11; Greenland, 73; Kelly and Scott, 148.

49. "Route 66," *Shield*, 23 (Londontown Music); Greenland, 73; Kelly and Scott, 149.

50. Dedera, "Route 66," 11; Melinda Guiles, "Laugh No More at 'Klean Kabins,': Archaeologists of the Early Auto Age," *Wall Street Journal*, 10 November 1988.

51. "Route 66," *Shield*, 23; Greenland, 73; "Route 66" [song title], *Phono-Log*, 10 August 1988.

52. Bobby Troup, telephone conservations with author, 18 December 1988, 10 February 1989.

Contributors

CAROL AHLGREN is an architectural historian with the Nebraska State Historic Preservation Office in Lincoln. She received a B.A. in history from Beloit College, Beloit, Wisconsin, and an M.A. in landscape architecture from the University of Wisconsin at Madison.

MARY ANNE BEECHER is an adjunct assistant professor at Iowa State University, where she teaches interior design history. She received B.A. and master's degrees in interior design from Iowa State University. Her interests include popular culture and vernacular design, both urban and rural.

MICHAEL L. BERGER is head of the Division of Human Development at St. Mary's College of Maryland. He is the author of *The Devil Wagon in God's Country: The Automobile and Social Change in Rural America, 1893–1929,* which won the 1980 Thomas McKean Award. He is completing *The Automobile: A Reference Guide,* an annotated bibliography of books, articles, and dissertations concerning the car's impact on American history and culture, which will be published by Greenwood Press.

GERALD BLOOMFIELD is professor of geography at the University of Guelph, Guelph, Ontario. His interests cover a broad range of subjects in economic, historical, and urban geography. He is the author of *The World Automotive Industry* (1978) and *New Zealand: A Handbook of Historical Statistics* (1984). Over the past decade he has contributed several plates on the economic and social effects of the automobile to the *Historical Atlas of Canada,* volume 2, to be published in 1990.

DANIEL M. BLUESTONE, a board member of the Society for Commercial Archeology, teaches architectural history and preservation at Columbia University. He lives in Brooklyn, New York, one block from Coney Island Avenue.

ROBERT M. CRAIG teaches at the College of Architecture, Georgia Institute of Technology, Atlanta. He was born and raised in St. Louis, Missouri, and was educated in Illinois (B.A. in history at Principia College and M.A. in history at University of Illinois) and New York (Ph.D. in history of architecture and urban development at Cornell University). Because his father

taught high school in St. Louis and had a summer job each year in Maryland, Robert Craig annually traveled by car (east in June and west in September from the late 1940s to the mid-1960s) back and forth along the old National Road, U.S. 40, the Pennsylvania Turnpike, U.S. 50, and later Interstate 70. Auto archaeology has emerged as an inbred interest. Professor Craig's research and writing interests range from popular culture and regional (Southeastern U.S.) architectural history to English, American, and Modern architecture and to Chinese garden design.

PETER J. HUGILL is associate professor of geography at Texas A & M University. He was born in York, England, and holds degrees from Leeds, Simon Fraser, and Syracuse universities. His current work is on World System theory, and his forthcoming book from Johns Hopkins University Press will address the role of transportation technology in the development of the modern state.

RICHARD INGERSOLL is editor for theory and history of *Design Book Review* and is an assistant professor at the School of Architecture, Rice University, Houston, Texas. He conducts courses in the history of urban form and organizes studios devoted to the problem of the automobile and architecture.

JAN JENNINGS is president of the Society for Commercial Archeology; an associate professor in the Department of Art and Design, College of Design, Iowa State University; and a historic preservation consultant. Her research centers on vernacular environments; she is the coauthor of *American Vernacular Interior Architecture, 1870–1940* (1988) and *American Vernacular Design, 1870–1940* (1985).

FOLKE (TYKO) KIHLSTEDT is chairman of the Art Department and teaches art history at Franklin and Marshall College in Lancaster, Pennsylvania. He was an undergraduate at Dartmouth College and holds M.A. and Ph.D. degrees from the University of Pennsylvania and Northwestern University. His recent scholarly work has ranged from the Crystal Palace and world's fair architecture to the interactions of art and technology and of the automobile and architecture.

ARTHUR KRIM is chairman of the Geography Department at Salve Regina College in Newport, Rhode Island. He holds degrees in geography from Clark University and the University of Chicago. He is a founding member and past president of the Society for Commercial Archeology. His past work includes neon preservation in Boston and the imagery of Los Angeles.

SARA AMY LEACH is an architectural historian on the staff of the Historic American Buildings Survey/Historic American Engineering Record, a division of the National Park Service, U.S. Department of the Interior. She has a master's degree in architectural history and historic preservation from the University of Virginia and a B.A. in journalism and B.F.A. in art history from Ohio Wesleyan University. Her recent projects have included National Register of Historic Places nominations for Civilian Conservation Corps–built cabin camps of the 1930s and for the Baltimore-Washington Parkway. She also writes freelance magazine articles about local preservation efforts.

FRANK EDGERTON MARTIN is a landscape preservation consultant in St. Paul, Minnesota. He received a bachelor's degree in philosophy from Vassar College and a master's degree in landscape architecture from the University of Wisconsin at Madison. His interests include the history of vernacular gardens and American roadside architecture.

JAMES E. PASTER has a master's degree in photography from the Institute of Design in Chicago. He teaches photography and filmmaking at Sam Houston State University in Huntsville, Texas, and is completing an interdisciplinary Ph.D. in aesthetic studies at the University of Texas at Dallas.

KEITH A. SCULLE is a social historian of vernacular architecture, especially that of the roadside. He has published articles on this subject in *The Annals of Iowa, Journal of American Culture, Journal of Cultural Geography,* and *Pioneer America.* He has been the coeditor of the *Commercial Archeology News Journal* and currently is its book review editor. He is with the Illinois Historic Preservation Agency.

R. STEPHEN SENNOTT is a Ph.D. student in the Department of Art at the University of Chicago. He has B.A. and M.A. degrees in art history from the University of Wisconsin at Madison.

He has taught history of art and architecture at the University of Illinois at Chicago and has taught writing in the College and the Humanities Division at the University of Chicago. His research interests include modern American and British architecture and design of the late nineteenth and early twentieth centuries, particularly the Arts and Crafts movement, the Prairie School, and American architectural clubs.

MAGGIE VALENTINE is completing a Ph.D. in architecture at the University of California, Los Angeles. Her dissertation is on the movie theatres of S. Charles Lee.

DAVID K. VAUGHAN is a member of the technical communications faculty at the Air Force Institute of Technology, Wright-Patterson Air Force Base in Ohio. He has given numerous presentations in the areas of technical communications and popular culture. He has published several articles on technology and transportation, children's literature, and the literature of flight. The author of a book-length study of the writings of Anne Morrow Lindbergh, he is presently preparing an edition of the diaries and letters of a World War I United States Air Service pilot for publication.

E. L. WIDMER, a Rhode Island native, is a Mellon Fellow and Ph.D. candidate in American Civilization at Harvard University. He has contributed to the *Boston Globe, Boston Phoenix, Rhode Island History, The Rhode Island Liar, Spy,* and *Harvard Magazine.*

Illustration Credits

1.1. Kenneth Frampton and Yukio Futagawa, *Modern Architecture 1851–1919* (New York: Rizzoli, 1983), 189

1.2. Richard Krautheimer, *Early Christian and Byzantine Architecture* (Baltimore: Penguin Books, 1965), copyright © Richard Krautheimer, p. 33, fig. 13. Reproduced by permission of Penguin Books, Ltd., and Richard Krautheimer.

1.3. C. Theodore Larsen, "The Citroën Automobile Sales Building, Paris," *Architectural Record* 67 (May 1930):541, copyright 1930 by Mcgraw-Hill, Inc. All rights reserved. Reproduced with permission of the publisher.

1.4. James W. Hanberg, "Novel Auto Body Advertises Home Building," *Building Age and the Builder's Journal* 45 (Feb. 1923):66

1.5. "Better Homes in America Small House Competition, 1934," *Architectural Forum* 60 (Mar. 1934):184

1.6. "Vernacular Forms," *Architectural Record* 81 (May 1937):21, copyright 1937 by McGraw-Hill, Inc. All rights reserved. Reproduced with permission of the publisher.

1.7. With permission of Paul Rudolph, architect.

1.8. Courtesy of Buckminster Fuller Estate, Los Angeles, and reprinted from James Ward, ed., *The Artifacts of R. Buckminster Fuller,* vol. 1 (New York: Garland, 1985), 87, with permission of the publisher.

1.9. With permission of Bertrand Goldberg and Associates, Chicago, Ill.

1.10. With permission of Albert Kahn Associates, Architects and Engineers, Detroit, Mich.

1.11. *Architectural Record,* January 1933, copyright 1933 by McGraw-Hill, Inc. All rights reserved. Reproduced by permission of the publisher.

1.12. Kauffman and Fabry, Co. Permission granted by K and S Photo Graphics, parent company of Kauffman and Fabry Co.

1.13. Heinrich Klotz, *Vision der Moderne* (Munich: Prestel Verlag, 1986), p. 364, fig. 503. With permission of the publisher and by Jan Kaplicky and David Nixon of Future Systems, London and Santa Monica, Calif.

1.14. With permission of Daniel Scully, architect.

2.1. "Ramsgate Municipal Airport," *Architectural Review* 82 (July 1937): 3

2.2, 2.4, 2.5, 2.8–2.10 © Robert M. Craig
2.3 *California Arts and Architecture* (Jan. 1935):1
2.6 Richard J. S. Gutman
2.7 St. Louis County Department of Parks and Recreation
2.11 Airstream, Inc.

3.1, 3.4, 3.6, 3.7, 3.9, 3.12. Photo: Peter J. Hugill; with permission of the Henry Ford Museum, Dearborn, Mich.
3.2, 3.5, 3.8, 3.11 Peter J. Hugill; data from Automobile Quarterly, *The American Car since 1775* (New York, 1971).
3.3 Advertisement, *Country Life* (America) 9 (Nov. 1905):83.
3.10. Advertisement, ca. 1910; reprinted in Cyril Posthumus, *The Story of Veteran and Vintage Cars* (London: Phoebus, 1977), 55.

4.1. Gerald T. Bloomfield, data from Allan Nevins and Frank E. Hill, *Ford: Decline and Rebirth 1933–1962,* vol. 3 (New York: Scribner's, 1963), app. 1
4.2–4.13 Gerald T. Bloomfield

5.1–5.10. James E. Paster collection

6.1. National Archives, 16-G-97-2-S-14561C
6.2. National Archives, 16-G-S-14156
6.3, 6.4. Washington County Free Library, Hagerstown, Maryland
6.5. National Archives, 83-G-13193
6.6. National Archives, 16-G-S-97-3-4
6.7. National Archives, 83-G-15059

7.1. Clarence Young, *The Motor Boys in Mexico* (New York: Cupples and Leon, 1906), 128. Charles Nutall, artist
7.2. Laura Dent Crane, *The Automobile Girls along the Hudson* (Philadelphia: Altemus, 1910), 67
7.3. Laura Lee Hope, *The Outdoor Girls in a Motorcar* (New York: Grosset and Dunlap, 1913), 13
7.4 Franklin W. Dixon, *The Great Airport Mystery* (New York: Grosset and Dunlap, 1930), 8. Walter S. Rogers, artist. Copyright © 1930. Reprinted by permission of Pocket Books, a division of Simon and Schuster, Inc.
7.5. Carolyn Keene, *The Sign of the Twisted Candles* (New York: Grosset and Dunlap, 1933), 74. Russell H. Tandy, artist. Copyright © 1933. Reprinted by permission of Pocket Books, a division of Simon and Schuster, Inc.

8.1. The Lester S. Levy Collection of Sheet Music, Special Collections, Milton S. Eisenhower Library, The Johns Hopkins University, Baltimore, Md.
8.2. Photo courtesy of the Country Music Foundation, Inc.
8.3. Photo provided by Graceland Division of Elvis Presley Enterprises

9.1 William Phillips Comstock, *Garage and Motor Boat Houses* (New York, 1911), 29

9.2 "A Garage of Terra Cotta Blocks with Plastered Exterior," *Building Age* (Nov. 1911):589
9.3 Advertisement, *Keith's Magazine* (Apr. 1920):225
9.4 The American Architect, *Garages, Country and Suburban* (New York, 1911), 20
9.5 Southern Pine Association, *Southern Pine Garages and How to Build Them* (New Orleans, 1926), cover. Courtesy of Southern Forest Products Assn.
9.6 "Cement Construction for the Private Garage," *Building Age* (Apr. 1911):217, and "A Garage and Studio Building of Cement Exterior," *Building Age* (Nov. 1912):557–60
9.7 "Cement Garage for the Suburbanite," *Building Age* (July 1911):368
9.8 William A. Radford, *Radford's Garages and How to Build Them* (Chicago, 1910), cover
9.9 "Portable Garage of Concrete Construction," *Building Age* (June 1910):261
9.10 "The Attached Garage," *Building Age and the Builder's Journal* (June 1924):81
9.11 Charles Alma Byers, "The Garage Bungalow," *Building Age and the Builder's Journal* (July 1923):51

10.1–10.6, 10.8, 10.9. Courtesy of Robert M. Trachte, Trachte Company, Inc.
10.7, 10.10 Frank Edgerton Martin

11.1. Mary Anne Beecher; illustrations (top to bottom): "Tourist Cottages An Active Field," *American Builder* (May 1937):88; "Flamingo Court," *American Builder* (May 1941):76; "Grande Vista Tourist Homes," *American Builder* (June 1937):79; "Attractive Setting Helps Tourist Court Set Income Record," *Architectural Record* (July 1940):100; "Two Ocean Front Resort Motels," *Architectural Record* (July 1940):170; "Roadside Cabins for Tourist," *Architectural Record* (Dec. 1933):457. The latter three copyrights 1940, 1940, 1933, respectively, by McGraw-Hill, Inc. All rights reserved. Reproduced with permission of publisher.
11.2. Postcard, Mary Anne Beecher collection
11.3. "'Flamingo Court' Tourist Cottages," *American Builder* (May 1941):77
11.4. "Tourist Cottages—An Active Field," *American Builder* (May 1937):88
11.5. Postcard, printed by MWM, Aurora, Mo.; Mary Anne Beecher collection
11.6. "Attractive Setting Helps Tourist Court Set Income Record," *Architectural Record* (Aug. 1940):101, copyright 1940 by McGraw-Hill, Inc. All rights reserved. Reproduced with permision of the publisher.
11.7. "Texas Motor Court Has Modern Appeal," *American Builder* (Aug. 1940):59
11.8. "Trim Design Attracts Auto Court Trade," *American Builder* (Mar. 1940):76
11.9–11.11. Mary Anne Beecher

12.1. Courtesy of Mr. and Mrs. L. H. Lindsey, Jr.
12.2. Courtesy of Raymond Bransetter
12.3. Keith A. Sculle
12.4, 12.6. Courtesy of Vetra Long
12.5, 12.8. Postcards, courtesy of Vetra Long
12.7, 12.10. Postcards, courtesy of A. P. Young, Jr.
12.9. Postcard, courtesy of Mrs. Paul L. Young

13.4, 13.5, 13.12. Maggie Valentine
13.1–13.3, 13.6–13.11, 13.13–13.16. Courtesy of Department of Special Collections, University Research Library, University of California, Los Angeles (13.1, 13.3, 13.16: S. Charles Lee; 13.2: Mott Studios; 13.8, 13.13: Julius Shulman; 13.11: C. "Pop" Laval; 13.14: Hoffman-Luckhaus Studio)

14.1. Right: Le Corbusier, *The City of Tomorrow* (1922); Richard Ingersoll
14.2. Courtesy of Las Colinas, Inc., Irving, Tex., brochure
14.3. Courtesy of Houston Metropolitan Research Center, Houston Public Library
14.4. *Civics for Houston,* Jan. 1929, 6
14.5. Drawn by Randall Stout (1989)

15.1. Courtesy of Chicago Historical Society (ICHi 04788)
15.2. From *Motor Age* 2 (20 Nov. 1902):1. Courtesy of Chicago Historical Society
15.3. *Architectural Record,* September 1907, copyright 1907 by McGraw-Hill Inc. All rights reserved. Reproduced with the permission of the publisher.
15.4. *Inland Architecture and News Record* 50 (Aug. 1907):23
15.5. Daniel Burnham and Edward H. Bennett, *Plan of Chicago* (Chicago: Commercial Club, 1909). Courtesy of the Art Institute of Chicago.
15.6.–15.8. Graham, Anderson, Probst, and White, Chicago, *The Architectural Work of Graham, Anderson, Probst and White and Their Predecessors,* vol. 1 (London: B. T. Batsford, 1932), plates 80, 72, 77
15.9. Courtesy of the Art Institute of Chicago. © 1989 The Art Institute of Chicago. All rights reserved.
15.10. Courtesy of Chicago Historical Society
15.11, 15.13. *The Jewelers Building* (Chicago: Poole Brothers, n.d.), 19, 16
15.12. M. J. P. Smith, "Parking Carcasses," *Inland Architect* (Nov./Dec. 1988):61

16.1, 16.2, 16.7. Postcards, Donald C. Jackson and Carol Dubie collection
16.3. Elizabeth Frazer, "Roadside Markets," *Satur-day Evening Post* 197 (20 Dec. 1924):11. Photo: Library of Congress. Reprinted from *Saturday Evening Post* © 1924 The Curtiss Publishing Co.
16.4. Herbert Johnson, cartoonist, in Kenneth L. Roberts, "Pests," *Saturday Evening Post* 202 (30 Nov. 1929):21. Photo: Library of Congress. Reprinted from *Saturday Evening Post* © 1929 The Curtiss Publishing Co.
16.5, 16.8. "Roadside Beauty: What Has Happened to It? What Can Be Done about It?" *Roadside Bulletin* 5 (1937):4, 3. Photos: Library of Congress
16.6. John B. Allison, artist, in *Roadside Bulletin* 1 (1931):9. Photo: Library of Congress
16.9, 16.10. "Elevating the Standing of the 'Hot Dog Kennel,'" *American City* 38 (May 1928):100, 99. Photos: Library of Congress
16.11. Advertisement, *Standard Oil Bulletin* 12 (Oct. 1924), inside cover. Courtesy of Chevron Corporation. Photo: Library of Congress
16.12. "A Service Station 'Before and After,'" *Standard Oil Bulletin* 11 (May 1923):16. Courtesy of Chevron Corporation. Photo: Library of Congress
16.13. New England Regional Planning Commission, *The Problem of the Roadside* (Boston: National Resources Committee, 1939). Photo: Library of Congress
16.14. "Filling Station Architecture," *Country Life* 51 (Apr. 1927):102. Photo: Library of Congress
16.15. Photo: Library of Congress

17.1, 17.6. National Capital Park and Planning Commission, *Annual Report,* 1930
17.2. National Capital Planning Commission
17.3. Rock Creek and Potomac Parkway Commission, "Estimates on the Development of Rock Creek and Potomac Parkway: Revised 1928 Estimates and Designs for the Development of the Parkway," July 1929

17.4, 17.8, 17.10. Sara Amy Leach
17.5. Maryland-National Capital Park and Planning Commission
17.7. Edward C. Gibbs, Edward Curtis Gibbs Collection, Alexandria, Va.
17.9. National Archives

18.1. United States Department of Agriculture, Bureau of Public Roads, June 1931
18.2. From 1926 *Auto Road Atlas.* © copyright 1926 by Rand McNally and Co., R.L. 88-S-189
18.3. Arizona Highway Department, October 1926
18.4, 18.8. Courtesy of Phillips Petroleum Co.
18.5. From Marathon Road Map of Missouri. © copyright 1934 by Rand McNally and Co., R.L. 90-S-72
18.6. Copyright by the Automobile Club of Southern California. Reproduced by permission.
18.7. Dorothea Lange and Paul S. Taylor, *An American Exodus* (New York: Reynal and Hitchcock, 1939)
18.9. From 1960 *Road Atlas.* © copyright 1960 by Rand McNally and Co., R. L. 88-S-189
18.10. Map, *U.S. Geological Survey,* 1969
18.11. Arthur Krim; data from *Hot Rod* magazine, 1987–89
18.12. Photo: Bobby Troup. With permission of Bobby Troup and Cynthia Troup

Index